# MANAGERS NOT MBAS

**FT** Prentice Hall
FINANCIAL TIMES

In an increasingly competitive world, we believe it's quality of thinking that will give you the edge – an idea that opens new doors, a technique that solves a problem, or an insight that simply makes sense of it all. The more you know, the smarter and faster you can go.

That's why we work with the best minds in business and finance to bring cutting-edge thinking and best learning practice to a global market.

Under a range of leading imprints, including *Financial Times Prentice Hall*, we create world-class print publications and electronic products bringing our readers knowledge, skills and understanding which can be applied whether studying or at work.

To find out more about Pearson Education publications, or tell us about the books you'd like to find, you can visit us at
**www.pearsoned.co.uk**

PEARSON
Education

# MANAGERS NOT MBAS

*A Hard Look at the Soft Practice*
*of Managing and Management Development*

Henry Mintzberg

**FT** Prentice Hall
FINANCIAL TIMES

*An imprint of* **Pearson Education**

London • New York • Toronto • Sydney • Tokyo • Singapore
Hong Kong • Cape Town • Madrid • Paris • Amsterdam • Munich • Milan

PEARSON EDUCATION LIMITED

Edinburgh Gate
Harlow CM20 2JE
Tel: +44 (0)1279 623623
Fax: +44 (0)1279 431059
Website: www.pearsoned.co.uk

First published in North America by Berrett-Koehler Publishers Inc., San Francisco in 2004

First published by Pearson Education Ltd in 2004

This edition is not for sale in North America

ISBN 0 273 66324 0

British Library Cataloguing-in-Publication Data
A catalogue record for this book is available from the British Library

Library of Congress Cataloging-in-Publication Data
Mintzberg, Henry.
    Managers not MBAs : a hard look at the soft practice of managing and management
    development / Henry Mintzberg.
        p. cm
    Originally published: San Francisco, CA : Berrett-Koehler, 2003.
    Includes bibliographical references and index.
    ISBN 0-273-66324-0 (alk. paper)
        1. Executives--Training of 2, Experiential learning. 3. Active learning. 4.
    Management--Study and teaching (Graduate) 5. Master of business administration degree.
    6. Business education. I. Title.

    HD30.4.M56 2004
    658'.0071'1--dc22                                                    2004047203

10 9 8 7 6 5 4 3 2
08   07   06   05   04

Printed and bound by Biddles Ltd, Kings Lynn

The publisher's policy is to use paper manufactured from sustainable forests.

*This book is dedicated to the "Why not?" people who brought the International Masters Program in Practicing Management to life:*

- *The thirty-two managers of the first class who came into this unknown with energy and enthusiasm: Pierre Arsenault, Gerhard Böhm, Marc Boillot, Jane Davis, Luc DeWever, Massar Fujita, Jacques Gautier, John Geoghegan, Kevin Greenawalt, Abbas Gullet, Kentaro Iijima, Vince Isber, "Rocky" Iwaoka, Terry Jenkins, Thierry Knockaert, Gabriela Kroll, Narendra Kudva, Silke Lehnhardt, Y. B. Lim, Steve Martineau, Jane McCroary, Brian Megraw, Edmée Métivier, Kazu Mutoh, Hiro Nishikawa, David Noble, Harald Plöckinger, Morten Ramberg, Nagu Rao, Roy Sugimura, Alan Whelan, and Torstein Wold*

- *The companies that took a chance when all we could offer them were ideas: Alcan, BT (in partnership with Telenor), EDF and Gaz de France, Fujitsu, The International Federation of Red Cross and Red Crescent Societies, Lufthansa, Matsushita, and the Royal Bank of Canada*

- *My colleagues of the original "mob of six" for never being selfish or shy in their determination to get this right: Roger Bennett, Jonathan Gosling, Hiro Itami, Ramesh Mehta, and Heinz Thanheiser, supported by Bill Litwack*

# CONTENTS

*Preface    ix*

Introduction    1

### PART ONE
## NOT MBAs

### PART TWO
## DEVELOPING MANAGERS

# PREFACE

I don't exactly have an MBA—the MIT Sloan School of Management called it a masters of science then. But I did exactly teach MBAs, for about fifteen years, until I had enough and asked our dean at McGill in the mid-1980s to reduce my teaching load and salary accordingly. I was simply finding too much of a disconnect between the practice of managing that was becoming clearer to me and what went on in classrooms, my own included, intended to develop those managers.

In these feelings, I have found myself not alone. Over the years, I asked colleagues all over the world and especially in the United States what they thought about teaching conventional MBA students. I have been surprised by how many agreed with me. A well-kept secret of business schools is how many of their faculty have had it with teaching MBAs. (We shall hear from the others, if not these.)

So in the 1980s I began my rants, speaking my mind about MBA programs, including a chapter entitled "Training Managers, Not MBAs" in a book I published in 1989. But then people started asking the embarrassing question: What was *I* doing about it? Academics are not supposed to be asked such questions, so it took me a while to respond. Then it took McGill a while to respond. But eventually we put together a group to do something about it: create a masters program truly for practicing managers.

Realizing we would do better in partnership, we approached Insead in France, where I was jointly appointed at the time. But that did not get far, so I called Jonathan Gosling at Lancaster University to see whether that school might be interested. He had to check with a couple of people, he said, including the dean. He called back an hour later!

I duly drafted a memo to Insead admitting defeat. Gareth Dyas noticed it on our common secretary's desk and said, "You can't do that!" I realized then that my proposal had been too simple; Insead needed something complicated. So I proposed a partnership of five schools. That they liked!

Next I faxed a letter to Hiro Itami at Hitsosubashi University in Tokyo, not realizing he was then dean. "Sit down before you read this," it began. "Why not?" began his reply the next day.

And so it was that our little fledging group of Jonathan, Roger Bennett and myself from McGill, and Heinz Thanheiser from Insead headed out to Tokyo, to convince Jiro Nonaka, the dean of management academics in Japan. We might never have gotten the chance had the madmen who gassed the subway cars in Tokyo that morning chosen to do so on the same line in the other direction, as we headed out to Hitsosubashi.

From there we went to the Indian Institute of Management in Bangalore, where Roger had done a reconnaissance trip earlier. "An interesting idea, but we'll never see them again" was the response to that trip (we found out years later). But they did see us again, and the partnership of five was confirmed (in Japan including the faculty of several schools).

Then we had to recruit companies to send their managers—no easy task when all we could offer were ideas (with no resources to back up our personal efforts). But thanks to the companies noted in the dedication, we managed to get going, although it didn't look like we would a month before startup. Thus in the spring of 1996 the International Masters Program in Practicing Management (IMPM) was launched, and it continues to be the delight of my professional life—as you will notice from my enthusiasm in Chapters 10 through 14.

This constitutes one of three main subjects of this book—what can be done to develop managers in a serious educational process. Another is my critique of the MBA, which is business education that I believe distorts managerial practice. And the third considers the practice of management itself, which I believe is going off the rails with dysfunctional consequences in society. So this little package called a book—four years in the writing, fifteen years in the developing, and thirty-five years in the thinking—draws together a great many of my ideas.

It must sound corny to read all the claims in such pages about how this and that book has been a collective effort, when everyone knows that nothing is more personal than the writing of a book. But the claim happens to be more than usually true here.

I dedicate this book to the "Why not?" people who got the IMPM started, but I wish to single one of them out in particular. This book would not have been worth writing had I not met Jonathan Gosling and developed such a wonderful working and friendly relationship with him. His ideas and imagination infuse this book, far beyond the many attributions to them. Perhaps people associate the IMPM with me because my name is better known in the literature, but there would have been no IMPM without Jonathan.

And there would not be the same IMPM without many others—faculty, participants in our eight classes to date, company people, administrators, and others. I mention here in particular Frank McCauley of the

Royal Bank of Canada, who not only supported us from the outset (and who prided himself in having sent our first check) but provided so many insights, as will be seen in Part II; Thomas Sattelberger, who at Lufthansa lit a fire under us to get things going; Bill Litwack, who set up some rather clever administration arrangements to deal with our complicated partnership and helped set the tone at the early modules; Colette Webb, who followed him as administrator of the program and has been its cheerful heart and soul ever since; Dora Koop, who has been there from the very first meeting at McGill to the current operation of the McGill module, and Kunal Basu, who was part of those early efforts; Nancy Badore, who has been so full of wonderful ideas and moral support; a number of our young faculty Turks, notably Quy Huy, Kaz Mishina, Taizoon Chinwalla (a graduate of the program and later co-cycle director while at Motorola), and Ramnath Narayanswamy, who were often truer to the fundamentals of the program than its founders, myself included; and Oliver Westall, who is extending the IMPM idea to the E Roundtables for existing EMBA programs.

My wife Saša and I have spent a good deal of time in Prague since late 1999, where I have written most of this book—about five times! Her support has been inspiring. Every once in a while I would announce to her energetic delight that I had finished the book. In fact, no book is ever finished until you hold it in your hand. Ask Santa, my personal assistant. Every time she finished typing the last chapter (I *write* books; Santa types them), I appeared with revisions to the first one. How she has remained so good-natured is a mystery I dare not investigate. Further help was provided by Chahrazed Abdallah, known as ChaCha (imagine life with a wife named Saša, a personal assistant named Santa, and a research assistant named ChaCha!), Elise Beauregard, Chen Hua Tzeng, and Rennie Nilsson. Nathalie Tremblay was brilliant in chasing down lost references.

It has, once again, been my pleasure to work with Pearson Education. This relationship goes way back, which is becoming increasingly rare in publishing these days. In particular, I would like to express my deep appreciation to Richard Stagg and his team, who are thorough in the very best sense of the word.

Helpful comments on parts or all of this book were provided by Charlie Dorris, Jeff Kulick, Bob Mountain, Andrea Markowitz, John Hendry, Joe Raelin, Dave Ulrich, Paola Perez-Alleman, Colette Webb, Oliver Westall, and Jonathan Gosling. Bob Simons offered some especially valuable comments on Chapter 2, far more sympathetic than my treatment of his school (Harvard) but successful in making my arguments somewhat more honest. Bogdan Costea provided in his doctoral thesis and private discussions ideas that have informed this book; Dan LeClair of the AACSB was very helpful in providing statistics on enrollments in business programs; Joe Lampel worked hard on the analysis of the nineteen Harvard CEOs discussed in Chapter 4. I must also mention the various IMPM participants who allowed me to quote from their material, as cited in the text.

Some years ago the dean of a prominent business school (Richard West of New York University) claimed, "If I wasn't dean of this school, I'd be writing a book on the bankruptcy of American management education" (in Byrne 1990:62). I have never been the dean of a business school. But I have worked with a number. Needless (if necessary) to say, the ideas expressed in this book represent neither their views nor those of their schools. But my deans and colleagues have been well aware of my views and never discouraged my expression of them in any way, while encouraging our efforts with the IMPM.

Thank you all!

Henry Mintzberg
*Prague, November 2003*

# INTRODUCTION

This is a book about management education that is about management. I believe that both are deeply troubled, but neither can be changed without changing the other.

The trouble with "management" education is that it is business education, and leaves a distorted impression of management. Management is a practice that has to blend a good deal of craft (experience) with a certain amount of art (insight) and some science (analysis). An education that overemphasizes the science encourages a style of managing I call "calculating" or, if the graduates believe themselves to be artists, as increasing numbers now do, a related style I call "heroic." Enough of them, enough of that. We don't need heroes in positions of influence any more than technocrats. We need balanced, dedicated people who practice a style of managing that can be called "engaging." Such people believe that their purpose is to leave behind stronger organizations, not just higher share prices. They do not display hubris in the name of leadership.

The development of such managers will require another approach to management education, likewise engaging, that encourages practicing managers to learn from their own experience. In other words, we need to build the craft and the art of managing into management education and thereby bring these back into the practice of managing.

Follow the chapter titles of this book into the chapters, and you will read about management education—Part I on what I believe is wrong with it, Part II on how it could be changed. But look within the chapters, and you will read about management itself—again what I believe is wrong with it and how it could be changed. To pick up on the subtitle, here we take a hard look at the soft practice of managing, alongside that of management development. There are plenty of books that provide soft looks at the hard practice of managing. I believe we need to face management as it is, in a serious way; it is too important to be left to most of what appears on the shelves of bookstores. Easy formulas and quick fixes are the problems in management today, not the solutions.

I have written this book for all thoughtful readers interested in management education and practice: developers, educators, managers, and just plain interested observers. I mean this to include MBA applicants, students, and graduates, at least ones who harbor doubts about this degree. If what I write here is true, then they especially should be reading this book.

Readers interested in management education will get the messages about management practice as they go along. Readers interested in management itself—this hard look at that soft practice—can focus on particular parts of the book. Chapters 4, 5, and 6 contain the essence of this material. Before reading this, however, I suggest you look at the introduction to Part I and the first part of Chapter 1 (pages 5–13) as well as, from Chapter 2, pages 36–42, 48–56, and 67–68. Beyond Chapter 6, I recommend pages 259–264 and especially 273–275 in Chapter 9, pages 299–312 in Chapter 11, and pages 333–336 and 344–345 in Chapter 13.

I should add that there are all kinds of illustrative materials in the boxes that accompany the text. Reading these will give much of the flavor of my arguments.

Part I of this book is called "Not MBAs." Some people may see it as a rant; I wrote it as a serious critique of what I believe to be a deeply flawed practice. If you have anything to do with MBAs, whether hiring them, supporting them, teaching them, or being one, I urge you to read this, if only to entertain some dark thought about this ostensibly sparkling degree. And if you are a manager or have anything to do with managers (who doesn't in this world?), I hope that reading this will open your eyes to a vitally important activity that is going out of social control.

The chapters of this first part flow as follows. What I call conventional MBA programs, which are mostly for young people with little if any managerial experience ("Wrong People," Chapter 1), because they are unable to use art or craft, emphasize science, in the form of analysis and technique ("Wrong Ways," Chapter 2). That leaves their graduates with the false impression that they have been trained as managers, which has had a corrupting effect on the education and the practice of management as well as on the organizations and societies in which it is practiced ("Wrong Consequences," Chapters 3, 4, 5, and 6).

There has been a lot of hype about changes taking place in prominent MBA programs in recent years. Don't believe it ("New MBAs?" Chapter 7). The MBA is a 1908 degree based on a 1950s strategy. The real innovations in management education, mostly in England but hardly recognized in America, serve as a bridge from the critique of Part I to the positive ideas for "Developing Managers" in Part II.

There is a great and unfortunate divide between management development and management education. While a full discussion of management development would require a book unto itself, the presentation of a framework of basic practices ("Management Development in Practice," Chapter 8) can open up vistas for management education.

The discussion of the book to this point suggests a set of general principles by which management education can be reconceived ("Developing Management Education," Chapter 9). These principles have been brought to life in a family of programs that can take management education and development to a new place, by enabling managers to reflect on their own experience in the light of insightful concepts (five aspects of "Developing Managers," Chapters 10 through 14). No one can create a leader in a classroom. But existing managers can significantly improve their practice in a thoughtful classroom that makes use of those experiences.

All this suggests that the business schools themselves need to be reconceived, including a metamorphosis into management schools ("Developing True Schools of Management," Chapter 15). But will these agents of change be able to change?

### PART ONE

# Not MBAs

I T IS TIME to recognize conventional MBA programs for what they are—or else to close them down. They are specialized training in the functions of business, not general educating in the practice of managing. Using the classroom to help develop people already practicing management is a fine idea, but pretending to create managers out of people who have never managed is a sham. It is time that our business schools gave proper attention to management.

This may seem like a strange contention at a time when MBA programs are at the height of their popularity, when MBA graduates are at the pinnacle of their success, and when American business, which has relied so heavily on this credential, seems to have attained its greatest stage of development. I shall argue that much of this success is delusory, that our approach to educating leaders is undermining our leadership, with dire economic and social consequences.

Every decade in the United States alone, almost one million people with a credential called the MBA descend on the economy, most with little firsthand knowledge of customers and workers, products and processes. There they expect to manage people who have that knowledge, which they gained in the only way possible—through intensive personal experience. But lacking that credential, such people are increasingly relegated to a "slow track" where they are subjected to the "leadership" of people who lack the legitimacy to lead.

Considered as education for management, conventional MBA programs train the wrong people in the wrong ways with the wrong consequences. This is the argument I shall pursue in Part I of this book. It contains seven chapters. The first is about the wrong people, the second about the wrong ways, the next four about the wrong consequences. Chapter 7 considers recent changes in MBA programs, concluding that most of these are cosmetic. A "dominant design" established itself in the 1960s and continues to hold most of this education firmly in its grip. The notable exceptions are found mostly in England, whose innovations provide a bridge to Part II of this book.

Some clarifications to begin. First, by "conventional" MBA, I mean full-time programs that take relatively young people, generally in their twenties, and train them mostly in the business functions, out of context—in other words, independent of any specific experience in management. This describes most MBA programs today, in the United States and around the world. With a few exceptions, the remaining ones (usually called EMBAs) take more experienced people on a part-time basis and then do much the same thing. In other words, they train the right people in the wrong ways with the wrong consequences. That is because they mostly fail to use the experience these people have.

Second, I use the words *management* and *leadership* interchangeably. It has become fashionable (after Zaleznik 1977) to distinguish them. Leadership is supposed to be something bigger, more important. I reject this distinction, simply because managers have to lead and leaders have to manage. Management without leadership is sterile; leadership without management is disconnected and encourages hubris. We should not be ceding management to leadership, in MBA programs or anywhere else.

Third, I refer to the schools in question in three ways: usually as "business schools," in reference to what most of them are; sometimes as "management schools," in reference to what they could be; and, especially in the last chapter, as M/B schools, in reference to what I conclude is the appropriate role for most of them—balanced attention to both management and business.

The MBA was first introduced in 1908; it last underwent serious revision based on two reports published in the late 1950s. Business schools pride themselves in teaching about new product development and strategic change, yet their flagship, the MBA, is a 1908 degree with a 1950s strategy. Part I of this book develops this conclusion; Part II proposes some real change.

Part I is highly critical of MBA education. I do this at some length because I believe the case against the MBA as education for management has to be made thoroughly, to counter some deeply entrenched beliefs and their consequences. One of the most interesting articles ever written about the MBA appeared in *Fortune* magazine in 1968. In it, Sheldon Zalaznick claimed, "The idea that the graduate school of business is the principal source of top executive talent has been allowed to flourish, unexamined . . ." (169). It has been allowed to flourish unexamined ever since. . . .[1] Not here.

---

[1] In 1996 (221), Aaronson reported on a search for articles about graduate business education. Of the 693 she found, only 12 criticized that education.

# 1

# WRONG PEOPLE

*It's never too late to learn, but sometimes too early.*
—CHARLIE BROWN IN *PEANUTS*

There are no natural surgeons, no natural accountants. These are specialized jobs that require formal training, initially in a classroom. The students must, of course, be able to handle a scalpel or a keyboard, but first they have to be specially educated. Then they can be foisted on a suspecting public, at least for internship or articling, before being allowed to practice on their own.

Leadership is different. There are natural leaders. Indeed, no society can afford anything *but* natural leaders. Leadership and management are life itself, not some body of technique abstracted from the doing and the being. Education cannot pour life experience into a vessel of native intelligence, not even into a vessel of leadership potential. But it can help shape a vessel already brimming with the experiences of leadership and life.

Put differently, trying to teach management to someone who has never managed is like trying to teach psychology to someone who has never met another human being. Organizations are complex phenomena. Managing them is a difficult, nuanced business, requiring all sorts of tacit understanding that can only be gained in context. Trying to teach it to people who have never practiced is worse than a waste of time—it demeans management.

## Management as a Practice

Were management a science or a profession, we could teach it to people without experience. It is neither.

Management Is Not a Science    Science is about the development of systematic knowledge through research. That is hardly the purpose of management. Management is not even an applied science, for that is still a science. Management certainly applies science: managers have to use all the knowledge they can get, from the sciences and elsewhere. But management is more art, based on "insight," "vision," "intuition." (Peter Drucker wrote in 1954 that "the days of the 'intuitive' manager are numbered" [93]. Half a century later we are still counting.) And most management is craft, meaning that it relies on experience—learning on the job. This means it is as much about doing in order to think as thinking in order to do.

Put together a good deal of craft with a certain amount of art and some science, and you end up with a job that is above all a *practice*. There is no "one best way" to manage; it all depends on the situation.

Effective managing therefore happens where art, craft, and science meet. But in a classroom of students without managerial experience, these have no place to meet—there is nothing to *do*. Linda Hill (1992) writes in her book about people becoming managers that they "had to act as managers before they understood what the role was" (67). In other words, where there is no experience, there is no room for craft: Inexperienced students simply cannot understand the practice. As for art, nothing stops that from being discussed, even admired, in the conventional MBA classroom. But the inexperience of the students stops it from being appreciated. They can only look on as nonartists do—observing it without understanding how it came to be.

That leaves science, which is what conventional MBA education is mostly about, at least in the form of analysis. So, as will be discussed in Chapter 2, conventional MBA students graduate with the impression that management is analysis, specifically the making of systematic decisions and the formulation of deliberate strategies. This, I argue in Chapter 3, is a narrow and ultimately distorted view of management that has encouraged two dysfunctional styles in practice: *calculating* (overly analytical) and *heroic* (pretend art). These are later contrasted with a more experienced-based style labeled *engaging*—quiet and connected, involving and inspiring.

MANAGEMENT IS NOT A PROFESSION    It has been pointed out that engineering, too, is not a science or an applied science so much as a practice in its own right (Lewin 1979). But engineering does apply a good deal of science, codified and certified as to its effectiveness. And so it can be called a profession, which means it can be taught in advance of practice, out of context. In a sense, a bridge is a bridge, or at least steel is steel, even if its use has to be adapted to the circumstances at hand. The same can be said about medicine: Many illnesses are codified as standard syndromes to be treated by specific techniques. But that cannot be said of management (Whitley 1995:92). Little of its practice has been reliably codified, let alone certified as to its effectiveness. So management cannot be called a profession or taught as such.

Because engineering and medicine have so much codified knowledge that must be learned formally, the trained expert can almost always outperform the layperson. Not so in management. Few of us would trust the intuitive engineer or physician, with no formal training. Yet we trust all kinds of managers who have never spent a day in a management classroom (and we have suspicions about some others who spent two years there, as will be discussed in Chapter 3).

Ever since the 1910s when Frederick Taylor (1911) wrote about that "one best way" and Henri Fayol (1916/1984) claimed that "managerial ability can and should be acquired in the same way as technical ability at school, later in the workshop" (14), we have been on this search for the holy grail of management as a science and a profession. In Britain, a group called the Management Charter Initiative sought to barrel ahead with the certification of managers, not making the case for management as a profession so much as assuming it. As its director told a newspaper, the MBA "is the only truly global qualification, the only license to trade internationally" (Watts 1997:43).

The statement is nonsense, and the group has failed in those efforts. It is time to face a fact: After almost a century of trying, by any reasonable assessment management has become neither a science nor a profession. It remains deeply embedded in the practices of everyday living. We should be celebrating that fact, not depreciating it. And we should be developing managers who are deeply embedded in the life of leading, not professionals removed from it.

Those fields of work discussed earlier can be divided into ones in which the person doing it truly "knows better" than the recipients and others in which acting as the expert who knows better can get in the way. Upon being wheeled into an operating room, few of us would be inclined to second-guess the surgeon. ("Could you cut a little lower, please?") No matter how miserable the bedside manner, we accept that he or she knows better. But a schoolteacher who acts on the basis of knowing better can impede the learning of the student. School teaching is a facilitating activity, more about encouraging learning than doing teaching.

Managing is largely a facilitating activity, too. Sure, managers have to know a lot, and they often have to make decisions based on that knowledge. But, especially in large organizations and those concerned with "knowledge work," managers have to lead better, so that others can know better and therefore act better. They have to bring out the best in other people. The idea that the chief does it all, coming up with the grand strategy and then driving its implementation by everyone else, is frequently a myth left over from the mass production of simple goods. Yet it is one of the impressions left by MBA education. "Our goal is to create an environment where students learn how to tackle difficult, complex problems. . . . Students learn what it feels like to exercise judgment, make decisions, and take responsibility" (in "Message from the Dean," Harvard Business School Web site, 2003).

Because grade schoolteachers can easily carry their skills from one classroom to another, they can still be called professionals. But not so managers, who can hardly carry their skills from one function to another within the same organization, let alone across organizations or industries. In other words, knowledge about context is not as portable in management as it is in education or engineering or medicine. That is why so many managers who have succeeded in one place fail in others (which is hardly true of teachers or engineers or physicians—so long as they stick to the skills they have).

A GUEST MANAGER?    Imagine a guest manager. The very idea seems absurd. How could anyone just come in and manage something? The manager must have a deep understanding of the context. Yet we accept substitute teachers who take over classrooms for a day, and Doctors without Borders who set up hospitals in hours. But temporary managers?

The one obvious example is instructive—a guest conductor. A few rehearsals, and off go the musicians performing at the most prestigious concert halls in the world. The reason is simple: the whole exercise is so highly programmed. Mozart is pulling the strings; everyone plays to his highly orchestrated score. We shall have professional management as soon as other organizations become as programmed as the symphony orchestra, playing their strategies like scores from Mozart, with all the obedient employees and customers sitting in neat rows responding on cue.

The practice of management is characterized by its ambiguity. That is why, despite its popular use, the metaphor of the conductor on the podium is wholly inappropriate (at least during performance, if not necessarily rehearsal; see Mintzberg 1998). Most work that can be programmed in an organization need not concern its managers directly; specialists can be delegated to do it. That leaves the managers mostly with the messy stuff—the intractable problems, the complicated connections. And that is what makes the practice of management so fundamentally "soft" and why labels such as experience, intuition, judgment, and wisdom are so commonly used for it. Here is how a successful manager at a major airline described her MBA husband to me: "He has the technique, thinks he knows best. But he is frustrated because he doesn't understand the complexities and the politics. He thinks he has the answers but is frustrated by being unable to do anything about it." He never learned management in the business school.

## "EXPERIENCE" IN MBA ADMISSIONS

Most business schools today require "work experience" of their MBA applicants, typically up to about four years. Some, in fact, are openly biased against much more than that, and Harvard apparently made the decision recently to reduce that to about two years and accept some applicants straight out of undergraduate studies.

But what is the use of a few years of experience, especially when it is not managerial? Can that install the necessary depth of understanding about how organizations work and what management means?

Imagine dropping a young MBA student into a classroom of experienced managers, even in a course on a specialized business function such as marketing or finance. So long as the class remains with theory and technique—in other words, remains at a generic level—the student would be fine. But as soon as the discussion turns to application—to nuance and appreciation—the student would be lost. In this respect, a classroom full of such students is always lost. "If you know how to design a great motorcycle engine," quipped Richard Rumelt, a professor of strategy at UCLA, "I can teach you all you need to know about strategy in a few days. If you have a Ph.D. in strategy, years of labor are unlikely to give you ability to design great new motorcycle engines." Business is about motorcycle engines: strategy is the means; motorcycle engines are the end. Conventional MBA programs are about strategy in the absence of motorcycle engines.

## Wrong Time?

Of course, this lack of experience suggests that the problem is not the wrong people so much as the wrong time. Do MBA programs teach the right people at the wrong time?

I think not, for two reasons. First, too early can make the right people wrong. Giving them a questionable impression of managing can distort how they practice it subsequently. Chapters 4 and 5 present some evidence on this. My colleague Jonathan Gosling has made an intriguing suggestion in this regard. The MBA appeals to people who are just gaining their independence from family and roots. Going "global," for example, sounds good to them. Yet management is about something quite the opposite—namely, the acceptance of responsibility. So MBA programs may be inadvertently encouraging an attitude of independence that is fundamentally antithetical to the responsible practice of management.

Second, I argue that MBA programs by their very nature attract many of the wrong people—too impatient, too analytical, too much need to control. These characteristics together with the MBA credential may get them into managerial positions. But with what consequences? That is the subject of Chapters 3 through 6.

## The Applications Charade

At the time of this initial writing, with a great deal of publicity and considerable help from McKinsey & Company, a new business school was being set up in India. The Indian magazine *Businessworld* (Gupta 2000) reported on its application criteria: "Students must be smart team players with proven leadership qualities and two years of work experience." How to select for such "proven" leadership qualities after only two years? "Selection criteria: GMAT scores, college performance, extra curricular and work experience."

This is typical of how people get into MBA programs. In the first instance, they select themselves, presumably in the belief that leading is better than following (and pays better). In fact, many people apply to MBA programs not just to move *up* but to move *out*—to find a better job somewhere else; in other words, to get away from the source of whatever limited experience they do have. Should that be telling us something?

The business schools choose from this pool. They select from among these self-selected leaders. The schools may look for evidence of leadership potential (e.g., posts held in extracurricular clubs, etc.), but when they boast about the quality of their students, they almost inevitably cite GMAT scores and grade point averages. Nicely numerical, all these—the business schools' own bottom lines. But do they measure managerial potential?

*GMAT* stands for Graduate Management Admission Test, and it assesses one's ability to give fast answers to little numerical and verbal problems (e.g., "If Mario was 32 years old 8 years ago, how old was he $x$ years ago? (A) $x - 40$, (B) $x - 24$, (C) $40 - x$, (D) $24 - x$, (E) $24 + x$" [GMAT 2000]). This is accompanied by an analytical writing task. Since how well you do depends on how well everyone else does, you had better prepare by buying a special book or taking a special course, because that is what everyone else is doing. "Take [the Kaplan exam preparation program] and get the score you need to get into the school you want," claims one big provider on its Web site (2003). So instead of practicing management, the would-be manager practices tests.

Good managers are certainly intelligent, and the GMAT certainly measures intelligence, at least formalized intelligence. But nonmanagers can be intelligent, too, as are no small number of dreadful managers. So the GMAT constitutes a useful but insufficient screening device, more useful, in fact, to identify successful students than successful managers. The latter have to exhibit all kinds of other characteristics that are not measured by such scores—indeed, many that are not adequately measured by *any* scores.

An MBA student at my own university once reproached me for having mentioned intuition in regard to the selection of MBA students. How can you possibly select for intuition, he insisted, when you can't even measure it? How indeed. Another asked whether the use of judgment in the selection process would not introduce bias. Sure, I replied, because bias is the other side of judgment. The best way to get rid of bias is to get rid of judgment. MBA programs that rely on these numerical scores get rid of judgment, and so, too, do they get rid of assessing managerial potential. In the process, they introduce their own bias—for science over art and craft.

Sure, the schools need some way to select the right people. But not from a pool of the wrong people. And not by the use of superfluous criteria. There is another way to select, which will be discussed in

Chapter 9: from a pool of practicing managers, based on their demonstrated success as managers.

## THE WILL TO MANAGE VERSUS
## THE ZEST FOR BUSINESS

In a classic *Harvard Business Review* article published over three decades ago, "The Myth of the Well-Educated Manager," Sterling Livingston (1971:84) wrote that many people who "aspire to high-level managerial positions . . . lack the 'will to manage.'" Not the *need* to manage but the *will* to manage. They "are not motivated to manage. They are motivated to earn high salaries and to attain high status."

Successful managing, in Livingston's opinion, is not about one's own success but about fostering success in others. "Universities and business organizations that select managerial candidates on the basis of their records as individual performers often pick the wrong [people] to develop as managers. . . . Fewer and fewer [management graduates] are willing to make the sacrifices required to learn management from the bottom up; increasingly, they hope to step in at the top from positions where they observe, analyze, and advise." Interesting words from 1971!

Some of these applicants do have another important characteristic, which Alfred North Whitehead, in another important article about business schools, published in 1932, labeled the "zest for business" (which is not the same as the zest for riches). Business schools have been effective at encouraging people with that zest and sometimes at encouraging others to get it; that may be their most important contribution to the economy. But they have also allowed this zest for business to be confused with that will to manage. In a sense, the former is about getting the most out of *resources*; the latter is about tapping the energy of *people*. (That people have become "human *resources*" in business schools and so much business practice is further evidence of this problem.)

As shown in Figure 1.1, there are people who have both the will to manage and the zest for business, just as there are people who have neither. The former would seem most suitable for leadership positions in large corporations, just as the latter are suitable for no leadership positions. Those who have the will but not the zest may be suitable for public and social sector organizations.

The problem is in the remaining box, with those who have the zest for business but not the will to manage. Such people are numerous in MBA programs. They may make good investment bankers, financial analysts, or consultants, which is what many of them in fact became

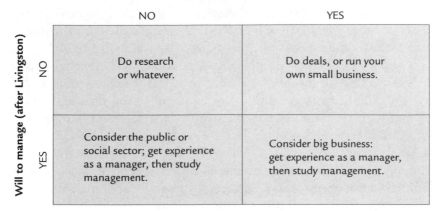

**Zest for Business (after Whitehead)**

|  | NO | YES |
|---|---|---|
| **NO** (Will to manage, after Livingston) | Do research or whatever. | Do deals, or run your own small business. |
| **YES** | Consider the public or social sector; get experience as a manager, then study management. | Consider big business: get experience as a manager, then study management. |

FIGURE 1.1

Business or Management?

(a famous one is discussed in the accompanying box), but often in the hope of running big corporations. I cite evidence in Chapter 4 suggesting that a surprising number of those who succeed in that hope fail in those positions. They should have remained where they were or else run their own small businesses (although other evidence cited there suggests that the record of MBAs as entrepreneurs is not strong).

## NOT MUCH WILL TO MANAGE, BUT PLENTY OF ZEST FOR BUSINESS!

"I didn't know what to do after the Navy. I didn't have any better idea than doing an MBA," said one holder of this degree, from Stanford (quoted in Crainer and Dearlove 1999:78). Not much will to manage, apparently. But he certainly did have a zest for business. He didn't end up as a manager. But he did do well in his chosen field, gaining great fame and making much money. His name is Tom Peters.

"[T]he MBA degree is not a magic wand that transforms inexperienced and immature undergraduates into licensed managers." So said Arnoud de Meyer et al. (1992:28), as head of the Insead MBA program. His counterparts, however, have generally thought otherwise. "This program is designed to develop high-potential managers," claims the University of Virginia Darden School on its Web site (2003). The Baruch

School in New York describes business schools as "incubators for the business leaders of tomorrow." And a faculty member of that new school in India said, "We will be interviewing people with the notion that we are training them to be managers" (Gupta 2000:53–54).

The business schools take this rhetoric seriously. They welcome people with the zest for business—or for power, or for riches—assume they have the will to manage, fill them up with courses on finance, marketing, and so forth, sprinkled with a few *about* management (not *on* managing), and then tell them that they are ready to manage. If the schools take this seriously, then why shouldn't the graduates? Most damaging of all, many of the hiring corporations, or at least people in their "human resource" departments, eager for a convenient source of managerial talent, take it seriously, too. It is, to repeat, a sham.

To conclude, we need leaders with human skills, not professionals with academic credentials. In the larger organizations especially, success depends not on what the managers themselves do, as allocators of resources and makers of decisions, so much as on what they help others to do.

So what should I tell Robert, a young man who came to see me about doing an MBA? It is with this question, discussed in the accompanying box, that I conclude this first chapter.

## What Should I Tell Robert?

Robert came to see me, the son of an old friend. He wanted to do an MBA. Where should he go?

That question comes up all the time. Bright young people, bored with a year or two of full-time work and looking for a better position somewhere else, see the MBA as a launching device. And I always give the same answer: Earn your leadership. Find an industry you like, get to know it, prove your potential, and practice management. *Then* get educated in management. Conventional MBA programs, I tell them, are a waste of time for managerial work; in fact, they can distort true managerial potential.

The eyes always glaze over at this point. No one actually says, "I came to find out which school to go to and you tell me this," but that is what seems to be on their minds. Instead, they say (in good years), "But look what awaits me if I get an MBA from a good school: a big salary, an important job, recruiters falling all over me, maybe even a

signing bonus like a football star—the fast track, the good life."
How could I tell Robert not to do the MBA?

Don't worry. I haven't done any harm in all this, because I doubt that a single one ever took my advice. They were all intent (as was I at that stage) to do the degree.

Until Joe came along. Same question. Same answer. But Joe's eyes didn't glaze over. At least he left wondering.

I've stayed in touch with Joe for several years now. A few months later he was accepted at a good business school. He decided not to go. Instead, he changed jobs. He loves his new work, he told me, and is learning a lot. He has doubts about the MBA now and is considering other options for further education.

Maybe there is hope.

# 2

# WRONG WAYS

*The secondhandedness of the learned world*
*is the secret to its mediocrity.*
—ALFRED NORTH WHITEHEAD

There are no right ways to develop the wrong people. We could, therefore, stop here and have a really short chapter. But the problem goes much deeper; and so does this chapter and those that follow. The MBA programs not only fail to develop managers but give their students a false impression of managing that, when put into practice, is undermining our organizations and our societies. Indeed, the ways of the MBA—the contents of the programs and the methods by which they are taught—are so entrenched that they are regularly used, with similar consequences, for the right people—namely, practicing managers in so-called Executive MBA and shorter management development programs.

In this chapter, I will discuss how MBAs are educated, first the content of these programs and then the methods used. I will consider the dysfunctional consequences of this education on management practice in the next chapters. But first a brief review of the history of business education, which will help explain why business schools today use the content and methods they do.

# A Brief History of Business Education

Business education began on a rather positive note but later deteriorated up to the 1950s, when some remarkable changes began to take place. We live with these changes today.

## The Formative Years

Business education is usually traced back to the University of Pennsylvania, which set up a bachelors program in business in 1881, thanks to the efforts of businessman Joseph Wharton. In a paper on the origins of business education (see also Redlich 1957), J. C. Spender (1997) argues otherwise, tracing this effort back to the Prussian school of bureaucratic statecraft, which developed an agenda that sounds very much like business schools today: "the application of the scientific method, meaning rigorous measurement, data collection, record keeping, statistical analysis and the development of rational-legal modes of order, decision-making and control over social activities" (13). Something akin to cases was also used, as well as field studies, and a debate arose over "whether such training should be for administrative technicians, staffers, or business leaders," which continues to this day—and in this book.

Joseph Wharton was an American businessman who learned German and visited Prussia. He is thought to have carried these ideas straight into his proposal for the business school that bears his name. He criticized the "learning by doing" (Sass 1982:22) common in the American commercial colleges of the day, and he insisted that the University of Pennsylvania curriculum include accounting, mercantile law, and economics; soon after, finance and statistics were added. When Edmund James, who did his doctorate in Germany, became dean in 1887, "The Wharton School was well under way" (Spender 1997:20) in Prussian tradition. "[E]mphasis shifted over the years that followed," but Sass [1982:294] records that when he accepted the Deanship in 1972 Donald Carroll embraced the school's original Jamesian vision (Spender 1997:21).

Enter the MBA   Dartmouth College was the first school to offer a masters degree in business, in 1900, when it "allowed a few undergraduates

. . . [to extend] their . . . course work by an additional year" (Schlossman et al. 1994:6). Harvard University followed in 1908 with the first
program called a Master of Business Administration (which the president's office apparently referred to as an "ugly label" [Heaton
1968:71]). Stanford introduced the second in 1925, although undergraduate education in business had by then been firmly established in
the United States. (The American Association of [now Association to
Advance] Collegiate Schools of Business [AACSB], later to become the
accrediting agency, was established in 1916.)

But neither Harvard nor Stanford had an easy time, having "to con-
tend with unenthusiastic sponsors from the business community, bois-
terous and skeptical students, and jealous and cynical university
colleagues and trustees," not to mention financial troubles (Schlossman
et al. 1994:9–10). Thirty-three students enrolled in the Harvard MBA
program in 1908; only eight returned for the second year. Four MBA degrees were granted in 1919 (15, 17).

Interestingly, "the principal impetus for [this] university-based business education" came from academics—"economists, psychologists, sociologists, and political scientists"—most of whom "lacked firsthand
knowledge about business and, indeed had few ties to businessmen."[1]
Nevertheless, "they were confident that they could discover an underlying 'science' of business, convey that science to the future leaders of corporate America, and thereby develop a new profession of management." Even at Harvard, "All four founders were academics with limited
business experience" (10, 11), including Edwin Gay, the first dean, who
had also done his doctoral thesis in Germany.

THE ADVENT OF CASES    Early on, there were "two competing themes,"
one based on "general knowledge about business conduct," the other,
"specialized knowledge about operations of specific industries." Harvard, for example, had required courses in principles of accounting,
commercial law, and economic resources of the United States, as well as
electives in fields such as banking and railroad operations (Schlossman
et al. 1994:13, 14).

Mostly the lecture method was favored at Harvard, except in commercial law, where examples were taken from public court decisions.
Gradually this use of examples became more widespread and was seen

---

[1]This situation has continued. In 1999 (October 18, p. 78), *Business Week* published the percentage of faculty of twenty business schools with at least five years of
business experience. Harvard ranked second lowest (after Insead), with 8 percent
(Stanford was at 20 percent; Wharton, 10 percent).

as giving rise to the case study method. But the real impetus for the widespread use of cases seems to have come from a Chicago business-man named Arch Shaw. He first used them in the undergraduate busi-ness program at Northwestern University and subsequently approached Gay (Gleeson et al. 1993:15). Cases first entered the Harvard MBA in a second-year required course called Business Policy, which became part of the curriculum in 1912. Individual businessmen were invited to pre-sent and discuss "a problem from [their] own desk." Two days later, "each student handed in a written report embodying his analysis of the problem and his recommended solution," which the businessman subsequently discussed with the class (Copeland 1954:33). The stu-dents apparently liked this, but the use of cases was not to spread until after World War I, under a new dean named Wallace Donham, a banker.

Donham later remarked about his arrival, "I had no theoretical knowledge of business, and my faculty, I found, had little practical knowledge of business. It was a difficult problem to fit the two to-gether" (in Gleeson et al. 1993:17). Shaw's idea solved Donham's prob-lem, and another as well: pressures from the students, who "stomp[ed] their feet when lectures became boring." Donham named Copeland, "a notoriously poor lecturer and a victim of foot-stomping protests," to run Harvard's Bureau of Business Research and "told [him] to convert it from statistical data to case collection." Copeland converted his market-ing course, too, and "miraculously, the foot stomping stopped" (18).

Donham did not force others to use the method, but Harvard's "enormously successful effort to mass produce cases created consider-able pressure on the faculty to include them, and by the mid-1920s cases had infiltrated most courses" (Gleeson et al. 1993:18), where they remain today. (At Northwestern, meanwhile, where the administration "never took a formal position on the case method," the use of cases "remained [and remains] highly individualized" [Gleeson et al. 1993:25].)

CASES FOR THE SAKE OF THEORY   Donham "assumed that cases would be used to introduce theoretical issues . . . [in a] palatable, down-to-earth manner." He also believed that the writing of cases "would en-courage the generation of theory." In fact, he described the case study as "simply a method of interesting the student," with "no magic," just a way to carry the student "much farther into theory" (Gleeson et al. 1993:31). His faculty, however, had other ideas and took the school's use of cases somewhere else, where it remained for most of the rest of the century and, to a considerable extent, today.

According to Gleeson et al., three groups comprised the faculty. First, the *industry specialists*, often prominent businessmen, taught the popular courses on specific industries, many of which Donham managed to eliminate. Second, the *functional specialists*, in areas such as marketing, finance, and production, were encouraged by Donham in his early years to combat this industry specialization. He insisted, largely in vain, that they discuss their functional problems "within the context of the entire firm." Finally, the *"homegrown" faculty* came in as case writers (often having used them to get the new doctoral degree). They saw cases differently, "as being most valuable when they encouraged students to abandon the search for theory and to learn how to make realistic and difficult decisions on their own" (32). Donham tried to counter this third group by reducing the expenditures on case writing (by almost two-thirds) and by promoting social science research, involving in the school such illustrious scholars as Elton Mayo, Joseph Schumpeter, and Talcott Parsons. But his was a losing cause: "Generalizable business theories did not spring forth from the case studies" (33).

So early on the stage was set for the great debate of business education: the theory of the original Wharton, rooted in scholarship, versus the practice of Harvard, rooted in experience, ostensibly that "learning by doing" so roundly criticized by Joseph Wharton. Yet a look at the courses offered by Harvard, from the outset, gives cause to wonder whether these differences in approach were all that significant.

ON TO MARKET SUCCESS AND ACADEMIC FAILURE    From these origins, the business schools rose to prominence in the United States. From about 40 in 1915, the next ten years saw the addition of 143 more (Cheit 1975:91); 110 masters degrees were granted in 1920, 1,017 in 1932, and 3,357 in 1948 (Gordon and Howell 1959:21).

But the academic quality did not follow. Harvard persisted with its case studies (and by 1949 had graduated almost half of all MBAs [Aaronson 1992:168]), but most schools descended into a kind of dark age of business education. "By the end of the 1930s . . . much of [Stanford's] graduate program was perilously close" to undergraduate studies (Gleeson et al. 1993:35), while Columbia experienced "the triumph of vocationalism"—the teaching of "job specific skills" (Aaronson 1992:163, 164). At Wharton, professors more interested in consulting than researching "conspired with the practical concerns of job-conscious students to frustrate Joseph Wharton's broad intentions" (Mast 2001:297). Management itself was taught in business schools as a collection of vague principles, akin to folk wisdom—for example, that the manager's span of control should not exceed seven. (See Simon's [1957] critique of these principles.) "By the late 1940s, the inability of even such elite institutions as Harvard, Stanford, Columbia, and Chicago to respond to the clarion call for a new type of manager was obvious." Business was changing rapidly, but "the knowledge available to students through both textbooks and cases" was not (Schlossman et al. 1994:3).

## THE RETURN TO ACADEMIC RESPECTABILITY

THE CARNEGIE MONASTERY    The Irish monastery of the business school Dark Age was a remarkable place in Pittsburgh, Pennsylvania, called the Graduate School of Industrial Administration (GSIA) at the Carnegie Institute of Technology (now Carnegie Mellon University). GSIA did not, however, keep the light of academia shining so much as turn it back on in the 1950s.

The precipitating event was the 1946 hiring of an economist named George Leland Bach, after wartime service in the Federal Reserve, to restart Carnegie's economics department. Bach brought in William Cooper from the field of Operations Research (mathematical applications to systems problems), which had become prominent in wartime applications, and they hired Herbert A. Simon, a brilliant young political scientist, to direct the undergraduate program in business. Zalaznick (1968) later wrote in *Fortune* magazine that Simon's hiring "was a signal to the academic community that a business school might be an appropriate place in which to work on . . . profound . . . if less immediately relevant" problems (206).

Pressures were building during the Cold War to improve U.S. management capabilities, and when a grant of almost $6 million came from William Lorimer Mellon to endow a new school of industrial administration at Carnegie, Bach became its first dean, bringing along his economics department.

The vision was clear from the outset (and not unrelated to the original German and Wharton efforts, let alone some of Donham's unrealized beliefs):

1. Systematic research matters; teaching follows. "Research was their fundamental engine of progress" (Gleeson and Schlossman 1995:14).

2. Research should be descriptive above all, especially to understand business and organizations; prescription could follow, in practice.

3. Such research should be rooted in a set of underlying disciplines, notably economics, psychology, and mathematics. These should also be central to masters-level courses as well as being the foundations of such business functions as finance, marketing, and accounting.

4. The classroom is a place to ground the students in the skills of analytical problem solving, in the style of operations research, or "management science."

5. Particular attention should be given to doctoral studies, to stimulate research and have the graduates carry these ideas to other schools.

One thing, however, did not much figure in all of this: the development of managers. GSIA was more concerned about getting the academic house in order and its professors properly respected. So it had to look inward, to its status in the university, not outward, to the needs of practicing managers. But this was a problem not so much ignored as assumed away, as it has been ever since: that properly respectable academic schools would produce properly practicing managers. Besides, if to manage is to make good decisions, then developing students' analytic skills could only improve the practice of management.

The GSIA faculty researched a remarkably broad and interesting set of issues, but never those just discussed. They never tested their own assumptions. Indeed, over time they retreated into the disciplines, and management (called administration), which had been the focus of early attempts at integration, simply disappeared.

GSIA in those years staffed itself with people—very smart people— educated largely in the social science disciplines. Bach was an economist; Simon, a political scientist; Cooper, a statistician. All became famous, as did many of their subsequent hires: Richard Cyert, economics; James March, political science; Harold Levitt, psychology; Allan Newell, mathematics; Franco Modigliani and Morton Miller, economics/finance. (The last two together, and Simon, separately, eventually won the Economics Prize named for Alfred Nobel.) Bach described GSIA (in Gleeson and Schlossman 1995:13, 23) as a "hardball place," with "no room for second-rate work," where "everyone debated everything." Well, *almost* everything.

Most important, GSIA faculty worked together, integrating around the disciplines as well as the newly emerging information technology of the computer. Some of their most important work focused on organizations. Although important work on them had been done earlier, notably by Max Weber, the great German sociologist (see Gerth and Mills 1958), GSIA, led especially by Simon, put "organization theory" on the map (see especially Simon 1947, 1957; March and Simon 1958; and Cyert and March 1963; see also the Starbuck review, 2002).

With the faltering of the other business schools, GSIA became the great hope. Here was academic respectability for the offering, fully up-to-date, with computers and mathematics. This could not only link the schools with established academic disciplines but also make them centers for the integration of some work in those disciplines. GSIA most certainly did this, at least in its early years. Its research output and conceptual insights, across psychology and economics, especially about organizations, were extraordinary: GSIA during the 1950s was undoubtedly the most exciting center of scholarship that has ever been seen in a business school. And it leveraged that effort to produce a steady stream of doctoral students who eventually had enormous influence on other business schools, many as deans.

THE TURNING POINT OF 1959    When two major studies were commissioned in the late 1950s to consider the dire straights of the American business schools, one by the Ford Foundation (Gordon and Howell 1959), the other by the Carnegie Corporation (Pierson 1959), it should come as no surprise that GSIA served as their model. In fact, Bach was closely associated with both reports (Gleeson and Schlossman 1995:26) and contributed a chapter to the Pierson report that argued for "analytical, rational" decision making as the key to management education (Bach 1959).

Gordon and Howell (1959) describe business education as "gnawed by doubts and harassed by the barbs of unfriendly critics," finding "itself at the foot of the academic table. . . . They search for academic respectability, while most of them continue to engage in unrespectable vocational training" (4). The proposed solution was "a sophisticated command of *analytical* and *research* tools derived from the fundamental *disciplines,*" as well as "[s]ound training in the physical and social *sciences* and mathematics and statistics, combined with the ability to apply these *tools* to business problems" (100, italics added), supplemented by cases and the like to "give the student *some limited experience* in dealing with the kinds of problems he will encounter in the business world"

(135–36, italics added). The report also called for "releasing more faculty time for scholarly activity and formal research" (391), and it urged business schools to develop closer cooperation with the underlying disciplines, by "seeking to interest more behavioral scientists, mathematicians, and statisticians in business problems" and offering "more training in these related areas for doctoral candidates . . . [and] present faculty members" (392).

The Pierson report conveyed much the same message, with perhaps more concern for integration among the various subjects, talking of increased "academic standards," "serious academic work" (ix), and "the prime role" for research (xv). The assumption once again, as articulated later by Whitley (1995), was that "research . . . would produce general scientific knowledge, which could be directly applied to . . . managerial tasks. Effective managers could thus be 'made' through formal university training programs" (81). But the report referred to business and businessmen more than managing and managers—which has proved to be an important distinction.

If ever words on paper have rendered significant changes, these two reports are certainly examples. Their spirit and much of their specific content (save their calls for what we now call "soft skills" and for integration across the functions) were widely adopted by business schools across the United States and then around the world. (The Ford Foundation also injected $35 million between 1954 and 1966 to create "centers of excellence" at Carnegie, Stanford, and a few other schools [Mast 2001:9].) The pendulum thus swung with a vengeance, from the practical to the academic—indeed, to the very place where Joseph Wharton had tried to secure it almost a century earlier.

Like the Phoenix, the business schools thus arose from their own ashes. Stanford, for example, having been in "stalemate" between 1945 and 1958, "the epitome of what [the] reformers sought to replace," "was transformed" and captured a leading role in the vanguard of what Gleeson (1997:8, 22) has called "the New Look," as did Wharton itself.

With these changes came "new academic respect on campus" (Cheit 1985:46). Research came to the forefront, and doctoral programs flourished as business schools took their place alongside the accepted professional schools and scientific disciplines. The U.S. government even issued a commemorative postage stamp in 1981 (Cheit 1985:46–47) to honor the one-hundredth anniversary of Joseph Wharton's initiative. It read "Professional Management."

RESEARCH YES, BUT TEACHING?    That stamp should have read "Business Research" (except who would have bought it?), for it was in research that these two reports brought about their revolution. While management hardly became a profession—or, indeed, received much attention in the business schools at all—research, especially in the functions of business, flourished. Scholars from all sorts of backgrounds gathered in business schools to address issues of marketing, finance, analysis, human behavior in organizations, and so on.

James March, who went to the Stanford Business School some years after he left Carnegie, has made a case for the importance of such research, but with an interesting twist. Hardly one to avoid provoking, March claimed not only that the business school's "primary role" is to produce research ("contribute to knowledge") but that this beneficially happens through the "subterfuge" of "[l]arge expenditures on research . . . concealed within the rhetoric and accounting of education" (in Schmotter 1995:59).

MBA students could hardly be expected to embrace March's point. Indeed, some early GSIA students themselves described their colleagues as having become "skeptical" about the "professional relevance" of the faculty's research agenda: At a "1958 conference . . . devoted to learning about recent faculty investigations, it became apparent that the alumni no longer cared much—and perhaps never had cared—about the school's research output" (quoted in Schmotter 1995:140).

But no matter: With the MBA's newfound respectability, enrollment took off. From 4,041 business masters degrees granted in the United States in 1958 (most of these MBAs) and 6,375 in 1964, the numbers more than doubled in the next two years, to 12,998. Ten years later, in 1976, they reached 42,654. The year after that, *Forbes* magazine called the MBA "second in esteem only to the coveted Doctor of Medicine as a passport to the good life" (quoted in Cheit 1985:46). The numbers continued to grow rapidly, although not at that pace. By 1997–1998, they passed the 100,000 mark (AACSB Web site, November 2001).[2] At this rate, the United States alone now produces upwards of a million people per decade who believe that they have the capacity to manage by virtue of having spent two years in an academic school of business. It is to this unexamined yet flourishing proportion that we now turn.

---

[2]U.S. Department of Education figures put the number of business masters degrees in 2000–2001 at 116,475, of which 82,430 in the categories of "business general" and "business administration—and management" are probably MBAs (according to Dan Leclair of the AACSB, in personal correspondence, who believes it likely that some other MBAs are reported in other specialized categories).

# QUESTIONING THE CONTENT

When a pendulum swings too far in one direction, its inertia generally sends it swinging back the other way. Not so the business school pendulum, which has been stuck in one direction for almost half a century. Pierson wrote in his 1959 report:

> If business schools in increasing numbers move in the . . . direction [prescribed], the charge will doubtless be made that their work would soon become too academic, and thus lose much of its value in terms of specific career training. Again, viewed against the record to date, the likelihood that this will occur is remote indeed. (xiii)

Too bad Pierson could not have assessed this concern against the record to come, for it has proved to be not remote but prophetic. "[H]ow strong is the gravitational pull of 'respectability,'" Murray (1988:71) wrote, even if "the only business that could seem to benefit [from such attitudes] would be the business school business!" In correcting the earlier problems, these two 1959 reports created other ones.

## THE DOMINATION OF THE BUSINESS FUNCTIONS

The business school most often ranked top in the popular magazine polls at the time this was first written in its MBA brochure for 2000–2002, "Wharton has top-ranked departments in more areas than any other business school, including finance, entrepreneurship, insurance and risk management, marketing, real estate, and business law." Everything but management!

UP WENT THE WALLS    Carnegie may have focused on the social science disciplines, seeking to integrate them around concerns of "administration," but something happened on its way to other business schools. Indeed, something happened on Carnegie's own way to the future. After a few years, the seams of this hoped-for integration began to split, soon to metamorphose into walls. By the "early 1960s, GSIA's various intellectual groups had boiled down to two main camps . . . the economists

. . . [and] a loose combination of organizational theorists and management scientists," with a "profound" rift between them (Gleeson and
Schlossman 1995:29). Bach resigned the deanship in 1962 and not long
after left for the Stanford Business School.[3] After Simon withdrew to
the psychology department and Modigliani left the university, the rift
grew wider.

More significant, perhaps, as the walls went up in other schools,
much as at GSIA, the social science disciplines came down. In some
places, such as Wharton (Sass 1982:289), they departed to other parts
of the university; in others, they were absorbed into the business functions (even if they sometimes dominated them, most notably the economists of finance). Soon these functions came to dominate the business
schools, around which all its activities were organized. And as these
functions became increasingly powerful, they also became increasingly
disconnected from each other. Today, as such, they are rock solid in the
business schools. Each pushes its own angle, its own content, its own
biases, and, at the limit, its own ideology: "shareholder value" in finance, worker "empowerment" in organizational behavior, "customer
service" in marketing, and so forth. Students are consequently left with
what Whitehead (1983) once called the "passive reception of disconnected ideas" (2, 11).

## THE BUSINESS SCHOOL AS A COALITION OF FUNCTIONAL INTERESTS

Almost everything done in almost every business school today takes
place in terms of the specialized functions, whether an idea researched,
a program designed, a course taught, or a professor hired. This has less
to do with any proven best way to manage or even to conduct business
than with the structure of the business school itself. Each functional department gets a piece of the action.

This is not to say that business schools do not teach material that
cuts across the specialized functions, only that they do so *within* particular functions. So collaborative teamworking, for example, gets taught
within organizational behavior, without collaboration or teamworking,
and new product development gets taught in marketing or else in strategy, with the result that the schools rarely engage in new product development of their own. We know about the dangers of doing such things

---

[3]On a personal note, in 1973 I was a visiting professor at GSIA for a semester. There
I found doctoral students, many of them European, walking the halls looking for
that famous GSIA administrative theory. By then almost everyone interested in it
had left.

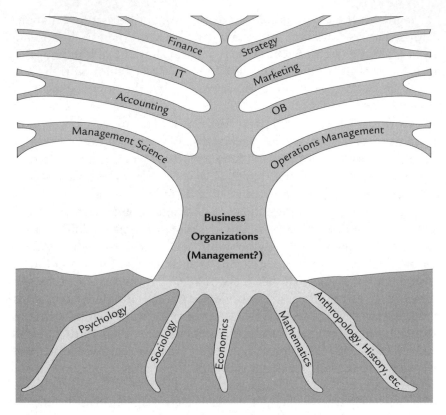

FIGURE 2.1

Concept of the Business School Inherited from GSIA

in business practice—indeed, we teach about these dangers—while we succumb to them in our own practice. As businesses work valiantly to bust down the walls between their "silos," business schools work valiantly to reinforce them. Business schools teach a great deal about managing change, notably that it has to get past the existing categories. Yet because business schools themselves cannot, they remain more or less where the two foundation reports of 1959 put them.

The genius of the original GSIA was its work across the disciplines and functions. As depicted in Figure 2.1, the disciplines were the roots, and research as well as the very notion of business and organization, (also administration, or management?) comprised the trunk, feeding out to the business functions, as branches. Now each of these branches has taken root on its own and stands apart from the others.

## AND WHATEVER HAPPENED
## TO MANAGEMENT?

Business managers certainly have to understand the business functions. At the very least, the functions constitute a need-to-know "language of business." Moreover, especially for students with work experience in a single function (e.g., sales or production), classroom exposure to all the functions can broaden their understanding of the practice of business. But the practice of business is not the same as the practice of management. Management is not marketing plus finance plus accounting and so forth. It is *about* these things, but it is not these things. Pour each of these functions, of a different color, into that empty vessel called an MBA student, stir lightly, and you end up with a set of specialized stripes, not a blended manager.

In 1984, Leonard Sayles wrote an important yet forgotten article entitled "Whatever Happened to Management . . . or Why the Dull Stepchild?" It expressed surprise that management was not taught in the management schools. Harvard still had its required course called "Business Policy," introduced in 1912, but Stanford dropped the one it had offered in the 1930s, and a number of the other prestigious schools, such as MIT, had none.[4]

That problem was eventually solved, too, much like the others. Courses came to be offered *about* management, initially often called "Business Policy," after the Harvard course.[5] But they hardly taught

---

[4]When I arrived at the MIT Sloan School in 1963 to do my master's degree, there was no professor of management, no area of management, no regular course in management. But Ned Bowman, a respected professor of operations management, had just returned from a year off to work with the head of Honeywell Computers, and he offered an elective in "Management Policy," which I took. I subsequently proposed to do my doctorate in the area, and Ned proposed to supervise me—to find out whether there was any future in this area, he said. One day he told me he thought not. I replied that he would change his mind. (Years later, he became the chaired professor of strategy at Wharton.) Ned left MIT the next year, and my thesis was supervised by another professor of operations management (Don Carroll, cited earlier when he became dean at Wharton), a professor of accounting, and a professor of labor relations. When I was interviewed at GSIA in 1967, they did not like my thesis on the nature of managerial work (Mintzberg 1973), and did not offer me a job.

[5]When I joined the McGill University Faculty of Management in 1968, I introduced a course called "Management Policy," designed to be compatible with the GSIA approach that McGill had adopted. I taught that course for about fifteen years. It set out to be integrative and teach about management, but I am not sure how much either aim was accomplished, at least with the less experienced students.

management.[6] They were touted as "capstone," or integrative, courses, but they hardly accomplished such integration and, in that respect at least, were soon gone.

HOW MANAGEMENT BECAME STRATEGY   These courses about management were not so much eliminated as converted to something more compatible with the rest of the MBA curriculum. And ironically (or perhaps not), the replacement, right up the alley of the theory-oriented business schools, came from Harvard.

Michael Porter received an MBA from the Harvard Business School and then crossed the river to do his doctorate in the economics department before returning as a professor in 1973. In 1980, he published *Competitive Strategy*, offering a solid if narrow analytical framework, and it took the policy courses by storm. The book quickly displaced the popular *Business Policy* text by Porter's colleague (originally Learned et al. [1965], but including Porter in the 1982 edition by Christensen et al.), made up primarily of cases, with some basic text dating mostly back to 1965.

Strategy combines missions and markets, products and process into some coherent "theory of the business," to use Drucker's (1994) phrase. Surely, then, it must be about synthesis. But not in Porter's view. "I favor a set of analytic techniques to develop strategy," he wrote in *The Economist* in 1987. Analytic techniques to analyze strategy, perhaps, or to feed information into the strategy process. But analytic techniques to develop strategy? Chief among these were what Porter called "industry analysis" and "competitive analysis." The book also contained a great deal of text that was remarkably reductionist in nature (checklist upon checklist). Moreover, for Porter in that book, strategies were not ideas to be invented so much as categories to be selected. He wrote at length about "generic strategies."

What all of this did, of course, was take strategy exactly where earlier efforts had taken marketing, finance, and other functions—to a place compatible with what business schools had generally become: Porter taught the business schools to develop analysts, not strategists.

---

[6]In his history of the Wharton School, Sass (1982: 298–337) describes at some length its various efforts to find some kind of general management focus. For example: "Whatever their ultimate scientific value . . . it has become clear by the mid-1970s that disciplines such as decision sciences and organizational behavior were not about to unlock the essence of managerial success" (323). One professor even "intended to make the study of collective bargaining . . . the foundation for the study of management in general" (299). By the time of the writing of his book in 1982, "No one course of study . . . succeeded in capturing the essence of modern management" (333).

For obvious reasons, the business schools embraced Porter's view. Even Harvard embraced it (although not without considerable conflict, which forced Porter and his followers to break away from what had come to be called the General Management group and to form a new one, called Competition and Strategy). MBA students loved it, too: Here, finally, was some real analysis under the guise of management, something they could sink their analytical teeth into, and that would give them an advantage over experience, especially as consultants. At Harvard, Porter's book became the basis for a first-year required course and an extremely popular second-year elective. By 2000, after eighty-eight years in the Harvard MBA curriculum, the required "Business Policy" course was gone (and a second required course in finance was added!).

Professors of management the world over embraced Porter's approach, too. It allowed them to gain the respect of their functional colleagues, by dropping soft management in favor of hard analysis. It also provided them with a new basis to do respectable research. Instead of writing stories about strategy—cases in one way or another—strategy professors could analyze the hard data of industries to hypothesize about which generic strategies worked best where. So as policy metamorphosed into strategy, and strategy later into "Strategic Management," the field mushroomed as never before, with new courses and new journals, the latter ever more academic. Indeed, the new problem for the field was success: Colleagues in other functions adopted the word *strategy*, as well as many of Porter's uses of it, every which way—in marketing strategy, financial strategy, IT strategy, and so forth—to the point where the "strategy" people began to feel besieged on all sides.

MANAGEMENT AS YET ANOTHER FUNCTION    It is important to appreciate exactly what this meant. With this shift from policy to strategy, and from concern for synthesis to focus on analysis, the one field in the business school that was supposed to be about general management itself became narrowly specialized. The very label "Strategic Management" implies that the management of strategy is something apart from management itself (another form of reductionism that has proven terribly destructive in practice, as I shall argue later). In other words, management found its place in the contemporary school of business by becoming yet another specialized function—in other words, by disappearing once again.

As a consequence, these days if you are interested in teaching and researching about management, you may have difficulty finding a job in a business school. The old functions won't want you, and the new function of strategic management may shun you as well. Of course, there is always "organizational behavior." But this area has not always shown great interest in management, either; for example, research on the practice of managing itself remains rare—let alone on the behavior of organizations. For organizational behavior is mostly about the behavior of people in organizations. Indeed, it has often become functional in recent years, too. As "human resources" have replaced people in its lexicon, "human resource management" has replaced organizational behavior (Costea 2000:146).

To conclude, the typical business school today is about specialization, not integration, concerned with the business functions, not the practice of managing. Courses exist *about* management, but they are not particularly mainstream. There have been continuous efforts to have more of them, but as shall be discussed later, they have not met with great success.

Does this mean that managerial skills are absent from the MBA curriculum? Not quite. And that brings us to the heart of the problem.

## MANAGEMENT BY ANALYSIS

That old joke about the MBA standing for *m*anagement *by* *a*nalysis is no joke at all.

Analysis means "the process of separating something into its constituent elements" (*New Oxford Dictionary of English*). Indeed, the word analysis itself comes from a Greek root meaning to unloosen. Separating things into parts, unloosening them from the whole, is what MBA programs are about. Business becomes a collection of functions; strategy, a set of generic strategies and competitive analyses; even people become analytical things. Here is what a popular organizational behavior textbook out of Harvard had to say about people:

> [W]e view human resources as *social capital*. The implication is that the development of work-force capabilities, attitudes, and international relations must be thought of within an investment paradigm. . . . As with other investment decisions, a long-term perspective, sometimes well beyond the current accounting period, is required. (Beer et al., 1985:12, 13)

NO SYNTHESIS IN ANALYSIS    The danger of breaking things apart, as Humpty Dumpty discovered to his chagrin, is that it may not be possible to put them back together. Business schools have not been able to put things back together again because that has to happen in context—in specific situations.

Synthesis is the very essence of management. Within their own contexts, managers have to put things together in the form of coherent visions, unified organizations, integrated systems, and so forth. That is what makes management so difficult, and so interesting. It's not that managers don't need analysis; rather, it's that they need it as an input to synthesis, and that is the hard part. Teaching analysis devoid of synthesis thus reduces management to a skeleton of itself. This is equivalent to considering the human body as a collection of bones: Nothing holds it together, no sinew or muscle, no flesh or blood, no spirit or soul. Accordingly, *Mastering Management*, a book produced as a kind of composite MBA in conjunction with Wharton, The London Business School, and IMD, opens with the following statement:

> *Mastering Management* is about general management but that subject itself is not covered as such since general management is the synthesis of many management functions, such as accounting and marketing, which are covered in their own right in other modules of *Mastering Management*. (*Financial Times* 1997:3)

Even if we were to accept this silly claim, the question remains of where the synthesis comes from. The usual, dismissive, answer is the students: They will put it together. Think of this as the IKEA model of management education: The schools supply the pieces, neatly cut to size; the students do the assembly. Unfortunately, the schools don't supply instructions. Worse still, the pieces don't fit together. They may look neat, but in fact they are cut every which way. And the students don't know what to build, because that depends on the situation, and in the classroom there is no situation, or else several a day in cases. Real management is closer to playing with Lego blocks—there is an infinite number of ways to assemble the pieces, and the interesting structures take time to build.

And so we have this comment from a business school dean, that the prominent consulting firm in which he used to work "officially gave up on the notion that graduates of the Harvard Business School or Stanford knew anything more about thinking integratively about business problems than a Swarthmore or Amherst or Williams undergraduate in philosophy" (Roger Martin of the University of Toronto, interviewed in the *Financial Times*, September 11, 2000). He added in another interview, "They were clever and knowledgeable, but had no overarching framework to apply to problems that ran across the academic disciplines they had studied" (in Schachter 1999:51).

There is one MBA program that may have a valid claim to synthesis, and it highlights the problem. At Rochester, everything is built around economics. "Using the discipline of economics as the basis for studying management permits us to offer the most integrated MBA curriculum of any leading business school."[7] That might well be true; the trouble is that management is not economics! (Even if the dean does claim in his letter that the "school prepares you not just for a job, but for a lifetime career in management.")

REDUCING MANAGING TO DECISION MAKING AND DECISION MAKING TO ANALYSIS    It is perhaps more reasonable to argue that the practice of managing is not so much excluded from MBA programs as reduced to one particularly narrow dimension of itself: decision making as analysis. To quote a prominent Stanford professor, "I would estimate that about 80% of the MBA curriculum in top-rated American business schools . . . is concerned with just [the] issue of analytic problem-solving" (Leavitt 1989:37).

One might have expected Carnegie and its followers to reduce managing to decision making. But Harvard did exactly the same thing. For example, that *Business Policy* textbook referred to earlier (Christensen et al. 1982) repeatedly used the words *choice* and *decision* to describe the strategy process, as if creating a strategy is equivalent to making a decision (which it, of course, is in a case study classroom). Even the *Harvard Business Review* used to describe itself on its cover as "the magazine of decision makers." As noted earlier, while managers certainly have to make decisions, far more important, especially in large networked organizations of knowledge workers, is what they do to enhance the decision-making capabilities of others.

Reducing managing to decision making is bad enough; reducing decision making to analysis can be far worse. Formally at least, there are various stages in the decision-making process: identifying the issue in the first place, diagnosing its character, finding and inventing possible choices, evaluating them to select one, and seeing that one through to action. Most of these stages are soft (see Mintzberg et al. 1976) and so not amenable to systematic analysis. The one exception is the evaluation of possible choices, so this is where decision-making-treated-as-analysis is focused. It is a narrow view indeed.

In his article on "The Myth of the Well-Educated Manager," Livingston wrote:

Formal management education programs typically emphasize the development of problem-solving and decision-making skills . . . but

---

[7]This quote is from the 1995–1997 brochure; similar words appear in 2002–2004.

give little attention to the development of skills required to find the problems that need to be solved, to plan for the attainment of desired results, or to carry out operating plans once they are made.

In Livingston's opinion, this "distort[s] managerial growth" by "overdevelop[ing] an individual's analytic ability" while leaving his or her "ability to take action and get things done underdeveloped" (89).

REDUCING ANALYSIS TO TECHNIQUE    There is a fine line between teaching analysis and promoting technique. That line is crossed when the illustration becomes the application, so that thinking gets reduced to the use of a formula. (A *technique* might be defined as something that can be used in place of a brain.) There is a great deal of mindless application of techniques these days, especially in North American management practice, and the blame has to be laid on MBA education alongside aggressive consulting, insecure managers, and a superficial business press hungry for easy answers.

MBA programs tend to attract pragmatic people in a hurry: they want the means to leap past others with experience. Techniques—so-called tools—seem to offer that, so this is what many such students demand, and what many of the courses offer: whether portfolio models for financial resources, competitive analyses for strategic resources, or empowerment techniques for human resources. Offer enough of this, and you end up with schools of business technology.

The trouble, here once again, is that technique has to be tied to context—it must be modified for use in a specific situation. Frederick Taylor had it right back in 1908 when he refused a request by the dean of the new Harvard Business School to teach his famous "Scientific Management." He claimed it could only be learned on the shop floor (Spender 1997:23).

Technique applied with nuance by people immersed in a situation can be very powerful. But technique taught generically, out of context, encourages that "rule of the tool": Give a little boy a hammer and everything looks like a nail. MBA programs have given their graduates so many hammers that many organizations now look like smashed-up beds of nails.

Think of this as a problem of *push*. MBA programs push theories, concepts, models, tools, techniques in a disconnected classroom. Management practice, however, is about *pull*—what is needed in a particular situation. Managers can certainly use a toolbox full of useful techniques—but only if they appreciate when to use each. As the chief executive of a pharmaceutical company told a group of MBA students, "My problem is that when I face a problem, I don't know what class I'm in."

THE MATHEMATICAL MANAGER?    This whole problem of analysis is highlighted by the business schools' requirements for mathematics. In their 1959 report, Gordon and Howell complained about the many business school students who lack "the mental ability to acquire the analytical tools that are increasingly necessary. These students will never rise far in the business world" (101).

Well, that problem, too, was solved, with a vengeance. To get into, and out of, most reputable MBA programs, you must demonstrate an ability in mathematics. And so the corporate world is crowded with calculating managers.

The assumption behind this—that one cannot be a proper manager without mathematical ability—would come as a great surprise to the legions of managers who have succeeded without that ability. Indeed, it should come as a great surprise to all of us, including the most hard-nosed business school professors, since we all admire many such managers, just as we all know our share of dismal managers who have risen far in the business world with great mathematical skills.

These requirements tell us more about the business schools than about the practice of managing. For one thing, as noted in Chapter 1, mathematics provides a reliable measure of one form of intelligence. The schools need some measures to select among applicants without managerial experience, even if it tells them nothing about managerial potential. Second, mathematical ability is needed for the teaching of all that analysis and technique, even if this breeds a distorted picture of managing. Thus, Wharton announces on its Web site (2003) that, "All students take a mathematics proficiency exam at the beginning of Pre-Term to ensure they are prepared for the core curriculum." And if they are not prepared for that, they get another course on "basic arithmetic and algebraic skills . . . and the basic notions and techniques of differential and integral calculus."

And so, to do an MBA, you must undergo this rite of passage. "Make the most of your experience," reads the headline of a University of Chicago brochure for its Executive MBA program (1999), below which is written, "With participants sharing a solid background in basic algebra, business mathematics, and spreadsheet skills, courses can quickly move from basic instruction to advanced strategy and analysis."

## WHERE ARE THE SOFT SKILLS?

In her book *Becoming a Manager*, Linda Hill (1992:274) cites a study in which almost two-thirds of the graduates of business education reported "that they used their MBA skills marginally or not at all in their first management assignments"—precisely when such skills should have been most useful. Hill concludes from her own research that "the education many business schools provide does little to prepare managers for their day-to-day realities" (275). Asked for one improvement in the MBA, the respondents called for more teaching of the "soft skills." They always do.

These calls for soft skills seem well founded. After all, managing, as discussed earlier, is mostly about the soft stuff—working with people, doing deals, processing vague information, and so forth. But the fact is that business schools have been trying to teach the soft skills for years, yet the calls for more never cease. What is going on?

The soft skills simply do not fit in. Most professors do not care about them or cannot teach them, while most of the younger students are not ready to learn most of them. And few of these skills are compatible with the rest of the program—they get lost amid all the hard analysis and technique. So rather than *teaching* the soft skills, the business schools have tended to "cover" them, in the two meanings of the word: review them and obscure them. They have courses on the soft skills, develop theories about them, and use cases to illustrate them. They just have not embraced them, internalized them. For example, you do not develop leaders by dropping in a course on leadership amid all the others depicting managers as analytical decision makers.

I once met someone from a large airline who said, "Every time we have a problem, we create a department to deal with it. If you want to see all problems we have faced over the years, just look at all our headquarters' departments!" The business schools have often followed suit: hear a complaint; add a course. That will "cover" it. In a paper called "Motivation: That's Maslow, Isn't It?" Tony Watson (1996) writes of the "contract of cynicism" between student and professor: "A student would say something like 'Oh yes, we have *done* Taylorism.' I would then ask, 'So you know all about it then?' to which there would be a reply along the lines, 'Well, no, but we don't really want to have to go over that again, do we?'" (448).

Impressive efforts have certainly been made in some places to teach certain soft managerial skills in MBA programs.[8] And some of these soft

---

[8]For an example of one of the better textbooks, see Whetten and Cameron (in its various editions 1998, 2002); for a particularly imaginative set of classroom exercises ("for sensitizing students to aspects of Japanese culture and business practice"), see Van Buskirk (1996); and for a rather ambitious program heavily rooted in the soft skills, at Case Western Reserve University, see Boyatzis et al. (1995b).

skills are in fact potentially teachable, because they can draw on non-managerial experience that young students do have—working in teams, for example, or conducting negotiations. (A table in Chapter 9 offers a list of skills for managers.) But even these have rarely become mainstream in MBA programs.[9]

Aaronson (1996) concludes in her review of the teaching of perhaps the most popular skill that "there is no consensus [among the prestigious schools] on how to teach leadership, if leadership can be taught, or even what leadership means" (219, citing an AACBS publication).

INFILTRATING ETHICS    Much the same can be concluded about the teaching of ethics, if not a skill, then at least part of the soft side of managing. Time and again cries have gone up to teach MBAs about ethics, and time and again courses have come down to "cover" ethics. Said the dean of a prominent business school (Darden) in a *New York Times* panel (Kurtzman 1989:34), "We have concluded that ethics [is a] discipline much like marketing." But what is the use of a course in ethics amid all the other courses extolling shareholder value? One student who referred to ethics as "the biggest dud" in the MBA program commented on hearing in the other courses "that taxes were always hateful and that one could profitably choose currency trades based on which nations were crushing street riots" (Applebaum 1993:1, 2).

But then again, to what extent can students with little experience appreciate serious ethical dilemmas? In a study called *Can Ethics Be Taught?* (Piper, Gentile, and Parks 1993), the authors interviewed an entering class of Harvard MBAs and concluded that they were hindered by "a lack of experience in making value-based decisions, a lack of comprehension regarding the consequences of their actions on society . . . , and an inability to articulate their own values in a leadership role" (72).

So the soft skills and the soft issues end up as questionable content in the MBA programs, not because they are unimportant, but because the rest of the content and the nature of the students marginalize them.

---

[9]Our own experience at McGill is perhaps indicative. After completing my doctoral dissertation on managerial work, which included discussion of the teaching of skills (Mintzberg 1973: 188–93), I worked hard to have a course on skill development included in our MBA curriculum. It became a requirement in the second year (see Waters 1980), but it never extended beyond this one course, nor was it appreciated by much of the faculty; and when no one was left to teach it, it was dropped.

# QUESTIONING THE METHODS

Let us turn now from the content of the MBA to its pedagogical methods.

## IN SEARCH OF THAT "REAL WORLD"

The easiest way to teach is to lecture and then call for questions. Business schools, like the rest of the university, do their share of this so-called chalk and talk. If the professor said it, the students must have learned it (at least until the exams are over). Thus are those empty vessels called students filled up.

To their credit, business schools have not been inclined to stop there. They have looked far and wide for other pedagogical methods, especially in search of that "real world" of managing.

The problem is that the "real world" is not out there, to be plucked from some tree of practice. It has to exist in here—not just in the classroom, but in the head of the learner. The real world, in other words, exists as lived experience. Visit a classroom where practicing managers get to reflect on their own experience, and you can appreciate immediately how "real" a learning situation that can be. So the solution depends on the people, not just the pedagogy. But we should review the various pedagogies to appreciate what they can do, if not necessarily what they have done.

## GAMES BUSINESS STUDENTS PLAY

The business simulation, or game, has been particularly popular since computers came along to process large quantities of data. Students are formed into teams to make decisions about prices and production on a "quarterly" basis as they compete for profit and market share. Sometimes these games are used as that "capstone" course to integrate the MBA program; sometimes these courses are called "management." That is because the students play managers, usually with the fancy titles of an executive team.

Thus, in Carnegie Mellon's "Management Game," teams of students "act as senior managers and make strategic decisions involving marketing, finance, production and research and development. Each team meets with a board of directors three times to report its activities and seek permission for new plans" (Web site 2003). The school has described this (in a brochure of the late 1990s) as "learning by doing . . . relating knowledge through instruction to real world situations and implementing the acquired skills in a real-world environment." One student is quoted as saying that the "Management Game gave me a great perspective on running a company. The roles you play and the interaction between team members expose you to all aspects of running a company, and give you a grasp of all the areas you are going to manage."

Such claims are patent nonsense. That they are made at all suggests how distant such schools are from management practice. Making a sequence of pat decisions on fixed parameters every few minutes so that a machine can tell you instantly how well you have done is not quite like managing in that real world. Indeed, it only compounds the problems created in other courses, by giving the impression that managing is far more orderly and analytical than it really is. While managers out there work in "calculated chaos" and "controlled disorder" (Andrews 1976), students in here write numbers down on fixed forms.

Playing at management is not management. Management is a responsibility, not a game played in a classroom. There are no clear rules out there, no great computer in the sky determining who wins and who loses. Some companies win because they invent new rules, others because they apply the old ones more carefully than their competitors. (I especially appreciated the way a group of students I knew at MIT played the business game—as a game unto itself. They did not set out to win by the rules so much as to infer what those rules were—what parameters were programmed into the machine. The first group to figure that out won the game [both games]. Here were people destined to succeed in business!)

Recognized for what it is, the business game can have an appropriate role in the business school. It can be an effective way to learn how to apply the concepts of accounting and also to illustrate concepts in marketing, finance, and operations. In this respect, the business game *is* a capstone, for precisely what the MBA teaches. But it does not teach management.

## PROJECTS BUSINESS STUDENTS DO

In recent years, growing numbers of MBA students have ventured into that real world, sent by their schools to do fieldwork projects, even consulting assignments, in real companies. Here everyone generally has a good time. The students are freed from the drudgery of lectures or yet another case, they get to see a bit of the messiness of the real world for themselves, and they have to dig out their own data. The professors, too, get to see some sort of real world, at least through the eyes of their students. Even the companies are usually pleased: They have done a service, welcomed the bright eyed and the bushy tailed, and so tend to be lavish with their praise. And they do sometimes receive good ideas. These are, after all, smart students with well-honed analytical skills.

But step back and ask yourself what is going on here. Certainly not managing. Not quite consulting, either (although I have seen my share of consulting no more real). And if this is real experience, then why do it from a university? People in real jobs do such projects all the time. After graduation, most MBAs will have their fill of them. So what is it about doing this in school that makes it better—or makes it learning?

There is an evident answer—in principle. The university is a place to reflect, to step back from experience and learn from it. But with such projects, that is no simple matter. It has to be done carefully, deeply, experience by experience, team by team, with the help—and a great deal of time—of a skilled faculty. For a class of, say, two hundred students in groups of five, that could amount to the full teaching loads of more than two professors.[10] How many business schools have been prepared to invest that? Indeed, how many of their professors have been able and willing to do that? And without this, the projects are just projects—they have nothing to do with education. Joe Raelin (1993a), one of America's foremost scholars on business pedagogy, has concluded that "enjoyable" as such activities may be, they "do little to advance the [students'] need for critical reflection, reframing, and testing" (5).

It has been said of bacon and eggs that while the chicken is involved, the pig is committed. MBA students play chicken in these projects, not pig. About a "turnaround" her group supposedly brought about in a company, an IMD student proclaimed in one of its brochures (1999), "We couldn't have lived something more practical, down to earth and with more impact than this project." Compared with a lecture or case in the classroom, perhaps. But compared with doing that in a real job? The head of her school said of these projects that the students "not only learn about management and business practice, they live them." This "living" was composed of four stages: "industry analysis," "company analysis," "issue analysis," and "implementation" (earlier IMD brochure).

---

[10]I have assumed ten hours of debriefing per group, also that, without the need for the preparation time of conventional teaching, each professor could do double the load of 160 classroom hours per year.

Whetten and Clark (1996) have written that "students whose learning is restricted to experiential exercises often arrive at invalid conclusions" (155). So do their schools, apparently.

Some schools have tried to simulate entrepreneurship. The students pretend to create businesses (sometimes they really do), work out strategies, draw up plans, even present them to investment bankers for comment. At Chicago, Davis and Hogarth (in a pamphlet, no date, circa 1992) describe a "total immersion event" in which teams of incoming MBA students were "required within 48 hours, to create a new consumer product or service and to develop a comprehensive business plan for market introduction," which was presented to a panel of investors. "The presentation also includes lessons learned from the experience about the process of managing" (22). Again, hardly managing, although certainly business related, and again playing chicken rather than pig, although perhaps useful: better to get shot down here than later for real.

There is, of course, one more pedagogy, which has been almost as popular in business schools as lecturing, but more pragmatic, it is claimed, by bringing that real world of managing into the classroom.

## MEANWHILE, BACK AT HARVARD'S CASES

Through the revolution inspired by Carnegie in the 1960s and beyond, the Harvard Business School kept on course—its course. The school's commitment to cases kept it off the roller coaster of down with the principles of management and up with the rigor of the underlying disciplines. Harvard simply had too much invested in the case study method, strategically, culturally, materially—and, for that matter, still does. "Eighty years after the first case was written, the case method is as much as ever at the center of teaching and learning at HBS. . . . Approximately 350 cases are developed at the school each year," claimed to be the majority of such cases produced worldwide (from the school's Web site, 2003).

To its credit, Harvard sustained its focus on teaching. While other schools were turning to research, often at the expense of teaching, Harvard professors continued not just to write cases (or at least supervise their writing) but also to spend significant time preparing and coordinating their teaching of them. As a faculty member told a *New Yorker* journalist, the professors spend "hours and hours—I can't count that high—discussing the courses we're going to teach" (Atlas 1999:44). A requirement to do anything close to that in many other schools would have caused mutiny. But a requirement to publish research in academic journals might have done likewise at Harvard a couple of decades or more back. To quote from the 1965 edition of the Harvard *Business Policy* text, "research has been for some time under way, but is not yet advanced enough to make more than a modest claim on our attention. . . . the most valid literature for our purpose is not that of general statements but case studies" (Learned et al. 1965:6).[11] And with its emphasis on cases, Harvard maintained its claim to developing general managers, sometimes alongside digs at other schools about being more concerned with training staff specialists.

All of this gives the impression that management education bifurcated into two camps by the 1960s, with many of what became the prestigious schools, such as Stanford, Wharton, and Chicago, adopting Carnegie's academic approach, while some others copied and remained true to Harvard's more pragmatic case orientation.[12] In a sense, the Carnegie schools treated management as a science, while Harvard saw it more like a profession. However, in reviewing and criticizing the case study approach, I wish to show that these differences have proved more apparent than real.

---

[11]That comment survived virtually intact to the 1982 edition of the book, the most significant change being that by then the research "begins to make a claim on our attention" (Christensen, Andrews, and Porter 1982:6). The text went on to say that "the books referred to [in the footnotes] comprise a relevant but incidental source of knowledge." It is instructive to consider those sources. Of the thirty-nine references to theoretical works in the footnotes of the 1982 edition, thirty-one were by faculty members or doctoral students at the Harvard Business School. Other research apparently still made a "modest claim" on the authors' attention!

[12]The Pierson report, for example, drew attention to this in 1959 (247–48). In fact, Fraser made such a distinction, at least in terms of pedagogy, back in 1931: "The teaching methods of business schools in the United States are beginning to divide into two systems which are radically different in both theory and practice . . . the method of precept, or the lecture system, and the method of experience, or the case system" (*The Case Study Method of Instruction* book, cited in Dooley and Skinner 1975:1). And at Carnegie in the 1950s, Cooper and Simon "were adamant in their criticisms of case method as the sole vehicle for developing students' problem-solving abilities, and they viewed the entire Harvard tradition in business education as an anachronism in the postwar environment. Cooper argued that all a student learned by reading one hundred cases was just that: one hundred unrelated bits of information, void of any generalizable knowledge that could inform action in a new situation" (Schlossman et al. 1994:118).

## THE CASE FOR CASES

A case is a sheaf of paper, of about ten to twenty pages, composed of mainly words in the text and often numbers in the appendices, sometimes with a few pictures, that describes a business situation, usually in a single company with a protagonist at some sort of crossroads, having to make a decision. The case may have been investigated and written by a professor, but more often it has been done by an assistant working under a professor's supervision. The *New Yorker* article describes the Harvard cases as having a "uniform look. They also tend to have a common formula, beginning like a feature story in a magazine" (Atlas 1999:43).

A good deal of information is compressed into those pages, at least information susceptible to this form of presentation. For a large company with a rich history in a complex industry, this means a great deal of information has to be left out. These pages thus become a kind of snapshot of a company facing an issue.

Be that as it may, as one student who wrote a book about his experiences at Harvard put it, "they just kind of dump the whole mess into your lap—tables, columns, exhibits, and all—and you can't run away from it because tomorrow ninety-four people—the entire section—will be waiting for your decision" (Cohen 1973:17). Over the course of their two years at the school, Harvard students face case after case, in course after course, two or three time each day, hundreds of times in all. (At one time it ran as high as nine hundred; the Harvard Web site in 2003 says approximately five hundred.) To quote that student further: "There are no lectures, no labs, few textbooks even. Only Cases, Cases, and more Cases. . . . You almost read yourself to death, just to find out what the *problem* is. And then, of course, you need a *solution*. . . . The name of the game is to make a point" (16, 17, 20).

This is a view from 1973, and it is what some Harvard people today might describe as the conventional approach to case teaching: using the case to drive the students to take a position on the issue. But with the opening up of staffing in the last twenty years or so beyond faculty who have been Harvard and case trained, all kinds of other uses are now frequently made of cases, particularly in second-year electives—for example, to illustrate a conceptual point or assess a particular technique. Yet the Harvard Web site of 2003 still describes case studies as an "inductive reasoning process to arrive at answers."

Key to this approach to cases, for which Harvard has long been famous, is that the student must take a stand. Good managers are decisive, so good management students have to take a stand. To quote from the "HBS Survival Guide" for the students of 2003, "It is your job to read the case, review the exhibits and construct a logical argument for what the protagonist should do" (47). As Ewing (1990) tells it, when one student said that he needed more information, the professor responded, "Don't you ever come to my class again without having made a decision. As a businessman, you will often be in a situation where you would like to have more information. That doesn't make any difference. You have to be able to act upon what's available at the time" (20). Even if that consists of twenty pages written by someone else about a situation for which you have no experience.

In required courses now, eighty-eight students sit in rows of seats tiered in the shape of a U, so that as many as possible can see each other, although they all focus down on the professor. He or she stands in the open space at the bottom, sometimes called "the pit." Behind is plenty of blackboard space to fill up with the points the professor wishes to record. They all have eighty minutes to discuss the situation and decide what the company should do.

In this approach, the students come well prepared—or as best they can, given the other cases to prepare for that day—because they know that one of them will be called on to open the discussion at some length (known as the "cold call"). This is how Harvard ensures preparation in a class of eighty-eight. Woe to the student who comes ill prepared.

After those opening comments, according to a book by two other students, "all hell breaks loose, with [all the] students scrambling to argue how they would deal with the situation differently and why their approach would work better" (Kelly and Kelly 1986:14). Class participation as judged by the professor constitutes a significant component of the grade, but with less than one minute per student per class, on average, that does not allow much time to make an impression. So these managers-to-be have to leap in and be sharp:

> One professor tells me that a student in her class came in to see her at midterm. "I said to him, 'You don't participate.' The student tried to explain—he raised his hand but I never saw him, he would be about to make a point when someone else in class would beat him to it. I said, 'I'm not interested in excuses. Either you participate or you don't.' The student never did break the pattern, and I gave him a category four [failing] at the end of the term." (Ewing 1990:38)

Trace that into practice and you may have an explanation for some of the consequences of MBA education discussed in Chapter 4.

The discussion is overseen/guided/directed/driven by the professor—depending on his or her style of teaching and your perspective on the process. Typically the professor will ask a sequence of questions—some prefer rapid, machine-gun-like fire, while others favor a more thoughtful approach—to bring the discussion to some point of culmination, when he or she will make summary comments. There is usually a point to be made, a lesson to be drawn, decided in advance by the professor, based on the case.

Following are the assumptions claimed to underlie the case study method of teaching:

1. *It brings the reality of management practice into the classroom.* "The primary form of instruction at Harvard Business School is the case study method, which *captures the essence of leadership.* Participants analyze and discuss *actual* management situations by *placing themselves* in the positions of the managers involved" (from the 1999 brochure for the General Manager Program at Harvard; italics added).

2. *It exposes students to "the big picture."* "[T]he view that Harvard Business School wants its students to be able to grasp" is "the big picture." Ewing, managing editor of the *Harvard Business Review,* went on in his 1990 book to ask his readers to "think of a pyramid," where, halfway up "you have an expert, close-up view of one section," while on top, "your view becomes quite different," you see the pyramid "as a whole" (79).

3. *It develops the skills of the general manager.* Case studies allow the students "to think, talk, and act as the actual general manager would"; to "feel at home in any management situation and know at once how to begin to understand it"; "to participate in risk taking"; to "learn by doing"; to "take responsibility for decisions"; and to "step in and make matters better without waiting years and years for everyday experience to soak in" (Christensen interview in *Harvard Business School Newsletter,* 1991; Christensen et al. 1982:6; Christensen and Zaleznik 1954:213; Kelly and Kelly 1986:15; Ewing 1990:272).

4. *It "challenge[s] conventional thinking"* (quote from brochure for the General Manager Program, Harvard, 1998).

5. *It is participative.* This "democracy in the classroom" transfers the attention of the students "from the teacher to each other"; "students and faculty teach and learn together"; the "instruc-

tor" has to "work at . . . making sure that students 'own' the discussion. The dialogue is theirs"; the task of the instructor "is to moderate, to lead" (McNair 1954:11; Dean Clark's letter in the Harvard MBA brochure, 1997; Ewing 1990:199).

## THE CASE AGAINST CASES

Reflect on all these points for a moment and then ask yourself whether they make the case for the case study method or against it. Dozens of students sitting in neat rows pronouncing on stories they read the night before "captures the essence of leadership," exposes the "big picture," gives them "responsibility for decisions," promotes "learning by doing," puts the students "at home in any management situation," turns them into "risk takers," and makes them "general managers." It all sounds a bit silly, except for the fact that tens of thousands of graduates have left Harvard believing it.

Of course, when compared with the "chalk and talk" at Stanford and elsewhere, some of these claims can be appreciated. But is that the right basis of comparison? Shouldn't we be comparing the case method with the practice of managing?

In her review of graduate business schools, Aaronson (1992) refers to this method as "probably as close to practical experience as one can get in a classroom" (179). As close as most business schools have gotten, perhaps, but hardly as close as they can get. Take a good look at a case study classroom, and what you in fact see is another form of chalk and talk—quite literally. "Keep the boys talking" became a famous comment attributed to one of Harvard's early deans.[13] Or, as Harvard professor John Kotter (1982) has remarked, "My students 'make' more big decisions in their case discussions in one day than most of the [general managers he studied] could be seen making in a month" (80).

REDUCING MANAGING TO DECISION MAKING AND ANALYSIS: ONCE AGAIN    The skills developed in the case study classroom are the skills of decision making—just like in the theory-oriented schools. And, again, even these skills are highly circumscribed: The data for the decisions are

---

[13]Although Copeland (1954) reported it slightly differently: "As I was coming from a meeting of the class, I met Dean Gay . . . [who] asked me how things were going, and since at the moment, I was feeling optimistic I told him that I had found enough to talk about so far. 'Humph,' was Dean Gay's rejoinder, 'that isn't the question. Have you found enough to keep the students talking?'" (27).

given, while tacit knowledge of the situation is absent and so ignored. The students analyze these data—"sucking up vast quantities of disorderly data and ordering them faster than a computer," according to one consultant about a Harvard-trained colleague (cited in Cohen 1973:43)—and debate their conclusions through carefully articulated arguments. All this about a situation that everyone in the room has read but no one has experienced, for decisions that can be made but never implemented. Some decision making! Some managing!

The use of cases in law, where such practice began, is in fact a more reasonable simulation of reality. That is because lawyers, particularly in the courtroom, don't deal with events; they deal with the accounts of events. So law schools can reconstruct them, mainly through the use of words—logical arguments. A simulation in the classroom of the simulation inherent in law practice seems reasonable enough.

But management is something quite different, or at least it should be. Effective managers do more than talk, convince, and make decisions; they create events, by leaving their offices, getting involved, stimulating others; they see and feel, experience and test, firsthand. Harvard may keep the boys (and girls) talking, but effective practice keeps managers listening and looking. (Ewing's comment about being on top of the pyramid is especially interesting, because from that high up, you can barely make out what is on the ground. As for "seeing the whole," you can hardly make out the shape of the pyramid, let alone what is inside.)

Reaching a logical conclusion and knowing how to convince others of it are certainly important aspects of managing. And the case study method can certainly help develop such skills. But overemphasized, as they are in the case study classroom, they can distort the whole managerial process. Managers have to sense things; they have to weave their way through complex phenomena, they have to dig out information,[14] they have to probe deeply, on the ground, not from the top of some mythical pyramid. The "big picture" is not there for the seeing, certainly not in any twenty-page document; it has to be constructed slowly, carefully, through years of intimate experience. Ewing's claim that discussing cases in a classroom can replace "years and years [waiting] for everyday experience to soak in" is just plain nonsense. Debating

---

[14]Contrast this with Dean Donham's claim in 1922 that "[t]here are far too many [facts]," so "it is advisable to present both relevant and irrelevant material [in cases], in order that the student may obtain practice in selecting the facts that apply to the case at hand"; also that "the case ordinarily should not require the student to collect new facts not included in the statement"; instead, the "known facts" should be studied (60).

the implications of other people's experience may give the impression of experience, but that is not experience. The practice of managing cannot be replicated in a classroom the way chemical reactions are replicated in a laboratory.

What the case does simulate (and encourage) may be precisely the problem with so much managing today: the executive office where people sit around discussing words and numbers far removed from the images and feel of the situation under consideration, the verbal in place of the visual and the visceral, management as some kind of artifact distant from the situations it so mighty influences. "The damn guy just sits there waiting for a case study," remarked a manager about a Harvard-educated colleague. Here is how Kaz Mishina, who taught for six years at the Harvard Business School before returning to Japan, characterizes the process:

> At the beginning, most students with sober mind are painfully aware that they barely know anything about the company and the decision at hand even after careful readings of the case they have received, and experience a great deal of difficulty in publicly stating their judgment, not to mention sensibly defending their position. Interestingly, though, they quickly learn to suppress this sense of uneasiness, possibly forever, in an environment where cases keep coming at them asking what they would do and where "I don't know" is not an acceptable answer. (www.impm.org/Mishina)

Words are life reduced to categories, numbers reduce the words to ordered categories. These take on meaning only when embedded in the rich experience of life, the world beyond the executive office and case classroom. Malcolm McNair (1954), one of Harvard's best-known marketing professors, wrote about the need for managers to "have the ability to see vividly the potential meanings and relationship of facts" (8). True enough. But how vividly can anyone see in a case study classroom? How is insight to come from debates about products no one has ever touched for customers no one has ever met? (See the accompanying box.)

"Practically all business of a routine nature may be reduced to the making of decisions based on specific sets of facts." So wrote Harvard's Dean Donham in 1922 (58). Yet he also wrote of the difficulties of using cases in "factory management" to present material "in such a way that the student may visualize the facts clearly." Not so in marketing and banking, he claimed, which require "no stretch of the imagination for the student to obtain a clear conception of the case from a printed page" (61). Does that help explain why so many MBAs have gone into the

## SEEING THE COLUMNS

I recall vividly one event in my own masters degree. The professor was a seasoned person in operations management, more concerned with practice than theory. One day he asked one of us how many columns there were in the entrance hall of the building, a place we all walked through many times every day. The student didn't know. So the professor suggested he go have a look. When he came back, the professor asked him, "What color is the floor?" Next time the student came back, he could tell you everything about that hall. The professor's point was made—but all too rarely: we are just not trained to *see* in business schools.

specialized functions of marketing and finance, and so few into the line operations?

And what about the making of strategy? Reducing it to decision making, as did that Harvard *Business Policy* text, with formulation neatly separated from implementation, may be convenient for the case study classroom, as was Porter's further reduction of it to the industry and competitive analyses of generic strategies. But what justice does that do to strategy? Is this why we find so many MBA graduates practicing "strategy" in consulting jobs and planning departments or (as will be discussed in Chapter 4) as CEOs formulating simple grand strategies from on high that came crashing down?

Managers certainly have to make decisions and have to be concerned about strategy. And we certainly hope that these are informed by logical arguments. But can managing stop there, where the case study method stops?

SOFT SKILLS IN CASE CLASSES? It is claimed that the case study method does not stop there. It also teaches "implementation," "leadership," "ethics"—all those "soft skills." But does it?

There are certainly case discussions about these things. But in them the students do exactly what they do in the other cases: they read and discuss solutions. Back to analysis and decision making. Here is how a 1998 brochure described the Harvard Program for Global Leadership:

The case-study method . . . captures the essence of leadership. Case studies in themselves provide intense leadership training by requiring participants to analyze facts and situations, think on their feet, commit to an action plan, and sell colleagues on the merits of their position.

Boss-ship perhaps, but leadership?

And then there is that course on implementation, again through cases. But verbalizing about implementation no more teaches implementing than verbalizing about decision making teaches action taking. In fact, it is telling that the strategy formulation courses at Harvard have been far more successful than those on implementation, which have always been problematic. The reason is obvious. Formulating is easy in a classroom, especially a case study classroom. Everyone can pronounce on the company's future strategy reduced to a decision. But how do you teach implementation in a place where nobody can be implementing anything, even if everybody can be formulating everything? Hence we had that Harvard *Business Policy* text describing implementation as "primarily administrative" (Learned et al. 1969:19), while those two Harvard graduates, Kelly and Kelly (1986:32), reduce it to "giving the orders."

Separating implementation from formulation may be convenient for the classroom (not to mention the consulting firm and planning office), but that often violates the needs of practice. Strategy is an interactive process, not a two-step sequence; it requires continual feedback between thought and action. Put differently, successful strategies are not immaculately conceived; they evolve from experience. The idea that someone pronounces from on high while everyone else scurries around implementing has often proved to be a formula for disaster (inevitably blamed on implementation). Strategists have to be in touch; they have to know what they are strategizing about; they have to respond and react and adjust, often allowing strategies to *emerge*, step by step. In a word, they have to *learn*.[15]

Formulation connects with implementation in two basic ways. Either the "formulator" controls implementation directly, as entrepreneurs often do, so that they can adapt their strategies en route. Or else the "implementors" play a key role in "formulation," which is common in high technology and other venturing situations. Here management's

---

[15]For strategy as a learning process, see Mintzberg, Ahlstrand, and Lampel (1998: chap. 7). For it as a process of designing, planning, and positioning, see chapters 2, 3, and 4. (Chapter 2 contains a detailed critique of the separation of formulation from implementation.) See Mintzberg (1987a) and Mintzberg and Waters (1985) for discussion of emergent strategy.

role is less to *formulate* than to *facilitate*—to encourage the strategic initiatives of others, listen carefully to their results, and help consolidate the best of these into emergent strategies and coherent visions. In a sense, management is more creative in the first approach, more generous in the second. Under the case study approach, students are instead encouraged to be analytical.

SECONDHANDEDNESS    This chapter opened with Whitehead's quote from 1929 that "[t]he secondhandedness of the learned world is the secret of its mediocrity." The thirdhandedness of the theory schools hardly justifies the secondhandedness of the case study schools. (The Harvard Web site of 2003 describes its cases as "firsthand accounts of actual business situations." The experience may have been firsthand; the recording of it in a case was not, nor, once more removed, is discussion of that in class.)

Sterling Livingston used this Whitehead quote in his 1971 article "The Myth of the Well Educated Manager." As manager turned Harvard professor, Livingston was not happy with what he saw around him. "Fast learners in the classroom often . . . become slow learners in the executive suite," he wrote. That is because managers "are not taught in formal education programs what they most need to know to build successful careers in management"—namely, "to learn from their own firsthand experience" (79, 84). Instead, "They study written case histories that describe problems or opportunities discovered by someone else, which they discuss, but do nothing about." Even "what they learn about supervising other people is largely secondhand . . . what someone else should do about the human problems of 'paper people.'" Without responsibility or the chance to take action, they cannot "discover for themselves what does—and what does not—work in practice" (84).[16]

---

[16]McNair recognized some of these problems in his 1954 book on the case method, which he claimed to be outweighed by its advantages:

> Although the case method has realism, it is by no means identical with reality. The case writer has made a selection of the facts for the student, who gains little practice in seeking and recognizing pertinent facts and relationships in the continuum of daily detail that makes up the life of people in business. The medium, the printed, page, is restricting and incapable of conveying many subtle but important overtones of human personality and conduct. Finally, the student faces a given problem for a relatively short time and without operating responsibility. In the actual situation, of course, operating personnel must live with their problems. (86)

All of this he referred to as "lack[ing] some realism," but he concluded that the case method still "seems to convey more of the essential notion of business administration than any other method," again presumably in reference to lecturing.

PARTICIPATION?    In a 1981 article, Harvard professor Arthur Turner leveled his own criticism especially at that "democracy in the class-room," which he saw as highly orchestrated by the professor, who "in a very real sense is 'conducting' the discussion" to demonstrate some kind of model or analytical scheme. Accordingly, the instructor senses who to call on, and which comments to record on the board, in order to make his or her point. A method thus described since Donham (1922:55) as "inductive"—where the learning is induced from the experience—may in actual fact be deductive, where the conclusion is deduced from the conceptual framework. This can apply even to the writing of the case. For example, if the case writer has been taught that the chief executive is *the* strategist (as did Harvard's *Business Policy* text),[17] then he or she will be inclined to focus a case about strategy on that person.

Bear in mind, too, that Harvard's main courses are taught in many parallel sections by different professors who spend a great deal of time coordinating their message. That hardly encourages a classroom of discovery. "How normative should we be in the session?" asked the lead professor in one of these meetings, who later "summed up the various responses that discussion leaders could expect, which were based on his experience in previous years. . . . 'The important thing is not *just* to give an answer but to *make* them feel and see the plant—that it's big and dirty and unsafe'" (in Atlas 1999:44, italics added).

A "Teaching Note" available for each case "walks the instructor through the purpose of the case." For example, the one "for a well-known accounting case suggests what issues the instructor might write on the board and how he or she might want to have the class discuss the issues raised, in what order and with what results" (Ewing 1990:226). Ewing describes such notes as "crucial to quality control. . . . After all, students in all sections [at Harvard] will get the same examination at the end" (227).

Turner (1981) concludes that the skills managers learn in the case study classroom are "relevant to the situation they are in" but "mostly irrelevant to what managers do" (8). They include, for example, "how to speak convincingly in a group of 40 to 90 people," to "impress [them], and especially the instructor." To Turner, this "suggests a disturbing hypothesis: the more skillful the instructor and the more pleased the students with the process, the less useful may be the learning" (7).

---

[17]Hence, Andrews (1987), on page 3, associates the whole field with the "point of view" of the chief executive or general manager"; on page 19, he includes a section entitled "The President as Architect of Organizational Purpose"; adding on page 361, "other key managers . . . must either contribute to or assent to the strategy if it is to be effective."

Perhaps even harsher is Chris Argyris, a well-known professor of organizational behavior jointly appointed in Harvard's Schools of Business and of Education. Also wondering about this democracy in the classroom, he observed a three-week executive development program that selected its faculty from among the "stars" of case teaching at Harvard and other schools.

Argyris (1980) counted the comments students made to each other compared with those made to and by the faculty member. In all but one session, the number of student-to-student responses was "significantly lower" than those to and from the professor. ("A flurry of hands went up, wagging for attention," Ewing [1990:23] wrote of one Harvard MBA case discussion. Turner [1981] described the process as "not really a 'discussion' so much as a series of instructor-student dialogues" [6].) As a consequence, Argyris describes the class discussions as "a series of games and camouflaging of the games" (195): faculty members established controversy; they "induc[ed] students to generate incorrect solutions"; they made sure to reveal principles only at the end of sessions. Asked why key questions were not given ahead of time, one faculty member responded, "That would blow the whole game." The point for them was to keep "control of the learning" (291, 292).

In one session, Argyris noted that "some of the most vocal executives felt they had been manipulated by the faculty member in competing with each other." As a result, "during the next class, one of the most vocal members announced that he wasn't going to get 'caught' again." He "retreated from future discussion," and the participation of the other executives in that session "diminished significantly. . . . [T]oward the end of the course, one executive asked the faculty member in a matter-of-fact manner: 'Are you in the phase of getting us to vote or trying to get us to take sides, or do you want general comments?' The faculty member appeared a bit flustered" (294).

BIASES IN THE CASES    Earlier I mentioned possible biases in the writing of cases, with the example of building a strategy case around the CEO when the case writer has been taught that the CEO is the strategist. While I know of no study of biases in business cases, there is one in public sector cases, which the authors believe follows "the business school model" (Chetkovich and Kirp 2001:284).

Chetkovich and Kirp (2001) studied the ten best-selling cases in American public sector programs for the year 1997–1998. These were produced by the Kennedy School of Government at Harvard, "which enjoys a near monopoly in the field" (286). Their reading of these cases uncovered a disquieting set of lessons:

The policy world is depicted as a domain where high-ranking officials, usually organizational outsiders, deal with narrowly constructed policy problems. Historical and social context are of limited relevance. Action is individualized rather than socially embedded, and conflict is more common than collaboration. Lone heroes get by with little help or input from politicians, the public, or organizational subordinates. (286)

Especially applicable to business cases may be these comments: "almost invariably, [the protagonists] are heroes," while middle-level managers do not figure prominently, and these are mostly unnamed; lower-level members are rarely "mentioned even as useful sources of knowledge" (288, 290). "In this policy universe, decisions are made only by individuals acting as individuals"; there is also a focus on "newcomer[s] brought in to bail out a failing institution"; "a top-down, or outside-in, model of action predominates" (289, 290).

Particularly damning is the comment "Four of the nine full-length cases provide no historical data beyond what must be given to produce a comprehensible story"; the others "barely sketch a complex history." The impression left is "that history does not matter much" (297). Can any manager hope to appreciate the future without a deep understanding of the past?

NOT CASES SO MUCH AS THE POPULAR USE OF CASES    To conclude this discussion, I wish to emphasize that my quarrel is not with cases per se. Cases as stories—as chronicles of experience—can be useful, so long as they respect the richness of the situation, including its history. Cases can be powerful means to expose people to a wide variety of business situations—if they are recognized as supplements to experience, not replacements for it. (See the accompanying box for a related view, which gives an idea of what else can be done with cases.)

## CASES AS PERSPECTIVES

*(prepared for this book by Jeanne Liedtka of the Darden School)*

One of the most interesting advantages of the case method is the opportunity to use it to encourage and develop perspective taking on the part of students. Too often, students are asked to play only one role in a case conversation—that of the "executive" asked to make a decision of some sort—and the quality that we value as instructors is a kind of "decisiveness" born of a willingness to ignore the complexity of the situation at hand. Understandably, this approach makes a lot of us nervous about the real messages that we are sending to students in case method classrooms.

Yet, the potential exists within the case method to do exactly the opposite—to give students real practice at looking at any given situation from varied perspectives, at uncovering the richness of the many ways that different people make sense of the same situation. After all, every case already has (or can be tweaked to include) a whole cast of characters who are likely to see the world in ways quite startlingly different than that of the "executive" in question. By asking students to help each other try on these multiple hats as they diagnose a situation and search for solutions, and by challenging facile interpretations of the views and motivations of others, we endorse a view of decision making in organizations as complex, nuanced, and multifaceted, and target a set of skills that we know will stand students in far greater stead in the years ahead than a naïve decisiveness.

But when cases are used in place of experience, devoid of history, and force people to take stands on issues they know little about, in my view they become a menace. I summarize this concern with a little concocted case of my own.

## JACK'S TURN

*[In lecture courses, students] are waiting for you to give "the answer." There's a built-in bias against action. What we say with the case method is: "Look, I know you don't have enough information—but given the information you do have, what are you going to do?" (Lieber 1999:262, quoting Roger Martin, dean of the University of Toronto business school)*

"OK, Jack, here you are at Matsushita. What are you going to do now?" The professor and eighty-seven of Jack's classmates anxiously await his reply to the cold call. Jack is prepared; he has thought about this for a long time, ever since he was told that the case study method is supposed to "challenge conventional thinking." He has also been told repeatedly that good managers are decisive, therefore good MBA students have to take a stand. So Jack swallows hard and answers.

"How can I answer that question?" Jack begins. "I barely heard of Matsushita before yesterday. Yet today you want me to pronounce on its strategy.

"Last night, I had two other cases to prepare. So Matsushita, with its hundreds of thousands of employees and thousands of products, got a couple of hours. I read the case over once quickly and again, let's say, less quickly. I never knowingly used any of its products. (I didn't even know before yesterday that Matsushita makes Panasonic.) I never went inside any of their factories. I've never even been to Japan. I spoke to none of their customers. I certainly never met any of the people mentioned in the case. Besides, this is a pretty high tech issue and I'm a pretty low-tech guy. My work experience, such as it was, took place in a furniture factory. All I have to go on are these twenty pages. This is a superficial exercise. I refuse to answer your question!"

What happens to Jack? At Harvard, I'll let you guess. But from there, he goes back to the furniture business where he immerses himself in its products and its processes, the people and the industry. He is an especially big fan of its history. Gradually, with his courage to be decisive and to challenge conventional thinking, Jack rises to become CEO. There, with hardly any industry analysis at all (that would have come in a later course), he and his people craft a strategy that changes the industry.

Meanwhile, Bill, sitting next to Jack, leaps in. He has never been to Japan, either (although he did know that Matsushita makes Panasonic). Bill makes a clever point or two and gets that MBA. That gets him a job in a prestigious consulting firm, where, as in the case study classes back at Harvard, he goes from one situation to another, each time making a clever point or two, concerning issues he recently knew nothing about, always leaving before implementation begins. As this kind of experience pours in, it is not long before Bill becomes chief executive of a major appliance company. (He never consulted for one, but it does remind him of that Matsushita case.) There he formulates a fancy high-tech strategy, which is implemented through a dramatic program of acquisitions. What happens to that? Guess again.

*Readers [of Kelly and Kelly's book,* What They Really Teach You at the Harvard Business School *(1986:46)] are probably asking,* Read the case and do that analysis in two to four hours? *Harvard's answer is yes. Students need to prepare two to three cases each day. . . . So [they] must work toward getting their analysis done fast as well as done well.*

## LEARNING FROM BOK

The discussion of this chapter has switched back and forth between Harvard's cases and other schools' theories, toward a conclusion that I hope is becoming increasingly evident. Before starting it, I wish to review an experience at Harvard that is particularly revealing, not just about how Harvard has viewed its case method and responded to a particular criticism of it but also how it has evolved since then—which takes us straight to our final conclusion.

Derek Bok, as president of Harvard University, chose to comment in his 1979 report on the Harvard Business School. To anyone familiar with the two 1959 Foundation reports, his remarks were rather tame and pretty obvious. But at the Harvard Business School, there was outrage, manifested in a fifty-two-page response to the twenty-three pages that Bok had written. These revealed problems at the school far better than did the president's own words.

Bok, from Harvard's law school, wondered whether the business school might consider the "limitations" of its case study method and build in more conceptual material to its courses, more theory. In a nutshell:

> Although the case is an excellent device for teaching students to apply theory and technique, it does not provide an ideal way of communicating concepts and analytic methods in the first instance. In fact, by concentrating on the discussion of detailed factual situations, the case method actually limits the time available for students to master analytic techniques and conceptual material. . . . [Moreover] the enormous effort required by the case system can leave little time [for faculty] to anticipate longer range issues or engage in intensive work to develop better generalizations, theories, and methods. (24)

The day after Bok issued his report, the *New York Times* ran a front-page story on it; *Fortune* come out with a cover story soon after (Kiechel 1979). Particularly upset with all this was a man named Marvin Bower (Harvard MBA, 1928), who had built up and still headed the McKinsey & Company consulting firm. According to one observer, McKinsey had "the most to lose" if the school cut back on its use of the case study method, since it had hired "more than a thousand fresh MBAs from 1937 on," to become "the preeminent management-consulting firm" (Mark 1987:58–59, 60).

It was decided that the alumni would respond. Bower put together a blue ribbon committee of seven executives from major companies

(AT&T, Ford, etc.) and had a report prepared for them by fifteen younger Harvard MBA graduates. Entitled "The Success of a Strategy" (Associates, Harvard Business School 1979), the report opened by quoting Benjamin Disraeli: "The secret of success is constancy to purpose." At Harvard, that purpose had been "to be a teaching school dedicated to preparing enlightened general managers for business firms," of which "the world needs an almost unlimited number" to achieve "the goals of every organization—profit, non-profit and governmental" (vii).

The report repeatedly emphasized training "designed to meet the . . . needs of general managers, not technical specialists" (vii). Yet of the report's fifteen own authors, seven were consultants (with McKinsey), two worked in financial institutions, and four were in staff units of large corporations; only one or perhaps two were line managers ("Associate Product Manager," General Food Corporation; "Manager," American Telephone and Telegraph Company). In rather arrogant terms, the report dismissed technical specialists as "available to managers," such that Harvard's role was "to ensure that its students know enough to direct such specialists"; and to "understand and work with quantitative decision-making aids" but with "little need . . . to become technically adept" at using them (21).[18]

The report referred to the "school's research program [as] the most extensive of any graduate business school," yet at one point it confused research with case writing and at another simply dismissed research: "the development—in an academic setting—of better generalizations and abstract theories for the general manager runs counter to the basic nature of the managing process in business" (28). And the authors provided no research or theory in support of that conclusion. (It might be recalled that this conclusion ran counter to the beliefs of Dean Donham, who had brought the case study method to Harvard in the first place and expected it to be used in conjunction with theory, although he lost that battle to faculty members who had the least amount of business experience.)

---

[18] The authors claimed to have "found" no significant evidence that the general manager needs, or will need, "the degree of quantitative/theoretical knowledge" taught in the other schools. "To test this point in a limited way, we surveyed [Harvard Business School] directors on their reading of journals with a quantitative content. Of the 25 who replied, almost none read such publications regularly and only a few read them occasionally, whereas most were regular readers of *Harvard Business Review*" (21). A survey of the Harvard directors, most with Harvard MBAs and so having had little quantitative training about their reading of quantitative journals, challenges Bok's claim that Harvard students needed better mastery of analytical technique!

The report concluded, "[W]e urge the school to keep the case method dominant," this "distinctive, student-centered learning instrument . . . superior to the lecture in preparing general managers" (vii).

The Harvard Business School remained sensitive about the Bok Report for some time. "If you raise it with the dean he will be very upset," a *New York Times* reporter was told when he visited the campus five years later (in Mark 1987:63). Yet gradually, perhaps not even consciously, the school did virtually everything the Bok report had suggested and the Bower report had dismissed:

- "Dropping in the [business press] ratings and pressured by its students, who felt less confident about their analytical and technical abilities than other grads" (Byrne and Bongiorno in *Business Week*, October 24, 1994), the school initiated curriculum reforms in the mid-1990s. As noted earlier, strategy had already come to be taught from a more systematically analytical perspective.

- By the mid-1990s, the number of cases in the MBA program had been reduced (to about five hundred, from a high of nine hundred), although they remained predominant in the curriculum, much as Bok had recommended. (The case method's "virtues are much too obvious and far too central to the mission of the School" to abandon [Bok 1979:25].) In words that might have been anathema to Bower, the dean's letter in the 1997–1998 MBA brochure stated, "The case method is not our only teaching method."

- After an early abortive attempt, in the late 1990s the school finally put its students on line with PCs: "We were like, way, way behind," Dean Clark told a *New York Times* reporter (Leonhardt 2000a).

- From the mid-1980s, the school also began a concerted effort to reduce inbreeding, hiring young faculty—particularly research-oriented faculty—from other schools, to the point after 2000 when the dean requested greater consideration of the schools' own doctoral graduates. It also brought in a number of established research "stars" and strengthened its doctoral activities by rooting many of them in Harvard's disciplines of psychology, economics, and others across the river.

- Perhaps most telling of all, as noted earlier after eighty-eight years, the school dropped its once "signature" business policy

course (Leonhardt 2000a) and concurrently added a second required course in finance.

# CONVERGENCE IN
# BUSINESS EDUCATION

If not before, then now my conclusion should be evident: The business
schools of Harvard and Stanford are separated mainly by geography.
Walk into a case study classroom at Harvard where a professor is leading a discussion about a company, and it certainly seems different from
a lecture theatre at Stanford where an economist is pronouncing on
game theory. Listen to their rhetoric, and it sounds like one is concerned
with management as a profession, the other with business as a science.
But step back, and perhaps you can appreciate how remarkably similar
these two approaches really are: Their students have little or no "management" experience yet are supposedly being trained as managers; the
management they learn takes the form of decision making by analysis,[19]
taught largely through the business functions; both schools believe in research and scholarly publication, and they hire each other's doctorates
to do it; together they pour out graduates mostly for specialized jobs
many of whom nonetheless expect to end up as general managers, supposedly able to manage anything. And so it goes. (Harvard and Stanford
now cooperate on their customized executive programs.) As the dean of
the MIT Sloan School concluded back in 1968, "the differences between
one business school and another . . . derive not from where the schools
are going but where they came from" (in Zalaznick 1968:202).

While Harvard itself maintains a rather strong commitment to case
study teaching, it has few real clones left. Thirty years ago, a number of
schools copied its every move; today few do. Not that imitation is gone.
Quite the contrary; it is stronger than ever. But in place of two models is
one, a blend of those two. In other words, in almost every well-regarded

---

[19]In fact, Bach's chapter in the Pierson et al. (1959) report opened by attributing to
Harvard and its use of cases the "focus[ing of] central emphasis" on decision making in management education (319). Bear in mind also that the citations earlier in
this chapter to two of the most baldly analytical approaches to the teaching of management—Porter's work on strategy and Beer et al.'s approach to organizational behavior—come from professors at Harvard, not from one of the theory-oriented schools.

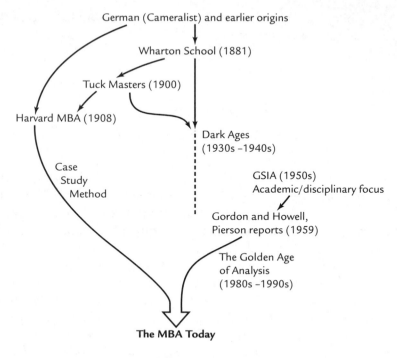

German (Cameralist) and earlier origins

Wharton School (1881)

Tuck Masters (1900)

Harvard MBA (1908)

Dark Ages
(1930s –1940s)

Case
Study
Method

GSIA (1950s)
Academic/disciplinary focus

Gordon and Howell,
Pierson reports (1959)

The Golden Age
of Analysis
(1980s –1990s)

**The MBA Today**

FIGURE 2.2

Passing the Baton: The Development of the Business School

business school today can be found a prominent place for the basic disciplines, for research, for theory, and for cases. Case study teachers rely more on concepts, or perhaps I should say they do so more transparently, while theory-oriented faculty use more examples, including cases.

As shown in Figure 2.2, Harvard, Stanford, and all the others have ended up in a remarkably similar place. That place is about B, not A. These schools teach the functions of business and the analysis of decision making while trying to give the impression that they are developing managers—for business and everything else. They do not. In a world rich with experience, in a world of sights and sounds and smells, our business schools keep the boys and girls talking, and analyzing, and deciding. In a world of doing and seeing and feeling and listening, they develop our leaders by thinking. In the final analysis, what they master is not what we need. These schools may be broadening their students' knowledge about business, but they are narrowing their students' perceptions of management.

Summarized in the accompanying box is the impression of management left by MBA training. Millions of people have carried this impression into practice, the consequences of which are discussed in the next four chapters. They suggest that no one should be allowed out of a conventional MBA program without having a skull and crossbones stamped firmly on his or her forehead, over the words "Warning: NOT prepared to manage!"

## THE IMPRESSION LEFT BY MBA EDUCATION

1. Managers are important people who sit above others, disconnected from the work of making products and selling services. The higher "up" these managers go, the more important they become. At the "top" sits the chief executive who *is* the corporation (even if he or she only arrived yesterday).

2. Managing is decision making based on systematic analysis. To manage, therefore, is significantly to deem. It is more science than art, with no mention of craft.

3. The data for such decision making comes from brief convenient packages of words and numbers, called cases in school and reports in practice. To make decisions, the numbers are "massaged" and the words are debated, perhaps with some added consideration of "ethics."

4. Under these managers sit their organizations, neatly separated like MBA programs into the functions of finance, marketing, accounting, and so forth, each of which applies its own repertoire of techniques.

5. To bring these functions together, managers pronounce "strategies," which are very special and, however mysterious, can be understood by people who have been taught industry analysis and given the opportunity to formulate many of them in case study classrooms.

6. The best strategies are clear, simple, deliberate, and bold, like those of the heroic leaders of the most interesting cases.

7. After these MBA managers have finished formulating their strategies, all the other people—known as "human resources"—must scurry around implementing them. Implementation is important because it is about the taking of action, which managers must control but never do.

8. This implementation is, however, no easy matter, because while the managers who have been to business school embrace change, many of those human resources who haven't resist it. So these managers have to "bash bureaucracy," by the use of techniques, and then to "empower" whoever is left to do the work they have been hired to do.

9. To become such a manager, better still a "leader" who gets to sit on top of everyone else, you must first sit still for two years in a business school. That enables you to manage anything.

# 3

# WRONG CONSEQUENCES I
## *Corruption of the Educational Process*

*Education, n. That which discloses to the wise and disguises from the foolish their lack of understanding.*
—AMBROSE PIERCE, *THE DEVIL'S DICTIONARY*

There was some good news in the last chapter: that recognized as education for specialists in the functions of business, MBA programs can train some of the right people in some of the right ways. The bad news now is that because these programs are rarely so recognized, they create all kinds of negative consequences. These extend beyond the graduates who become managers into the organizations they manage and out to a world shaped by these organizations. We simply cannot afford to have a society of elitist leaders trained in analysis and promoted on "fast tracks" beside the daily work of making products and providing services. All of this undermines our organizations and our social fabric as well as our educational institutions.

This may sound like an awfully broad condemnation of a rather innocent degree. I think not, and I set out now to demonstrate why. Indeed, I hope to demonstrate that the consequences of MBA education are far more influential and disturbing than most people realize. David

Ewing (1990) opened his book with the claim that "The Harvard Business School is probably the most powerful private institution in the world" (30). It would be easy to dismiss this as the overblown rhetoric of an insider. The worrisome thing is that Ewing may have been right.

I shall not be arguing that the MBA ruins every recipient for life. All sorts of people do the degree for all sorts of reasons with all sorts of consequences, some minor, some major, some positive, some negative. Rather, my argument is that the overall effects have been profoundly more negative than positive.

MBA programs are not solely responsible for all the dysfunctional aspects of managing we now see around us, from the exaggerated executive compensation schemes and the failed strategies and mergers to the scandals of dishonest corporate behavior, all indicative of a demise of leadership. A hyped-up business press and questionable consulting practices have contributed, too. But they have done so in conjunction with the educational programs, which have both legitimized and encouraged some of the very behaviors they should be challenging.

Destruction is so much easier than construction. It takes nine months to grow a human being and a moment to destroy one, years to build a great organization and months to run it down, centuries to establish a democratic society and decades to undermine it. Leadership is an old phenomenon; the managership promoted by the MBA is a rather new one. In my opinion, it has contributed to what will be described here—and I have chosen the word carefully—as a pervasive corruption, from education through management to organizations and into society.

Because I have much to say about these consequences, I have divided them into four chapters, on each of these aspects, beginning here with the corruption of the educational process.

"There are four things a student should want from a business school," James March, a prominent business school professor at Carnegie and then Stanford, told an interviewer in 1995:

> One is to learn something about business disciplines like organizations, accounting, finance, production, and marketing. The second is to deepen an intellectual understanding of the relation between activities in business and the major issues of human existence. The third is to be able to signal that you're the kind of person who goes to a certain kind of business school. And the fourth is to lay the basis for a set of personal connections. (in Schmotter 1995:58)

March maintained that any business school can teach the business disciplines. But he claimed the other three points require more than an ordinary business school, including the one about deepening an understanding about those "major issues of human existence." This is certainly a noble intention, but a good deal of evidence presented in this and the next three chapters suggests that even the famous schools end up achieving the exact opposite effect. That leaves us with March's other two points—namely, "establishing that you're one of the very smart folks, or of putting you in contact with other very smart folks to build a national or international network of personal contacts" (58). These alone, I maintain, corrupt the educational process.

Later in the interview, March referred to the business school as "less a factory than a temple . . . justified by the way it symbolizes things we value." What, then, do the acolytes of these temples, the MBA students, value?

## Some Student Reactions to MBA Studies

On this question, let me quote from three books written by MBA students about their experiences: one awfully simplistic and positive, a second superficially suave and mixed, the third rather sophisticated and mostly negative. Each damns the educational process in its own way.

Of course, books may not be representative—book writers have their own axes to grind, I am told. So the second set of reactions comes from surveys of large numbers of MBA students, specifically about what they value and how that changes over the course of their studies. That message is no better.

Francis Kelly and Heather Kelly (1986) wrote a book about their experiences called *What They Really Teach You at the Harvard Business School*. It is hardly encouraging. For example, they describe two of their courses in the following terms: "In the marketing class, students learn how to develop a product that meets a real need" (11). Human resource management "has emerged [in the 1980s] as a 'real business' hot topic. Managers realize that generating profits in an environment of increasing competition depends on human resources. . . . [This, however] is one of the more difficult tasks required of managers. As with every decision, trade-offs exist" (143).

Kelly and Kelly provide "a group of five or six key questions to ask about any organization so that readers will be able to do a simple, fast HBS-style analysis of their own business and business situation." They refer to this as "the essence of what HBS seeks to give its students" (26,

27). For example, a question for the policy course reads, "Can the company's overall corporate strategy and market position be summarized in two or three sentences?" (49). A more general question, mentioned earlier in the book for all areas, is "How does one do a quick check on a decision before it is implemented to make sure it is the best possible?" (11). I hope this is not "the essence of what HBS seeks to give its students," but it does seem to be what these two students got.

At Stanford (home to Professor March), a student wrote a book called *Snapshots from Hell* (Robinson 1994). Mostly about the first year of the program, it is thin on course contents but thick on student attitudes. Much of this sounds more like grade school than grad school, with students panicking about exams and stomping out of courses they do not like. (The *New York Times* review of this book, entitled "Boot Camp for Yuppies," commented on the "insanity of the modern American tendencies to transform practical tasks into academic disciplines" [Lewis 1994:7].)

The moment of truth for this student came in a marketing class, which "got down to where people lived, down to Pringles and Cinch" (257). Cinch was a fiasco, admitted the Procter and Gamble executive who came to class. "Even the big guys like P&G make mistakes," he told the class. This was a revelation for Robinson, who repeated the sentence in italics, explaining, "Those words were the most exalted I heard uttered at Stanford. They were my MBA epiphany. From then on, everything at business schools was different for me." Hardly one of March's "major issues of human existence," but, again, what this student got.

An earlier book by Cohen (1973), *The Gospel According to the Harvard Business School*, is far more sophisticated and more negative than the other two. For example, about the WACs (Written Analyses of Cases), due every other Saturday, Cohen wrote, "The incredibly tight rules of a WAC strangle your thoughts. No leaps of faith allowed; no grandiose assumptions permitted. You've got to slug it out, covering all your bases" (48). When the results come back, "You will look frantically for the little white slip, and you don't care what Petra Cement [a case company] should or could have done, what your mistakes were, or the flaws in your argument," but that you received "a P (for Pass) on the slip; that you have made it past yet another one, and that thank God— five WACs down. Only six to go" (53).

The atmosphere of Harvard classes comes through in Cohen's book as demanding, strident, individualistic: "Whatever happens, jump at the argument as if it were a loose ball. Develop a unique pattern of waving your hand. And most of all, be unscrupulous" (21). One student talked about "the feeling that this is a mob, not a group. We are people when we're outside of class, talking to each other. And suddenly, when we walk in there and sit down, we're all transformed. We become lions." Using fear "to get people to learn . . . just doesn't make sense" (133–34).

A major event occurred during Cohen's time at Harvard, concerning the Vietnam War, certainly a major issue of human existence. Harvard College students from across the river held a mass meeting in the stadium, next to the business school. "[W]hile ten thousand people across the street were wondering what their world was coming to, the staff of Corporation 7 [a business game] was busy figuring out ways to increase their profit." Cohen described his disassociated classmates as exhibiting "the mixture of disdain and fear that came from not really understanding what a crowd, an emotion, are all about." Later, he commented, "The school doesn't want to hear the tumult outside. . . . Can't hear because it is up against the worst obstacle to progress—success." It may have been putting in more cases "on pollution and social responsibility. But it isn't really doing anything to change the mood, the attitude, or the place . . . the school remains more concerned about placing its graduates and getting business's financial support than about whether business is using the nation's productive resources for the good of the nation" (328–29).

Times have changed since this was written. Business schools have made greater efforts, for example, with courses in ethics. And the result, by any reasonable account: the situation has gotten worse.

In 2002, the Aspen Institute published a pamphlet entitled "Where Will They Lead?" (Initiative for Social Innovation through Business, 2002). This presents the results of a survey of the attitudes toward business and society of almost two thousand MBA students from thirteen leading schools. The key finding, in a nutshell: "There is a shift in priorities during the two years of business school from customer needs and product quality to the importance of shareholder value" (3). Over 70 percent of the students ended up choosing "maximize value for shareholder" as one of the "primary responsibilities of a company," while 50 percent chose "invest in the growth and well-being of the employees." Just over 30 percent chose "create value for the local community" (8). Hardly any included improving the environment. In fact, twice as many students identified the primary benefit of companies fulfilling their social responsibilities as "better public image/reputation" as did those identifying a "stronger/healthier community" (9). *Business Week* (online, March 11, 2002) reported, "The schools say the students apparently aren't learning what is being taught." They sure are—in finance, not ethics.

More telling, perhaps, another survey of MBA students from the highest-ranked schools found that they "appear less concerned about social issues than current executives" (Filipczak et al. 1997:16) and more opposed to government action aimed at encouraging responsible social behavior (13). Indeed, while 24 percent of the executives identified "compassion" as the most important characteristic of future leaders, only 4 percent of the MBA students did. The report's author, Thomas Dyckman of Cornell, concluded that "Apparently experience teaches compassion. Maybe business schools should too" (16). But can they?

## Confidence − Competence = Arrogance

Humility is not a word often pegged on MBAs. Arrogance is. That the label has been used so often is not an indication that all MBAs are arrogant, only that a noticeable number of them are. Cohen (1973) quoted one of his classmates with two years' experience as a plant engineer: "Like the typical Business School student, I want to start at the top. . . . I don't want to wait around for five years. . . . I don't think I have any long-range objectives beyond what I've already said" (203). But then again, "Once one has tasted the executive suite, even if it's only in the classroom, it is naturally a bit frustrating to take a cubicle in the back room" (Kelly and Kelly 1986:28). Businessmen in eighteenth-century Germany expressed concern "that university training would render the students haughty and therefore unfit to rise in commerce" (in Spender 1997:29). Today that haughtiness *enables* them to rise in commerce.

The word *confidence* appears again and again in reports by MBA graduates about the benefits of their education; for example, the program "has given me the confidence I needed" and "the EMBA experience expanded the breadth and scope of my self-confidence" (in Hilgert 1995:69). As for competence, employers "failed to utilize [their] new competences," so most of these MBAs left their jobs! (73)

The title of this section means that confidence without competence breeds arrogance. Perhaps the proverbial arrogance of the MBA reflects feelings of vulnerability—inner worries that they do not deserve their success. "Parker displays the hollow self-confidence of a man who has never been seriously challenged," Cohen (1973:67) wrote of another of his classmates.

Imagine a $2 \times 2$ matrix of confidence and competence. The effective people have both, the sad ones neither. The unfortunate people have competence but lack confidence. They are worth worrying about, however, because a small boost in confidence can have great benefits. The dangerous people, especially in this hyped-up society, are the remaining group: those whose confidence exceeds their competence. These are the people who drive everyone else crazy. MBA programs not only attract significant numbers of such people but encourage their tendencies, by boosting their confidence to manage while providing little competence to do so.

As a student was quoted in her school's brochure (1999): "The IMD project gave me the confidence to tackle virtually any problem which comes my way, even if it is outside my experience." After a talk I gave to Insead students about MBA education, one woman put up her hand and said that while it is true that the program might not teach them that much about managing, it did give them the confidence to manage. I thanked her for making my point!

If the business schools were really doing their job, were truly creating leaders, their graduates would be known for their humility, not their arrogance. Certainly they would graduate with an acute appreciation of what they do not know. Instead, we hear from a recent graduate of Harvard Business School about a professor who told her class that "in the future, we would be among those who set the rules and have the conversations about what should and shouldn't be done in the way business is conducted." She and her classmates "gave him a standing ovation." No doubt! Why is Harvard publishing this (on its Web site, 2003), instead of hiding it?

It is "understandable" that Harvard students "attain a high degree of self-confidence," wrote Kelly and Kelly (1986): "For two years, they have been beaten down, then puffed up, told that after they have survived Harvard they can afford to consider themselves the best young management talent the country has to offer" (16–17). Good stuff for getting to the executive suite, perhaps. But what happens there? We'll get back to that.

## THE MINDLESS MARKETING
## OF CRITICAL THINKING

These kinds of student attitudes have been keeping good company with a growing corruption of the business schools themselves. Open the back of *The Economist* and look at the ads touting MBA programs like the latest potions of snake medicine. A few years ago, the most prestigious schools may have been the worst. "Flying Lesson, Wharton Style," headlined one ad above three of its notable professors in front of an executive jet. "Let Wharton's management faculty help you fly above the clouds for a global perspective on your business." Another urged readers to "Seize the Chicago advantage." Claimed the London Business

School, "The fast track to success just got faster"—at least if "you've got what it takes" and can "stand the pace." Finish the course, and "you'll rank as one of the most highly qualified professionals in the world." So simple.

"Smelly breath? Try Colgate Mouthwash. Problems with your career. Get an MBA." So wrote two professors about the promotion of MBA programs in the Malaysian press (Sturdy and Gabriel 2000:998).

"Newest," "world class," "know how," "fast moving managers," "mastering the skills," "manage in the new millennium"—these words come from just the first paragraph of a letter from the head of IMD in its 1998–1999 EMBA brochure. "Turbulent times" and "constant change" appear in a University of Chicago brochure, as they do in most others, including the word *global.* All of these are labels that stop thinking, not start it. Wharton's brochure for 2000–2002 shows a group of students trekking up "the imposing trails of Mt Everest. While not all the WE[World Executive]MBA students take on this physical challenge," the brochure continues, "they all share an equally rigorous experience that tests their critical thinking . . . [in this program that] can carry you to new heights." Perhaps such comments carry the empty rhetoric to new depths.

It might be easy to dismiss all this as just more of the mindless marketing that has gripped so much else in society. But academic institutions have a particular role to play in society—namely, to promote that critical thinking. They should be the very places that challenge such inanities. That they use them so casually bears witness to their own corruption.

What effect does all this have on serious attempts to raise the level of thoughtfulness in the classroom? I hope little, but I'm not so sure. If the first thing an applicant to a business school sees is this promotion, then what mindset can he or she be expected to bring to class? When people have read that Wharton will help them fly above the clouds for a global perspective, how are they to be educated on the ground, not least to reflect critically on vacuous words like global?

How often do we now hear reference to business schools as businesses, their names as brands to be exploited? The head of the IMD quoted earlier is President, not Dean. He told the *Financial Times* that "the faculty help me run the business" (Bradshaw 2003c). John Byrne of *Business Week* has commented on business schools not having cared "about the perceptions of their customers, the people who actually buy their product" (in Mast 2001a:18). But what other "business" examines its "customers" and dismisses them when they fail? When I recently heard someone from one of the most prestigious business schools talk in these terms, I thought, For what purpose? The school is phenomenally wealthy and can distribute no profits. It has no worthy project short of funds, no successful member of faculty without a "chair." Is expansion just a way to keep score? If so, that has to come at the expense of scholarship. Business schools do not exist to grow and diversify, to run around the world creating alliances, to exploit their brand and sell their name (see the accompanying box). They exist to generate knowledge and encourage wisdom. Nothing more.

## THE HIGH COST OF SELLING A BUSINESS SCHOOL

Oxford University sold the name of its new business school to Wafic Said for £20 million in 1996. (Templeton College had been established at Oxford with a £5 million grant from John Templeton in 1984. The two schools battled for years.) Said also tried to buy the board of trustees; he demanded the power to appoint six of its ten members. That "caused disquiet" in the university (according to *The Economist*, November 9, 1996), so he accepted *less* power over appointments at the school (Crainer and Dearlove 1999:147). *The Economist* claimed that this "shows how much Oxford needs a course in management, especially if it is to prosper in a world where academia is becoming a business." Perhaps *The Economist* needs a course in education, to appreciate that not everything is a business.

## THE SCHOOLS' OWN TOP LINE

Now the business schools have their own bottom line—which is really a top line—and it may be aggravating the problem. The schools get rated and ranked by the business press, regularly and relentlessly. Crainer and Dearlove (1999:178) found thirty-four different rankings.

There are two perspectives on these rankings, which I believe lead to the same conclusion. The favorable one is that they make the schools more responsive, because their students and recruiters get polled. Certainly this can counter the academic tendency toward insularity, especially in favoring research over teaching. The question is whether these assessments drive the schools to the right place.

The unfavorable perspective of the rankings is that they encourage a standardization of curricula beyond that required by the accreditation agencies. *U.S. News & World Report,* for example, uses the GMAT score as a determinant of how selective schools are, thus reinforcing a measure that we have seen has little relation to managerial potential. Moreover, innovation may be discouraged because high rankings are earned by conforming to the standards more than breaking away from them. The truly novel programs don't even get ranked—they don't fit. Even slight variations can get punished. Stanford "fell two spots, to ninth," reported *Business Week* in 1998, "due in part to the ire of recruiters frustrated because students abandoned them for tiny Silicon Valley startups" (Reingold 1998:87).

Most seriously perhaps, as with any ranking, these may evoke more manipulation than illumination. "I can tell you," said John Byrne who started all the rankings, at *Business Week*, "the schools lie" (in Mast 2001a:23). Much like some students, the schools play games to get better grades. *Business Week* reported how Chicago's response to having been "slammed" by recruiters two years earlier: besides bringing in new staff, the dean "added . . . valet parking and a concierge desk" (Reingold 1998:90).

And then there is a measure of the starting salaries of the graduates. Woe to the school with a student who goes to a nongovernmental organization in a developing country or, for that matter, a student from such a country who takes a job with a company back home. We can fix that problem, the magazines may claim. Sure. They can fix any problem; they are constantly fixing. And the deans are constantly manipulating. (For advice from a particularly candid ex-dean, see the accompanying box.) Maybe the real problem is the very notion of a top line, the idea of measuring things instead of judging them. Just as it is in managing itself.

## GAMES BUSINESS SCHOOLS PLAY

*(excerpted from "Ten Easy Steps to a Top-25 MBA Program," by Andrew J. Policano, former dean, University of Wisconsin-Madison, 2001)*

If your MBA program is in the unenviable group that *Business Week* and *U.S. News & World Report* rank below the top 25, you are undoubtedly under constant pressure from your students, alumni, and donors to move into the top 25. The following . . . steps [among others] can get you there. . . .

- *Provide a wide variety of students' services for MBA students,* including free breakfasts and luncheons . . . and free parking. . . .

- *Increase the average GMAT score of your MBA class to above 650 . . .* You will need to decrease the number of students in the MBA program . . . and never admit students who have low GMAT scores, even if they otherwise show strong potential. . . .

- *Increase services to recruiters,* including valet parking, free meals, gift baskets in hotel rooms, and a comfortable lounge area. . . .

- *Eliminate not-for-profit programs and other MBA majors that produce graduates who are placed in low-salary positions.* . . .

- *Entice everyone who inquires about [your] program, especially unqualified students, to apply.* . . . (*U.S. News* uses the number of admits divided by the number of applicants as a selectivity measure.). . . .

- *Increase the budget for the MBA program substantially; $50,000 per student is a good target.* . . . you will need to reallocate funds . . . [for example, by decreasing] the size and/or the cost of delivery of your undergraduate [and doctoral] program[s] [and diverting] resources from the support of faculty research to the MBA programs. . . .

If you think that these suggestions seem tongue-in-cheek, think again. They are only a fraction of what many deans over the years have described to me as their "rankings strategy."

The object of the exercise is not placement or salaries or valet parking; it is not how schools are perceived to be doing. The object is learning, developing more thoughtful people who can improve the practice of managing. And who is measuring that?[1] Those major issues of human existence quite literally don't count in all of this. But how can they? Who can measure what really matters, such as how much someone learns in a classroom? (More on this in Chapter 13.)

---

[1]Interested readers can see the *Financial Times* (Bradshaw 2003c) list of the criteria used by five major rankings: its own, Economist Intelligence Unit, *Wall Street Journal, Business Week*, and *Forbes*. On the rankings of research, the paper noted "huge variations."

On balance, the rankings have certainly opened up the business schools, to some things they should be worrying about and others they shouldn't. The bigger problem is that the rankings have distracted them from the most important issue—namely, how effectively they are developing responsible managers, businesspeople, and citizens. To get to that will require something beyond top and bottom lines, beyond numbers, toward values, beliefs, judgments.

# 4

# WRONG CONSEQUENCES II
## *Corruption of Managerial Practice*

*"Unhappy is the land that has no heroes."*
*"No, unhappy is the land that needs heroes."*
—BERTOLT BRECHT, *LIFE OF GALILEO*

With so many people receiving the MBA these days and so many of them making it to senior positions, the influence of the degree on the practice of managing has become enormous. Yet it has hardly been investigated.

In this chapter, we look first at how the graduates enter the workplace, their leap to the real world, most notably into consulting and investment banking, or else to what is "hot" (often just as it cools down). Then we consider how increasing numbers of MBAs get into managing—by going around most of it, straight into executive positions. The next section addresses what I believe to be the key consequence of MBA training in general—putting the practice of management out of balance, in favor of calculating and heroic styles. That leads to the final section, which presents results on the performance of some of the most prominent MBAs who made it to CEO. To the claims that so many of them get there, I counter with data on how the supposedly best of them perform there. Not very well, according to some startling evidence.

# FIRST: THE LEAP TO THE "REAL" WORLD

Do an MBA and, in a good year, you might double your salary—at least if you are willing to change employers and industries, especially to consulting or investment banking. In other words, ignore any experience you might have, and forget about learning the practice of management. That can come later, when you run a company.

## GETTING THE GREATEST JOB BANG FOR YOUR EDUCATIONAL BUCK

The *Oxford Dictionary* defines mercenary as "working merely for money or reward." Does the MBA promote a mercenary approach to management?

"[M]ost people go to business schools to get rich, not to improve their minds," concluded *The Economist* in 1996 (July 20). A few years later, *Fortune* magazine wrote that "MBAs want more money . . . for fewer days of work . . . and then—maybe—they'll make a commitment"—of "3–5 years to their next employer" (Branch 1999:79). This is backed up by various studies over the years—for example, that money was the key criterion for 77 percent of graduating MBAs (Dearlove 1997), that "Fully 76% of MBAs don't plan to stay with one employer for more than five years" (Koudsi 2001:408, in *Fortune*), and that actual turnover within five years of graduation ranges from just over one-half to two-thirds in two studies (Dougherty, Dreher, and Whitley 1993:544).

The next employer, of course, is usually another employer. Upon graduating, MBAs don't go back so much as move on. Hence, Whitley et al. (1981:157) have referred to business schools as "switching institutions."

To help move these MBAs along, *Business Week* ran an article entitled "Getting the Most for Your B-School Money" (Dunkin and Enbar 1998). It showed how to calculate return on investment—salary gained for money spent—and rated schools accordingly. The "winner" was the University of Pittsburgh, whose MBA offered a 38 percent return on investment "because its MBA program lasts only one year" (177). Less is apparently more (money at least, if not learning). "Business school looks like a better deal than it was in 1996" (176), the article concluded. So long as you don't mind turning education into a farce.

The MBA is a hot commodity, the saying goes; its holders are "the supermodels of the business world" (Dearlove 1997). In the same year, a *Fortune* article titled "MBAs Are Hot Again—and They Know It" (Branch 1997:77) described six-figure salaries plus signing bonuses and tuition reimbursements. One student talked of finding "an opportunity where I can directly impact the direction of an organization," although the article characterized his group as "a pretty risk adverse bunch." Well, not everyone: "A top [Northwestern] student didn't like the fact that a recruiter kept glancing at a clock during an interview. So the student jumped up from his seat, ripped the clock from the wall, and dumped it on the table. A students' market indeed" (79). A perverse world indeed.

## WHY SO HOT?

What exactly makes MBAs so "hot," at least when the economy is good? What have the companies been buying? The answer, according to many people involved, on both the educating and hiring sides, is not a process of educating so much as a method of screening. The MBA is a convenient credential to justify hiring choices. After all, if she comes from Harvard or he went to Stanford, how can a recruiter go wrong? Blame the school if the graduate fails.

Accordingly, business schools have been described as "expensive employment agencies" (Samuelson, in *Newsweek*, 1990:49) and "mere hiring halls" (from a survey of employers [Martin 1994:20]; see also Aaronson 1996:213). Even some prominent deans have concurred. Said Richard West at Dartmouth some years ago, "Business schools are like bottling plants. . . . The product is about 90% done before we ever get it. We put it in a bottle and we label it" (in *Time*, May 4, 1981). Most telling of all is a *Business Week* survey of six hundred senior executives that "revealed that the majority felt an MBA has little to do with job performance and makes little difference in employee merit or ability. However, these same executives admitted that their companies interviewed only MBAs for their management-trainee position" (McGill 1988:76). For more of this kind of logic, see the accompanying box, entitled "Who's Fooling Whom?"

In a 2002 journal article entitled "The End of Business Schools? Less Success Than Meets the Eye," Jeffrey Pfeffer and Christina Fong of the Stanford Business School draw some interesting conclusions. In sharp contrast to those return-on-investment figures cited earlier, which

## WHO'S FOOLING WHOM?

*Business Week* published a poll in 1986 (March 24, p. 63) about "How Executives Rate a B-School Education." Among the findings:

| | | |
|---|---|---|
| Business schools teach students a lot about management theory but not much about what it takes to run a company. | Agree<br>Disagree<br>Not sure | 86%<br>10%<br>4% |
| It makes sense for people with MBAs to get higher salaries than people with the same work experience but no degree. | Agree<br>Disagree<br>Not sure | 33%<br>64%<br>3% |
| Younger employees with MBAs tend to have less loyalty and job-hop a lot more than employees without the degree. | Agree<br>Disagree<br>Not sure | 63%<br>25%<br>12% |
| Business school graduates tend to have unrealistic expectations about how fast they will get ahead in their careers. | Agree<br>Disagree<br>Not sure | 78%<br>18%<br>4% |
| If your son or daughter were planning a career in business, would you advise him or her to get an MBA, or not? | Would advise<br>to get an MBA<br>Would not<br>Not sure | <br>78%<br>17%<br>5% |

were based on reported salaries for the first job, Pfeffer and Fong found "almost no economic gains for an MBA degree unless one graduates from a top-ranked program" (82). And they questioned whether there is more learning in these top-ranked programs, since "the course of study, even the textbooks used, are remarkably similar across schools of different degrees of selectivity" (82). Nor do grades in the program seem to matter much "to subsequent performance in business" (83). "In today's prestigious business schools, students have to demonstrate competence to get in, but not to get out" (83, citing Armstrong 1995). Indeed, Pfeffer told an interviewer that "there is not much evidence that actual education does very much" (in Sokol 2002). Pfeffer and Fong conclude that "it is not education in business but selectivity that is being assessed" (82).

Of course, the recruiters get more than the credential. They get people who have chosen to do a degree in business and have sat still for two years in the process. So they are likely to be interested in business and cooperative at work, at least until they move on.

But if this is true, then why bother with the expensive education? Why don't companies just pay the business schools to screen people? As Samuelson (1990) has mused in *Newsweek*, imagine if "all MBA programs vanished. Companies would have to be more thoughtful about how they recruit and train future managers" (49).

One particularly candid Japanese executive, himself with an American MBA, provided another perspective on this:

> In practice . . . the only thing we immediately expect from Japanese graduates of American MBA programs is that they be able to speak English because we often have our MBAs interpret for foreign businessmen visiting the company. These employees don't return to Nissay with significantly better business skills—they don't generally learn much in an MBA program that they couldn't learn on the job. (in Linder and Smith 1992:30)

He also commented that the degree teaches "a lot about the workings of American society, law, and culture." But so would a degree in theatre—perhaps better. "An MBA is sort of like a designer suit," he added, "an attractive status symbol that also wears well" (31).

## CONSULTING AND INVESTMENT BANKING INSTEAD OF MANAGING

These status symbols appear to have worn particularly well in consulting and investment banking, where many of the graduates have traditionally gone—63 percent of them from the twenty-five schools ranked highest in the *Business Week* survey of 1998 (October 19). *Fortune* also reported in 2003 (April 28) that all five of the employers most preferred by MBA candidates came from these two industries. "Harvard has become a finishing school for consultants and investment bankers," said one of its faculty members in 2000 (Clayton Christensen, cited in Jones 2000:28).

Of course, this should come as no surprise, given the nature of the education and the inclination of the students. Both industries look good and pay well, no matter what one's prior experience. Following on MBA studies, they offer great opportunities to do analysis and apply techniques—numbers galore—with little responsibility for implementation or direct management. Instead, the graduates go in and out of client firms, as they did in their case studies, providing advice without having to suffer its consequences. And where better to make use of the "old boys" network than in consulting and investment banking?

## WHAT'S HOT ISN'T COOL

"What's hot?" seems to be the mantra of the MBA looking for a job. And consulting and investment banking have long been hot. Recall from Chapter 2 for just how long McKinsey & Company has been hiring so many Harvard MBAs.

The trouble with most things hot is that they can cool rather quickly—no matter how "cool" they were when hot.

An interesting article appeared by J. L. Pfeffer in the *International Herald Tribune* in 1994. If you wish to know where *not* to put your money, the writer suggested, "Keep an eye on people long on greed, long on debt and short in foresight"—namely, "graduating MBAs":

> These debt-laden pinstripes have a history of chasing after the latest hot and soon-to-be-overvalued job in the latest hot and already overvalued industry. The equation can be observed time and again in industry after industry: The longer and bigger the boom, the higher the starting salaries, the greater the number of MBAs and the harder the crash.

The writer presented data on five industries. In four of them (health care/pharmaceuticals, entertainment/media, computer systems, and investment banking), as annual returns grew and then fell, the percentage of the Harvard class accepting jobs in them continued to rise, at least for a time. Only in consulting did the two figures rise steadily.

That was in the mid-1990s. A few years later, this thesis was confirmed with a vengeance. Along came the hottest new industry of all— the dot-coms—and schools raced to revise their curricula while students flocked to the new courses. Jobs in consulting became "less cool among MBAs" (Taylor 1998:66), as those in the dot-coms heated up. For a while, anyway.

"Harvard has been wildly enthusiastic about e-commerce," wrote a recent graduate in the *New York Times* (Buchanan 2000). Four months later, *Fortune* headlined that "MBA Students Want Old-Economy Bosses" (Koudsi 2001). "In 1999 and 2000, only 12 or 15 students attended Ford's presentations" at Northwestern; "this year the event was standing room only" (407). In a companion article, Harrington (2001:410) wrote that "last winter, Stanford's new e-commerce elective was the hottest thing . . . on campus. . . . This quarter there are empty seats. . . . Clearly MBA students know how to read a stock chart."

A stock chart perhaps, but not a crystal ball. Perhaps not even a tennis ball, not when their eyes are focused on the scoreboard. Are their schools any different? A Harvard associate dean told the *Fortune* writer, "We need to change—indeed get out in front of the parade—to continue to attract these bright 25 year olds." But Harvard is supposed to be the drum major of this parade. It seems to have no better idea where to go than anyone else.

To be a leader means to think for yourself, to break away from the crowd, and entice it to follow, in other words, to lead. Leaders don't imitate. People who hop onto moving bandwagons are not leaders. Nor are the schools that cater to them.[1]

"So where do MBAs want to work?" *Fortune* asked in 2001 (Koudsi 2001:408). Its survey put the "internet/e-commerce sector" down to third place (tied with consumer goods, to be discussed later), behind— did you guess?—management consulting and investment banking![2] Except that this time, once again, they may have been a little too late.

## E Tu, BCG

We have seen repeatedly, from Harvard's response to the Bok Report to the discussion just above, that consulting and investment banking have been not only the most enthusiastic proponents of MBA education but in a sense the very pillars of its support. So a shifting in that support can

---

[1]That recent graduate quoted earlier wrote his piece in the *New York Times* to make the point that while Harvard may have been "wildly enthusiastic" about e-commerce and saw such changes as putting the school "on the cutting edge of the new economy . . . responding to the demands of its customers," his own conclusion— in retrospect—was that "the customer isn't always right . . . [does] not have the perspective to see the big picture. . . . I realize that I needed more grounding in the old economy before I tried to understand the new one—even if I 'demanded' something else" (Buchanan 2000).

[2]Firms in these industries comprised four of the five "most coveted" employers—the exception being Cisco Systems, soon to encounter its own problems! They were five of five in *Fortune*'s 2003 ranking (April 28), while accounting firms were absent— recall Enron, Anderson, and Homeland Security—and the CIA made the list of the top 50 for the first time!

be a significant sign indeed. That is precisely what has been happening over the past decade. Some of the most prestigious consulting firms have been turning increasingly away from MBAs, toward more eclectic hiring—of people from the sciences, the arts, law, and so forth. A senior partner of McKinsey told me in 2002 that 70 percent of their new hires were not MBAs and were doing "exceedingly well"; he predicted they would soon make up over half the professional staff. A formal study at the firm, of people on the job one, three, and seven years, found that at all three points those without the MBA were as successful as those with the degree, while the Boston Consulting Group reported that the non-MBAs they had hired "were receiving better evaluations, on average, than their peers who had gone to business school" (Leonhardt 2000c:18).

There are signs of similar happenings in investment banking. The *Financial Times* ran an article in 2003 about Henry Kravis of KKR, the firm famous for its leveraged buyouts. Kravis waxed eloquent about the MBA, especially his decision not to quit the Columbia program after a few weeks. The article went on to say that "although he is a big fan of business education, KKR does not usually hire MBA graduates. Instead, for the past seven or eight years, the buy-out firm has run a program whereby it takes on as analysts people with two years experience on Wall Street" (Murray 2003:5).

But there is worse news for the business schools: Consulting firms are educating their non-MBA hires themselves—in BCG's case, for example, in just three weeks. Leonhardt (2000c) reports on this—what some firms call their "mini-MBA"—in his *New York Times* article:

> There was a doctor from Boston and a lawyer from Chicago, a philosopher from Australia and an engineer from France. There were people who had Ph.D.'s in mathematics, sociology and astronautics. In fact, in the tiered classroom filled with 50 clean-cut, casually dressed people in their 20's and 30's, there seemed to be just about every graduate degree imaginable, except one: the M.B.A.
>
> Yet within a few weeks, this hyper-educated crowd would go forth as certified management consultants, advising the executives of multibillion-dollar companies. . . .
>
> To prepare, the neophyte consultants had come to the campus of Babson College here in this western Boston suburb for a three-week crash course in the basics of business. It was run by their new employer, the Boston Consulting Group. . . . "This," said one student . . . "allows me to get a business education without getting a degree." . . .

All of this raises an interesting and disquieting question: What is the point of an M.B.A., anyway? (18)

Perhaps the most ominous comment of all came from the dean at the University of California at Berkeley's business school: "'Oftentimes the problems [these people are] trying to solve, really do require a deeper level of analytic skills' than many MBAs have."

## HANDS OFF

The jobs that MBAs have considered hot or cool are not the real activities at the heart of business. Companies generally do only two things of ultimate consequence: They make things, and they sell things. Not market things, not analyze things, not plan things, not control things. These support the physical making of something, or the provision of some service, and then getting some final customer to buy or use it. It can thus be said without great overstatement that MBA programs take people who have hardly ever made anything or sold anything and then make damn sure they never will.

Even when MBAs join companies that make and sell things—most commonly consumer goods, for reasons to be discussed later—it is rarely in the realm of making and selling. They tend to take positions in the staff (strategic planning, information technology, human resources, etc.) or else go into the specialized functions of marketing and finance. In other words, they are drawn to the hands-*off* activities, because that is where prior experience in the industry is least necessary and where the abstractions of aggregates—money in finance, targets in planning, statistics in marketing—shield them from the messiness of people and products. This amounts to an extension of that secondhandedness of business education into the world of work.

Production (or, as it is now called, operations management) has long been a marginal area in many business schools, with relatively little attention from the students and often not much more from the faculty. And selling has been totally absent. Not marketing, selling. There is an important difference. Selling takes place one-on-one. It is inductive, rooted in the specific, the concrete. Salespeople have to roll up their sleeves and face customers. So they live by their wits and draw on their experience. Marketing, in contrast, is removed even from markets, let alone customers and products. It works in aggregate terms, one-on-many. And so it tends to be more generic and more deductive, as well as more reliant on technique and analysis. As a result, MBAs have tended to favor marketing over selling. And so, too, perhaps, have the companies managed by MBAs.

# NEXT: THE END RUN
## AROUND MANAGING

You might think that beginning a career in this way—detached from making and selling, and managing itself—would hardly launch people on the road to leadership positions in large enterprises. Yet the evidence is the opposite. MBAs are becoming CEOs in increasing numbers (figures will be presented later), often moving laterally from finance, marketing, or planning into senior management positions, or—especially popular in recent years—leaping to that position straight from consulting. By going into that field, wrote a *Fortune* reporter in 1997 (Branch 1977: 77), "students get to put off committing to a specific industry." But not to running a company eventually—in some industry or other.

In his book that traces the careers of the Harvard class of 1974, John Kotter (1995) disputes the claim that MBAs have abandoned big business and especially large manufacturing companies. No, "instead of acting as employees, they are suppliers, distributors, bankers, landlords, and consultants" (81). For example, by 1993 a quarter of the class of 1974 were "mostly financial deal makers." And consulting was "seen as offering a way to get executive positions in firms without having to work oneself" up. Avoiding promotion "up tall, bureaucratic, and political hierarchies" may be "the only way [some headstrong individuals] would get an executive position in a large company today," Kotter writes (89).

Kotter seems to think all of this is a good thing: Their schooling trains people to serve big business rather than engage in it, at least until some of them get to run it. "Learn the business at the top," seems to be the formula. Indeed, after years of consulting and financial deal making, "Learn the practice of managing at the top" might be included.

This amounts to the ultimate consequence of separating leading from managing. MBAs haven't been trained to manage, and many don't have the will for it. But they are determined to lead. So a trajectory has been developed to take them around management into leadership. The trouble, as we shall discuss later, is that many of these people make dreadful leaders, precisely because their hands are off the business. In fact, the landscape of the economy is now littered with the corpses of companies run by headstrong individuals who never learned their businesses.

There are, of course, other MBAs who make their way up the hierarchy—but too often laterally rather than vertically. Instead of proving themselves in one place, they move from business to business, industry to industry, not staying around for the consequences. Like the education they received, they keep solving new problems without having to face the consequences of implementing the previous ones. In his critique of management education, Livingston (1971) referred to this "job-hopping" as "usually . . . a sign of arrested career progress, often because of mediocre or poor performance on the job" (81). Now such job hopping has become a sign of *accelerated* career progress!

## MERCENARIES IN THE EXECUTIVE SUITE

A human being is more than skin and bones; we have souls and spirit. So, too, a company is more than structure and systems; it has culture and competences. What, then, is the effect of parachuting into its leadership someone who has no appreciation of its history, no sense of its culture? What is the effect of imposing a detached outsider on committed insiders? And what is the effect of such a person whose experience has been in carrying out consulting projects or doing financial deals or hopping from one industry to another? Sure, a new broom sweeps clean. But that is precisely the problem: these brooms have been more adept at sweeping out experienced people than sweeping in new ideas. All that mindless downsizing with so little creative strategizing.

Mercenary soldiers flit from one battle to another, chasing the money. Mercenary managers do likewise in business. The result is a corruption of the very essence of corporate leadership, which has become more a means to get ahead personally than to make an organization a better place.

This may sound strong, but current practices in executive compensation, manipulation of financial statements, casual dismissals of "human resources" at the drop of share price, and the cash-in-and-run tactics of many of today's chief executives indicate that we are in a crisis of corporate leadership. Leaders are supposed to engage others, to foster teamwork, to take the long view, not to grab the lion's share of the rewards for themselves. Imagine a chief executive saying to the board, "We have talked a lot about the long-term health of this company. Why, then, am I being rewarded for short-term gains in the stock price? And why just me? How can I foster teamwork when a disproportionate share of the benefits comes to me? Why not reward all of us equally?" That would be leadership. How much of it do we see in large American corporations today?

Doing an MBA hardly makes someone a mercenary. But these programs do attract a disproportionate share of people with these characteristics—impatient, aggressive, self-serving—and then launch them on fast tracks to positions of influence in society. Because the education is rooted in no industry or organization, is anchored in no particular context, it encourages a style of management that is likewise impatient, aggressive, and self-serving, obsessed with being "on top" to manipulate the "bottom line," "downsizing" to raise "shareholder value." This, in other words, is a style of management devoid of leadership.

# Consequently: Managing Out of Balance

To appreciate how people educated in MBA programs are inclined to manage, let me return to the framework introduced in Chapter 1, of management as a practice that combines art, craft, and science. Figure 4.1 shows these three dimensions as poles of a triangle within which different styles of management can be mapped. The point I wish to make is that, while effective managing requires some balanced combination of the three, MBA education, by focusing on only one, distorts its practice.

## Balancing Art, Craft, and Science

Table 4.1 lists various characteristics of managing under art, craft, and science. Art encourages creativity, resulting in "insights" and "vision." Science provides order, through systematic analyses and assessments. And craft makes connections, building on tangible experiences. Accordingly, art tends to be inductive, from specific events to the broad overview; science deductive, from general concepts to specific applications; and craft is iterative, back and forth between the specific and the general. This is expressed most evidently in how each approaches strategy: as a process of visioning in art, planning in science, venturing in craft.

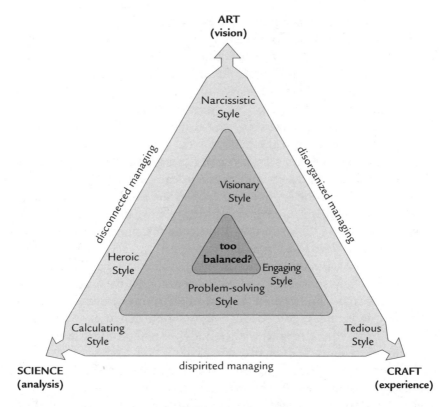

**FIGURE 4.1**
A Managerial Style Triangle

TABLE 4.1    THE THREE POLES OF MANAGING

|  | SCIENCE | ART | CRAFT |
|---|---|---|---|
| Based on | Logic (the verbal) | Imagination (the visual) | Experience (the visceral) |
| Relies on | Scientific facts | Creative insights | Practical experiences |
| Concerned with | Replicability | Novelty | Utility |
| Decision making as | Deductive | Inductive | Iterative |
| Strategy making as | Planning | Visioning | Venturing |
| Metaphor | The Earth (rational) so can get stuck | The air (spiritual) so can get lost | The sea (sensual) so can go adrift |
| Contribution | Science as systematic analysis, in the form of inputs and assessments | Art as comprehensive synthesis, in the form of insights and visions | Craft as dynamic learning, in the form of actions and experiments |

Clearly, effective managing requires all three. They needn't exist in perfect balance, but they do have to reinforce each other. Accordingly, Figure 4.1 labels the styles at each of the poles of the triangle in negative terms: *narcissistic* at the pole of art, namely art for its own sake; *tedious* at the pole of craft, where a manager may never venture beyond his or her experience; and *calculating* at the pole of science, with relationships that can become dehumanized. To use the metaphors listed in Table 4.1, art, as spiritual, rises into the air but risks getting lost in the clouds; craft, more sensual, floats on the sea but can go adrift; and science, so rational, sits firmly on the ground, where it can get stuck.

Figure 4.1 labels the styles along each of the three lines of the triangle negatively, too, since each combines two of the dimensions but leaves out the third. Art and craft without the systematic scrutiny of science can lead to *disorganized* managing. Craft and science without the creative vision of art can lead to *dispirited* managing, careful and connected but lacking spark. And art with science, creative and systematic, without the experience of craft, can produce rootless, impersonal, *disconnected* managing. Figure 4.1 also shows a particular example of the latter, labeled *heroic*, closer to science but with a hint (or illusion) of art, a prominent style that will be discussed later.

Effective managing, then, tends to happen within the triangle, in what is shown on Figure 4.1 by the inner triangle—where the three approaches coexist, even if there may be a tilt toward one or two. (A third, smaller triangle is shown at the center to suggest that too much balance of the three may also be dysfunctional, since it lacks any style.)

Many functional styles are possible within this middle triangle. The figure shows three in particular. One, near the top but toward the right side, is labeled *visionary*. It is largely artistic but rooted in experience, and it is supported by a certain level of analysis (or else it would go out of control). This suggests that the "big picture" of art does not appear as some kind of apparition but has to be painted, stroke by stroke, out of the tangible experiences of craft. The visionary style seems to be especially common among successful entrepreneurs.

A second style, labeled *problem solving*, especially combines craft with science. It seems to be common among first line operating managers, such as factory foremen and project managers. This style may be significantly analytic, but it is also strongly rooted in experience and dependent on a certain capability for insight as well.

And toward the lower right is shown a people-oriented style, labeled *engaging,* favored by managers who do a good deal of coaching and facilitating. This is mostly craft, but with enough art to make it interesting and enough science to make it viable. (More on this style in Chapter 9.)

## THE UNBALANCED MBA

The conclusion reached in Chapter 2, in these terms, is that MBA education is unbalanced. It is devoid of craft; indeed, it denigrates experience in favor of analysis. The students themselves have little experience, or else they are not able to make use of the experience they do have in a classroom disconnected from practice. And MBA education is weak on art as well. Not that it denies art—indeed, many of the cases glorify visionary leadership—just that it can do little with it. Insight, vision, and creativity come alive in action, not in admiration. Art and craft are based largely on the tacit, while the MBA classroom focuses on the explicit, in the form of analysis and technique as well as formal theory.[3]

The conclusion developed so far in this chapter is that many of the graduates of MBA programs carry this imbalance into their careers: They choose jobs that favor analysis removed from the experience of craft, and carry this to positions in the executive suite. There, as we shall now discuss, they have been inclined to practice two of the dysfunctional styles of managing just introduced. For many years, it was the calculating style, which so closely mirrors their MBA training. More recently the heroic style has become popular. My point is not only that many chief executives with MBAs have exhibited these two dysfunctional styles, but that by virtue of their sheer numbers, they have helped make these styles fashionable. Because of their consequences, each merits discussion at some length, together with examples of well-known people who have practiced them.

## THE CALCULATING MANAGER

In his book *Voltaire's Bastards: The Dictatorship of Reason in the West*, John Ralson Saul (1992) describes vividly what he calls the "new man of reason," the calculating manager who places all his faith

---

[3]Back in the heady days of Carnegie, Herbert Simon "struck the tone of optimism common among his colleagues when he declared himself 'positively exhilarated by the progress we have made . . . toward creating a viable science of management and an art based on that science'" (Sass 1982:303). Somehow the art got lost.

in the "system"—in technique and the obsessive numerical calculations required to support it. But "when he ventures outside the protective defenses of the system," into the real world of "common sense," this new man is lost (89).

Saul and others have pointed to Robert S. McNamara, Harvard Business School's most famous graduate of his day and recipient of its first "Alumni Achievement Award" (199), as the epitome of this "new man." As Zalaznick wrote of the MBA student of 1968: "His mind is keen, his ambition is endless, and his guru is Robert McNamara" (169). If McNamara is no longer anyone's guru, then how he got from there to here, told in the accompanying box, may contain a critically important message about the consequences of MBA education.

## CALCULATING MANAGEMENT INTO A QUAGMIRE

Robert Strange McNamara received his MBA from the Harvard Business School in 1939, two years after completing his undergraduate studies. He then joined the faculty for three years before serving in World War II as a statistical control officer (Shipler 1997). From there, he teamed up with a group of veterans, who came to be known as the "Whiz Kids," looking for a company to run. Henry Ford II, who had just succeeded his grandfather in a difficult situation, took them on, and two of them, including McNamara, eventually became president. "The Whiz Kids accomplished what he hired us to do," McNamara wrote. "The value of the stock increased dramatically" (12).

But it was subsequent to this, as American Secretary of Defense during the Vietnam War (1961–1968), that McNamara became famous—and infamous.

To that job he brought, in his own words, "a limited grasp of military affairs, and even less grasp of covert operations" (26). What he did bring to the Defense Department was PPBS, which sought to combine strategic *p*lanning, *p*rogramming, and *b*udgeting into a single *s*ystem. It was heavy on measurement, seeking to compare the quantified costs of proposals with their quantified benefits, much like capital budgeting in business.

PPBS spread to other U.S. government departments and later to other governments around the world. It was by far the most ambitious effort ever undertaken to impose rational analysis on government. As the man who conceived it claimed, "systematic analysis is essential . . . whenever the relevant factors are diverse and complex. . . . [U]naided institution is incapable of weighing them and reaching a sound decision" (Hitch and McKean 1965:56).

So, apparently, was PPBS. Despite enormous efforts to apply it, in the words of its most distinguished critic, "PPBS has failed everywhere and at all times" (Wildavsky 1974:205).

But not before McNamara applied it to the Vietnam War, most famously in the "body counts" of dead Viet Cong soldiers (or at least people who looked like Viet Cong soldiers). To McNamara, the numbers were paramount. David Halberstam (1972) wrote in his book *The Best and the Brightest*, about McNamara and the group that surrounded him in these years:

*When [civilian advisers] said the Diem government [of South Vietnam] was losing popularity with the peasants . . . McNamara asked, well, what percentage was dropping off, what percentage did the government have and what percentage was it losing? He asked for facts, some statistics, something he could run through the data bank, not just this poetry they were spouting. (256)[4]*

McNamara's stated view of the strategy process came straight out of the Harvard Business School: "We must first determine what our foreign policy is to be, formulate a military strategy to carry out that policy, then build the military forces to successfully conduct this strategy" (quoted in Smalter and Ruggles 1966:70). This is what he did in Vietnam, except that successful conduct of the strategy translated into failed conduct of the war. McNamara the formulator sat in his Washington office while implementation was collapsing in Asia.

According to his chief adviser on PPBS, the Secretary of Defense was fully briefed in his Washington office. The "machinery" of the System took care of that. Key was "a systematic flow of information," said Alain Enthoven (1969), and "we are organized to provide this information" (273). Meanwhile, in the rice paddies of Vietnam, the enemy was gathering, eventually to overrun the country. As Wilensky (1967) describes what he calls the "ghoulish statistics" of Vietnam:

---

[4] According to a later article in the *New York Times Magazine* (Shipler 1997), "During the war [McNamara] was so impressed by the logic of statistics that he tried to calculate how many deaths it would take to bring North Vietnam to the bargaining table."

*[A]nalysis of the easy-to-measure variables (casualties suffered by the Viet Cong and the South Vietnamese) was driving out consideration of the hard-to-measure variables and long-run costs (the nature of popular support for a South Vietnam government, the effect of the war on the Western Alliance and on domestic civility, the effect of bombing on the will to resist). . . . Kill ratios and the like represent a touch of spurious certainty in a highly uncertain world. (188)*

Colonel Harry Summers Jr. (1981) of the U.S. Army concluded in his book on the Vietnam War that all of this represented "an educated incapacity to see the war in its true light" (29). McNamara believed in "consistency", and "war is not . . . consistent." [Recall from Chapter 2 the opening of the Bower report in response to Harvard President Bok that "the secret of success is constancy to purpose." At least when one understands the situation.] McNamara prepared his plans and left the rest "mostly to the staff." But those plans preempted the staff's ability to maneuver, and, according to Saul, turned the military officers into bureaucrats—"from self-sacrifice to self-interest" (82).

Harold Leavitt (1989) of the Stanford Business School wrote, "[We do not] remember Mr. McNamara as a great visionary" (36). Certainly not in the Defense Department. Nor subsequently as head of the World Bank, again with a dramatic new strategy, dependent on numerical calculations, where, according to Saul, "his actions have resulted in uncontrollable disasters from which the West has still not recovered" (1992:81; Saul also details what he saw as the disastrous effects of McNamara's nuclear strategy in the Defense Department [82–86]).

If not a visionary, then what was McNamara? "His most memorable skill was as an analyst . . ." (Leavitt 1989:36).

McNamara's story has been especially prominent. But its thrust is not especially unique. Indeed, with growing attention to the bottom line over the succeeding years, this kind of obsessive calculating has become more common, not less. And MBA curricula, if anything, encourage it more than ever. Back in 1973, Cohen quoted one of his Harvard classmates that "it seems you almost lose part of your humanity. . . . You become more calculating. . . . I could see a definite change in myself" (89). The Aspen study cited earlier shows how prevalent that now has become across MBA programs.

In a sense, MBA education has been providing managers with new clothing, like the tailors did for that emperor in the Hans Christian Andersen story. The trouble is that once these managers move into the executive suite, their nakedness becomes apparent. So they grab on to what they know best—the numbers that worked back in school, the techniques that ordered complexity, at least on paper. These have become the fig leaves for the naked manager-emperors.

"STRATEGIC PLANNING" AS A FIG LEAF    The most popular of these leaves has been so-called strategic planning. The system will do what the managers' imagination cannot: synthesize a strategy. The problem is that the technique offers only analysis.

Analysis provides order, which, as shown in Figure 4.2, can be helpful before and after the creation of strategy: before to provide systematic inputs, "hard data," and after to order strategies into plans—that is, to *program* them. But not during. The creation of strategy requires invention more than calculation, from connected minds that are able to *see* a different future. So managers who rely on calculation tend not to create strategies so much as copy them—from other organizations, especially what is fashionable, or by extrapolating, with modifications, the strategies of their own organization. In other words, such managers analyze and plan like mad; they just don't strategize. (See my *Rise and Fall of Strategic Planning* [Mintzberg 1994].)

The all-too-common consequence of this approach is that the strategy process reduces to a game of business chess in which generic pieces are moved between established locations: Companies are bought and sold; budgets are thrown at research departments; the organization is structured and restructured.

William Agee was another of Harvard's infamous calculating managers. About a book written by Mary Cunningham, also a Harvard MBA, who worked alongside him as CEO of Bendix, a *Fortune* reviewer wrote:

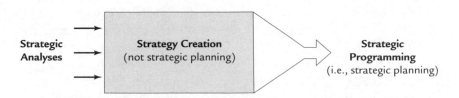

FIGURE 4.2
Strategic Analysis around the Black Box of Strategic Creation

What little discussion there is of actual business consists mainly
of genuflecting in front of a deity called *The Strategy*. . . . Near as
I can tell, it consisted of getting Bendix out of a lot of fuddy-duddy
old-fashioned products and into glitzy high tech. What makes this
a terribly ingenious idea, let alone a good one, she does not say.
(Kinsley 1984:142)

High tech is no more a strategy than is profitability (which is a number). And global is not a vision any more than are restructuring and
downsizing (which are often cop-outs). Visions do not follow the
crowd; they take companies to unique places. Warren Bennis has remarked that when a company truly has a vision, the first time you are
exposed to it, you will never forget it. (Recall the first time you visited
IKEA, the novel furniture store.) Compare this with all the eminently
forgettable strategies of the calculating managers (including those of
Agee in his next job, as described in the accompanying box).

## THE COLLAPSE OF A CALCULATING MANAGER

*(excerpts from "Agee in Exile," in* Fortune *[O'Reilly 1995])*

[Bill Agee had become] CEO of Bendix, a $4-billion-a-year auto
parts maker, when he was just 38, in 1976. The company fared well
under him at first; he was facile with finance and accounting,
shrewdly selling assets and investing in other companies. . . . [But
after] Bendix's ill-conceived effort to go high tech: a takeover attempt
. . . backfired, leading to the sale of Bendix [52].

[From there Agee went to Morrison Knudsen, where he] made
some dreadful business decisions [53]. More substantively, Agee
never fixed [the company's] core construction business. Much of the
$35 million or so in annual earnings that MK reported in the first
years of Agee's regime derived from accounting decisions and nontra-
ditional sources such as investment income. . . . MK executives say
the company boasted earnings by tens of millions of dollars [using
questionable accounting practices]. Some managers came to believe
they had to produce optimistic projections or lose their jobs. Says a
high-ranking MK official: "Four years ago I watched Agee pressing
on a strategic planner. Bill kept chewing on him to produce better

numbers. The guy said, 'Bill, you can make what numbers you want. Here's what we can do.' Bill got mad and walked out of the meeting, and the next day the planner was gone" [60].

[Agee tried to take the company from heavy construction into] railcars and locomotives . . . but the plunge . . . was badly flawed. MK had virtually no experience in passenger railcar design [61].

After three years of so-so earnings, MK lost $7 million in 1992. . . . [Then] in succession, many of the pet projects that Agee hoped would save Morrison Knudsen fell apart. . . . [Yet his method of reporting] "operating income". . . gave the impression that MK's construction and rail operations were doing well [65].

[Eventually] a mutiny began . . . [of] a handful of top executives, shareholders, and MK retirees [who forced the board to act] [70]. [Agee left and the company declared bankruptcy soon after.] . . .

Agee's fatal flaw was his weakness as a manager. A CFO at heart, . . . he relied on buying and selling assets so much that he obscured MK's problems. . . . "He was a dealmaker, not a manager," says one Wall street analyst. "He never thrived in a line business." Agee didn't understand the construction business [74].

NOTHING BUT THE FACTS: NOTHING BUT THE PRESENT    An obsession with "facts" blinds the calculating manager to everything but the present. It is certainly true that calculation derives from "hard data" of the past. But such data tend to be categorical more than nuanced, often reducing complex realities to simple measures, mostly recent. (See the accompanying box on the soft underbelly of hard data.) They caused McNamara, for example, to see only a shallow past in Vietnam and likely impeded him from being a visionary. It takes a deep appreciation of the past to develop a rich vision for the future. As a consequence, calculating managers tend to get stuck in the present. As Saul (1992) wrote about McNamara, "when things didn't work out," he "simply walked away . . . in protest against a war out of control, as if by that simple act he had washed his hands of it all . . . had removed himself from the history of the war" (86).

The characteristic common to the modern man of reason is this loss of memory; lost or rather, denied as an uncontrollable element. . . . The past, when it involves a failed system . . . disappears from the

## The Soft Underbelly of Hard Data

*(adapted from Mintzberg 1994:257–66)*

1. *Hard information is often limited in scope, lacking richness and often failing to encompass important noneconomic and nonquantitative factors.* Much important information never becomes hard fact. The expression on a customer's face, the mood in the factory, the tone of voice of a government official—all of this can be information for the manager but not for the formal system. Hence, while hard information may inform the intellect, it is largely soft information that builds wisdom.

2. *Much hard information is too aggregated.* The obvious solution for a manager overloaded with information is to have it aggregated. The problem is that a great deal of information is lost in such aggregating. How much does the bottom line tell about the condition of an enterprise; what do patents registered reveal about what is going on in a research laboratory? It is fine to see forests, but only so long as nothing is going on amid the trees.

3. *Much hard information arrives too late.* Information takes time to "harden"—time for trends and events and performance to appear as "facts," more time for these facts to be aggregated into reports. Often managers cannot wait.

4. *Finally, a surprising amount of hard information is unreliable.* Something is always lost in the process of quantification—before those electrons are activated. Anyone who has ever produced a quantitative measure—whether a reject count in a factory or a publication count in a university—knows just how much distortion is possible, intentional as well as unintentional.

Of course, soft information can be problematic, too—speculative, distorted, and so forth. But that only highlights the key point here: that *all* information must be scrutinized carefully. The danger with hard information, as pointed out by Devons (1950) in his wonderful study of British aircraft planning during World War II, is that once information becomes hard, especially called "statistics," it tends to acquire "the authority and sanctity of Holy Writ" (155).

mind. Devoid of memory, anchored in the present, inescapably op-timistic about the future, rational models always have great diffi-culty adjusting themselves to simple reality. (85, 88)

TOO SMART? PEOPLE SMART?    Calculating managers are usually smart. But is smart enough, this kind of smart, in a complex, nuanced world?

The calculating manager's problem seems to be with so-called people smarts. As Livingston (1971) wrote in the "Myth of the Well-Educated Manager," many such managers "fail because their affinity with other people is almost entirely intellectual or cognitive. . . . They are emotion-blind just as some [people] are color-blind" (87). Of course, people smarts honed as managers work closely with others, cooperatively on teams and in projects. But does the trajectory of MBAs that we have been tracing in this chapter encourage that?

Asked whether the members of the Harvard class of 1974 were "team players," John Kotter remarked, "I think it fair to say that these people want to create the team and lead it to some glory as opposed to being a member of a team that's being driven by somebody else" (Vogel 1995:30). But that is the very antithesis of teamwork and underlines the central problem with the MBA: its self-centered individuality. As a Wharton dean put it some years ago, "Our system has a built-in ten-dency to reward the aggressive loner" (Friedrich 1981:4).

A BALANCED TEAM    A study by Patricia Pitcher (1995, 1997) in a large financial services company highlights the people problems of the calculating manager. Pitcher was interested in the three poles of manag-ing discussed earlier but, unlike our Figure 4.1, saw only one as negative. She labeled managers at our science pole "technocrats" and described them with rather cold words ("no-nonsense," "controlled," "serious," etc.), in contrast with the exciting words she used for the "artists" ("bold," "daring," "volatile," etc.), and the warm words for the "craftsmen" ("helpful," "wise," "reasonable," etc.).

As she tells the story, the company was built by an artist, who sur-rounded himself with other artists as well as craftsmen and technocrats. It was "outward looking." But when a technocrat took over, he drove out the other artists and marginalized the craftsmen, surrounding him-self instead with other technocrats. In other words, calculation took over, and imbalance. "The by-product . . . was centralization [which in turn produced] demoralization." The annual reports described the strat-egy as "profitability." But "losing the artists, the company lost vision. Losing the craftsmen, it lost its humanity." As a result, "profits did not go up." Eventually the company was "absorbed by a more ambitious rival" (Pitcher 1993).

Pitcher's key finding here is that balance in the managerial team is critical—that others with different styles can compensate for the weaknesses of a chief executive. But only if the chief executive respects other styles. Calculating managers, she concludes, do not. Is this what we have been seeing from many of those "aggressive loners" weaned on analysis?

## THE RISE OF THE HEROIC MANAGER

The calculating style of management was prevalent for years in industries such as automobiles and telecommunications, whose markets favored mass-produced products and services while sometimes tolerating mediocre quality and/or the absence of innovation. Under such conditions, calculating chief executives could get by. But conditions have changed in many of these industries.

Partly demand arose for better quality (as in automobiles, largely because of Japanese competition), or for innovation (as in telecommunication, with its technological breakthroughs) with a requirement for more knowledge work. But another factor appeared, too: the rise in investor expectations, driven by the ascendancy of "shareholder value." And shareholder value has trumped quality and innovation. Rather than discouraging the calculating style, it has promoted another style that only masked that one, a style that has become pervasive and destructive.

Under shareholder value, publicly traded companies have had to perform better, dramatically better. But performance has taken on a special meaning—not about producing better products or improving customer service or doing more innovative research; no, just about raising the price of the stock. Of course, the assumption continues to be made that doing all these things raises the price of the stock. It is just that many companies have been doing opposite things to raise the price of the stock, at least temporarily. To make the immediate numbers look good, so as to catch the attention of journalists, analysts, and ultimately stockholders, products have been rushed to market, brands have been depreciated, customers have been exploited, research has been curtailed, employees have been fired—many, many employees—and financials have been manipulated. In other words, many companies have been driven to superficiality, sometimes in the form of spin and drama, sometimes outright theft, at the expense of honest substance.

Accompanying this—in fact, driving it within the corporations—has been another shift, in a sense away from hard analysis but not away from calculating management. On our Figure 4.1, chief executives have been encouraged to move up the right side of the triangle, toward the artistic pole, along the line labeled disconnected managing. But most did not get very far: Their lack of imagination stopped them in the place labeled the heroic style. In Pitcher's terms, the technocrats have pretended to be artists.

What encouraged them to do that was the assumption by boards of directors that shareholder value could not capture corporate behavior without elevating the chief executive to heroic status.

How can a large corporation get its people to respond to something as abstract as the maximization of shareholder value? Who is supposed to get excited about making money for people they have never met, some of whom are buying the stock in the morning and selling it in the afternoon? The answer has been to concentrate power in the hands of a single individual who can act rather arbitrarily to bring everyone else in line—someone who can order them to improve numerical performance and fire them when they do not. The CEO has thus become king.

THE EASY, FAULTY ASSUMPTIONS OF SHAREHOLDER VALUE    But how to ensure that these kings themselves do the shareholders' bidding? That, too, seemed simple enough, once the board accepted a massive set of easy assumptions: that the chief executive *is* the enterprise, that he or she alone is responsible for its entire performance, and that this performance can be measured and the chief executive rewarded accordingly. In other words, the shareholders have bought off the CEOs: they have empowered them to disempower everyone else. They just never realized that the CEOs would take it all so seriously—for their own benefit, at the expense of the shareholders themselves. It is an awfully naive view of the corporation, but it has served greedy chief executives well.

Power in corporations has thus become centralized around the CEOs to a degree not seen for decades, reminiscent of the captains of American industry a century earlier. Sure, all the rhetoric has continued about empowerment and decentralization, knowledge workers and networked organizations. But practice has been driving a wedge between the so-called leaders sitting atop their pedestals, detached and generously rewarded, and everyone else awaiting their next dramatic move with trepidation. All that progress made since the Hawthorne studies of the 1930s, to engage people in their enterprises, was undermined in the 1990s.

But how could these CEOs, flesh-and-blood human beings like the rest of us, deliver on such ambitious expectations? This has required another easy if massive assumption: They have simply become heroic. The CEOs are expected to ride in on their white horses to do the dramatic deals that save the day and up the share price. Again—for a while.

THE CONSUMPTION OF HEROES    In this myth, the boards and shareholders have been joined by an all-too-willing press with its insatiable appetite for heroes. Calculating managers, even craft managers doing their job quietly, hardly make for good stories, compared with those engaged in bold mergers and massive firings. (See the accompanying box.) Of course, real artists provide drama, too. But there are not many of them to go around, at least ones whom conventional boards of directors are willing to appoint. So we get pretend artists instead: all the drama of art with little of the beauty. Or else we get regular flesh-and-blood managers, simply trying to do their job, hoisted onto heroic pedestals.

A couple of examples from *Fortune*, otherwise one of the more thoughtful business magazines, give the idea (April 14, 1997, and March 1998): "In four years Gerstner has added more than $40 billion to IBM's share value." All by himself! "When Merck's directors tapped Gilmartin, 56, as CEO four years ago, they gave him a crucial mission: create a new generation of blockbuster drugs to replace important products whose patents were soon to expire. Gilmartin has delivered." In the labs, beside his office?! And in just four years, which has to be a record for the pharmaceutical industry—or for mindless journalism. (*Fortune* did not refer back to this when it wrote three years later [Nee 2001] that "Merck has what Wall Street analysts refer to as a 'pipeline problem.' This year five of Merck's best-selling drugs are expected to lose their patents. When that happens sales will plummet.")

And where were the business schools in all this? Again complicit, overtly and covertly. Many of their case studies did much the same as the press: put the individual leaders atop pedestals, at the expense of others in their organization (as discussed in Chapter 2), often giving the impression that the chief executive somehow does it all. Sometimes the schools just said it: the Harvard General Manager Program (1997–1998) "looks at leaders 'in action' to see how they develop a vision of the future, align the organization behind that vision, and motivate people to achieve it. It examines how leaders design effective organizations and change them to achieve superior performance." All by themselves!

## GIVE US DRAMA, NOT RESULTS

An article in *Canadian Business* magazine (DeCloet 2000) goaded John Cleghorn, chairman of Canadian's largest bank, the Royal, to make a dramatic acquisition in the United States. The author referred to the company's strategy as "timid," looking "like the 98-pound weakling who goes to the beach and gets sand kicked in his face." Later he added "everyone is wondering when the ever-cautious Cleghorn is going to do something a little bolder."

The article concludes as follows:

*The whispers have already started that Cleghorn, 58, is past his prime, that he lacks the courage to take a bold gamble. Since he took over as CEO in 1994, Cleghorn has steered the bank to some impressive profits [the highest of any corporation in Canadian history, as a matter of fact], but he's never been able to close the big deal. If Royal Bank really wants to fulfill its American dream, maybe it should find someone who can.*

When you stop and think about it, all this hero stuff sounds rather silly. But how many chief executives today stop and think about it? Not enough, apparently, to discourage the shift from the age of calculating management to the cult of heroic leadership. "There is something quite compelling about this scenario of foot-loose, buccaneering, symbolic analysts making lucrative deals throughout the global village," Locke (1996b) has written. "There is also something quite depressing about it as well, for the symbolic analysts are the only ones to profit from the system" (217). So recall the experiences of Sculley at Apple and Lorenzo at Continental Airlines; read about Fiorina at Hewlett Packard (in the accompanying box).[5]

---

[5]Lest anyone think this is just an American phenomenon, read about Lukas Muhlemann, a Harvard MBA and seventeen-year McKinsey veteran—"the new breed of Swiss business figures"—who moved in 2000 into the CEO position at Credit Suisse, one of that country's great banks. He was "not afraid of making bold moves" and "started with a bang," closing "nearly a third of [its] domestic branches and slash[ing] its workforce." The big mergers followed soon after. Then his troubles began, timing a big acquisition badly, failing "to rein in [the] buccaneering management in the U.S.," and getting involved in the Swissair bankruptcy, on whose board Muhlemann sat. "The final strain seems to have been the loss of confidence among Credit Suisse staff"(*Financial Times,* September 20, 2002). Muhlemann was fired in 2002.

## A Textbook Case of Heroic Management

Were a textbook case to be written about heroic management, following all the steps in sequence, Carla Fiorina's stewardship at Hewlett Packard (to the time when this was first written, in mid-2002) would be a strong contender. The company was "looking for a savior," *Fortune* noted (Nee 2001), but "the risk is especially high if the newcomer is eager to play that role, as Fiorina showed herself to be at H.P."

Fiorina arrived at HP from Lucent Technologies (just before it went into crisis) with her strategy all worked out, according to a cover story in *Business Week*. This was intended to "'reinvent' HP from the ground up" (Burrows 2001b:76) in three phases of about a year each.

In Phase I she "Spread the Gospel," in "'Coffee with Carly' sessions in twenty countries, to boast morale" and "spark innovation . . . away from incremental product improvements and toward big bang projects" (74). Phase II reorganized, from eighty-three product divisions into four units, thereby "dismantl[ing] the decentralized approach honed through HP's 64 year history" (72). Commented former CEO Lewis Platt with regard to the company's founders, "Bill and Dave did not feel they had to make every decision" (80). Phase III was intended to build new markets: "woo customers" by offering "soup-to-nuts solutions" from teams across HP (74).

"Not content to tackle one problem at a time, Fiorina is out to transform all aspects of HP at once, current economic slowdown be damned," concluded *Business Week* (72). It then asked, "Will her grand plan work?" and replied, "[T]he initial results are troubling."

Most troubling were the promises she made to the financial community. An earlier article in *Fortune* (Loomis 2001) on "the delusion" of "brash predictions about earnings growth" (48) singled out Fiorina at HP, who within months of her arrival was announcing earning growth targets, which she kept upping in the months that followed, eventually to a "sky high" figure of 17 percent. But a little over a year into her job, two weeks *after* the end of the fourth quarter, she "was obliged to tell a shocked world" that the company would not make its fourth quarter projections. In three days, the company lost $23 billion in market value, more due to its "credibility" than its shortfall (53). And this despite Fiorina's "marathon multi-day sessions to figure out how to cast the financials in the best light" (*Business Week* 2001:76). But Fiorina held fast: She informed analysts she was raising the growth targets for fiscal 2002. "In blackjack," she told HP employees in a broadcast, "you double down when you have an increasing probability of winning. And we're going to double down" (71). Two months later the company announced that profit and earning estimates for the quarter would drop to about 5 percent.

Major layoffs followed, from a "company that . . . [had] always avoided major layoffs" (Poletti 2001). These came shortly after promises that would not happen—indeed, after Fiorina had asked employees to take work cuts to avoid layoffs. "More than 80,000 people signed up, saving the company $130 million. A month later, Fiorina cut 6,000 jobs. Many employees felt betrayed" (Poletti 2001).

After that came McKinsey, "to look at strategic options," followed by the great merger—"the biggest in high tech history" (Burrows 2001a), with Compaq. This was to involve fifteen thousand more layoffs, a "conservative" estimate of the synergies, Fiorina told analysts in a flyer. Walter Hewlett and Dave Packard, sons of the founders, declared their opposition to the merger as a violation of their fathers' legacy, and a vicious proxy fight ensued. In a sense, it pitted these guardians of the old New Economy against the champion of the new Old Economy.

Hewlett and Packard lost. Fiorina won: rumors circulated about the huge bonus she earned for the merger (not its consequences). Did Hewlett Packard win? Fiorina reported near the end of 2002 (Musgrove 2002) that the merger was proceeding well: the target of laying off 10,000 people by November 1 was already 2,500 ahead of schedule! Stay tuned.

SOME GAMBLERS!    As quoted in the story, Fiorina has been fond of the gambling metaphor. "[S]he says she plans to keep upping her bets," *Fortune* concluded in an article (Nee 2001).

This is a popular metaphor among heroic leaders—except that these people engage in a particular form of the sport: They gamble with other people's money. Not only that, but the cards are stacked so that they win both ways. If the stock rises, they cash in their options. If it falls, they bail out with a golden parachute.

Mergers are the perfect bets for such gamblers: they are big, often bet-your-company size, with the promise of huge payoffs—for themselves, at least. Frequently, as in the HP story, they receive huge bonuses just for consummating the merger—in other words, they collect for putting down other people's money, before the cards are even turned. And what happens when these cards are turned? The record on these big mergers, in wave after wave, decade after decade, has not been good.[6] Yet the heroic managers keep trying, and failing.

Why do they keep trying? "Why not?" may be the better question. In a world "where egos rise faster than share prices," what do they have to lose? In addition to the financial rewards is the status. To chiefs in executive offices (not to mention students in classrooms), "the day-to-day running of a business is difficult, grudgingly hard work and often very boring. By contrast, a takeover is exciting and glamorous, promising even the dullest managers their brief moment in The Sun" (Hilton 2003). If that sounds good to you, then read the accompanying box.

### RULES FOR BEING A HEROIC LEADER

- Look out, not in. Ignore the existing business as much as possible, since anything established takes time to fix. Leave that to whoever was not downsized.

- Be dramatic. Do the deal and promise the world, to catch the attention of the investment community. In particular, merge like mad: go after other established businesses—the devils you don't know.

---

[6]This is one of those subjects where the academic researchers have tied themselves in knots. (See, e.g., Andrade et al. 2001.) One scholar of the subject, Maurizio Zollo of Insead, concludes (in personal correspondence) that "the empirical evidence is a 'tie': acquirers do not make abnormal returns (i.e., better than competitors) but they also do not consistently destroy value. . . . [T]he [perceptual] estimates of a failure rate vary from 50% to 75%." The popular press, aware of the dramatic failures, has tended to be more negative; for example, in *Business Week online* (October 14, 2002): "fully 17 out of 21 'winners' in the heady merger spring of 1998 were a bust for investors who owned their shares" (Henry 2002); and in the *Wall Street Journal*: "in the current weak economy the stocks of the top 50 acquirers have fallen three times as much as the Dow Jones industrial average" (cited in Sonnenfeld 2002).

- Focus on the present. The past is gone, dead, and the future is distant. Do that dramatic deal *now*.

- Inside the company, favor outsiders over insiders; anyone who knows the business is suspect. Bring in a whole new "top team." Rely especially on consultants—they appreciate heroic leaders.

- To assess the insiders, use the numbers. That way you do not have to manage performance so much as deem it.

- Promote the changing of everything all the time. In particular, reorganize constantly; it keeps everyone on their toes (instead of planted on their feet). Refuse to change this behavior no matter what the consequences.

- Be a risk taker. Your golden parachute will protect you.

- Above all, get that stock price up. Then cash in and run. Heroes are in great demand.

## Result: The Bottom Line for the MBA—Performance at the Top

A calculating manager reading this chapter might point out that much of the evidence so far cited on management failures has been idiosyncratic—about individual CEOs and the like. Where are some hard facts?

In fact, the hard facts most commonly cited point to an opposite conclusion: that a great many MBAs succeed by making it to the "top" —they constituted 42 percent of the Fortune 100 CEOs in 1998 (consistent with our own tabulation of 40 percent in 2001), up from 33 percent in 1991 (from the *Economist Intelligence Unit*, reported in the *Observer*, November 8, 1998, and *The Economist*, March 2, 1991). The Harvard Web site claimed in 2003 that its "alumni currently comprise about 20% of the top three executive positions of Fortune 500 companies."

But all this indicates success in getting there. What about success in being there? Shouldn't we be assessing how MBAs perform *as* CEOs, rather than *in becoming* CEOs?

## GETTING THERE

There are some obvious reasons why MBAs get there. These are intelligent and aggressive people to begin with, dedicated to business. In their MBA studies, they learned the language of business and how to use it quickly and impressively—not bad skills in a world of moving targets. As one Harvard student put it, "They teach you to be a great salesman here" (in Atlas 1999:47). Add to this the confidence instilled in their studies, which makes these people even more aggressive. All that rationality in Harvard's cases and Stanford's theory can be awfully seductive, leaving the feeling that "if you just want to there is nothing you can't do" (Cohen 1973:21). At least, once again, in getting there. And then, upon graduation, at least from the prestigious schools, that "old boys" network kicks in. Enabling Harvard to place so many people at the top is the fact that Harvard already has so many people at the top.

But what happens at this "top," where there is nowhere else to go (except sideways)? What happens to some of this disconnected rationality and questionable confidence when real things have to happen? With so many MBAs being produced, doesn't the relationship between the classroom and the boardroom deserve careful attention? It has not had it, not from business school researchers who spend so much time studying every other form of performance. "I've seen no serious studies that have attempted to link an investment in management education to shareholder value or a company's share price," commented the recently departed dean of the London Business School. On the facing page of the same journal, a professor and the President of the IMD business school wrote, "The answer to the question Does Executive Education really improve business performance? is obviously 'yes'" (Quelch 2001; Gilbert and Lorange 2001).

## PERFORMING THERE

Accordingly, in the mid-1990s, I began my own little investigation. I started rather informally: I went around asking people knowledgeable about American business to name the really great chief executives, the ones who made or were making a major *sustained* difference.

---

Stop here and ask yourself the same question
if you know American business well.

---

I then took the names mentioned and checked their backgrounds. Rarely did any of them have an MBA. The names that came up most frequently then, aside from the Sloans and Watsons of earlier times, were Gates of Microsoft, Galvin of Motorola, Grove of Intel, and Welch of GE. The first two never finished bachelors degrees; the last two, as it happens, both completed doctorates in chemical engineering. (Galvin, incidentally, refers to the father of the recently resigned CEO of Motorola. The latter has an MBA from Northwestern.) There were certainly a lot of famous MBAs out there—McNamara, Agee, and Sculley, to cite a not-so-random sample. But, as you might imagine, they did not get mentioned. (On September 22, 2003, *Business Week* [Merritt, 2003] ran a cover story survey on the MBA class of 1992 from the 30 top-rated programs. As self-reports of the 31% who responded—likely the most successful—questions can be raised about the generalizability of some of the conclusions. But one is especially revealing—a list of the "most-admired business leaders" [Warren Buffett, Herb Kelleher, Michael Dell, Bill Gates, Jack Welch, and Oprah Winfrey]. Not a single one has an MBA!)

Duly encouraged, I looked for more systematic evidence. I found it in a 1999 *Fortune* article entitled "Why CEOs Fail." Written by Ram Charan and Geoffrey Colvin, it discussed thirty-eight chief executive officers who ran into major, often famous, difficulties. All of these "highly ineffective CEOs" were "pushed, saw their companies bought, or left a company that had lost its way" (33).

We removed the non-American companies from the list, since the MBA is less common elsewhere, and looked up the credentials of the thirty-three CEOs who remained: Thirteen of them had MBAs, almost exactly their proportion in the Fortune 100. No worse than the average, to be sure, but isn't the purpose of the degree to make people better than average?

Charan and Colvin offered two key explanations as to why the CEOs failed: "bad execution" and "people problems"—exactly where we have seen MBA selection and training to be the weakest. About bad execution, Charan and Colvin made a telling comment in light of our discussion of heroic management:

Keeping track of all critical assignments, following up on them, evaluating them—isn't that kind of . . . boring? We may as well say it: Yes. It's boring. It's a grind. At least, plenty of really intelligent, accomplished, failed CEOs have found it so, and you can't blame them. They just shouldn't have been CEOs. (36)

Or as a Harvard MBA graduate told *Time* magazine some years ago, in case discussions "you get into the habit of thinking you can deal with any problem quickly. In real life you don't have the luxury of skipping over details" (May 4, 1981:44).

Then I came across David Ewing's (1990) book *Inside the Harvard Business School*. Ewing saw himself as just the person to write such a book, since he had "seen the school from the inside out for four decades, personally known most of its leaders, taught, and had a hand in many of its struggles." So he set out "to answer such questions [as why the school has become so important] from an insider's viewpoint" (7).

Early in the book (4–5), Ewing presented his list of Harvard alumni who "had made it to the top" in business—nineteen people in all, Harvard's superstars, presumably. (Robert McNamara was conspicuously absent, even from another list of those who distinguished themselves in government.) A biased sample if ever there was one. So I decided to use it as such.

Actually, my attention was piqued by certain names on that list, notably William Agee, who has already been discussed, and Frank Lorenzo, who became famous for his troubles at more than one airline. (Both, incidentally, were on the Charan and Colvin list of failed CEOs.)

I had the advantage of hindsight: More than a decade had passed since the list was published. "[T]he real test of the [Harvard Business School] is . . . how its alumni perform," Ewing wrote (274). How, then, did Harvard's presumably best alumni perform, not in getting there but in being there?

In a word, badly. Looking at the record as of late 2003 (see Table 4.2), ten of the nineteen seem clearly to have failed (meaning that the company went bankrupt, they were forced out of the CEO chair, a major merger backfired, etc.). The performance of another four could be called questionable at least. Some of these fourteen CEOs built up or turned around businesses, prominently and dramatically, only to see them weaken or collapse just as dramatically. None of the fourteen left behind solid sustainable businesses.

So, of Harvard's nineteen presumed best of 1990, only five left their jobs with an apparently clean record. If any bottom line gets closest to the ultimate performance of the MBA, this is it!

TABLE 4.2   EWING'S NINETEEN OF 1990:
THE PERFORMANCE OF HARVARD'S BEST?

| NAME | COMPANY | PERFORMANCE |
|------|---------|-------------|
| William Agee | Morrison Knudsen | Departed after company ran large losses; company declared bankruptcy shortly thereafter |
| Warren Batts | Premark | Successful |
| Roy Bostock | D'Archy Masius Benton & Bowles | Retired in 1997 after a decade as CEO; company—an institution—closed down in 2002 |
| Robert Cizik | Cooper Industries | Gave up CEO position after major acquisition ran into difficulties; retired from chairman's position and company shortly thereafter |
| Marshall Cogan | Knoll International Holdings and subsequently Foamex | Forced out in 1999; company declared bankruptcy shortly afterward; lawsuits concerning "looting" |
| Lou Gerstner | RJR Nabisco and subsequently IBM | Successful |
| Robert Haas | Levi Strauss | Gave up CEO position when company ran into severe difficulties |
| Robert Hauptfuhrer | Sun Exploration and Production (later Onyx Energy) | Questionable: serious performance problems when stepped down; "scorn" from Wall Street analysts |
| Richard Jenerette | Equitable Life | Questionable: persistent turnaround problems |
| Victor Kiam | Remington | No clear evidence of failure, but company sold by Kiam's heirs as too small |
| Frank Lorenzo | Eastern Airlines, Texas Air, Continental Airlines | Major failures in all three airlines; one sold, two bankrupt; major conflicts with employees |
| Vernon Loucks | Baxter International | Gave up CEO position under pressure from shareholders frustrated by poor performance and unsuccessful merger; company convicted of a felony |
| Robert Malott | FMC Corporation | Questionable: performance problems and questions raised about strategy |
| Joseph McKinney | Tyler Corporation | Forced into retirement after the conglomerate he built through aggressive acquisitions fell on financial hard times and was dismantled |

TABLE 4.2 *continued*

| NAME | COMPANY | PERFORMANCE |
| --- | --- | --- |
| Jerry Pearlman | Zenith | Forced to retire after failing to restore the company back to health; company sold shortly thereafter |
| James D. Robinson | American Express | Dismissed by an "agitated" board |
| John Rollwagen | Cray Computers | Questionable: management may have been resourceful in the circumstances, but the company was in a downturn as he left, incurred a huge loss three years later, and was sold the following year |
| Richard Thomson | Toronto Dominion Bank | Successful |
| William Timken | Timken | Successful so far as can tell |

*Note*: In a number of these cases, such as Agee, Lorenzo, Pearlman, and Robinson, the problems have been widely discussed in the business press (some also earlier in this chapter). Some of the sources used for this table include Laing (1995), O'Reilly (1995), Nudd (2002), *Adweek* Magazine's Newswire (2002), *Marketing Week* (2002), Norman (1994), *Mergers & Acquisitions* (1998), Santoli (2000), Button (1992), *Forbes* (1987), Sutter (1999), Munk (1999), Himelstein (1998), *The Economist* (1997), Bloomberg (1996), DiNardo (1995), Rudnitsky (1992), MacFadyen (2003), Ivey (1990), O'Reilly (1999), *Time* (1990), Castro (1990), Roeder (1999), Jaspen (1998), Byrne (1992), Machan (1994), de Rouffignac (1997), Yoshida (1996), Peterson (1995), Button (1993), Dolan (1999), Saporito (1993), *Investment Dealers Digest* (1993), Stedman (1992), *Wall Street Journal* (1993), Dorfman (1993), and Mitchell (1992).

BACK TO THEIR EDUCATION? Can we trace the problems of so many of these chief executives back to their education? We can certainly trace them back to the criticisms of that education presented in this book. The following are excerpts from articles about some of these people:

- "A perceived lack of focus was one of the many factors that made investors skeptical of [Baxter International] for a number of years. And Wall Street, rightly or wrongly, blamed . . . longtime Chief Executive Vernon Loucks for the problem" (Roeder 1999). "Baxter . . . pled guilty in 1993 to a felony charge for violating the 1977 U.S. anti-boycott law" (Jaspen 1998).

- "Barbis [of NatWest Securities Corp.] said that Onyx new chairman and CEO, Robert Keizer, had used 'the same old rhetoric often heard from his predecessor (Robert Hauptfuhrer)' in announcing 'yet another corporate restructuring, including a massive $958 million writedown . . . the sale of high cost assets . . . and a very questionable accounting charge'" (DiNardo 1995).

- Concerning the shutdown of D'Arcy Masius Benton & Bowles, an institution among advertising agencies: "'I think what's behind all of this is a group of managers who wanted to make a lot of money,' [Jack Bowen, former CEO] charged. . . . Bowen would not discuss the performance of [Roy] Bostock, his hand-picked successor. But as staffers anxiously awaited word of their fate, one particularly bitter employee accused managers of 'creating equity literally on the backs of people who didn't get a dime'." (*Adweek*, 2002).

- "Twice last year [Marshall] Cogan attempted to 'merge' the apparent cash cow [Foamex] with his debt-laden Trace International Holdings. Twice he was snared in shareholder lawsuits that claimed he intended to loot Foamex to pay Trace's debts" (Brickley 1995; see also Berman 1999). "The judge presiding over the case ruled that Marshall S. Cogan, the founder, chairman, CEO and controlling shareholder of Trace International Holdings Inc., a bankrupt, privately held Delaware corporation, along with his co-defendants, breached their fiduciary duties under Delaware law and held the group personally liable for damages in excess of $40 million" (Lenson 2003; see also Fabrikant 2003).

- "Continental Airlines Holding Inc., the US 5th largest airline company, filed for bankruptcy on December 3, 1990, for one simple reason: [CEO Frank] Lorenzo had loaded it with too much debt and an unseemly reputation. . . . Ultimately [Hollis] Harris [the following CEO] must convince the disinterested business traveler that Continental has left behind the Lorenzo days of chaos-as-usual" (Ivey and O'Neal 1990).

- "In the last year of [Joseph] McKinney's 30-year tenure beginning in 1966, the company entered a tailspin that hasn't stopped yet. McKinney managed to take the company to a high of

$1.1 billion in sales with solid earnings and then down again"
(de Rouffignac 1997).

- "It was about five years ago when Equitable, crippled by bad
  real-estate loans and unprofitable insurance products sold in the
  1980s, saved its skin by converting to a public company. . . .
  For a while, the turnaround seem to be working, generating
  kudos for then Chairman Richard Jenerette, the plan's master-
  mind. But then something happened. The stock stalled in 1993
  after Equitable failed to deliver big sales of its hot new product,
  variable annuities, and hasn't moved much since. Mr. Jenerette
  left a year ago" (Pulliam and Scism 1997).

Joseph Lampel, who joined me in this assessment of the performance of these nineteen CEOs, noted an often-fatal tendency to pursue a formula—some kind of generic technique—in disregard of
nuance and in spite of . . . well, those people and execution problems
again. As someone named Berger once remarked, "In science, as in
love, a concentration on technique is likely to lead to impotence." Inexperienced students who seek "practical" applications in the classroom seem to become disconnected managers who seek easy answers
on the job—especially financial ones that make the company look
good, for a time.

On the Ewing list, Bob Cizik, who grew Cooper Industries through
a program of aggressive acquisitions, turned postmerger integration into a
formula that entered the business vocabulary as a verb: the company did
not merely acquire companies; it "cooperized" them. At least until the acquisition that refused to be cooperized put an end to Cizik's tenure (Norman, 1994).

At Levi Strauss, Robert Haas, formerly of both the Peace Corp and
McKinsey, had more ambitious beliefs—namely, that social responsibility and group decision making should come first. But even for this Haas
had a formula, since he was an evangelist in a hurry. At one point, he
brought together two hundred of the company's best managers with one
hundred consultants to redesign the supply chain. In the process, Levi
Strauss suffered the corporate equivalent of a nervous breakdown.
Reengineering with a human face was in the end just reengineering—
and badly done at that (Munk, 1999). Haas learned in business school
about human resources and marketing; did he learn on the job about
human beings who make and buy jeans? What we seem to have here is
the manager who *knows* better rather than *learns* better and so is more
controlling than facilitating.

So what do we conclude from all this? Again, not that the MBA is a dysfunctional degree that ruins everyone who gets it. There are graduates of these programs who are doing fine,[7] just as there are those MBAs who have failed miserably. The evidence presented here is not definitive. But it should make us all highly suspicious about this influential degree. Having an MBA should no more qualify people to manage than it should disqualify them. But the data provided here should certainly sound some warning bells: that the MBA confers important advantages on many of the wrong people. Put differently, people should be earning their managerial stripes on the job; their progress should not be speeded up by their having spent time in any classroom. No company should tolerate that "fast track."

My own conclusion is that those MBAs who succeed do so in spite of the distorted image of managing left by their education. And those who fail may be the ones who have taken that image most seriously. The very characteristics that have gotten the latter into senior positions undermine their performance once there: They are too smart, too fast, too confident, too self-serving, and too disconnected. Many of the white knights of heroic management turn out to be the black holes of corporate performance.

---

[7]See *Business Week* (September 23, 2002) on "The Good CEO," the ones with a focus on the companies more than themselves. Four of the six discussed have MBAs, but, significantly, they were "unfamiliar names" who were not running "glamorous companies." One, Reuben Mark of Colgate-Palmolive (Harvard MBA, 1963), "wouldn't even comment for this story, citing his belief that talking to the press does nothing to improve his operations." (Likewise, he "wouldn't even cooperate with *Fortune* [another article, Schwartz 2001], explaining he'd rather have the spotlight on Colgate's thirty-eight thousand employees.) Nor were these people "change agents . . . charged with remaking culture or strategy." Their tenures on the job averaged eighteen years!

# 5

## WRONG CONSEQUENCES III
### *Corruption of Established Organizations*

*The trouble with being in a rat race is that
if you win, you are still a rat.*

—LILY TOMLIN

Ok, that calculating manager might continue, the MBA is not trained for management, and many MBAs fail as CEOs. So what. Look at the American economy, enamored as it is with MBAs. It hasn't exactly been doing badly, has it?

It had been doing rather well when I first wrote this (around 2000). It is doing less well now, as I revise this for about the fifth time, in April 2003. The question is the extent to which this economic success, and failure, is influenced by the prevailing style of management in America, which is influenced by the prevalence of MBA training.

Clearly this is a difficult question to answer with any precision, certainly here and perhaps anywhere. Many factors contribute to the performance of an economy. Economic ones, such as productivity, have received a good deal of attention, because economists usually discuss *such* issues. Management factors have not.

This chapter takes a look at two concepts, exploration and exploitation, and how MBA-educated managers tend to tilt them out of balance. It is not two economies that is at issue here so much as two cultures of managing, and the exploiting one may be undermining the long-term health of the economy.

Next we look at MBA managers in different spheres of the economy, first in "fast-moving consumer goods," often their preferred sphere, then as entrepreneurs, where their record is less impressive than business schools like to believe, and finally in high technology, where their increasing prevalence as CEOs may be especially problematic. This chapter concludes that we may be seeing the spread of a new form of dysfunctional bureaucracy, fostered by MBAs.

## Exploring and Exploiting

James March (1991) has written about the distinction between exploitation and exploration, as follows: "*Exploitation* refers to . . . short-term improvement, refinement, routinization, and elaboration. . . . It thrives on focused attention, precision, repetition, analysis, sanity, discipline, and control." Performance measurement is emphasized, and people "focus energy on relatively short-run concerns." In contrast, "*Exploration* refers to experimentation . . . in hopes of finding alternatives that improve on old ones. It thrives on serendipity, risk taking, novelty, free association, madness, loose discipline, and relaxed control." This "is risky. Success is not assured, indeed is often not achieved."

Exploitation sounds like calculating and heroic management as well as the consequences of MBA education in general. Here is where we find the managers in a hurry, with a short-term, fast-track view of the world, who grab what they can as fast as they can rather than taking the time to build long-term capabilities. Often removed from context, they tend to exploit other people's experience in the absence of their own. (A letter about this follows later.)

Every economy obviously needs both exploration and exploitation, one to create, the other to realize the benefits of creation. But so, too, I shall argue, does every company—to some degree, at least. The danger lies in tilting too far in either direction. Economies and companies that favor calculating and heroic styles of managing tilt too far in the direction of exploitation—of efficiency at the expense of discovery. It is not that they lack people with a flair for invention and innovation so much as that they stifle those they have.

For exploration, getting there is the hard part: doing something different, something interesting. Exploitation, on the other hand, thrives on being there—on extracting gains from what already exists, climbing aboard existing bandwagons to ride them to greater fortune. This is a lot easier, and so there is no shortage of people prepared to do it. The trouble is that you can't *be* there unless somebody *got* you there. Without exploration, there is nothing to exploit. Is that where we are headed as a society?

EXPLOITING THE ECONOMIES, "OLD" AND "NEW"    The economist Frederic Scherer (1992), in a study of the R&D activities of American corporations in the 1970s and 1980s, described the "failure of some U.S. businesses to meet technical challenges from abroad" as "first and foremost a managerial failure," perhaps attributable to the rise of MBAs as managers:

> At key points, the managers of U.S. companies did not allocate re-sources needed to remain technologically competitive, carried exist-ing developments into the market too slowly, and failed to main-tain an organizational environment conducive to innovation. Doing these things is not easy. But failure is more likely when top man-agers lack an appreciation for, and skill in, making innovations happen. Our statistical analyses suggest that R&D support is greater, and reactions to rising import competition are more ag-gressive, when top managers are educated in science or engineer-ing. In view of this, it is disconcerting to find, at least for our sam-ple of R&D-oriented corporations, a shift away from technically educated leaders during the 1980s . . . [and] toward leadership by executives with MBAs (for our company sample, increasing from 24 percent in 1971 to 42 percent in 1987). (182)

Scherer was, of course, writing prior to the boom of the 1990s. But a more recent report in the *International Herald Tribune* (Belson 2002) gives particular poignancy to his conclusion. It lists the "top 10 patent winners in the United States" for 2001. First was IBM and fourth was Micron Technology. No other American company appears on this American list. Seven of the others are Japanese, the eighth Korean.[1]

---

[1]According to *Business Week*, Carla Fiorina "goosed innovation by creating an in-centive program that has doubled the number of patents HP filed this year" (Bur-rows 2001). A letter on the Web gives one perspective of this (www.interesting-people.org/archives/interesting-people/200203/msg00106.html):

> HPs top brass points to an increase in patent filings: up between 67 and 100 percent, depending upon who is making the claim. How did this happen? Very simple. HP gutted the internal patent review process. In early 2000

Consider in this regard one industry famous for its exploration—pharmaceuticals. According to *Business Week* of December 10, 2001, "Drugmakers have upped research spending in recent years . . . but with no big payoff. . . . Big Pharma is licensing more drugs from biotech companies." Indeed, the CEO of Merck, cited earlier for its problems with research, told a *Fortune* reporter (October 30, 2000:91), "Scale has been no indicator of the ability to discover breakthrough drugs. In fact, it has been the other way—you get bogged down." Yet scale in the industry keeps rising. Is this more exploitation at the expense of exploration? A rather remarkable view of research came from the soon-to-be CEO of Pfizer (Henry McKinnel, Stanford MBA, 1967), who pointed "to the newly doubled library of two million compounds that the company can now screen for possible new drug combinations. We now have essentially twice the chances of finding a quality candidate in the *discovery* process" (87, italics added). Exploration by calculation!

ROBERT LOCKE ON MBAs IN THE ECONOMY    Several studies by historian Robert Locke over two decades on what seem like the "old" and the "new" economies shed further light on this issue.

In one paper (1996b; see also his book, 1984), Locke addresses three questions. First, "Did American graduate schools of management and their MBAs have anything to do with the creation of the reputation of American management?" His short answer: "not much" (4). Locke points out that America's prowess in management was established by the 1940s, long before MBA education was prevalent—indeed, when business schools were widely regarded as weak. It was, he argues, engineers and the like who built American business, thanks to their logistics abilities. Indeed, Locke points out that while the MBA programs expanded in the 1960s and 1970s, "the reputation of American management went into eclipse," as the German and Japanese economies surged ahead. He describes "management" in this sense as "a cultural peculiarity" of America that "never played the role in economic success that managers believed" (1).

And that leads to Locke's second question: "Did the most successful rival capitalist economies to the American after the war, namely the German and the Japanese, base their success to any extent on a copied American-style system of management education?" Despite both being

---

management was given a new directive, to raise the number of patent filings substantially . . . employees were encouraged to file just about any idea and let the US Patent Office decide the matter. The net result is more patent filings, but it proves little about HP's inventiveness.

"eager pupils" of management, and America a particularly "enthusiastic teacher of management" (6), neither country developed any MBA education to speak of (to be discussed in Chapter 7). As Locke (1989) has noted elsewhere, the innovativeness of many high-technology German manufacturing firms, in contrast to Scherer's conclusion about American ones at the time, may have derived from the fact that "German managers willingly participate in the work of the technical and scientific community" (276).

Locke's third question is "Could American-inspired form of graduate management education in fact be said to have done more harm to management than good?" Here his answer is more suggestive than definitive. He points out, for example, that "American business school research and teaching have contributed almost nothing to the most significant development in the business world during the past half-century—the quality revolution" (1996b:17). He also argues that the creation of a managerial "elite is detrimental to the sort of unit cohesion that . . . is critical to success at the operational level," precisely where he claims American practice to have excelled earlier. Back to Kotter's graduates of 1974 who have to lead the team.

Locke's article, too, was written before the American economy resurged, while those of Germany and Japan slowed. Was this, then, the revenge of the MBAs, finally coming into their own in the so-called New Economy? Not if one of Locke's more recent papers (1998) is any indication. Here he looks at the semiconductor and microcomputer industries, and especially at tendencies for the inventive founders to be succeeded by MBAs.

Locke (1998:20–22) writes, "Managers tried always to convert tacit knowledge into formal knowledge," starting with Frederick Taylor's time studies and continuing into more sophisticated efforts. So "business schools taught a standard curriculum (accounting, finance, marketing, decision theory, etc.) meant to serve the management elite operating in the knowable environment of Fortune 500 companies." Here the focus has been on a "hierarchical, production-driven model," which emphasizes volume and scale, control, and cost reduction—in other words, exploitation.

Interestingly, the rapidly developing semiconductor and microcomputer companies of the 1980s succumbed to this, too, by adopting the various systems of control—"budgets, accounting based financial reporting systems, cost control instruments." And that "seemed" to work—until "the unexpected happened." First, they "suffered grievous losses because of Japanese competition," their share of worldwide semiconductor revenues falling from 80 percent to 33 percent between 1983 and 1990. "Then the semiconductor business moved away from a commodity-driven business to one of specialist chipmakers, high valued added, high tech, customized semiconductors" (7). As a consequence, out went the possibility to rely on a "detached analytical thinking in executive quarters" and in came the need for "experimental behaviors" (quoting a study by Eliasson 1998:6–8), which had to make use of the tacit skills and innate abilities of the workers.

Locke concludes, much like Scherer, that "start-up entrepreneurs . . . in interactive IT could not have gained their entrepreneurial insight in some MBA program. Consciousness about the market possibility of a technology or a product depended on a thorough grasp of IT acquired on-the-job" (9).

Locke takes this point beyond the companies themselves, to the venture capitalists behind them. He contrasts the risk-averse ones of the East Coast, who did not know the technologies well, with those of Silicon Valley, whose knowledge ran deep. As a former Wall Street executive commented, "In New York, the money is generally managed by professional or financial promoter types. Out here [Silicon Valley], the venture capitalists tend to be entrepreneurs who created and built a company and then sold out. When problems occur with any of their investments, they can step into the business and help out" (9).

Even within firms, this "East-West management dichotomy affected interactive IT start-up":

> Xerox top management in the East ignored computer research in its Palo Alto Research center. The firm's chief executives in the 1970s, one a Harvard MBA, the other a Stanford MBA, had recruited their management team from finance people at Ford Motor Company and marketing people at IBM. One of the two CEOs, Archie McCardell, installed a "phased program planning" process for project evaluation brought from Ford when he came to Xerox. He, like the members of his team, believed that "if you sat on something long-enough and hard enough . . . you could control the outcome." "The Easterners were 'so risk adverse and numbers-bound that meaningful change seemed impossible. [They] had become nothing more than bean-counters bound to heartless formulas without factors for enthusiasm, faith, or finesse.'" (9, citing Smith and Alexander 1988:157, 33)

So here, in Locke's two studies, various of our conclusions about MBA-style managing come together: the propensity to exploit and so discourage exploration, with negative consequences for future development; the dangers of a management not steeped in the business; and the consequences of obsessive calculating and overreliance on formulas. Notice that Locke's conclusions come together for both ostensible economies, old and new.

## Two Cultures, Not Two Economies

The danger of talking about an old and new economy is that, once again, it focuses attention on the present in ignorance of the past—there is *always* a new economy, whether based on locomotion, electricity, or electronics. More serious is the implication that exploration belongs in the new economy, exploitation in the old. This view, I maintain, is proving increasingly destructive.

Certainly, developing industries have greater need for exploration. But they can hardly do without exploitation, just to get their products out the door. So, too, established industries that have to rely more on exploitation cannot forget exploration, or else they will eventually wither. For a famous example of a company that for so long got that balance wrong, see the box on the Swinging Apple.

### The Swinging Apple: Between Exploration and Exploitation

In the mid-1970s, Steven Jobs together with Steve Wozniak created the proverbial high-technology startup—quite literally in a garage. There they had the audacity to develop their Apple, the first personal computer. But IBM eventually struck back, developing a PC of its own. In the opinion of most aficionados, it was not as good as the Apple had become, but with its power and appeal to big business, IBM soon passed Apple in dollar sales of the PC.

Jobs was too much the explorer. The company had an array of somewhat uncoordinated products, innovative though they were. According to an article in *Fortune*, the company needed "discipline—controlling costs, reducing overhead, rationalizing product lines," more effective exploitation of its innovations, as well as stronger marketing and distribution (Morrison 1984:87). So in 1983, Jobs brought in, as president, a marketer from Pepsi Cola named John

Sculley (Wharton MBA, 1963), whose "innovations" there included "the introduction of large-size plastic bottles" and "the development of the Pepsi Challenge campaign" (Dreyfuss 1984:183).

At first there was cooperation between the "celebrated visionary" and the "driven corporate professional" (Uttal 1985:20). But soon they clashed, with Jobs "frightened that the blue-suited marketer with an MBA wouldn't understand [the] technological possibilities" of his new product (23). He should perhaps have been forewarned when, shortly after they first met, Sculley told him, "Just as Northern California was the 'technology center' for innovation in computers . . . the Northeast corridor was the 'management center' for innovation in business" (Sculley 1987:135). When Jobs tried to oust Sculley, Sculley in turn secured the support of the board and had Jobs ousted.

Immediately following, "Apple reorganized in a rush, fired 20% of its work force, [and] announced that it would record its first-ever quarterly loss." One insider said, "They've cut the heart out of Apple and substituted an artificial one. We'll just have to see how long it pumps" (Uttal 1985:20). The answer was eight years.

Things went fine as Sculley tightened up and exploited key developments that Jobs had left behind. *Fortune* reported that "in the year since Sculley went to Apple," (Dreyfuss 1984:180) it had "made a recovery dramatic even by the roller-coaster standards of Silicon Valley" (180). How had Sculley "managed to put his stamp on Apple in such a short time?" (183) *Fortune* asked. "I'm very comfortable absorbing a lot of complex information," (183) claimed Sculley, who elsewhere "declared that he would not read a memo more than a page long" (182). Soon he named himself Chief Technology Officer.

By the late 1980s, however, the press was noticing weaknesses on the company's technical side. The publisher of an industry newsletter claimed that Apple was selling "yesterday's products with flash and smoke and tomorrow's promises," while one article in the *Los Angeles Times* (Lazzareschi 1989) referred to Sculley's approach as "line extension," and another described this once "brash aggressive entrepreneurial success" as "a victim of swollen bureaucracy and sluggish technology" (Lazzareschi 1990). This article quoted the publisher of a PC newsletter that "[t]here is no basic leadership in product design."

In 1990, Apple reported its first loss since the problems of the mid-1980s. Sculley resigned the post of CEO but remained chairman. Perhaps he had explained the problem best, if inadvertently, back in 1984: "I think a company changes its culture not by any big decision, but by slowly making little compromises along the way" (Morrison 1984:100).

In 1991, *Business Week* (Buell 1991) described the company as "a disaster in the making," with stagnant sales and disgruntled customers plus "a revolving-door management [that] seemed oblivious to its problems." Sculley's newly appointed president stated, "[The low-end] strategy works if we can manage expenses as gross margins move down."

It didn't, and by 1993 Sculley was gone. After the failure of his second successor, Steve Jobs was back, "charming and hypnotic" as always, together with his "duplicity and arrogance," to quote from two very different newspaper articles (Deutschman 2000; Carlton 1998). The new iMac appeared soon after he did. It was a big hit, and Apple quickly became profitable again and highly innovative. Back to exploration!

The problem today, increasingly, is that we have two *cultures*—specifically, two very different approaches to the process of managing. This is the important message from Scherer and Locke, and it has also been articulated in an article by Fallows (1985), who wrote about "a war between two quite different cultures of achievement": one the *entrepreneurial*, "informal, outside-normal-channels, no-guarantee" and the other *professional*, representing "security, dignity, and order" (50). Fallows noted how status goes to the latter:

> At just the time when American business is said to need the flexibility and the lack of hierarchy that an entrepreneurial climate can create, more and more businessmen seem to feel that their chances for personal success will be greatest if they become not entrepreneurs but professionals, with advanced educational degrees. (50)

## FAST-MOVING MBAS FOR SLOW-MOVING TECHNOLOGIES

For those MBAs who do go into industry, which do they prefer? We would expect them to be most comfortable in those industries that rely on hard data, which suggest industries established enough to generate such data. We would also expect industries that favor knowledge of management technique over knowledge of company context, which tends to be true where the abstractions of marketing, finance, and planning take precedence over the specifics of sales, production, and R&D.

This points to mass production and mass service industries that exploit established technologies more than they explore new ones. The most evident example of this came out in the 2001 *Fortune* survey cited in Chapter 4 of the preferred jobs of MBAs: After consulting and investment banking came consumer goods. MBAs seem to be especially drawn to what marketing people call FMCGs, *fast-moving consumer goods*—everything from paper clips to potato chips. Thus, a student at Northwestern spoke "fondly" to a *Fortune* magazine interviewer (Branch 1997:78) about "his 'perfect' summer marketing gig with Pepsi Cola, where he helped drum up fruity drinks. And [for his graduating job] he's leaning towards Clorox, which has offered him a chance to work on its cat litter team." In such industries, even if MBA managers are not especially informed about the products or their manufacture, they can carry their marketing techniques from one to the other—as, for example, has James Kilts (Chicago MBA, 1974) from Oscar Mayer, to Kraft, Nabisco, and then Gillette—"a master at exerting financial controls while reinvigorating brands" (Griffith 2003).

FMCGs seem to change all the time. But much of that change is cosmetic: "New and Improved!" The goods may move fast, but the technologies tend to move slow, because they tend to be low-tech or at least well established. As a consequence, exploiting takes precedence over exploring: to keep the rather standardized products—the so-called brand—moving down established channels. As Ross Johnson put it as CEO of Nabisco, "Some genius in the past invented the Oreo Cookie and we're just living off the inheritance." In these industries, marketing is king, supported by finance, and the favored managerial style seems to resemble the fast-food cook more than the gourmet chef.

Fast-moving consumer goods tend to attract fast-moving managers. Fruity drinks today, cat litter tomorrow. Have technique, will travel: there is always a new and improved job somewhere else. As the British magazine *Management Today* (2000) puts it, "MBAs [themselves] are a branded, big-ticket, fast-moving consumer good."

But if the technologies move slowly to begin with, such managers may slow them down further, by focusing on marketing adaptations more than technological advances—Oreo Cookie Ice Cream. (Did Sculley see Apple's products as FMCGs?) Are there then limits to the exploitation model of managing, even in fast-moving consumer goods?

Clearly, MBA managers have had many of their greatest successes in these industries. Reuben Mark (Harvard MBA, 1963) of Colgate-Palmolive is one notable example (mentioned in an earlier footnote), but he has been chief executive for two decades. MBA managers have also had their share of failures, some directly attributable to this style of managing.

An overemphasis on any one function can send any company out of balance. Steve Jobs did it with development, and then John Sculley did it with marketing. Other chief executives have done it with finance. Marketing and finance are hands-*off* functions. An obsession with finance has been described as playing tennis by watching the scoreboard instead of the ball. An obsession with marketing might thus be described as watching the crowd instead of the ball. But being too hands-on can be no better: an obsession with development, for example, can be described as watching the design of the ball more than its trajectory. Business needs all of these functions, but focused on hitting the ball.

## MBAs as Entrepreneurs?

In this climate of educating people to manage "professionally," where will the new enterprises come from? Entrepreneurs, obviously. So once again, as in ethics and soft skills, the business schools have responded by introducing courses. They teach entrepreneurship, with the appropriate cases, exercises, and guest speakers. In this section, we look first at these activities in the schools, one in particular, and then at the record of MBAs as entrepreneurs.

THE SCHOOL OF SOFT KNOCKS    Starting up new businesses has not been the central focus of MBA training—running large established ones, or at least servicing them as consultants and investment bankers, has been. A good example can be found in Porter's (1980) popular book *Competitive Strategy*, which includes a discussion of how to consolidate fragmented industries, but no corresponding discussion of how to fragment consolidated industries—which is often where entrepreneurs thrive. But it has become fashionable in recent years for business schools to claim that they are training entrepreneurs, too.

Starting in 2000, Harvard required its entire first-year class to take a course called "The Entrepreneurial Manager," taught by its "Entrepreneurship Department" (with twenty-five members). According to an article in the *New York Times* (Leonhardt 2000a), it also offered eighteen elective courses on the subject in the second year, which accounted for a quarter of all elective enrollments.

If entrepreneurs have long prided themselves on attending the "school of hard knocks"—namely, learning from hard experience on their way to creating new enterprises—then MBA entrepreneurship courses might be seen as the school of soft knocks, not necessarily to circumvent the hard knocks of experience so much as to soften them. Harvard's Web site (2003) describes its Entrepreneurship curriculum as enabling "students to test their business ideas in a risk-free environment." But is it entrepreneurship if it is risk-free?

A closer look at this reveals a curious interpretation of entrepreneurship. Said the dean, "We think of entrepreneurship not as a personality type or as a stage in the life cycle of a business but as a way of managing." The faculty echoed his sentiments, according to the *New York Times* journalist: "Almost like a mantra, the professors repeat word-for-word a definition of entrepreneurship that they say applies to General Electric as well as it does to a dot-com operated out of a garage: the pursuit of opportunities beyond means that are currently available" (Leonhardt 2000a:8).

At that level of generality, who can argue with such a statement? It is its implication in practice that can be disputed, of how these opportunities are pursued, and by whom, in creating startups compared with running big businesses. To treat the two together is to repeat the major mistake business schools have been making all along: seeing management as something general, generic, removed from context. On the personal shoulders of the entrepreneur falls the enormous burden of getting a company going. To equate that with the managing of a large established business—being there, compared with getting there—is to belittle the task of entrepreneurship. And it perpetuates that cult of heroic leadership, that the chief executive is personally responsible for everything. The CEO who is parachuted into an established business arrives having been responsible for nothing!

THE ENTREPRENEURIAL RECORD    True entrepreneurs often have an artistic bent—they are visionaries with frequent insights. As such, as we shall see, many ignore MBA programs. These are individualists intent on breaking away from the crowd, while MBAs more commonly want to be in the middle of it.

So how do MBAs do as entrepreneurs? Crainer and Dearlove (1999) write in their book on the MBA, "If business schools were supposed to turn out entrepreneurs who would go forth and multiply—creating jobs and adding to GDP—then they have not succeeded. When it comes to successful business start-ups, with a few notable exceptions . . . business school graduates are conspicuous by their absence" (27). These authors cite a survey of Britain's top one hundred entrepreneurs, chosen on the basis of job creation and sales growth over five years as well as personal wealth. Only three among them had MBAs, two from the same company.

In the United States, Harvard claims that "about one-third of graduates who have been out . . . for at least 15 years own their own businesses" (Leonhardt 2000a:8). But there are all kinds of ways of owning your own business, from incorporating as a management consultant to building a major corporation. Some earlier data from Harvard suggest a significant amount of the former (Stevenson 1983). While the proportion of "self-employed" went up over time (from 11 percent for those who graduated in 1977 to 36 percent for those from 1942), most of this involved very small ventures: almost three-quarters had under fifty employees. In fact, almost half of it involved the industries of consulting (highest, with 16.7 percent of the self-employed alumni reports), real estate (12.2 percent), retailing (5.7 percent), investment banking (5.1 percent), and diversified financial services (4.8 percent). Stevenson in fact describes the first three industries as "at least as hospitable to self-employment as working for others" (3).

There was no listing for high technology, but many of the remaining categories seem likewise low-technology (e.g., agribusiness, wholesale trade, consumer products; the latter, incidentally, came in at only 2.5 percent, suggesting that MBAs rarely start up the companies they often run).

A later study by Bhidé (1996) of Harvard Business School (HBS) alumni up to 1992 reinforces these findings. Of those ten years out, 18 percent reported themselves to be "founders or major equity holders," while for those twenty-five years out, the figure was 31 percent. Bhidé describes this as a "gradual migration" toward "entrepreneurship," but again the industries line up much like those of Stevenson. Bhidé himself comments that the "HBS self-employed" are "attracted to fragmented industries with low capital requirements . . . 25% to 30% have gone into consulting or other advisory services that require little investment in fixed assets" (71).

Bhidé also reports on one hundred founders of the fastest-growing American companies identified by *Inc.* magazine. While 81 percent had college degrees, only 10 percent were MBAs (1; see also Bhidé 2000:94). A more recent study in *Inc.* of its full five hundred company list put the proportion of MBA founders at 15 percent (Greco 2001; a 2001 *Fortune* report on the forty richest Americans under forty had only one with an MBA—and he was a vice president, not a founder [Dash

2001]). So while there are certainly prominent MBA entrepreneurs, they are far less prevalent than might be expected, given the number of MBAs in total and the proportion (40 percent) of them heading up Fortune 100 companies.

More interesting still is a report that entrepreneurs with bachelors degrees in business outnumbered those with MBAs by more than three to one (Updike 1999). Of course, there are more people graduating in the United States with a bachelors in business than a masters—U.S. Department of Education figures for 2000–2001 put the ratio at 2.3:1. But shouldn't we expect the higher degree to produce many more entrepreneurs proportionally? Unless the potential entrepreneurs are reluctant to do the advanced degree, or those who do get discouraged from becoming entrepreneurs.

## MBA Entrepreneurs in Technology

We did our own survey to assess the presence of MBAs as founders of prominent American high-technology companies. NASDAQ categorizes its companies under various labels, including "Technology" (the New York Stock Exchange does not), so we used that. As of February 14, 2003, we took all of those headquartered in the United States with a market capitalization of over a billion dollars, founded since 1975 (by which time MBAs had become numerous in the United States). This gave us a sample of the rather successful American high-technology companies—presumably those contributing most significantly to U.S. economic development. For example, the list includes Microsoft (founded in 1975), Cisco, and Dell (both founded in 1984).

We ended up with ninety-three companies in all (we could not get founder information on four, all near the smallest end). MBAs founded fifteen of them (alone, in groups, or among others). This comes to 16 percent, interestingly almost the same proportion as in the overall *Inc.* 2001 list. (Ph.D. founders were slightly more numerous, at sixteen out of the ninety-three.) Half of these companies (eight) were at the small end, with market capitalization under $2 billion. Of all twelve companies with market capitalization above $10 billion, MBAs started two. So MBAs do not figure particularly prominently among the founders of high-technology companies.

Entrepreneurship as Dedication    Entrepreneurs tend to be highly dedicated to their companies and their industries, often to "their" people as well, in many cases obsessively so. It takes that kind of dedication—emotional, involved, intense—to see something through to its solid establishment.

Yet we have seen that many MBAs tend to be fickle in precisely these respects: not dedicated to particular companies or industries or even to the notion of startup. A report in *Fortune* after the bursting of the dot-com bubble found that MBA graduates were "no longer willing to take a gamble at a startup—only 7% said they would compared with 18% last year" (Koudsi 2001:408). Two years later, the *Financial Times* (Bradshaw 2003c) reported that "the hiring freeze imposed by banks and management consultancies means entrepreneurial ventures are once again proving attractive to MBA graduates." Next in the long list of MBA fashions!

For the serious entrepreneur, however, starting a company is not a fashion or a gamble but an imperative. It is not a question of calculation but of commitment: these people are engaged personally as well as professionally. An entrepreneurial friend of mine in India put it this way about one of his marketing people from a business school: "He doesn't have the fire in his belly!"

Perhaps people with fires in their bellies don't have the patience to sit still in a business school through two years of analysis. Said a highly successful American entrepreneur, "I went to night school to get an MBA. I should have utilized that time to set up more businesses. True entrepreneurs get out of school as fast as they can and get on with life" (quoted in Crainer and Dearlove 1999:40).

It might be said, then, that the entrepreneur practices a traditional style of managing: as the boss who knows the business deeply and gets involved in everything. Perhaps we keep getting these new economies thanks to that old style of managing.

Sure, entrepreneurs exploit, but not before they have explored, because they have to build companies to get there in order to be there. And sure, they have to calculate on the way, but often in their heads, informally, or on the back of that proverbial envelope; *scheme* might be a better word for what they do. Many are, in fact, attracted to industries too new or fragmented to generate the numbers required for fancy calculations. So they need the courage to act without the data, and MBA education hardly encourages that. How do you do industry analysis without industry data? Who can calculate the potential return on investment for a product that has never been to market?

Entrepreneurship is, therefore, largely an act of faith, requiring the imagination of the artist more than the calculation of the technocrat. So entrepreneurs go largely by inner belief, and that is their great strength as well as their debilitating weakness: They go where the calculating managers fear to tread, toward great successes sometimes followed by glorious failures. And that is where the MBAs come in.

## MBAs in Fast-Moving Technologies

It is, of course, failures like that of Steve Jobs the first time around that drive entrepreneurs out of their own businesses. Artists can be too dedicated, too exploring, not careful enough with the calculations, the exploitation. Then they may have to be replaced.

But by whom? The answer seems obvious, as in Sculley's replacement of Jobs: with people who can correct these faults, ones who are well organized, comfortable with numbers, not overly dedicated or emotional or intuitive—in other words, specialists in exploitation. But as we also saw in the Apple story, the obvious answer may be the wrong answer.

Our NASDAQ data indicate that MBA managers figure prominently among these replacements in the technology companies. We looked at the educational backgrounds of those running these ninety-three companies on February 14, 2003: Twenty-four had MBAs (26 percent). They may not have been as prominent as among the chief executives of Fortune 100 companies in general (40 percent), but they were certainly more prominent than among the founders of these high-technology companies in particular (16 percent). The question is, Do such people succeed by balancing the company's needs or fail by swinging the pendulum too far the other way?

Balance is obviously easier to maintain in established industries, such as those selling FMCGs. They don't need all that much exploration—some, but not much. But industries are called high-technology because their complex knowledge bases do not settle down but keep changing. And so they require a great deal of exploration. (Think of a Hewlett-Packard over the decades.) How, then, do the chief executives with MBAs who know all about management in general but often little about the technologies in question, do?

The evidence we have seen so far—the systematic studies of Scherer and Locke as well as the stories of companies such as Apple and Xerox—suggests that they do not do particularly well at all. But there are other stories, too—for example, of Gerstner (Harvard MBA, 1965) who took over IBM with no technical or industry background, and of Chambers at CISCO (Indiana MBA, 1976), who was doing well, although the situation is less clear at the time of this writing. As for Fiorina at Hewlett-Packard (Maryland MBA, 1980), it is too early to tell, if not to speculate.

It is tricky to assess managerial performance in any established company, in high or low technology. Under startup, success or failure may be more clear-cut: The company makes it or goes bankrupt. But once a company is established, it has momentum in its procedures and in the marketplace. So, how to tell whether the new chief executive is making things better or just exploiting the legacy of the founder (which is often readily exploitable, when there has been sloppy management)? Even in the fast-moving computer industry, it took almost a decade for Sculley's influence on Apple to become evident. But at least he stayed around for the consequences. In today's world of easy come, easy go, the chief executives are often gone with their bonuses before anyone can tell.

My conclusion is that we have reason to be skeptical if not dismissive about the growing phenomenon of MBAs taking over the leadership of established high-technology companies. Going from potato chips to fruity drinks is one thing, into silicone chips quite another, and on to nuclear reactors or hospitals something else again. *Fortune* magazine introduced an article entitled "CEOs Who Manage Too Much": "At their old Fortune 500 companies, they knew how to run the show. But when they take the reins at Internet startups, big-company migrants find the old rules no longer apply" (Gimein 2000:235).

The all-too-current "old" rules are heavy on calculation and light on commitment. Management technique is more important than industry technology. These rules are heavy on people, too; as that *Fortune* article notes, the "command and control" mentality just doesn't work in a world of "distributed decision making" (Gimein 2000:240). If the leader is not truly engaged in the technology, can he or she sustain the engagement of the experts?

A chief executive dedicated to an industry can easily make use of people who know management technique. The question is whether a chief executive who knows management technique can be equally successful in surrounding him- or herself with people who know the technology. (Recall Rumelt's quip about being able to teach motorcycle experts about strategy but not being able to teach strategy experts about motorcycles.) Put differently, the explorers can easily find exploiters, but the exploiters cannot simply hire explorers.

It seems that people who lead high-technology companies mostly have to feel the technology—to live it. Engagement cannot be feigned, not by a Sculley naming himself "CTO" or by a Fiorina recasting the famous old "HP Way" as "Rules of the Garage." Inventions do not come from imperatives to "Invent" (the last of these rules), least of all when coined by those most distant from the garage. They are stimulated by leaders who feel, not who deem.

So what could Apple have done to stop swinging in the 1980s—and so many other companies since? Perhaps it could have found a leader dedicated to the company and the industry if not quite so much to its particular strategy. A Steve Jobs with the edge off. With some balance on.

## NEW BUREAUCRATS FOR A NEW AGE?

It is fashionable to view the MBA as modern, progressive, change-oriented. And it is certainly true that most MBA programs make great efforts to keep current.

In sharp contrast is the image of bureaucracy. It stands for old, staid, change-resistant. MBAs are supposed to be the antithesis of this; indeed, the schools send them out to "bash bureaucracy."

I believe the reality is exactly the opposite: MBAs who take what they learned about management seriously end up being the bureaucrats.

I am not using the word for shock effect. *Bureaucracy* has a pejorative meaning and a technical one; I mean both here, quite literally. In the pejorative sense, time and again I have witnessed MBA managers acting like Dilbert's boss. Not all, but far too many. In the technical sense, classic bureaucracy has two main characteristics: formalization and centralization (see Mintzberg 1979, 1983). MBA programs promote both, and so therefore do many of their graduates.

Control of human behavior through the formalization of activities is the central guiding principle of classic bureaucracy. It is accomplished through plans, systems, and performance measures—all emphasized in MBA education and therefore favored by many MBA managers. To control in bureaucracy typically means to have it down on paper. A market is controlled if a high number appears next to "market share" on a report; quality is controlled if a low one appears next to "defects"; people are controlled if everyone is connected to a boss on a chart; the whole system is controlled if every action is anticipated in a document called a "plan," from the "strategic plan" on "top" to the most detailed budgets on the bottom.

There is nothing wrong with control, or formalization, or even bureaucracy per se. It is difficult to imagine any organization without some degree of them. Who, for instance, would fly an airline that did not rely on standardized procedures as well as clear divisions of responsibility? The problems arise—and the word *bureaucracy* takes on its pejorative meaning—when an organization tilts too far in this direction. It becomes impersonal and inflexible, its managers distant and disconnected. In my opinion, MBA education tilts too far in this direction. So do companies run by its graduates who fail to get past their education in their practice, who cannot offset their analytical training with the practices of art and craft.

As for centralization, I know of no MBA program that overtly promotes it, that is neither modern nor progressive. But are there any that do not covertly encourage it—by leaving the impression that managers are important people removed from the context of their managing, people who sit in offices to make carefully calculated decisions and pronounce immaculately conceived strategies for everyone else to implement? (Recall my counter in Chapter 2 to Ewing's metaphor of being on top of the pyramid: from there everything around looks awfully small, except the pyramid itself, the inside of which cannot be seen at all.)

John Ralston Saul (1992) was quoted earlier with regard to Robert McNamara that "[a] truism of all technocrats is that . . . they are wedded to centralization" (87). For good reason. Managers who focus on the numbers instead of the nuances, systems instead of subtleties, especially when parachuted into contexts they do not understand, feel insecure and so grab onto whatever controls are available. The consequence is overcentralization in some areas, through the making of decisions that should have been delegated, and overformalization in others, by expecting systems to control what direct decision making cannot. Such managers are too controlling and too disconnected at the same time, much like parents who cannot get the discipline right and so appear confusingly inconsistent.

Putting this discussion together, I believe that the numbers of MBAs in senior positions coupled with the cult of heroic leadership has made many of our large corporations more hierarchical, more centralized, and more formalized than they should be. All the efforts that developed from the 1960s through the 1980s to involve people more deeply in their work have given way to a callous and arbitrary reign of bureaucratic management. And this in a time, especially in high-technology industries, when we need to favor teamwork, collaboration, and networks.

WEBS IN CHAINS[2]    Consider the popularity of the concept *chain* in management education and practice. Of course, it is not the *vertical* chain that is fashionable, that "chain of command" running down a hierarchy, but the *horizontal* chain, of operations, popularized as the "value chain" in Michael Porter's 1985 book, *Competitive Advantage*.

---

[2]The following discussion draws on an article by myself and Ludo van der Heyden (1999).

It should be realized, however, that this ostensibly new horizontal chain in fact reinforces that old vertical chain.

The idea of depicting business operations as a horizontal chain comes from the most classic sphere of mass manufacturing, the automobile assembly *line*. Here all tasks sequence themselves in linear order, from the components coming in to the automobiles driven out. Since Porter generalized about the value chain of sequenced functions—from inbound logistics to operations, then outbound logistics, then marketing and sales, finally to services—all sorts of other operations have likewise been seen as chains.

Go into an airport or a hospital, a research laboratory or a project team, and look for such chains. Sure, you will find subprocesses that take this linear form. But the overall activity hardly looks like that. We call airports *hubs*, shown in Figure 5.1b, for a good reason: they are organized less as sequences of activities than as focal points, to and from which people, things, and information flow. So, too, can hospitals be seen as hubs, not only overall, to which people come, but also at each patient inside, to whom the services flow.

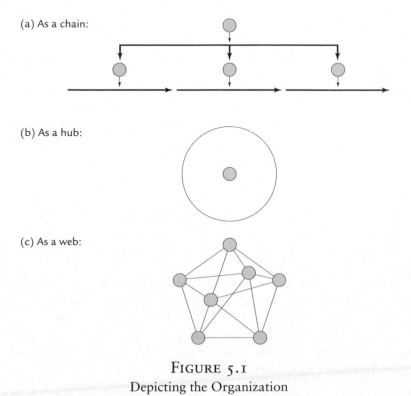

(a) As a chain:

(b) As a hub:

(c) As a web:

FIGURE 5.1
Depicting the Organization

Research laboratories and project teams, however, do not look like hubs, any more than chains, because they tend to have no obvious centers, any more than dominant linear sequences. They are better seen as webs, as shown in Figure 5.1c—loosely interacting networks of collaborative relationships that flow every which way. Depicting them as chains, even hubs, violates their complexity.

Now, where to put management in these different perceptions of organizations? In the chain, that's easy: on top, removed. As shown in Figure 5.1a, over each link is a manager, and over each manager is another manager. A manager for each and a manager for all! In other words, naturally laid over the horizontal chain of operations is the vertical chain of command. No wonder Porter's chains are so popular in MBA programs: The manager is on top. Of course, this is how management has been *seen* for a century, on top. But that has been a century significantly dedicated to mass production. (Joseph Lampel [in Lampel and Mintzberg 1996] tabulated all the industries used as examples in Porter's [1980] book *Competitive Strategy*. He found that 176 of the 196 were dominated by the "logic of aggregation," meaning mass production or the mass provision of services.)

In a world of increasing prominence of hubs and webs, however, we shall have to see management differently. Look at the figures and you will see why. Putting a manager on top of the hub or the web is silly: it just removes him or her from what is going on. So where to put the manager?

In the hub, that's easy: the manager is at the center. In Figure 5.1, that is a trivial change, rendered easily with a pencil. But in the world of organizations, that change is profound: It puts management in a different place. Seeing oneself at the center, instead of on top, changes the whole perception of one's managerial world. As Sally Helgesen (1990) put it in her book, *The Female Advantage: Women's Ways of Leadership*, women managers "usually referred to themselves as being in the middle of things. Not on top, but in the center; not reaching down, but reaching out" (45–46). So, for example, to get to strategy in a hub, managers have to reach out, to others; they cannot just deem them down, from on high.

Now, where to put management with regard to the web? Stop and take a good look at Figure 5.1c, and ask yourself that question.

When I ask it of people, they hesitate. On top? Obviously not on top—any manager on top of a web would be "out of it." At the center? There is no center in a web; creating one would "centralize" it and so undermine its free flow of information.

Then the answer becomes obvious: In the web, management has to be *everywhere*. It has to flow with the activity, which itself cannot be predicted or *formalized*. But there is an additional answer, less obvious but perhaps more profound: Management also has to be potentially *everyone*. In a network, authority for making decisions and developing strategic initiatives has to be distributed, so that responsibility can flow to whoever is best able to deal with the issue at hand. If this sounds overstated, then think about the "management" of the World Wide Web.

Put differently, in the web control has to give way to collaboration. "Bosses" and "subordinates" running up and down a hierarchy have to give way to the shifting back and forth between "colleagues" on the inside and "partners" on the outside. Sure, webs need formally designated managers. But to connect and contribute more than to command and control. And that means the managers have to get inside those networks. Not be parachuted in, without knowledge, yet intent on leading the team. No, they must be deeply involved, to *earn* any leadership they can provide.

"The dot.com's are structureless," claimed Paul Bracken, a professor of business. Not true, but indicative of the problem. Webs are not so much structureless as structured according to a different logic. (Take a good look at Figure 5.1c.) They seem structureless only to people with a conventional view of structure. (A caught fish might likewise describe its situation as "waterless.") To exercise effective management in a web, therefore, is to appreciate its own special structure. Of course, business schools can teach about this. But will it be appreciated by students who want to be on top?

The implications of this are profound. For here we find the main reason why MBA education, as well as the associated calculating and heroic styles of managing, are so antithetical to the important industries dependent on knowledge workers, teamwork, networks, and the like. What sense does it make to parachute onto webs bosses trained in management but ignorant of its context, all ready to make decisions and formulate strategies? That is as silly as it is common, saddest of all in high-technology organizations. *Here* is where bureaucracy needs to be bashed! And that means bashing conventional management education, which continues to go one way while much of the economy goes another. If the business schools really do believe in change, then they should be changing who and how they educate for management.

# 6

# WRONG CONSEQUENCES IV
## *Corruption of Social Institutions*

*Perfection of means and confusion of goals seem in my
opinion to characterize our age.*

—ALBERT EINSTEIN

I have been developing a central point in a series of steps: This seemingly innocent degree, to prepare people for the practice of management, actually does no such thing and in fact has a corrupting effect
where it does have influence. This begins in the educational process and
passes into the practice of managing and the organizations where that
happens. Now I shall discuss where it ends and where these effects may
be the most destructive: in society at large.

Here the discussion shifts from the economic consequences to the
social ones, which I believe significantly influence the economic. Certainly economic development facilitates social progress. But it also depends on social progress: Those societies most able to engage their
citizens have tended to generate the greatest economic wealth. How a
society selects and develops its leaders, and how these leaders exercise
their leadership, figure prominently in the engagement of all its citizens.
How we have been doing this in recent years has worked to disengage
our citizens. The social costs are obvious, but we may also be experiencing a decline in economic development without even realizing it.

## THE ILLEGITIMACY OF
## CONTEMPORARY LEADERSHIP

Do we stop to consider seriously the kind of leadership we need in our most important social institutions, including businesses? Do we give enough attention to the role of judgment, commitment, humility, generosity—and legitimacy? Do we consider what effect the prevalent form of educating managers, and consequently selecting them, has on all of this?

Leadership is not about making clever decisions and doing bigger deals, least of all for personal gain. It is about energizing other people to make good decisions and do better things. In other words, it is about helping release the positive energy that exists naturally within people. Effective leadership inspires more than empowers; it connects more than controls; it demonstrates more than decides. It does all this by *engaging*—itself above all, and consequently others.

To do so, leadership has to be legitimate, meaning that it has to be not only accepted but also respected by those subjected to it. Above the will to manage must be the right to manage. Abraham Lincoln said, "No man is good enough to govern another man without that man's consent." He was speaking about government, of course, but increasingly today people govern each other in organizations. If democracy is to have real meaning, it must extend to the organizations where most of us function every day. I maintain that the leadership promoted by our business schools violates this spirit by encouraging a separate, privileged elite—that culture of professionalism discussed earlier—usually imposed on people without their consent.

I am not making a case here for the election of managers (although it would be interesting to see how many of today's managers would win such elections).[1] Rather, I am arguing the case for reference to the led in the selection of their leaders—for example, through representation in the selection process—to ensure that the people chosen have earned their respect. That kind of input could bring a critically important perspective to the selection process, often by people who have worked alongside the candidates. Given the dismal record of so much manager

---

[1]For my earlier views on this, see in Mintzberg (1983) the section entitled "Who Should Control the Corporation?" especially chapter 27. I should add that no less a power in the corporate world than the McKinsey & Company consulting firm elects its managing director for a three-year term through a closed vote of its senior partners (called "directors").

selection, often by outsiders with only superficial understanding of the unit in question, and even of the candidates themselves, such input from insiders could result in quantum improvements in the quality of management.

A survey before the collapse of Enron and other corporations reported that only 47 percent of the employees of American companies saw their leaders as people of high personal integrity (*The Gazette*, October 9, 2000). A more recent study by Rutgers University of Connecticut found that "58 percent of workers think that most top executives are only looking out for themselves, even if it harms the company, while 33 percent think top executives are interested in doing a good job for their company" (in Greenhouse 2002). Can we really continue to tolerate this situation?

A New Aristocracy?    Is "Business Class" just a place in an airplane? Or has it become a class in and of itself in society, what *Time* magazine has described "a professional managerial caste that considers itself trained—and therefore destined—to take command of this nation's corporate life" (May 4, 1981:58)?

Near the close of his book on the history of the Wharton School, Sass (1982) makes the following comment:

> The success of the Wharton M.B.A. stood, perhaps, as the culmination, perhaps, of the school's century-old effort to raise a leadership class for industrial society. More thoroughly and harmoniously than in its past, the program amalgamated the three classic Western leadership types—the professional, the aristocrat, and the businessman—into a new social persona. (336)

How ironic that an America so proud of having thrown off the yoke of British aristocracy should find itself with an emerging aristocracy of its own two centuries later. Britain declined partly because of workers who rebelled against class privileges and the disconnected leadership of a landed aristocracy. Is the United States now following suit in its own way? (See Kelly 2001.)

In *The Case against Credentialism*, Fallows (1985) writes, "Through the years certain cultures have rewarded behavior that eventually proved ruinous to the society as a whole—the British upper class's desire to be free of the taint of commerce is the most famous example." He asks whether "a similar perverse process [is] at work here" in America, even if the cause may be not freedom from the taint of commerce but personal exploitation of it (52).

Can any society afford to have two tiers, one based on academic credentials, the other on connected experience? Should not the route to leadership be varied, and indeed idiosyncratic, by assessing the candidate for his or her own qualities, beyond credentials and affiliations, let alone a superficial ability to impress outsiders? I reproduce in the accompanying box a letter sent to me by a woman manager in response to something I had written. I have left most of it intact because it so articulately describes this serious problem.

## They All Wish to "Manage" Me

### A Letter from the Led

Dear Professor Mintzberg:

I was intrigued by your comments in the November/December 1992 issue of the *Harvard Business Review* regarding traditional MBA programs. . . .

A two-tiered system based on educational attainment definitely exists. . . . [However, in such a system, where] educational attainment is more valued than experience and is rewarded accordingly with higher wages and responsibility, the rational response of the recent college graduate is to pursue the advanced degree, foregoing the needed experience.

Many companies, even those who claim to value experience, still perpetuate the problem . . . [making] it impossible for a non-MBA or second-tier employee ever to earn management responsibility by performance alone, even when company policy dictated promotion from within. . . .

Unfortunately, I know from where I speak. I took the "get experience" approach (I'm a sales manager) to earning my management stripes, namely because I could not afford to return to graduate school. Last year I accepted a position in a . . . company that would allow me to develop an autonomous business unit. . . . My experience dovetails perfectly with the requirements of the job—having had seven years sales experience in [the industry], two years directly related previous experience in [the specific area]. My mandate was to grow a new initiative working with [certain customer] companies to produce custom products.

In the past year, I have more than doubled sales, written and implemented a marketing plan, built an entire database from scratch, initiated a direct mail program, begun a public relations program, and functioned in every position, from creative director to acquisitions editor to copyeditor to sales manager to file clerk. As might be expected, I received an "exceptional" rating at my 12-month review. However, this is just the sort of two-tier company you so accurately described in the *Harvard Business Review*.

No one has told me that I'm not going to advance any further with my current employer, promoting non-MBAs to positions leading to general management has simply never been done in this company. The most important rules in any company never appear in the employee handbook.

No further management responsibilities for me—the title, recognition and salary I have earned by my performance—are being contemplated by my employers, as we also employ a cadre of MBAs from the top schools (Stanford, Harvard, etc.) and even an Oxford University graduate.

This is not to say that my successes have gone unrecognized. My business school-educated fellow employees have recently informed me that I am a valuable member of the team and have in essence suggested that when they are done carving up the pie that constitutes the territory of my politically beleaguered immediate supervisor, "we will let you know exactly where your business unit fits in." Nine months ago, none of them would even invite me to lunch, now I have no lack of offers from those who wish to "manage" me. Perhaps I should be glad they have not simply upgraded my job to require a graduate degree and reorganized me out.

With respect to the experience factor, please note that . . . among our merry bank of MBAs, there is no one with any kind of [specific experience in this industry] (though one of them sold three-ring binders to junior colleges for a year before entering graduate school). . . .

It was not my intention in the latter half of this letter to whine about being victimized. I do not consider myself victimized and I also have something that an inexperienced fresh MBA graduate does not—a genuine and absolute faith in my ability to do productive work even when the odds are against me, because I have already accomplished that in the real world. I have learned another valuable lesson from this experience, a healthy cynicism—a significant factor in increasing my value to the market, not to mention personal maturity.

However, I am only one person and a realist at that—I cannot buck the system any longer. If the system rewards educational attainment, whatever the state of traditional MBA training, I can no longer afford to continue without a graduate degree. Next fall, my employer will lose a talented, motivated and experienced employee . . . to a full-time graduate program.

I hope you will counsel any undergraduate who asks to get an advanced degree. And if the system suffers as a result, do not blame MBA training, blame instead the employers who do not sufficiently recognize and reward homegrown talent—the fault is theirs.
Sincerely,
[reprinted with permission; name withheld on request]

## A Society Out of Balance

In recent years, we have been experiencing a glorification of self-interest perhaps unequaled since the 1920s. Greed has been raised to some sort of high calling; corporations are urged to ignore broader social responsibilities in favor of narrow shareholder value; chief executives are regarded as if they alone create economic performance. A society devoid of selfishness may be difficult to imagine, but a society that glorifies selfishness can be imagined only as cynical and corrupt.[2]

In effect, our societies have been tilting increasingly out of balance, in favor of the economic and against the social, correspondingly in favor of markets at the expense of other social institutions.[3] We need both but are finding ourselves increasingly dominated by one. MBA education plays a significant role in this.

THE DEGRADATION OF HUMAN VALUES    Perhaps nowhere is this problem more evident than in a widely circulated article by two prominent professors of finance. In it, Michael Jensen then at Harvard and William Meckling at Rochester (1994) introduce five models of "The Nature of Man." They quickly dismiss three that describe human behavior from the perspectives of sociology, psychology, and politics. A

---

[2]This and some sections that follow come from Mintzberg, Simons, and Basu (2002).
[3]I am preparing an electronic pamphlet entitled *Getting Past Smith and Marx: Toward a Balanced Society*, in which I attribute the problem to a mistaken belief that capitalism "triumphed" in the fall of communism. I argue that by failing to recognize that it was balance that triumphed, across government, business, and the social sector, compared with communist countries fully tilted to the power of government, we are now going out of balance the other way.

based in economics, they do not so much reject as fold into the fifth, which they give the rather convoluted name of "Resourceful, Evaluative, Maximizing Model," or REMM.

Under REMM, according to the authors, everyone "is an evaluator." People have all sorts of wants, and they "make tradeoffs and substitutions among them"—specifically among the "amounts" of each. (That the amounts of some wants, such as money and fancy cars, can be evaluated and measured more easily than other wants, such as trust and integrity, the authors do not discuss.) And these "wants are unlimited. . . . REMM cannot be satiated. He or she always wants more," so "each individual is a maximizer."

An important consequence of this is that the REMM has no absolutes. Specifically, "there is no such thing as a need" according to Jensen and Meckling. Everything is a trade-off (except, of course, the need for more). They illustrate with a rather startling example:

> George Bernard Shaw, the famous playwright and social thinker, reportedly once claimed that while on an ocean voyage he met a celebrated actress on deck and asked her whether she would be willing to sleep with him for a million dollars. She was agreeable. He followed with a counterproposal: "What about ten dollars?" "What do you think I am?" she responded indignantly. He replied, "We've already established that—now we're just haggling over price."

Startling is not the story—which is well known—but the fact that instead of qualifying it in any way, Jensen and Meckling follow it with this statement: "Like it or not, individuals are willing to sacrifice a little of almost anything we care to name, even reputation or morality, for a sufficiently large quantity of other desired things." In other words, pushed to the limit, everyone is a willing prostitute. Everyone, everything, every value, has its price. We cherish nothing. "REMMs are everywhere," claim the authors. How true. How sad.

Jensen and Meckling's article has been used in a great many MBA programs—it was required reading in what for years was the most popular elective course at Harvard, attracting a majority of all students. This, then, is the message untold numbers of MBA students carried away from their studies, alongside, of course, whatever corrective materials were supplied in that course in ethics. And the result is what we saw earlier in reports that the values of MBA students harden over the course of their studies, even compared with executives, away from social responsibility and toward "shareholder value"—in other words, toward "more" for the owners, and everyone else be damned.

ANALYTICAL IMMORALITY    The author of one of these reports puts the results down to a lack of experience: "Students like things to be clearcut, not messy and complicated. They want to focus on the bottom line and not let real life get in the way." He expects that this changes as "these students begin to gain experience" (in Keily, p. 13).

Robert McNamara gained a great deal of experience after his MBA, yet we saw that he always wanted things to be clear-cut, not messy and complicated. His experience is particularly instructive, for McNamara considered himself to be a good man, an ethical man, and in many respects he probably was. Yet the consequences of his most important responsibilities were decidedly unethical.

Is there something fundamentally wrong with the kind of education McNamara received? He wrote in his autobiography on "The Tragedy and Lessons of Vietnam" that

> The defining moments in my education . . . came in my philosophy
> and mathematics curricula. The ethics courses forced me to begin
> to shape my values; studying logic exposed me to rigor and preci-
> sion in thinking. And my mathematics professors taught me to see
> math as a process of thought—a language in which to express
> much, but certainly not all, of human activity. (1995:6)

McNamara was referring to his undergraduate education, but the implications for his graduate education and the practice that followed are evident. Can it be that thinking in precise, logical, mathematical terms about "much" of human behavior gets in the way of ethical values, those ethics courses notwithstanding?

David Halberstam's (1972) carefully documented history of the Vietnam conflict makes it clear that McNamara's was no ordinary failure of analysis, not yet another to be explained away in "implementation." Something was fundamentally wrong with the formulation, and with analysis itself. Here "the best and the brightest," to use the title of Halberstam's book—not politicians or public bureaucrats, but America's finest analytical talent, drawn from its centers of liberal intelligentsia—applied the latest techniques of analysis, and the result was a war both ill conceived and fundamentally immoral.

What went wrong? Could it have been the inability of analysis to handle the soft data—the expression on a peasant's face as opposed to a body count, the will of the enemy as opposed to the number of bombs needed to defoliate a jungle? Can immorality creep into analysis when the number of dead bodies or the acres of defoliated jungle are measurable while the worth of a human life is not? What happens to those REMMs who can measure material resources and capital assets but not the characteristics of trust or integrity?

Of course, McNamara and his team were only trying to be objective, like Jensen and Meckling. But it has been said that to be objective is to treat people like objects. It is also to treat people as well as objects without imagination, because imagination is subjective. Was McNamara's "precision in thinking," using "mathematics as a language in which to express much . . . of human activity," the very problem? Is that why he wasn't a visionary?

Facts become impregnated with value when they consistently line up behind one set of goals at the expense of another. In Vietnam, they supported the militaristic goals. The humanitarian ones, lacking hard data, got lost. We see the same in business when an obsession with cost reduction or market share supports narrow, short-term considerations, driving out softer but more lasting ones, such as product quality and investment in research.

Robert Ackerman (1975) studied the control systems intrinsic to the functioning of large, especially diversified corporations—bottom-line systems based on quantifiable, financial goals. He found that they discouraged consideration of social goals simply because these could not easily be measured. Ackerman concluded that

> the financial reporting system may actually inhibit social responsiveness. By focusing on economic performance, even with appropriate safe-guards to protect against sacrificing long-term benefits, such a system directs energy and resources to achieving results measured in financial terms. It is the only game in town, so to speak, at least the only one with an official scoreboard. (56)

Most significantly, Ackerman found this to be the case even when the chief executive sincerely believed in the social goals and wished to promote them. The very control system he or she used precluded attention to those goals. "Listen, boss, do you want me to treat people well or meet the targets?" Ackerman published his book in 1975, before the advent of shareholder value. Think of the situation now!

One response to the problem Ackerman raised is the "balanced scorecard" (Kaplan and Norton 1996). Find measures for all the things you care about. The trouble is that the game remains loaded—the economic things are much easier to measure than the social ones, the short-term payoffs much easier to measure than the benefits of long-term investments.

ECONOMIC IMMORALITY    There is another response to this problem, which has had far more influence because it so justifies self-serving behavior. This is the one long promoted by economists such as Milton Friedman (1962, 1970): that business simply has no business attending to social goals. These are for government. Let each stick to its own sphere of responsibility.

How convenient would be a world as black and white as this bit of economic theory. It does not exist. In the real world of decision making, the economic and the social get all tangled up. Find me an economist who would argue that social decisions have no economic consequences. Every economist knows that all social decisions cost resources. Well, then, how can any economist argue for economic decisions that have no social consequences? They all impact socially. So businesspeople who take this separation seriously create havoc with the social consequences of their actions. They do as they wish for economic gain while conveniently slipping the social consequences off their ledgers, as what economists call "externalities," meaning that the corporations create the costs while society pays the bills.

Put differently, there is always discretion in business decision making, to thwart social needs or to take them into consideration. Business may not exist to serve social needs, but it cannot exist if it ignores them. The Russian novelist Aleksandr Solzhenitsyn (1978) made this point with lucidity when he wrote while living in America:

> I have spent all my life under a communist regime, and I will tell you that a society without any objective legal scale is a terrible one indeed. But a society with no other scale but the legal one is not quite worthy of man either. A society which is based on the letter of the law and never reaches any higher is taking very scarce advantage of the high level of human possibilities. The letter of the law is too cold and formal to have a beneficial effect on society. Whenever the tissue of life is woven of legalistic relations, there is an atmosphere of moral mediocrity, paralyzing man's noblest impulses.

That is the atmosphere we live in today.

LEGAL CORRUPTION    The views of Friedman coupled with those of Jensen and Meckling, now represented by shareholder value, have manifested themselves most evidently in the collapse of companies like Enron. Their managers focused on the economic, played the numbers, maximized personal gain with a vengeance, and we all discovered how thin is that line below the letter of the law.

Enron was loaded with MBAs. "During the nineties, Enron was bringing in two hundred and fifty newly minted MBAs a year," notes Malcolm Gladwell (2002) in a *New Yorker* article entitled "The Talent Myth." Here he takes apart the "star system," which he calls "the new orthodoxy of American management"—hiring supersmart people with bonuses and the like, "fawning over them," giving them rather free rein, and promoting them "without regard for seniority or experience." This led to precisely the problem discussed earlier in the selection of managers. These stars moved so fast that "performance evaluations [weren't] based on performance." People got ahead based on their charm, energy, and self-confidence. As a result, Enron ended up with narcissistic leaders, even though "narcissists are terrible managers" who "resist accepting suggestions" and tend to "'take more credit for success than is legitimate'" (quoting Hogan et al. 1990:29, 30, 31).

"What if smart people are overrated?" Gladwell asks. What if Enron failed not in spite of its talent mindset but because of it? "The talent myth assumes that people make organizations smart. More often than not, it's the other way around." For example, "Wal-Mart is an organization, not an all-star team" (29, 32, 33).

It is important to realize that criminality is not the issue here. Criminality is the tip of the iceberg, easy enough to address in courts of law once exposed. The real problem is the *legal* corruption—the antisocial behavior below the surface of public awareness yet above the letter of the law. That is far more insidious, not only because it is more difficult to identify and correct but also because we are now so inundated with it.

That notion of externality carries these problems into society. When corporations are held accountable for only those antisocial behaviors that can be numerically attributed to them, we all pay for the rest. When laid-off workers become ill and their families collapse, they and society pay the bills. When pollution is released into the atmosphere, we all suffer the consequences. And when pharmaceutical companies charge what the market will bear—the "market" being sick people, often poor with no option but to die—then societies at both ends of the transaction become distorted. When all of this happens, the analysis behind such choices can no longer be called amoral: It drives even well-intentioned decision makers to make decidedly immoral choices.

Singer and Wooton (1976) studied Albert Speer's seemingly enlightened management of the Nazi wartime production machine and conclude, "It's not that managers are authoritarian themselves; rather . . . it may be that the process of management is authoritarian" (100). This is a critically important point, at least about the currently prevailing styles of management. Some years ago, Albert Shapero (1977) compared MANAGEMENT with plain old management, the former representing "an Analysis in Wonderland outlook where abstractions are reality and where people and things are ciphers or difficulties to be dealt with" (107). Maybe it is MANAGEMENT that is authoritarian, and we desperately need more management.

The "professional" manager claims to be the "hired gun," brought in to apply ostensibly neutral techniques to whatever needs managing. Too often, unfortunately, the metaphor applies almost literally. As in Speer's case, technique is not neutral when its use drives organizations to a narrow and greedy form of morality. Calculation is not amoral when many of the things that matter most to us cannot be measured. These drive us to an economic morality, precisely as described by Jensen and Meckling, which at the limit becomes a social immorality. We end up with an imbalanced society in which innocent people get run over by professional managers racing down the fast track toward their bottom lines.

A SOCIETY OF MEANNESS    That "lean and mean" has become so fashionable a term in business should be telling us something.

*Skinny* is a synonym for *lean*. Are we, therefore, creating bulimic economies, so "productive" that they will eventually collapse under the weight of their burned-out managers, angry employees, and used-up technologies? And are we creating a society that is just plain mean? If so, for what purpose? So that some of us can be economically rich while all of us are socially miserable? In a democratic society, we do not exist for our social and economic institutions; they exist for us.

On February 4, 2002, *Fortune* published its list of "The 100 Best Companies to Work For"—those that "tried to do right by their employees," based largely on a survey of those employees (Levering and Moskowitz 2002). The reader had to go down to number 15 before a familiar name appeared (Cisco Systems). Half of the fourteen companies had sales below $650 million (most below $250 million). The largest had $3.8 billion (CDW), which put it in the number 430 spot on the Fortune 500. Not a single one of these companies was listed on the New York Stock Exchange, only three on AMEX. The message is all too clear.

The Business Roundtable, a hitherto socially responsible group of chief executives of America's largest corporations, concluded in a "Statement on Corporate Governance" issued in 1997 that "the paramount duty of management and of boards is to the corporation's stockholders: the interests of other stakeholders are relevant as a derivative of the duty to stockholders" (3). The customer may be "king" and the employees may be the corporation's "greatest assets," but when it comes down to it, nothing matters except "value" to the shareholder (meaning price of the stock).

An earlier report of this group, issued in 1981, and then labeled "Statement on Corporate Responsibility," was rather different: "The shareholder must receive a good return but the legitimate concerns of other constituencies also must have the appropriate attention" (9).[4] That report went on to discuss "balancing the legitimate claims of all [these] constituents." But the 1997 report dismissed "the notion that the board must somehow balance" these interests as "fundamentally mis-constru[ing]" its role. It referred to this as "an unworkable notion because it would leave the board with no criterion for resolving conflicts" among the different interests (3–4). How about judgment?

Somehow between 1981 and 1997 the chief executives of America's largest corporations lost their sense of judgment. And that speaks legions about the shift in "leadership" in American corporations, accompanied by the scandals in executive compensation.[5] Out with the social and in with the economic, the chief executives deemed. Out with responsibility and in with greed, is what they meant. The chief executives who signed that Business Roundtable document were followers, not leaders.

Shareholder value is an antisocial dogma that has no place in a democratic society. Period. It breeds a society of exploitation—of people as well as of institutions. It is bad for business because it undermines its respect and credibility. Look at the Enrons, the Andersons, and all that followed.

Of course, shareholder value is not promoted as selfishness. Rather, it is claimed to be a "rising tide" that lifts all boats. In that convenient twist of dogma, selfishness becomes altruistic.

The facts, conveniently ignored by those so otherwise obsessed with calculation, tell a different story. In 1989, the United States had 66 billionaires and 31.5 million people living below the official poverty line. A decade later, the number of billionaires had increased to 268, while the

---

[4]We have a copy of both statements, which we first published in Simons, Mintzberg, and Basu (2002). The 1981 statement was subsequently removed from the Web site (www.brtable.org), and a telephone request for a copy was met with a reply of "not available."

[5]Over the course of the 1990s, corporate chief executive pay rose by 570 percent, while corporate profits rose by 114 percent and average worker pay by 37 percent (Anderson et al. 2001). In 1999, when median shareholder returns fell by 3.9 percent, CEO direct compensation rose another 10.8 percent.

number of people below the poverty line increased to 34.5 million (Collins et al. 1999:2). In 1996, 26 percent of all workers were in jobs paying poverty-level wages, a larger proportion than in the past (Misher et al. 2001:353). Overall, from 1979 to 1997, the top 1 percent of households saw their after-tax income rise by $414,000, while the bottom lost $100 (*Washington Post* editorial, June 6, 2001). Kelly (2001:xiv) cites figures that 10 percent of American households held 90 percent of the wealth in the late 1990s, and the wealthiest 1 percent doubled their share from 20 to 40 percent in the last two decades. Some rising tide! More like a shifting of the waters.

Business schools have not caused this so much as contributed to its causes, in the many ways already cited in this book. But that makes them part of the problem, not the solution. Is that acceptable for institutions created to promote social leadership? Where is *their* legitimacy?

## AN MBA FOR ALL SECTORS?

This discussion has so far concentrated on the social consequences in business institutions. But these consequences spill over to other spheres—namely, government and the social sector (of not-for-profits and nongovernmental organizations, etc.). Because organizations in these sectors are supposed to attend more to social goals, this corrupting effect may be far more damaging on society. And here the business schools are most directly guilty.

Of all the distortions emanating from the business schools, none is more flagrant than the claim that this degree in *business* administration prepares people to manage any organization. To the earlier quotes cited to that effect can be added the claim of two students mimicking the claims of their school: "The skills and perspective gained at HBS can . . . be transferred from the business world to the management of government, quasi-governmental and nonprofit organizations" (Kelly and Kelly 1986:30). Well, not quite all. There is one sphere outside business that has managed to select and develop managers in the traditional way. Perhaps that is because its people know too much. Its experience, described in the accompanying box, is instructive.

I argued in Chapter 2 that the MBA prepares people to manage nothing. But at least it imparts knowledge about business (marketing, financing, accounting, etc.) and may also enhance a zest for business, at least established big business. But how that carries over to government and the social sector constitutes a leap of faith that business schools have yet to explain. Instead, they conveniently assume that they have

## DO AS WE DO, NOT AS WE SAY

If you wish to know how managers should be developed and selected, then I suggest you turn to the experts. Not to what they say, but to what they do. After all, the business schools have been hugely successful. Perhaps they have a secret about managing unbeknownst even to themselves.

I addressed this issue some years ago, at a meeting of the European heads of business schools, some ninety deans and directors in all, more or less as follows:

"You will be pleased to know that we are introducing an MUA at McGill University, a Masters of University Administration. We shall take our students with a couple of years of experience—not necessarily in university work; any experience will do. Then we shall put them through the more or less standard MBA curriculum, with special attention, of course, to the managing of universities. (We are preparing a few cases on that.)

"In the management science course, for example, we intend to teach an algorithm for allocating faculty slots, to get rid of the politics in this once and for all. Portfolio techniques in finance will inform our students about maximizing trustee value, because values are very important in universities. I am particularly enthusiastic about our strategy course. We shall be applying Porter's competitive analysis framework to higher education, just as soon as we figure out who are the customers and who are the suppliers.

"The courses in organizational behavior, economics, and statistics will need no changes at all (not to mention the one in ethics). For example, we know who our human resources are, even if they do call themselves professors. And we know what statistics we need to collect: grade point averages of our students and publications by our human resources in refereed journals. Our managers-to-be will be taught to sit in their offices and read such things.

"Our graduates will emerge on a fast track to the top of university administration. We expect them to become deans within five years of graduation—medical schools, divinity departments, philosophy faculties, it hardly matters. What matters is that they do this by the age of thirty, or else how will they become university presidents by forty?

"We are, however, especially targeting the business schools. All deanships are ripe for the picking, but none more so than your very own. That is because most of you sitting here wasted your youth being professors, teaching and researching instead of going straight into university administration. Where you got this strange idea, I cannot imagine. Certainly not in any of your own classrooms. Being a professor in the hope of becoming dean is almost as silly as working with customers in the hope of running the company.

"At this point, you may have the impression that my story is apocryphal. Not quite. Only with regard to application. Because we do this to everyone else, even if we would never let anyone else do it to us."

magically metamorphosed into management schools. They don't teach much management, but somehow their graduates can manage anything. Learning how to market fast-moving consumer goods, how to conduct competitive analyses of industries, how to use algorithms for the raising of capital in financial markets, and so forth, somehow prepares young people to manage embassies, churches, and hospitals. It would be dismissed as ridiculous if not for all the government and social sector organizations that have taken it seriously (not to mention those MPA and MHA programs [in the public sector and health] that have copied the MBA).

Thus, we have MBA managers running around hospitals looking for "customers" to serve, merging like mad, and developing mission statements. (Anyone who needs a mission statement to understand a hospital should find work somewhere else.) Such behavior is particularly devastating in the social sector, which should not be relying, like business and government, on hierarchy so much as on the engagement of the people involved. In cooperatives, for example, those most involved—the workers—can be the owners; in so-called voluntary organizations, some of the people may be volunteering their time. So a two-tier system promoted by MBA education, which separates managers from others, is particularly antithetical to much of this sector.[6]

---

[6]Mirabella and Wish (2000) have published "A Comparison of Graduate Education Programs for Nonprofit Managers." They found eighty-three programs in all in the United States, in business schools, public administration, and social work. Those in the business schools tended to be the least adapted to the social sector and most like conventional MBA programs, albeit with some additions. (For example, only 7 percent of the MBA programs for nonprofit organizations had courses in "Philanthropy and the Third Sector," compared with about twice that number in MBA programs for nonprofit organizations and MNO programs [Masters of Nonprofit Organizations in Social Work]. And they had far more conventional MBA core courses like Marketing and "Decision Sciences.") While the authors cite arguments for a convergence of the social sector with business—for example, "the increasing commercial orientation of the nonprofit sector"—they find the differences significant—in legal,

THE OLD CORPORATE VALUES OF THE "NEW PUBLIC MANAGEMENT"
As for government, typical is this comment from the British head of the
Home Civil Service: "Departments will get a good return on their investment" if they send their people off to do an MBA. The notion of the
"gifted amateur" was at an end, he declared (Wood 2001). So, too, presumably, was that of the civil servant. When government is run by people with this mentality, then we all endure the problems of public policy
(such as environmental pollution) pending numerical "proof" of their
costs (presumably by more body counts).

Thanks to this sort of logic, much of the public sector has lost its
way, ambling around like an amnesiac pretending to be business. When
an official of the Bush White House Staff was questioned in September
2002 on a belated start to a propaganda offensive for action against
Iraq, he replied, "From a marketing point of view, you don't introduce
new products in August." War has become a new product. When this
administration named its secretary of the army, he promised to bring in
"sound business practice." He came from Enron.

Most influential in recent years has been the "New Public Management," a label for the old corporate values. Governments are supposed
to treat people like customers, to hold their managers accountable for
measured performance, to make decisions based on calculated costs and
benefits. It is all so simple, part of the prevailing—and destructive—
managerial correctness. Government is not business; treating it as such
demeans it.

Holding their managers accountable is supposed to get some of the
government agencies around the messiness of democratic politics. In fact,
by ostensibly empowering nonelected officials to make public decisions, it
often has the opposite effect, making politics messier. As for treating us like
customers, I expect a lot more from my government than that, thank
you. I am a citizen, not a mere customer. (See Mintzberg 1996.)

And about measurement in the public sector: Didn't we learn about
that from McNamara's body counting in Vietnam? The problem wasn't

---

economic, and social environment; functions performed by the organizations; governance structures; influence of the community; use of volunteers; the diversified sources
of funding; performance criteria; and the importance of collaboration over competition. As a result, "Nonprofit management curricula become lost in a business
school," which has an "implicit conceptual bias toward business in most [of its]
management courses" (221). Moreover, a survey of faculty, alumni, employees, and
funders associated with each program found that of those from the MBA for nonprofits, 43 percent "pointed to . . . the need for nonprofits to become more like
businesses," while those from other programs emphasized fund-raising, volunteer
management, working with boards of directors, and so forth (226).

the wrong measures; it was the assumption that measurement could re-place judgment, that generic analysis could substitute for situational knowledge. Many activities fall outside the realm of business precisely because their benefits don't lend themselves to measurement—for example, what a child learns in a classroom, what constitutes cure in psychiatry, the efficiency of an army. Sure, we can generate all kinds of measures for these things (e.g., IQ tests for learning). And just as surely do they distort when allowed to dominate (as have IQ tests with serious learning, and especially creativity). By its very nature, the goals of government are vague and conflicting, the political factors complicated, the benefits (if not the costs) difficult to measure. So what sense does it make to treat government like business—and let it be infiltrated by business education?

"I would love to be involved in reinventing government and re-engineering federal agencies," proclaimed a Wharton MBA in one of its brochures (1998–1999). Wouldn't we all! But sure, why not: with all the damage already done by this kind of thinking, he probably wouldn't make things much worse. Maybe the problem with government in the United States is that it has become *too* businesslike.

In an article on correctional institutions, Gendreau (1998) labels this spread of the "MBA management syndrome" as "basically fraudulent." The managers know nothing about the agencies they are running, he writes, yet they run around fixing them, "grasping at any panacea that comes about" (73). The accompanying box reprints parts of another articulate letter that I received from a Canadian civil servant in 1999.

## THE NOT-QUITE UNIVERSAL STYLE OF MANAGING

Dear Professor Mintzberg:

. . . I am a 25 year veteran (or survivor) of employment in the federal government and so much of what you said today [in a CBC radio interview] struck a responsive chord.

For years I have decried the "businessification" of government. So often we have consultants with no understanding of the reality of government preaching to us. In the private sector if you do a better job you get more business and revenue and thus resources. In government you face raised demand, and if you are lucky, the same resources (and compensation—there is no commission). Whenever I point this out, the consultant gasps like a beached fish.

We are in the throes of introducing performance measurement yet again, so I enjoyed your comments about efficiency measurement. I was previously in a corporate crime investigative unit. We only had resources to investigate about 5% of valid complaints, so we had to justify our existence in terms of the general deterrent effect of those files we did take to court. . . . This of course was not quantifiable. The result was a sort of cobbled together fiction in which we tried to measure efficiency or effectiveness in terms of inputs only!

If I have to sit in another "brainstorming" session . . . to determine who our "clients" are, I'll be ill. It always turns out to be the subset of the public we serve directly, society as a whole, and THE MINISTER. Not necessarily in order of priority.

I am convinced that the government "surplus" is a misnomer. It is only a surplus if you continue to do the job the reasonable public expects you to, through increased efficiency. Taken to the extreme, we could fire the whole civil service (except the tax collectors), continue to tax, and have a huge surplus. This is what the government has done, subject only to public tolerance limits. . . .

Anyway, thank you for your insights.

[reprinted with permission; name withheld on request]

In summary, beyond the earlier critiques, the MBA carries a lot of tacit baggage that has no business outside business. MBA graduates who believe that they can manage anything are quite simply a menace to society.

Martin Sorrell (Harvard MBA, 1968), well known head of a design management firm in London, has commented (in Stern 2002) on his Harvard education. "[W]e were in a hothouse, having three case studies a day on what the chairman and CEO should do and why. We ended up believing we could do anything and rule the world." In a sense, one of his fellow Harvard graduates is doing just that, from a white house in Washington, D.C. Stay tuned.

## THE MBA AND THE BUG CLEANER

I was sitting in my office at the Insead business school near Paris a few years back when I received two knocks on my door, a couple of weeks apart. The first was from an MBA student about to complete his studies. He wanted to know about Bombardier, the high-flying Canadian company. He had heard good things about it and considered writing for a job there. Was it as good as they say, he wanted to know, and did I think it would sustain its success for another ten or fifteen years? (Another MBA risk taker!)

How was I to know, I answered. They are certainly doing well now. But who knows what will happen after the guy who built up the place retires or if it runs into some problem with one of its planes. (Later he did retire. And it ran into problems, with one of its trains.) Besides, I asked, why should they hire you? Do you have any experience in their fields of aircraft, transportation equipment, sports vehicles? Just because you have an MBA?

I am sure he found a good job, if not with Bombardier, then with some other company that was happy to have his experience, whatever it was.

A couple of weeks later, the knock was very different. It came from a maintenance man, sent to clean the bugs out of my fluorescent lights. He was a talkative fellow and well informed about the things he wanted to discuss. He read all kinds of OECD documents, he told me, and was worried about many of the trends he saw.

"When I first started to work, we worked as a team. There was a boss, of course, but he was the best informed; his job was to train the younger people." Now all of that has changed, he bemoaned; titles and status have taken over. The bosses often don't know what's going on. The old kind of leadership, which respected the workers and knew the work, was better. He was concerned that society was moving into a dangerous state.

When he left, he thanked me, saying that he felt much better for having discussed this. I thanked him, too. So did I, I replied, although I doubt he realized how much!

Here we have two very different views of leadership in society. Which would you choose? We do have a choice.

# 7

# NEW MBAS?

*Change the environment; do not try to change man.*
— R. BUCKMINSTER FULLER

There are certainly people in business schools aware of many of the consequences discussed in the last four chapters. And they have promoted changes in MBA programs in recent years to deal with them. Have these changes made major differences? That is the issue to which we now turn.

The automobile you drive has had many improvements over the years, probably hundreds in the last year alone. Yet it is fundamentally a Model T, the vehicle built by the Ford Motor Company starting in 1908. It does more or less the same thing in more or less the same way, carrying a few people on rubber tires propelled by a four-cycle internal combustion engine (or else a diesel engine, which is even older). Compare this with the development of computers over the past decade or two.

Products and services that take over a marketplace and stabilize like that are called *dominant designs* (after Abernathy and Utterback 1978). And there are few designs more dominant than the MBA of business education. Since the 1960s, and in certain ways long before, it has done much the same thing in much the same way with much the same consequences. A rather standardized composition of courses based on an established philosophy can be found from school to school and from country to country. (An article in the *Guardian* called the MBA "the world's first universally recognized qualification" [Williams 2002].) I looked at the textbooks used in one prominent European MBA program a few years ago. I found the fourth edition in finance, the sixth edition in financial accounting, the seventh edition in marketing, and the ninth edition in managerial accounting.

Some of this standardization has been driven by the accrediting agencies, such as the Association to Advance Collegiate Schools of Business, or AACSB (to the point that Jerry Wind [1999:24] of the Wharton School has described business education as a "regulated industry"). One university published a fancy brochure to announce its AACSB accreditation, "confirming that the faculty is among the world's leaders in business education." "Among the world's *followers*" would have been a more apt description.

There are certainly differences between schools, such as Stanford's theory and Harvard cases. But there are differences between hatchbacks and sedans too, which have little bearing on the rest of the vehicle. There are also the occasional programs that break the mold, just as there are automobiles powered by batteries. And they are hardly more common.

This chapter surveys recent developments in business and management education, while the next surveys activities in corporate management development. Together they seek real advances that can be combined to improve our ability to develop managers.

We begin this chapter with the advances over the past decade or so most highly touted by the business schools as well as a business press hungry for novelty, concluding that these have changed nothing fundamental in the MBA. In the early 1990s, the dean of Carnegie-Mellon's business school invited one of its most prominent graduates, Paul Allaire, the chief executive of Xerox, to speak. "The associate dean gave a presentation of the curriculum," recalled the dean. "Allaire said that what we presented was the same as he had studied in 1966" (in Crainer and Dearlove 1999:95). I believe that equivalent graduates today would conclude the same thing.

The second part of this chapter looks at some real innovation, most of it in Europe and especially England, but hardly recognized elsewhere. This provides us with a bridge from Part I to Part II of this book, from a negative critique of what is, to positive proposals for what can be. As we consider some of the truly novel programs in England, we move into the realm of developing managers.

## THE DOMINANT DESIGN

Open up almost any MBA brochure, from Boston to Bucharest,[1] and you will likely find a set of courses in a first year with labels such as economics, quantitative methods, marketing, finance, organizational behavior, operations, accounting, and international business, followed by an offering of electives, mostly listed under the same kinds of labels, perhaps with a required strategy course as some kind of "capstone."[2] Thus, in their carefully reasoned but ultimately rather conservative critique of MBA education, Porter and McKibbin (1988) question the extent of "*real* rather than apparent diversity" and note "a distressing tendency for schools to avoid the risk of being different. . . . A 'cookie cutter mentality' does not seem to be too strong a term to describe the situation we encountered in a number of schools" (314–15).

In 1996, Oxford University opened its MBA program. What an opportunity to break new ground: all that prestige and intellectual power behind a degree that had become so standard. According to the brochure for 1998–1999, Oxford offered a one-year, full-time program for people who averaged twenty-seven years of age. "A GMAT score normally in excess of 620" is required, and "a minimum of two years work experience is preferred." (One-third of the class was aged twenty-one to twenty-five.) The brochure referred to the program as "advanced and innovative"—indeed, "the most exciting development of management education in the 1990s." The facts in the brochure, however, suggest exactly the opposite (also that its authors were unaware of true developments taking place in England). "Integrated" courses such as "Managing Financial Resources" and "Managing Services and Products" sound like finance plus accounting and marketing plus operations; there were other courses in strategic management and economics, as well as electives plus a business project. All of this ostensible novelty (to-

---

[1]Costea (2000) lists among the places offering the MBA Bangladesh, Bulgaria, Croatia, Ethiopia, Fiji, Iceland, Macao, and Nepal.

[2]Interestingly, in a listing of the core courses at Chicago and Harvard in 1957–1958 (in Pierson 1959:245), seven of these nine appeared at Chicago (by identical or similar names) and six at Harvard. International Business appeared at neither, while strategy, called "Policy," appeared at Harvard, which did not have quantitative methods or economics.

gether with sixteen mentions of the Oxford name on the first page of the brochure) saw the program grow to over one hundred students by 2001 (*The Economist* 2001).[3]

## E FOR EXECUTIVE?

The so-called Executive MBA (I have never met an executive in an Executive MBA program) started at the University of Chicago in 1943, for part-time students with full-time jobs.[4] Later the idea spread extensively, particularly within the United States (to 190 accredited programs in 1999 [Reingold 1999:88]). Here again was real opportunity: classrooms filled with many of the right people: practicing managers with significant experience that could be used. And what did almost all of these schools do? Exactly what they did with their daytime students (Raelin 1994:307): they replicated a curriculum designed for people with little experience and no context.[5] Indeed, they boasted about it: "The Wharton Executive MBA Program is a true MBA program," said its brochure of 2000–2002. Students "cover the same curriculum and . . . complete the same coursework . . . the only difference is how it is delivered and the high level of experience of students."[6]

If there really were executives in these programs, or even people soon to become executives, why would they need all those courses in the business functions? They would be coming out of these functions. Why go to school to get pushed back in? Why not *do* something with that high level of experience?

In its EMBA brochure of 1998, the University of Southern California wrote proudly of a curriculum that "closely simulates the business environment," with "case analyses, computer simulations, industrial and group projects, field research," and so forth. But why the need to

---

[3]This brochure went out of its way to distinguish the school from the American tradition yet listed among the guest speakers at the Oxford Union Society Dan Quayle and O. J. Simpson!

[4]Longer established are the full-time Sloan Fellows Programs for experienced managers. They began at MIT in 1931 at the initiative of Alfred P. Sloan, chairman of General Motors. Two others followed, at Stanford and London Business School, which continue, those at MIT and Stanford for managers sponsored by their companies.

[5]A "benchmarking " study of seventy executive MBA programs found that 90 percent of them offered each of the nine standard core courses just mentioned (*Executive MBA Review* from the Executive MBA Council 1997:7).

[6]The list of core courses included all the usual functions and disciplines, as well as strategy, but no mention was made of any course in management.

"simulate" that environment when it is sitting right there in the class—in the students' own experiences? Why take the right people and repeat the wrong ways? In a second-year project, groups of participants "identify a local company and perform a strategic analysis." (It sounds like an appendectomy.) These people work for real companies that have all kinds of real problems; shouldn't they be analyzing what they know best? If these programs made natural use of their students' natural experience, the term *real world* would sound silly.

## Variations on a Theme

The automobile companies make a big fuss about whatever is new in their cars from year to year—a fancier hubcap, a bigger engine, some trendy new CD technology. So do the business schools, for much the same reason: to attract buyers and improve ratings. But none of this should be confused with "revolution," another word that has been bandied about for some years now.

*Business Week* described the early 1990s as the "revolution" in MBA programs, the period of "radical . . . curriculum overhaul" (Dunkin and Enbar 1998:64). Wharton led the way. As the outgoing dean had earlier told *Fortune* magazine, "We've got to make fundamental changes. We've been tinkering" (Main 1989:78). Accordingly, in 1991 Wharton modularized its curriculum, teaching intensively in weeks what had formerly been taught over months. The school was "*even* handing out only one grade per semester in the first year" (Byrne and Bongiorno 1994:64). Alongside this, once more, came integration—"trying to teach business as a complex whole instead of a set of disparate functions"—and the soft skills (teamwork, leadership, and quality, etc.).

But *Business Week* also wrote that "[i]n some ways . . . the makeover has been too ambitious." Wharton had to "scale back" some of the new offerings. "And the much ballyhooed integration of the core curriculum has run into serious obstacles at a school where the faculty is divided among 12 departments and 21 research centers" (Byrne and Bongiorno 1994:66). Nonetheless, for all its efforts at promoting change if not quite accomplishing it, Wharton was propelled to the top of the *Business Week* rankings in 1994—"this time," as the *Business Week* headline put it.

In recognition that there is always a next time, other business schools joined the "revolution." History does not record how many went so far as to give one grade per semester, but those modular courses in weeks instead of regular courses in months certainly spread, as did the new efforts to teach the soft skills and achieve integration. The business schools have never ceased to make the greatest fuss about the very things they are least able to deliver. The MBA is not soft; the MBA is not social; the MBA is not managerial; the MBA is not integrated. It favors the hard, the economic, the analytical, and the decomposed.

The more dominant a design, the more inclined are insiders to mistake adaptations for revolutions. Of course, put cosmetic changes into the hands of the promotional people—as business schools now do—and you get "revolutions" right and left. "The MBA is dead," proclaimed the dean of a business school (Horvath 1995:1). "Long live the MBA!" Exactly.

## Pedagogical Technologies

I would like to single out two particular areas of ostensible change in management education because, potentially at least, they could be important. One has to do with pedagogical technologies, the other with internationalization.

There are two perspectives on the new technologies, such as CD-ROMs, the Internet, and video conferencing: "Radicals talk of 're-inventing executive education around new IT capabilities,' while conservatives see it as an adjunct to traditional classroom delivery" (Jampol 1998:4). Here, as is often the case, conservatism dominates, by using the new means to deliver existing materials in familiar ways—for example, paper workbooks converted to electronic format, or lectures on video ("using IT simply to put [the] gurus on-line" [Crainer and Dearlove 1999:219]). Consider this comment in a Carnegie Mellon brochure, which is meant to sound radical:

> For the 1990s and beyond, GSIA is blazing new paths in business education. Through the use of leading-edge computer technology, students learn through decision-making in simulated environments. This computer-based experiential learning goes far beyond traditional case methods. Using international computer networks, our students interact and compete with other students from top business schools around the world. This is truly the new wave in international management education.

Running business games over electronic networks instead of in closed rooms may be another stream, but it was hardly a new wave.

The benefits of the new technologies, beside speed, are convenience and coverage: students can work at their own pace on their own schedule in their own place. This is the *how*, and it is new. But the *what* is not, simply because binary bits change nothing fundamental in the educational process. They certainly travel faster, but only until they reach the place that matters: our heads. There the technologies end, as our same old brains take over. Indeed, because in these technologies everything has to be reduced to those binary bits, a great deal that is critical to managing gets left out. It may not be critical to learning analytical technique, but again, let's not mix up analyzing with managing.

This leads to an important conclusion: that the new pedagogical technologies drive MBA education further along its established path—that is, toward analysis and away from management. (See the accompanying box.) So the more business schools adopt these technologies—and they are enticing—the farther away they are taken from management education.

"Interacting with 'faceless' classmates and professors in remote locations with disparate time zones, forces you to be creative and thoughtful," claimed a Hong Kong student in an international electronic MBA program. "My team in particular is quite close. We share jokes on-line and even send pictures to each other" (Austin 1997). But what makes this more thoughtful, or creative, let alone managerial?

## DUBBING BY DRUCKER

*(excerpted from* Forbes *(Drucker 2000:86)*

Alexander Brigham . . . has landed Peter Drucker for a series of interactive Web-based courses on executive management. . . . "We are now the Peter Drucker brand," declares Brigham, a 31-year-old former investment banker.

"We developed 30 hours of Internet-based educational material based on Peter's latest thinking," Brigham says. In the programs Drucker expounds on his principles, after which multiple choice questions appear on the screen. If viewers click the right answer, Drucker's dubbed voice responds in his heavy Viennese accent with comments like "excellent" or "very good." If the viewer flubs, Drucker says, "Sorry you are wrong." . . . Eventually [Brigham's company] and its competitors hope to offer accredited M.B.A. degrees.

PLACE AND SPACE    In this regard, Wallace et al. (2003:3) contrast "place" with "space"—education that occurs in a specific location, compared with virtual exchanges made possible by technology across distances, of which they describe two "approaches": correspondence courses in which the student works alone and the distance learning model in which students gather for lectures received on video links.

Wallace et al. combine all these in a Place and Space Model. "For example, information transfer can be most easily achieved through space. Dialogue and discussion can begin in place and continue in space" (3). Space allows more people to participate, while place provides the emotional context needed for learning together. Put place together with space, and, in their opinion, "the truly global school" becomes possible (6).

The Open University of the United Kingdom, founded in 1983, is a well-established space MBA program reinforced by place components. It claims to deliver "a full range of materials to satisfy [the student's] study needs, including textbooks, workbooks, videos, audio cassettes, and computer-based information" (brochure, 1999–2000), reinforced by personal tutoring and collaborative study groups that meet for periods of two to five days. (It also offers a space-only on-line MBA tailored for American students.) And Queens University offers a "National Videoconference EMBA," where participants sit around tables at various locations in Canada, with two-way video connections to the instructor. They receive the lectures and are able to ask questions as well as engage in discussions with their colleagues around the table. These alternate Friday and Saturday sessions are reinforced by two modules of two weeks each at Queens plus a two-week international study trip.

GEMBA    Perhaps most ambitious in the technological sense is the GEMBA program at Duke University, with which the authors of the place and space paper are affiliated.[7] The program is intended for experienced managers from around the world (hence the G for global). Its content is structured much like the conventional MBA. As one of its designers, Blair Sheppard, commented, GEMBA "hasn't triggered a rethinking of content at all." But in delivery of what he calls its "computer-mediated learning," it is radically different (although still "faculty-driven").

---

[7]The following is based on discussions I had at Duke with one of the designers and the technical director of the program in May 1997, followed up by correspondence in 2003.

Each of the five semesters begins with place: residential sessions of two weeks (two at Duke in North Carolina; the others in Europe, Asia, and South America). The courses, with fifteen to eighteen hours of class contact to establish face-to-face relationships, appear to be mostly regular MBA type, with "global" in their titles (and presumably content). Then each semester continues for another eleven to twelve weeks in space—in the Internet-mediated format. Here, the instructors prepare lectures, which are recorded for downloading at the students' convenience. Assignments are given weekly, and examinations are used.

Reinforcing all this are electronic discussions (in real time and not) among the students, while course "bulletin boards" focus on specific subjects, with faculty involvement. The instructors also have on-line office hours. They may also assign a theme for study by "virtual" teams, which bring their results back for class discussion (again, electronically). Needless to say, creating and coordinating all the electronic linkages, which includes supplying all students with a notebook containing the necessary software, was a complicated affair.

GEMBA may be a rather conventional MBA program in course structure and content, driven by a faculty from one U.S. campus, but it is certainly worth watching from a pedagogical point of view.


## VENTURING ABROAD

The words *international* and especially *global* have become mantras in today's business schools. Not a brochure must go out, it seems, or a press interview given without some mention of them. Domestic business is out, no matter how common it may remain; global business is in, whatever that means.

An MBA program can be international in at least four respects:

1. The students can be international (meaning rooted in various cultures, not drawn to one).

2. The faculty can be international (in their heads, not just their origins).

3. The context, philosophy, and culture can be international (i.e., eclectic, which is the opposite of global).

4. The location and control can be international (which means dispersed, not dominated by one country).

In these respects, so far as I know there is no international MBA program.[8]

INTERNATIONAL STUDENTS?    The most international of the American MBA programs generally claim to have about 25 to 35 percent foreign students. (European schools such as Insead, IMD, and Rotterdam show figures of more than 90 percent foreign students [from an EFMD fact sheet, September 2002].) Any program that is two-thirds or more native—and of a people hardly known for their timidity, least of all in this setting—is more accurately described as domestic.[9]

Thus, in a 1998 article entitled "The Melting Pot Still Has a Few Lumps," *Business Week* stated, "The culture of most U.S. Business Schools remains strongly American, both in the classroom and out" (Reingold 1998:104). The article quoted a student born in Hong Kong but raised in America: "There is a very aggressive social schedule here [at Stanford], and that is something most of the East Asian crowd stays out of." Another student at Berkeley claimed, "Domestic students made all the contributions to class discussion . . . so you don't know how business is conducted in Europe or the Pacific Rim" (108).

INTERNATIONAL FACULTY AND PHILOSOPHY?    As for the faculty, especially among the best of the American schools, it is often rather international. To their credit, U.S. schools have been very open to foreign nationals. But not to foreign training: almost all of these people have received their doctorates—and therefore been socialized to academia—in the United States. As a consequence, the foreign-born faculty have been less inclined to carry their home cultures to America, as teachers, than to carry American beliefs back to their home cultures, as visitors. (See the accompanying box.) Put differently, the international faculty in American business education has never demonstrated a particularly international mindset. Indeed, in my experience they tend to be the ones most inclined to promote a homogenous "globalization."

---

[8]As Jerry Wind (1999) of the Wharton School put it, if companies that become international evolve through four stages—"(1) domestic firm, (2) import and/or exporting, (3) joint ventures and direct foreign investment, and (4) a truly networked global organization"—then "most business schools are at stage 1" (10, 11). Some import and export students and faculty, and a few have gone further. Wind's conclusion: "The world is global, but most B-schools are domestic" (5).

[9]A Wharton brochure of 1997–1998 referring to the school as "a truly international community" presented figures that 25 percent of the graduates accepted jobs outside the United States and that 90 percent of those were not American citizens. It seems, therefore, that less than 4 percent of the Americans accepted jobs abroad.

## WHO HAS THE CATCHING UP TO DO?

Professor John Quelch, originally from Britain, spent many years as a professor of marketing at the Harvard Business School before returning for three years to head up the London Business School. Back at Harvard, he published a short piece called "Why Europe Has Some Catching Up to Do" (2001). Some excerpts follow:

*The general management qualification represented by the MBA has become the educational standard for US business in a way that has not yet happened in Europe. I believe Europe is catching up but that overall European business performance has probably suffered as a result.*

*. . . Harvard Business School is over 90 years old. You can see the results by comparing the number of chief executives with MBA degrees in the [London Stock Exchange] FTSE 100 with the percentage of Fortune 500 CEOs holding the degree.*

*. . . British business is still too finance and accounting orientated. In the US, many more top managers come up through the strategy and marketing ranks—something which is reflected in the more general coverage of the MBA—and in my view leads to greater risk orientation, a more entrepreneurial style and a willingness to see the glass as half full rather than half empty. . . .*

*. . . [T]here has been the disastrous Daimler/Chrysler merger which presumably made sense from the perspective of financial analysts but which in practice became embroiled in the soft issues of corporate culture. The skills to handle this sort of cross border integration are not ones you would expect to learn in an engineering or accountancy course—you would, however, study such challenges on a general management or on an MBA course. . . .*

*Some Europeans—certainly a section of the British business community—still see academia as remote and irrelevant to the business world. The attitude is reflected in the use of the dismissive British phrase "that's just academic"—a pejorative meaning you would never hear in the US. [!]*

*I'm certainly not saying US business schools are perfect—there's a myopia in the US about the rest of the world that I notice having been at London Business School for the last few years. At Harvard one of my jobs will be to stimulate the faculty to do more overseas research.*

It is remarkable how rare it is for business schools around the world—except in Japan—to pay attention to any domestic style of managing. Most are too busy trying to be "global." A few years ago, I did a video hookup with a Buenos Aires MBA class. At one point I asked the director whether his program teaches an Argentinean style of managing. No, he answered proudly, "we teach the *universal* style of managing." I suggested he meant the American style of managing.

INTERNATIONAL LOCATIONS?　As for international location, here the rhetoric tends to get farthest ahead of the substance.

It has become popular to send students' abroad for study trips. By 1993, *Business Week* could add to its table of the "highlights" of the twenty-five leading EMBA programs such phrases as "week-long seminar abroad," "global trip optional," and "overseas trip to Budapest." Jonathan Gosling of England's Exeter University (in a speech to the Association of British Business Schools on March 15, 2000) referred to this as "The Mir Experience": dropping in on another galaxy, from within one's own spaceship. Learning can certainly take place, but how much?

Beyond the study trip is the semester abroad. Gosling (2001) characterizes this as the "Alien Exchange," usually "approved on the basis of the content of [the students'] studies being as alike as possible to those they would have done at home." Accordingly, many business schools these days have a set of partner schools around the world, carefully selected to be of equivalent status. Of such activities, a director of the Wharton EMBA has commented: "We think people are substituting international residency for learning" (in the *Financial Times*, October 22, 2001).

More recently, some of the prestigious schools have moved beyond this, by replicating their home programs in other countries. Northwestern, for example, has set up "International Executive MBA" programs in various places. The one in Israel, in conjunction with Tel Aviv University, "modeled after the Executive Masters Program" back home, claims a class profile of 75 percent Israeli, 8 percent Palestinian, 3 percent Jordanian, and 12 percent other (Web site, 2003). The University of Chicago runs an "International Executive MBA" program in Barcelona taught by its own faculty. Asked at a conference why the school chose Barcelona, an administrator of the program said, "That's the beauty of it; it could be anywhere!" A consulting firm was apparently engaged to choose the site.

There are programs that go much deeper into the foreign context, but these are few, and, tellingly, some of the most interesting do not come exclusively from business schools.

At the University of Pennsylvania, the Lauder Program is offered jointly by the Wharton School and the School of Arts and Sciences. Students earn an MBA in management and an MA in international studies.

In addition to the MBA and MA courses, such as international political economy, students select a specialization in language and region—for example, in Spanish or Portuguese in Latin America—and spend at least 20 percent of the two-year program there. In the first summer, they study the language and culture; in the second, they do an internship with a local organization.

Similarly, at Capilano College in Vancouver, a two-year postgraduate program on Asia Pacific Management, ongoing since 1987, prepares students for work in that part of the world. Alongside some of the conventional management courses are others in Asian geography, legal traditions, art history, and so on, as well as more general courses in such areas as trade logistics and economic geography. Students must also study one of six Asian languages. The coursework is followed by a twelve-month internship in Asia. In 2002, according to the director, 73 percent of the students had offers to stay on with their Asian employers.

A step beyond going abroad is to replicate the school abroad, by creating a clone or encouraging a local school to be one. Harvard set up several of these years ago, but they pretty much all disappeared as such, whether by closing down or simply going their own way. A new wave is under way now, with Insead, for example, having created a second campus in Singapore. I shall discuss later why I believe such efforts are questionable.

INTERNATIONAL PARTNERSHIPS?    More popular now, and clearly more in the spirit of internationalization, is to partner with other schools in offering a joint degree. It should be noted that the most common examples of this, where a prestigious school, usually American, takes the lead, is not partnering so much as venturing. Partnership means balance. Indicative of this, although not a degree offering, was a program called Global Leadership 2020. A press release of 1998 (still on the school's Web site in 1993) described the program as an "alliance" of the Tuck School of Dartmouth with Templeton College Oxford and H.E.C. Paris, yet referred to "The Tuck Global 2020 Program." Not surprisingly, the partners of that "alliance" changed from year to year and eventually disappeared.

One example of balance seems to be the international masters in management offered by Purdue in the United States, Tilburg in the Netherlands, Budapest in Hungry, and the École Superior de Commerce of Paris. It was described in its 2001 brochure as being for "experienced professionals," with the six two-week residencies rotating among the four campuses, but appearing to offer conventional MBA materials. The newer "One MBA," offered by schools in Hong Kong, São Paulo, Monterey, Rotterdam, and North Carolina, appears to be similarly balanced, except that with students spending "the majority of their time at their home universities" (Schneider 2001), the international dimension is diminished. Chapter 10 discusses our own partnership, in a very different design, not called an MBA, of schools in Canada, England, France, India, and Japan, created in 1996.

## BUSINESS AT THE BUSINESS SCHOOLS

Where do these international activities take the business schools? Mostly to the wrong place, in my view.

In their 1988 report, Porter and McKibbin wrote that "a growing number of business schools are becoming involved in the development and marketing of educational products for international consumption" (312). Were business schools businesses, intended to market products for consumption, that would be fine. But they are supposed to be places of scholarship, intended to develop knowledge for edification. And so what would be expansion for a business amounts to contraction for a business school.

Going global, creating alliances, engaging in various forms of exporting and franchising, all of this "aping the behavior of large corporations," as Crainer and Dearlove (1999) put it, has to be judged solely on its capacity to enhance the quality of education—in other words, on the growth of intellect, not market share.

The better schools might argue that such activities extend the reach of quality education. But how, and for what purpose? Flying professors over to drop messages hardly enhances their research, unless they stay and get involved in the local culture. As for the local students, they may get exposed to famous faculty, but all too often generically, with little reference to their own cultural needs. Should we not be encouraging local schools to stand on their own feet instead? They should be welcoming advice, to be sure, but for purposes of developing what is best for their own people. Effective partnering brings people with different perspectives together to learn from each other, not to follow the leader.

As for schools that set out to replicate themselves in other places— create subsidiaries of a sort—in my opinion that leads to a "damned if you do, damned if you don't" result. The new campuses are set up as clones. If they remain clones, they will always be second-rate, because first-rate scholars will not be inclined to stay at them. And if they get past that and become centers of scholarship in their own right, then they will eventually seek their independence. For what self-respecting faculty will accept the curriculum decisions of the mother ship? Will its professors be satisfied to attend virtual faculty meetings? How long until they rebel? That is why the best clones of schools like Harvard, including Insead itself, eventually went their own way, while the few that have remained clones are not renowned for their scholarship.

The great places of education, from ancient Greece to contemporary Cambridge, have always functioned best as geographically tight communities of dedicated thinkers—students and teachers on a log, as someone once put it. Collegiality is a form of community, in place; it doesn't work the same way across space.

## MEANWHILE, ELSEWHERE

Imagine another world. Imagine, muses Jerry Wind (1999), if instead of management ideas flowing out from the United States, they flowed back in, to mitigate "U.S. centric concepts and methods" (11), through efforts to understand the management practices of other places. Imagine opening our eyes beyond globalization, to all the interesting things happening on this globe.

I was in Ghana recently, where I heard concerns about the controls exercised by the multinational corporations, not to mention the International Monetary Fund. "Just because it works in New York doesn't mean it will work in Accra." Imagine, in contrast, someone arriving in the United States with the claim "It worked in Accra, so it's bound to work in New York!"

There is no need to imagine. Kofi Annan was raised in Ghana and has functioned remarkably well in New York, as head of probably the toughest and certainly the most global organization in the world: the United Nations. He may have received much of his university education in the United States (including an M.S. in management from MIT), but his style, more engaging than heroic, seems to have been significantly influenced by his origins (see Mintzberg 2002). If Annan is the most prominent example of this, think of all the others of which we are unaware, managers doing interesting things all over the world from whom we can all learn.

GLOBAL LEARNING FROM LOCAL EXPERIENCE    In a talk to his fellow deans from business schools around the world, Gabino Mendoza (1990) of the Asian Institute of Institute of Management in Manila said, "For forty years or so, teachers of graduate management education in the developing world have wandered in the academic desert, starved, parched, mesmerized by mirages that have invariably faded in the sand. In their sojourn in the desert, three temptations have bedeviled them" (13).

The first, to which "most teachers of management in the developing world have succumbed," has been simply to "uncritically pass on to their students . . . [what has] been found to work in the industrialized developed countries of the west." But much of this, in Mendoza's opinion, has "little relevance" to their developing countries. Thus, Sturdy and Gabriel (2000), in a paper on "MBA Teaching in Malaysia," have described the visiting academics from the west as equivalent to the religious missionaries and military mercenaries of earlier times: "Knowledge became a major export industry for industrialized countries" (980). Old products are "sold in new markets through the franchising of ideas," using advertisements in the Malaysian press that "compete for space with advertisement for cars, watches, and cosmetics" (983, 986), with about as little differentiation for local consumption.

Mendoza's (1990) second temptation, which he calls "an invitation to despair," is to forget the whole business of business education. After all,

> [t]he Japanese, the Koreans, the Taiwanese, among others, formed their own unique management systems, educated and trained competent corps of managers, developed their economies, successfully competed with the industrialized West, and enriched their countries with little or no help from modern graduate schools for would-be managers. Why do your poor countries need such expensive, resource-intensive institutions? Why not just close them down and save some money? (13)

Mendoza's third temptation is for people in these nations to develop their own solutions. He cites as examples a Central American management institute that encouraged meaningful dialogue between the key institutions of business, government, labor, the military, and the church, and African schools that helped the revival of the local agricultural sector. His message is that every country has something to learn from its own managerial and business behaviors, and to teach it to other countries.

So let's look at some countries that have—or could.

BUSINESS EDUCATION IN JAPAN   Japan has certainly been the prime example, which helps explain its remarkable progress since World War II. (It must be pointed out that current problems in the Japanese economy do not discredit the Japanese style of management. Toyota, for example, so characteristic of this style, is widely regarded to be the best-managed automobile company in the world.)

The Japanese have business (or commerce) departments in their universities, but these have concentrated almost exclusively on undergraduate education, and they are "highly theoretical," according to Okazaki-Ward (1993:24). Management development in Japan has been mostly the concern of corporations themselves (and will be discussed as such in the next chapter).

MBA programs have remained rather rare in Japan (although that is now changing). One private university, Keio, has had one since 1978, still modeled after Harvard, while some foreign schools, such as Dartmouth and McGill, have set up Western-style programs. A 1995 survey of the Keio alumni (Ishida 1997) found that "the exchange of views and friendship with other students greatly exceeded what they had expected [upon entering], while learning advanced professional/specialized knowledge did not come anywhere near expectations" (191). (Hitsosubashi University, long respected as a Japanese center of scholarship in business and management, has a new MBA program since 2000. But its director, Hiro Itami, wrote to me recently [April 8, 2003] that the aim is to teach how to think and analyze and that he makes it quite clear to the students that they are not being educated as managers in two years. "The aim of our program [if not the title] is Masters in Business *Analysis*" [italics added].)

Japanese companies have also sponsored some of their managers to do MBAs in the United States. But by the late 1990s, they were cutting back, primarily because "too many returning MBAs have trouble readjusting to the local business culture" (Syrett 1995: 25). In personal conversations, executives of some large Japanese companies have complained to me about the high expectations of the graduates and their inclination to quit the company. (These figures are very low by American standards but unacceptable by Japanese ones.) Yet Japan can hardly be faulted for being closed to Western management ideas. Quite the contrary: Probably no country, including the United States, has adopted them more thoughtfully and effectively. Whereas many Western firms have grabbed at the latest technique, Japanese firms have been inclined to blend them carefully into their own cultures.

BUSINESS EDUCATION IN GERMANY    Germany has also gone its own way in business education and likewise has had a remarkable record of economic growth since World War II. Many of its companies became famous for quality and logistics, as well as for cooperation between research and marketing (Locke 1996b:98). Yet here, too, the MBA has been almost nonexistent (that is starting to change here too), although discipline-based undergraduate programs, including ones in business economics, have been very strong (see Locke 1996b). In fact, many Germans have been inclined to carry such specialized education right to doctoral level. Even back in 1988, Handy et al. (2) put the proportion of directors (senior executives) in Germany's hundred largest corporations with such doctorates at 54 percent.

Much like Japan, "the locus of German management is in the firm, not in the management profession itself" (Locke 1989:100).[10] But while Japanese companies have tended to move their best new recruits around so they can get to know different parts of the company, German companies have tended to promote them up single functional ladders. In fact, Locke (1989:276) suggests this may help explain the innovativeness of many high-technology German firms, since their line managers actively participate in the work of the technical and scientific community. He contrasts this with the educational systems of England and France, which he accuses of training "a self-conscious elite" of strategic generalists separate from the technically trained managers—a problem that may now be worse in the United States (as discussed in Chapter 5).

BUSINESS EDUCATION IN FRANCE     France is another story altogether, unlike Japan and Germany and in a sense beyond the United States. It has its share of university business schools and of the equivalent of masters programs in business. But the real status in that country goes to a limited number of "grandes écoles," in business, engineering, other fields, that, with one notable exception, focus on the equivalent of undergraduate education. From there, the graduates move fast, much like American MBAs, with many of the same consequences discussed in Chapters 5 and 6. "In France, the CEOs are selected as early as [age] 15, on the basis of their ability in math!" quipped Aix-en-Provence professor Pierre Batteau (in a speech prepared for the Academy of Management in 1998). A senior French manager put it more seriously: "We have to look for people who are going to develop into managers quickly. . . . [The top schools] turn out a high calibre of individual who can study a problem and come up quickly with an answer."

[10]See Locke's (1989) full discussion of "German obstinacy" on pp. 55ff. Yet even here, "It is rather astonishing to observe the extent to which American managerialism has gained a hold on people's minds . . . and stopped them from appreciating the German managerial alternative" (96).

The grandest of the grandes écoles (beside École Polytechnique for engineers) is École Nationale d'Administration, or ENA, so influential that its graduates are known as "*énarques*." They enter mostly just after their first degree, often from another grande école, and later move ahead in ways that put even Harvard to shame. Despite their small numbers—fifty to one hundred a year, at the discretion of the French government—these are the aristocrats of present-day France: they comprise an astonishingly high proportion of France's leadership, including (not uncommonly) the President and Prime Minister (at the time of this writing, and of this editing one administration later!), as well as many of the senior government officials and heads of major corporations (often the same people, parachuting back and forth). France's ultimate heroic manager of late, Jean-Marie Messier of Vivendi fame, is an énarque.

I have known many graduates of the grandes écoles; they are often brilliant, although not often creative. But again, does that brilliance reflect the education or the selection for the education? The answer is suggested by the fact that the graduates of these schools are known during their careers for their rankings on the tests *going into* these schools, not coming out of them! "Some recruiters admit that in new hires, they are primarily purchasing the entrance exam" (Barsoux and Lawrence 1991:63).

Perhaps the selection process works too well, because by favoring analytical intelligence without work experience, it evokes the same criticisms made of MBAs in the United States: these graduates are too Cartesian, too detached, too arrogant. As a senior French manager, also head of the French Association of Training Managers, commented, "it is difficult for them to manage people. . . . The fierce competition entailed in their education makes them highly individualistic and self-seeking" (in Handy et al. 1988:101, 102).

In his book *Voltaire's Bastards*, John Ralston Saul (1992) attacks the narrow rationality in and beyond the land of Voltaire, including the waves of énarques "with an undirected personal ambition . . . who knew nothing about the real world but were rapidly given real power" (127). Saul draws a parallel between ENA and HBS, both producing an "elite" who favor "abstract truths based on detached abstractions" (129). But France has taken this much farther: While it is everyone for him- or herself after Harvard, albeit with the help of that old boys' network, the French system works to move these people ahead in a much more privileged way. It is as if the whole country acts like one carefully controlled corporation, moving its "high potentials" along. Thus, the grandes écoles are highly attuned to the national interest, more than to any particular sector. And after that, the best of their graduates, particularly the énarques, get placed in influential staff jobs—for example, finance in government and planning in business—which become springboards to senior positions in management. From there they move easily across sectors, so that a senior civil servant can suddenly be found running a major French company—without prior business experience. Hence, Barsoux and Lawrence (1991), in their *Harvard Business Review* article "The Making of a French Manager," describe management in France as a "State of Mind"—a kind of "shared identity . . . of belonging to the French managerial class," called the "cadre," a term borrowed from the military.

This certainly serves the graduates. It may also serve the country in a certain way, although, as a narrow form of meritocracy, it hardly serves democracy and flexibility. "What Japan achieves through consensus and groupism, France achieves through elite convergence. . . . Because the French establishment is run by a core of like-minded people, it can take concerted action" (Barsoux and Lawrence 1991:66).

But this also breeds centralized bureaucracy, which in France can be stifling: French managers "like to communicate in writing," and they "are trained to distrust makeshift or intuitive solutions." Senior managers may also centralize because they "believe they owe their high position to their intelligence and cunning" (62). Locke (1998), who studied the impact of American MBA education on French nationals, concludes, "The elitist American business school experience only reinforced" the long-held French view that "power flows from the top down in a pyramidal organization" with a powerful chief executive (11).

BUSINESS EDUCATION IN THE UNITED KINGDOM    The United Kingdom probably stands second to the United States in per capita graduation of MBAs (about 11,000 in the year 2000, for a population about a quarter that of the United States).

As an English-speaking country with such close ties to the United States, it is inevitable that developments in American business education get rapid attention in the U.K. That is certainly happening, with the consequence that some schools quickly fall in line with changes in American practice. Yet ironically, this seems to be more common in some of the big name schools, such as London Business School and Oxford, than in a number of lesser-known ones, which, as we shall see, are doing all kinds of interesting things. Indeed, taking the latter into account, England is exploding with new ideas for business and management education.

How sad that so few professors and journalists in the United States are aware of this.[11]

Below I discuss two important trends in England, rather different but potentially complementary. The first, shared with many schools on the European continent, are highly specialized MBA programs. The second are programs for practicing managers.

## DIFFERENTIATION IN EUROPE

I have argued that MBA education could be the right way for the right people with the right consequences if it was recognized as specialized education for specialized jobs in business. That, in fact, is how much graduate business education is viewed in Europe (increasingly but not always labeled MBA)—specialized by function but also sometimes by industry, as discussed in turn.

THE MBF (IN FINANCE), MBC (IN CHANGE), MBA (IN ACCOUNTING), ETC. While an MBA student in the United States will typically complete a set of core courses in the first year and then select elective courses with some functional major in the second year, a student in, for example, the business school in Aix-en-Provence, France, can do a full masters-level degree in Internal Auditing, Quantitative Marketing, Management of Logistics Systems, Finance, International Business Law, or Project Management. Likewise, at Warwick, one of England's better schools, one can do a masters degree in Economics and Finance, European Industrial Relations, Organization Studies, and others. Less conventional but still functionally specialized are masters degrees in Design Management at Westminster, Organizational Change at Hertfordshire, and Management Learning ("for management developers") at Lancaster University. Think of these as MBA programs without the A—unless, of course, it stands for *Accounting*!

---

[11]Sometimes even the ones in Britain. On CareerPoint, on FT.com, I found a statement (September 24, 2002), about how "MBA degrees for working managers" were being taught in evenings and weekends until the "mould was broken" by the GEMBA program in Britain. In fact, modular programs of one or two weeks go back in England to at least the 1980s, a full decade before GEMBA. Recall, too, the earlier comment quoted in that Oxford brochure. How sad that supposed experts can be more aware of even minor changes in America than serious innovations at home.

Such specialized programs allow the entire design to be tailored to the function in question, not only in the obvious ways of curriculum and materials but also in linking the studies to practice. For example, the students can be sent out to do serious apprenticeships in their field; some of the French programs which usually run for a year, include several months of in-company training. Also, practitioners can be brought into the classroom and even into the design of the curriculum.

Moreover, such programs send a clear signal to both the graduates and their employers that these people have been trained as functional specialists, not general managers. So what is negative when claimed to be managerial—such as an emphasis on analysis—can become positive in specialized application.

Of course, specialized masters degrees are fairly widespread on the other side of the ocean too, but heavily focused on a few rather hard disciplines and not nearly as well known as the conventional MBA.[12] European practice, appears to be more varied and advanced on this front,[13] more widely recognized at home, and more inclined to break away from the dominant MBA design.

The University of Bath provides an interesting example of how far such tailored design can be taken. Its Masters Degree in Purchasing and Supply Management, created in 1993, brings in people already experienced in the field for two years of part-time study. It is "based on research," the school says, because of "the lack of advanced research and literature" in the field; the students are expected to create it! Over six months, they do five one-week "residential courses" (e.g., Strategic Purchasing, Marketing, and Networking), after which they dedicate a day a week to field research, plus a day a month to meetings of their "Action Learning Set" of six or so colleagues plus a faculty member. This is intended to result in "two publishable research papers" in addition to a dissertation, the topic of which is selected jointly by the student, the supervisor, and the employer.

---

[12]Statistics prepared by the AACSB (2002:9) of its membership show 245 schools reporting specialized masters' programs, with accounting being by far the most common (in 192 of the school reporting), followed by information systems (92), finance (67), taxation (63), and economics (51).

[13]Gosling has attributed this inclination to a different history, at least in the U.K.: Business schools came together from functional departments, which already had their own specialized programs (interview in the IIMB *Management Review*, 1998:168). Muller et al. (1991:85) have also claimed that the "European schools of business have been spared [the] homogenizing influence" of the American accreditation process.

THE MBF (IN FOOTBALL OR FASHION), MBC (IN CONSULTING), MBA (IN AEROSPACE), ETC.    Common as well in Europe is differentiation by target industry (perhaps more appropriately labeled segmentation than differentiation). Here students specialize by the industry under study, where they will find jobs, or have them already.

Ashridge in the U.K. and the Free University of Amsterdam offer graduate programs in management consulting; in France, the Centre de Formation Professionnelle des Journalistes has been giving an MBA in the management of journalism, while the École Supérieure de Commerce of Toulouse, city of the Airbus, offers an MBA in Aerospace. Bishop Grosseteste College even offers a masters degree in Church Management, while the University of Liverpool (where else?) offers an MBA in Football Industries. The MBA, which has been called "the luxury brand of the management educational world" (Crainer and Dearlove 1999:81), perhaps reaches its apex in another of the French grandes écoles, ESSEC, which offers a degree in Luxury Brand Management. (The brochure, oversized with the thickest pages of all, also offers the most enticing images: a graceful neck receiving a drop of perfume, an elegant hand accepting champagne in an even more elegant glass, and so on.) Lecturers are brought in from luxury brand companies, the brochure says, and students are sent out to do internships in them.

By focusing on a specific industry, like those on a specific function, these programs are able to break away from the dominant MBA design, although only some choose to do so.[14] Now we turn to programs that although neither functional nor industry-specific, do break away—toward management.

## INNOVATIONS IN ENGLAND

Like the United States, England has much conventional business education and, beyond that, an aggressive movement to certify management as a profession. But beneath this lies a good deal of intriguing innovation.

---

[14]In the course descriptions of this ESSEC program, the differences sound as cosmetic as the products. Core courses are offered in the usual business functions plus sociology as well as industrial and property law, while the electives sound mostly like the standard business functions (e.g., "Specific Marketing Tools and Techniques Used by the Luxury Sector").

A large majority of English MBA students stay on the job and study part-time.[15] Handy et al. (1988) note that the British "have always preferred to earn while they learn" (170). Even many of the full-time students are experienced people who are "investing their redundancy [layoff] payment to do the course" (Bradshaw 1996), while half are fully funded by their employers and another quarter partially so (Whiteley 2001).

As a consequence, instead of copying programs created for people with little experience, some English business schools have been designing programs for people in practice. Add to this the British inclination for thoughtful idiosyncrasy, and the result has been a hotbed of interesting developments. (A particularly unusual example is described in the accompanying box.)

## CRITICAL MANAGEMENT FOR MANAGERS

The University of Lancaster offers a masters of philosophy in critical management, aimed at practicing managers but not at their managerial skills. The purpose is to "question conventional wisdom" about management practice, writes Julia Davis, the program director: "it is less about quick fixes than about ways of thinking. . . . The principal aim of the programme is to provide a forum for informed reflection, debate and decision for those in positions of responsibility."

The brochure describes the program as a "part-time research" degree. Modules during the first eighteen months include Insight for Ecology, Ethics and Values, Change and Renewal, and so on, followed by "a rigorous piece of research" that also lasts eighteen months on a part-time basis. "We are offering" this program, claims the brochure, "because management is vital to the survival of organisations, yet we need to be critical of it in order to improve practise in an uncertain future."

---

[15]Whiteley (2001) puts figures for the year 2000 at 5,323 full-time (but only 1,250 of them British), 4,679 part-time (almost all British), and 3,300 distance learning. The average age is just over thirty. In the United States, figures for 2001–2002 reported by 60 percent of the AACSB membership put part-time MBAs at about 60 percent of the total, most coming for evenings and weekends (AACSB 2002:21), and therefore, by taking longer, making up a smaller proportion of graduates.

> Perhaps this is not practical in the conventional sense for the company, but it is most practical for a society that is so inundated with management!

Before discussing key characteristics of these developments—company collaboration, periodic modules, practitioner themes, and participant engagement—alongside examples from specific programs, one caveat. I have a masters degree, but only one. I have not attended any of the programs discussed here, or those described earlier, for that matter, which is really the only way to be sure of what is going on. I have studied their materials and have discussed some of them with knowledgeable people, but designs on paper can be quite different from practice in the classroom. And designs do change; some of these programs may be gone by the time this gets into print, while others more deserving of attention may have appeared. The purpose of this discussion, however, is not to review interesting programs—applicants beware!—so much as to suggest interesting developments that mark a shift from business to management education.

COMPANY COLLABORATION    This book has noted repeatedly that when the learner stays on the job, there is the chance to tie the educational experience to the working environment. Doing a degree while holding a job cannot help but have impact at work—negative in terms of energy but positive in terms of opportunity. So to treat the educational experience as something apart—done on one's own time, for oneself—is not only to lose that opportunity but also to drain away more energy. The learner and the employer both lose. In recognition of this, English companies have been inclined to engage themselves in the educational process—indeed, sometimes beyond what many American universities would accept.

*Consortium* programs are usually offered by one business school in partnership with a set of companies that take responsibility for filling the class. Warwick, Henley, and Lancaster, among others, have offered such masters programs.[16] How the Warwick program developed might come as a surprise in some of the better American schools, which have traditionally insisted on strict academic control: "The initiative came from three original consortium members: National Westminster Bank,

---

[16]CEDEP in France, affiliated with Insead, has also offered such an arrangement for over thirty years, but not as a degree.

BP, and Coopers and Lybrand." They wanted an MBA "focusing on practical applications and integrating their respective corporate management development programs," which they felt could not be done in traditional programs. "After the corporations made their needs known, several universities submitted applications. The Warwick proposal to be the academic member of the consortium was accepted" (Muller et al. 1991:86).

This ceding of considerable control to companies is not uncommon in England. A document about a masters program at the City University of London, circa 1990, stated, "Decisions in the area of fees, curricula, and implementation are vested in the Consortium Board," made up of four people from the university and one representative from each of the six member companies. The consequence of such arrangements can be rather close links. "'Theory-led' but 'practice-driven'" is the phrase used in a Lancaster brochure (2000–2002) for its consortium program, which invites in the line managers of students to explain the program's objectives and how they can help promote the learning. And "assignments are all based on actual situations," so the students can serve as "catalysts for change."

Closer to practice are *company-specific*, or *in-company* programs, where a school offers a degree program to participants from a single company. This, too, is common, increasingly so, although not unknown in the United States.[17] Such programs can, of course, drive corporate change agendas even more directly, but the danger can be a certain inbreeding, as well as possible compromises of academic standards. In the accompanying box, I discuss both of these consequences in terms of two personal experiences with the British Airways MBA run by Lancaster University.

PERIODIC MODULES   To stay on the job, practitioner students need to come to school in convenient blocks of time (unless they only self-study at home). The American EMBA programs have tended to run on evenings or alternate "weekends" (usually Fridays and Saturdays), which restricts participation largely to people nearby. There are programs like that in England, but more popular have been those where people come in modular blocks of one or two weeks' duration. (This should be distinguished from the "modules" of the American programs discussed earlier in the

---

[17] A *Wall Street Journal* article (Scannell 2001) described a Babson MBA offered in Intel with "company-specific cases and projects . . . woven into the curriculum." Another program at Lucent, in existence then for four years, allowed employees to earn a Babson masters degree in finance.

## GOING TOO FAR?

In early 2000, I received a request to submit a proposal for a module on strategy as part of the British Airways MBA program, run mostly at Lancaster University. The module was to be outsourced in a sense. I was not particularly sympathetic to such an approach, but at the urging of Jonathan Gosling of Lancaster as well as a friend who was interested in working on the module, I agreed to draw up a proposal and meet the evaluation committee—two people from Lancaster University and four from British Airways—in what turned out to be "Vendor Selection Day"! At least I would learn something about the process.

Back in 1991, I had given a talk at the British Academy of Management on developments in management education. I referred to some interesting things happening in that country but suggested that some seemed to go too far, and I mentioned MBA programs dedicated to single companies, such as the one for British Airways.

Someone came up to me afterward and introduced himself as Jonathan Gosling of Lancaster University, involved with that program. I should see for myself, he said, and invited me to one of his tutorial group meetings, with a few of his students, as "reflective practitioners" (as Jonathan wrote to me).

The meeting, held two months later, was dedicated mainly to preparing their "Strategy Projects." One concerned BA sourcing in the Far East; a second was about a strategy for Gatwick Airport; a third was on a competitive threat from an American airline. I was impressed with the nature of the topics and how they combined the conceptual thinking of the university with the practical problems of the company. These were not young students venturing into some sort of "real world" to play consultant, or even experienced ones discussing other people's cases. They were managers involved in the issues they were investigating and so were acutely aware of what they did not know.

Gosling was right! Our meeting led to a wonderful collaboration that continues to this day, manifested particularly in the International Masters in Practicing Management program described in Part II of this book. In it, we work closely with the participating companies but retain responsibility for the curriculum decisions: we have no "Vendor Selection Days"!

Incidentally, probably best for all concerned, we were not the "vendor" selected in that 2000 competition. The committee, as their representative reported to us, preferred something more conventional.

chapter, where full-time students do their courses in intense blocks.) Ashridge, for example, in its two-year part-time program, held ten residential modules, two of two weeks, the rest of about one week, interspersed with "in-company development" (1995–1997 brochure).

Coming to class for a full week or two, compared with evenings or weekends, allows for more concentration on studies. The students tend to be less tired and can get more deeply into the material. Of course, there is more time away from work, but these durations have not proved to be very disruptive. Most important, this format encourages the making of serious connections between the students' experience, fresh on the minds and soon to be renewed, and the concepts of the classroom. Here, in fact, is where some of the really significant innovations in English management education can be found.

PRACTITIONER THEMES    As discussed in Chapters 2 and 3, the dominant framework of the conventional MBA—around the business functions—has established a stranglehold on most MBA programs. Yet many experienced managers seek further education as they are coming out of these silos. Accordingly, a number of the English schools have broken away from them and organized around themes closer to managerial practice. For example, some of the modules in that Ashridge program were Global Business Environment; Achieving Operational Effectiveness; Business and Society and Implementing Change (1995–1996 brochure). Here and there around the world, other interesting frameworks can be found as well. The University of Capetown offers a fascinating EMBA in South Africa, which seeks to synthesize systems thinking with action learning. Managers focus on issues in the field while learning from each other in the classroom. Managerial activities are seen in three domains: value adding (using resources and capabilities efficiently), innovative, or strategic (sustaining the capacity to create value), and normative (long-term legitimacy, identity, and viability), developed in six modules. The MBA program at Sabanci University in Istanbul divides its first year into Globalization, Competition, Networking, Meaning

Management, Organizational Structuring, Product Management, Research Management, and Value Creation Management (2001–2002 description).

Another thematic approach, less cohesive but more practical, focuses program activities around current issues in practice. In the mid-1990s, for example, the EMBA program at ESCP, another of the French grandes écoles, scheduled sixteen weekend "workshops" of ten hours each on topics such as debureaucratizing the enterprise, defining the relationships between headquarters and subsidiaries, and establishing a European strategy.

The importance of these thematic reconceptions is that they see the world from the practitioners' perspective, rather than imposing a structure that suits the academics. There are two dangers, however. On one hand, the themes can be too general (e.g., Investigating the Future): it is easy enough, especially for academics, to come up with nicely labeled themes.[18] On the other hand, the themes can be too applied (e.g., total quality management), too close to practice to encourage the necessary probing beyond the obvious. Chapter 10 discusses a thematic framework that was designed to avoid both these dangers.

All of these characteristics—company collaboration, periodic modules, and practitioner themes—facilitate a shift from business to management education, but a fourth characteristic, concerning the pedagogy of the classroom, is necessary to ensure it.

PARTICIPANT ENGAGEMENT    It is when the educational process shifts from the teaching of the instructor to the learning of the student that real change happens. This requires a radical shift in pedagogy, beyond the "participation" of students in case discussions and field projects, and in a direction opposite that of the new technologies discussed earlier. The pedagogy has to become more engaging, more personal, and especially more customized. And here again, the English schools have been in the forefront.

At its limit—and that limit has to be approached to be appreciated—this kind of pedagogy gives experienced "participants" significant responsibility for their own learning, in its design as well as its execution. Pushing concepts onto (or into) the student may be appropriate for some structured material. But as noted earlier, management itself is not very

---

[18]Including ones that simply combine the traditional functions. As noted earlier, cross-functional is still functional. A dead giveaway of this is a matrix in the program materials that maps the new themes onto the old functions. A truly thematic curriculum gets past the old categories rather than rearranges them.

structured, and managers hardly learn in such passive ways. Active learning happens when the learner *pulls* new ideas into his or her realm of experience—to connect them, see them in context, use them naturally.

Two steps in this regard can be found in various business schools in England. The first uses some kind of *Action Learning* assignments on the job. We have already seen examples of this in the British Airways MBA projects and the University of Bath company studies. The participants choose what to do, perhaps in consultation with their managers, and do it in their companies. But as Thirunarayana (1992) has pointed out, they needn't make an actual change; they can also learn through investigation of some live issues.

Action Learning projects carried out by teams of practitioners have, of course, become very popular in nondegree management development programs, especially in the United States, as in General Electric's famous "Work Out" program. But as we shall see in the next chapter, too many of these have become exercises in action more than learning.

Second, under what is sometimes called *self-managed learning*, responsibility for much of the learning is turned over to the participants themselves, beyond just selecting assignments or projects. In its "Management MBA" (the title of which says something), the City University of London some years ago took customization rather far. "The workplace is the center of focus," said the brochure (1994), "not the campus," and so "the course is as mobile as the participants." First, "each student undergoes a rigorous process of assessment . . . to suit [the training to] the individual's needs." Then a few projects, "usually three," serve as the "central core" of the program, by which the knowledge and skills learned "are immediately put into practice." With the brochure's claim that "academics do not have the monopoly in business acumen" but that practitioners are often "the best people to help develop" the necessary skills, we find ourselves quite a long way from those game theory courses at Stanford, let alone the five hundred cases at Harvard!

How all of these things work—indeed, how well any of them work—only the participants can reveal. I have come across no systematic research on this. But these innovations can certainly help us consider more powerful ways to develop managers, as shall be discussed in several chapters in the next part of the book.

## A Tale of Two Programs

Let me conclude this discussion by contrasting two programs, both of which used a number of these innovations, but only one in a fully committed way. I experienced the first when I worked briefly with one of its classes some years ago; I followed the second over time through discussions with people involved, particularly a long-standing director.

In Dublin, the Irish Management Institute, in conjunction with Trinity College, offers an M.Sc. in Management Practice. This is a two-year program whose "object is to bring senior management through real-time general management development, centered around their own jobs and organizations" (Web site, 2003). Between ten and twelve people are accepted each year, and at this stage close to 250 have graduated. The participants are awarded the degree after submitting a thesis in which they have carried out a strategic analysis of their organization in its environment, have developed a change strategy for some aspect of the organization, and have described "the interventions made, progress achieved, and what has been learned from the experience (both specific and general)." To get a flavor of the authenticity of the initiatives, here are a few examples.

"Strategy Formation in a High Technology Irish Company" was written by a vice president at the end of the dot.com era. An attempt to redirect the company failed for various reasons, and these were explored. "Colonel to General—Why the Battlefield Looks Different" was written by the operations manager of a multinational subsidiary making the transition to the role of general manager. The HR director of an airline documented the management of change in the period of unprecedented uncertainty after September 11 and drew conclusions at a corporate and personal level.

Throughout the program, the emphasis is on "application of what is being learned to the individual's organization and job." Each month, participants submit a report that uses the ideas in the readings to describe their job and organization. There are also a number of seminars, averaging two days each, spanning two years, on strategy, financial analysis, organizational design, management of change, and others. Between seminars intense tutoring/mentoring takes place one to one.

I found it stimulating to work with this class. I recall one particularly articulate "student" bursting with interesting ideas and fully conversant with the theory—he was second in command at a major Irish utility company. He would have been a wonderful addition at a Stanford or a Wharton. But would it have been equally beneficial to him?

Not far away, in geography at least, was the MBA program developed at Cambridge University in the early 1990s. The ideas were innovative, but they went halfway, as a kind of hybrid between the conventional MBA and the programs described above.

This program also was directed at people on the job, but young ones, "typically in their mid-twenties." And in the original design they had to leave their jobs for long periods—nine to ten weeks in each of three years. There was an action learning component, too, but its very statement suggested a certain hesitation, pointing out, "Most of the students taking part in this course will not yet be in positions of significant management responsibility," but "even a share of responsibility" constitutes "a managerial component on which" to build learning. Elsewhere the brochure mentioned the program's "strong project orientation . . . [each] based on a real life management situation." No need to mention "real life" in Dublin! The course work was organized in themes called Foundation for Managing, Integrative Managing, and Managing in Context, with a good deal of conventional functional study.

This design ran into difficulty for some obvious reasons: disruptively long periods of time away from the job and many of the students too young to appreciate management or to get the endorsement of their employers. So over time the program was watered down, to the point where the Cambridge brochure for the year 2000 focused on a rather conventional one-year full-time MBA, and it mentioned the "Two Year Integrated" program, where the students take "a year off to work . . . either with your original employer or a different one" before returning to their studies.

## THE GREAT DIVIDE IN THE MB/A

This chapter in general, and these two stories in particular, indicate that there is a kind of knife-edge in graduate MB/A education. On one side is B: specialization in the *business* functions, mostly for younger people with little experience, whether recognized as such in the specialized European programs or not in the conventional MBA programs. And on the other side is A, for *administration*, meaning management: programs designed to educate practicing managers in context, and so adopting a wholly different approach.

Not only does there not seem to be a middle ground between the two, but the recent "innovations" described in the chapter seem to have driven them farther apart. On one side have been the new technological pedagogies, the efforts at internationalization, and the teaching of soft skills that, if anything, have taken the conventional programs even deeper into their analytical orientations and further away from managerial practice. And on the other side are the serious innovations of the programs for experienced managers, which show the way toward authentic management education.

We shall pick up on the latter in Chapter 9, where the conclusions of this chapter will be ordered into a set of propositions for the educational development of practicing managers. This will be followed in Chapters 10 through 14 by the description of a family of programs developed to bring these propositions to life. But first we need to take a trip to the other side of the process, to survey activities for the development of managers outside of formal education. There we shall see the benefits of combining the best ideas of management development with the true innovations in management education.

### PART TWO

# Developing Managers

I N THE SECOND part of this book, picking up on the ending of the first, we change focus, from conventional educational programs concerned with specialized skills to developmental activities to improve the practice of managing. We also change tone, from critical to constructive: from the problems of what are to the opportunities for what can be.

Part II contains eight chapters. Chapter 8 reviews management development practice, within and without the managers' own organizations. There is a richness here that begs to be married with management education. Chapter 9 suggests how this marriage might take place, in principle, while Chapters 10 through 14 show how it has taken place in practice, in a family of programs developed by a team of colleagues and myself. The final chapter of this book calls for renewal of the business schools—for some real development of their own—to become true management schools.

# 8

# MANAGEMENT DEVELOPMENT
# IN PRACTICE

*We all want mass customized action learning
for the individual.*
—HEINZ THANHEISER

From management education, we turn here to management development—something quite different, unfortunately. While the organizations that employ the managers rarely get involved in their education, beyond hiring and sometimes sponsoring them as students, they do take the lead in their development. This has resulted in more variety, and so more experimentation, also more practicality, and so more superficiality, too. But there is a great deal of thoughtful practice in management development, and the best of it should be informing management education more than it has.

## MAPPING MANAGEMENT EDUCATION
## AND DEVELOPMENT

Figure 8.1 provides a map to locate the various components of management education and development, as well as the various actors. Out of the left, from the business schools, comes the *push* of *management*

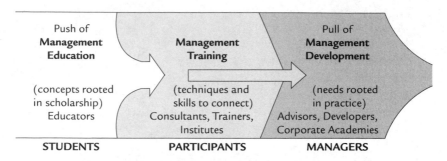

FIGURE 8.1

Map of Management Education and Development

*education*, with its theories, concepts, and so forth, offered to those who enroll. Mostly, therefore, people are educated outside the practice they are subsequently hired into, or return back to. This even applies to many of the shorter programs for managers, which are often designed as miniature replicas of degree programs—less intense, but not much more connected. Even the best-known business schools—or perhaps I should say especially the best-known ones—tend to tone down their academic materials rather than rethinking them for a different audience, offering them generically to whoever enrolls. Many schools certainly make claims about customization, but all too often that means the selection of components from a generic pool.[1]

Into the right of the diagram is the *pull* of *management development*, as organizations draw on whatever they find appropriate to further the development of their managers. Increasingly, in search of real customization, they do it themselves.

Between these two sits *management training*, offered by independent trainers, consultants, and various institutes. Often they develop their own practical repertoires of techniques, skills, and so forth; sometimes they adopt materials from the business schools.

An article in the *Financial Times* (Wood 2000) describes consulting courses as oriented to "tactical knowledge," more "vocational" than "academic." But there is quite a wide variety of offerings in this middle ground. Some course providers, such as the Center for Creative Leadership and the Aspen Institute, both in the United States, go beyond training, sometimes into rather unusual development, and on to education.

---

[1] A recent article in the *Financial Times* (Bradshaw 2003c) highlights a shift to "custom" programs but also quotes the heads of executive education at Harvard and Wharton about their enthusiasm for "open" (or public) programs; both schools had, in fact, recently added a number of new such programs even in the face of a declining market for them.

At their best, the providers in the middle connect both ways, acting as transmitters or cross pollinators, between the ideas of inquiry on one side and the needs of application on the other. They are able to see more clearly into practice than many of the academics and more broadly across practice than many of the companies. To the conceptual insights of scholars, they can add a greater facility with technique and a greater capacity to develop skills. At worst, however, they sit in a kind of no man's land, promoting disconnected technique as a kind of idealized "one best way."

Likewise, at its best management education connects with management development: push from the left joins pull from the right. Some of the English programs discussed in the last chapter are good examples of this. But mostly, as discussed in Chapter 2, management education sits worlds apart from management development. The broad conclusion that can be drawn from this is that while management development may rarely educate, management education rarely develops. That is unfortunate, because they are most powerful when they work in concert.

This second part of the book shifts our attention from push toward pull, more exactly from the push of conventional management education, criticized in Part I, to the combination of push and pull in management educational development. As can be seen in the accompanying box, this is not a new idea.

## DOWNHILL EVER SINCE?

*In* The Republic, *[Plato] set out his vision for training leaders for the ideal political state. Starting with good raw material, he felt, was critical to the success of his program. . . . But he also believed that training and work experiences were critical. His candidates . . . would undergo rigorous studies of arithmetic and geometry, with a healthy dose of athletics for balance. Afterward came work experience in public office or the military. This was accompanied by in-depth studies in philosophy. . . . Throughout their many years of preparation, Plato would have tested the candidates to determine which ones should advance to the next level of study and work experience. Finally, at age fifty—yes, fifty—Plato's candidates would be ready to rule. (Conger 1992:37–38)[2]*

Plato's dream never came to pass. But we do keep trying!

[2]Conger opens his article with this Plato quote and closes it with another: "Aristotle said he could do it in two [years]. His pupil was Alexander the Great" (64). But that still took two years!

This chapter reviews practice in management development. The discussion is not comprehensive—that would take another book (see, e.g., McCauley et al. 1998)—but rather seeks to identify and draw out the main approaches that can be considered in designing more effective management education. The five identified here are labeled Sink or Swim; Moving, Mentoring, and Monitoring; the Management Development Buffet Table (about courses); Learning in Action; and the Corporate Academies. The conclusion is that the interesting things happen not so much within any of these approaches as at the interfaces of them.

# "Sink or Swim"

Ask a group of managers, as I often have, what happened the day they first became managers, and the response is almost inevitably the same: a look of puzzlement, a shrugging of the shoulders, and then the common reply: "Nothing."[3] "Did they at least give you an article to read on managing?" I ask. "No." Management is treated like sex: You'll figure it out. And the initial results are frequently similar: all sorts of dire, unexpected consequences.

Being promoted from engineering the products to managing the engineers, or from delivering babies to chief of obstetrics, is quantum change. The tasks are wholly different. "I didn't have the slightest idea what my job was. I walked in giggling and laughing because I had been promoted and had no idea what principles or style to be guided by. After the first day I felt like I had run into a brick wall."

This comment is included in Linda Hill's (1992:15) insightful book, *Becoming a Manager*. Her topic, incidentally, is as rare in the literature as training is for new managers in practice—hardly anyone seems much to care. We talk endlessly about management, yet when it most matters, we do and write almost nothing about it. There may be something instinctive about managing, but it has to be learned, too, not just by doing it but by being able to gain conceptual insight *while* doing it. "The new managers obviously had their work cut out for them: Learning how to

---

[3] "Constable and McCormick (1987) estimate that of some 130,000 entrants to 'management' [in Britain] in any year . . . most . . . will receive either no formal introduction to the elements of business or will wait until mid-career at which stage over one-third will still receive nothing" (Mayon-White 1990:xiii).

be a manager was a formidable task. They have to make sense of complex, often conflicting, and demanding expectations" (47).

It is not surprising, therefore, that the most common management development practice, "sink or swim," ends up with a lot of sinking and not much swimming—and that more like splashing about frantically. (See the accompanying box.)

---

### SINKING AND SWIMMING IN MANAGEMENT

*(from Tony J. Watson,* In Search of Management *(1994:159)*

"I wouldn't regard myself as someone who has ever been trained to be a manager. I was thrown in at the deep end when I began. I didn't know how I was going to survive—sink or swim, like. I suppose I knew I could hack it at the end of the day though, using my native wits and all that. I think I soon learned to manage."

"To manage?"

"To keep my head above water. Oh I didn't mean to 'be a manager' in the sense you are talking about. I mean just surviving to the end of the week, or the month more like, without getting into too much trouble or upsetting too many folk."

"But is that really different from 'being a manager'?"

"Perhaps it isn't. I don't know. I must admit that in spite of all the courses I've been on and all that management book stuff that I've swallowed, I still rely on my wits, my devastating charm, to do the job. Sometimes I think I haven't learned anything and other times I think that I am learning all the time. I don't think I am as likely to sink beneath the tide as I might have been early on."

"You're a better swimmer than you were?"

"I like that: learning to manage is like learning to swim. It's sort of instinctive but you still need to learn; perhaps not learn, but become more confident. Yes, you get confidence as you try out different things."

---

Of course, no one starts with nothing. New managers have had their own managers, if not as role models then at least as examples of what managers do. But seeing this from outside that office is hardly the same as experiencing it within. And most new managers continue to have their own managers, who can help them—more or less—as mentors. Sometimes this is done seriously, even formally, which can render the learning a kind of apprenticeship. But more often it just becomes "get what you can from whomever you can."

Moreover, every manager is welcome to *self-develop* on his or her private time—buy a cassette, read a book, take a course, do a degree. In the United States, development is now seen increasingly as a personal responsibility. In this world of easy come, easy go, if you lose your job and cannot find a new one, that's your fault. So be prepared.

But by so separating the learner from the organization, the learning becomes separated from the practice, emotionally as well as conceptually. Managing thus gets treated as just another job, like programming a computer, rather than the essential glue that holds organizations together.

All managers certainly have to function in a world of sink or swim. But there are ways to help the swimming. We look at four in particular, concerning on-the-job development, course work, action learning, and more intensive formal development in corporate academies.

# Moving, Mentoring, and Monitoring

If management is a practice, then some sort of apprenticeship has to figure prominently in how it is learned. In other words, some formal learning should happen significantly on the job. In this respect, management is no different from any other complex work. Even surgeons, for example, despite extensive educating, need a great deal of developing on the job.

For the most part, organizations today do not encourage much apprenticing, at least in a formal sense. But under the label "on the job training," or OJT, some interesting things do happen. I discuss two in particular: systematic moving of "high potential" managers to maximize their opportunities for self-learning, and mentoring, or coaching, by more experienced managers to help this process along.

## McCall for Moving

Morgan McCall (1988; also McCall et al. 1988) has emphasized moving people about, "rotating" them, to facilitate learning. Key for developing managers, he and his colleagues believe, are "the lessons of experience" (97), a point supported by Ohlott (1998), who cites research indicating that managers "consider job experiences as *the* primary source of learning. . . . Executives were asked to identify crucial events in their development as leaders. Their stories showed that they felt they learned more from influential people at work and from the challenges inherent in their jobs than from formal training programs and other nonwork experiences" (128).

McCall (1988) especially emphasizes such challenges in the assignment of jobs. He refers to a study in one major company that "found a significant relationship between early job challenge . . . and subsequent managerial success" (2):

> In many of their significant learning experiences, managers came into the situation with *at least one missing trump*. They routinely faced unfamiliar functions, businesses, products, or technologies, sometimes they were too young, had the "wrong" background, or had to master computerese or financialese or legalese. Some found themselves in foreign countries, unable to speak the language or communicate with the people they managed. In all these cases, the challenge was not to let the missing trumps do them in; the development was in learning how to work around a significant disadvantage. (5)

"Meeting these challenges left little choice but to learn and develop new abilities." Accordingly, "development came from the inside," which led McCall to state his "first rule": "Development is not something you can do to or for someone. Development is something people do for themselves" (5). But his "second rule" is that challenge can be provided to encourage this self-development, notably by rotating people through a series of challenging jobs that stretch their abilities: from managing a start-up to learn about "providing strong direction in the face of ambiguity," to managing the turnaround of an existing business to learn about "overcoming resistance and incompetence" (9). Likewise, "small strategic assignments" can "shock" people "out of a parochial point of view by requiring them to go from an operational to a strategic perspective" (McCall's colleagues, Lombardo and Eichinger 1989:9). And, of course, international assignments help to broaden perspectives. Overall, "hardships" teach "because they tell us something about our limits." McCall adds, "In our research, managers told of making mistakes, getting stuck in dead-end jobs, having to fire people, and enduring the traumas of life. These events often caused managers to look inward and reflect on their humanity, their resilience, and their flaws" (3).

## BOETTINGER FOR MENTORING

Mentors, coaches, role models—call them what you like—can help all this along. "Having a good boss seemed to matter most in a manager's first supervisory job and in big scope jobs," especially "if they modeled an exceptional skill or attribute" (McCall 1988:4).

Such roles are viewed as rather informal in much of the practice as well as some of the literature (e.g., Fox 1997). An early and vigorous championing of formal apprenticeship, however, came in a 1975 *Harvard Business Review* article entitled "Is Management Really an Art?" written by Henry Boettinger, the Director of Corporate Planning at AT&T. "Intuition alone is insufficient for even amateur performance in the conventional arts," he claimed. Proficiency takes years of developing, through "methods . . . handed down from teacher to pupil . . . virtually never arrived at instinctively or without practice" (55). And "only someone who can actually perform or can act is qualified to teach it," Boettinger wrote. In management, however, compared with "the other arts," this does not get started at an early age, with young people working by the master. Boettinger did cite an exception, which he considered an ideal: the early days of the Indian civil service, where new members were associated with experienced ones, "who instructed them in their duties. The mentor gave them progressively [more] difficult missions, extricated them when they were over their heads, wrote confidential reports on their progress, and made recommendations for new assignments designed to develop strengths and eliminate weaknesses" (59).

Boettinger did make one distinction between some of those other arts and management which brought him to a conclusion quite opposite to that of McCall. "When the tools and materials of an art are inanimate, as in sculpture . . . development is a personal activity," whereas in management, where the "personalities, talents, and efforts" of others are at stake, "the education of its members becomes a social responsibility of the institution itself" (57). As Raelin (2000) puts it, in support of Boettinger's position, moving alone leaves the learning to the individual, whereas moving with mentoring turns it into a social process, which can make it more effective. He points out, for example, that stretch assignments, however challenging, do not necessarily give the manager much chance to reflect with others on the learning. "Experience, in other words, tends to teach in private, reinforcing the notion that learning [in organizations] is done individually, not collectively" (18).

While mentoring has long existed as an informal process, more formalized "coaching" has become popular in recent years. At least the word has become popular, and programs to encourage it. As Cappelli

(2000:22) notes in an excellent review article on employee commitment, there has been a decline in internal mentoring accompanied by an "exploding" rise in coaches and mentors for hire, by the managers personally. Yet there are interesting exceptions, one of which is discussed in the accompanying box.

## Mentoring, Red Cross Style

Some years ago, we held a meeting of management development people from companies involved in our masters program. We started with a go-around, and people from various large corporations described their elaborate efforts to develop managers. Then it came the turn of the representative from the International Federation of Red Cross and Red Crescent Societies (which sends teams into disaster areas for relief work). She apologized for what seemed to be their rather meager effort—not many courses, not much headquarters activity.

As it happened, I had recently spent time at one of their refugee camps in Tanzania, and I disagreed. The Red Cross was probably the most active developer of managers in that room, I suggested; it just took a very different form. Attached to each of its own "delegate" managers, in Tanzania and often elsewhere, was a "counterpart" member of the local Red Cross Society who worked alongside these more experienced managers to be trained by them. The delegates I observed spent a great deal of time working with their counterparts. This mentoring arrangement may have been somewhat informal, but it was personal and powerful. (See Mintzberg 2001, also *Depressing is hardly the word* under stories, on mintzberg.org.)

## Everyone for Monitoring

Assessment, on the other hand—monitoring the managers' performance, as well as determining their needs—tends to be carried out much more commonly and much more systematically. The tendency here is to focus on some popular technique, such as "360-degree feedback" from people all around the manager. As Milan, Kurb, and Prokopenko pointed out back in 1989 (79), the variety of relevant techniques for needs assessment alone is wide: tests and examinations, questionnaires, interviews, observation, diaries, self-assessment, management by objectives, and so on, in addition to performance appraisals and assessment centers. The literature on monitoring is likewise vast, but since the issues are somewhat aside from the concerns of the book, and well covered elsewhere, I shall not discuss them here (although I do have some things to say in Chapter 13 about numerical measures applied to management development).

## OJT IN JAPAN

Boettinger (1975:8) pointed out that successful companies allow—indeed encourage—their managers to take risks and make mistakes. In these, "movement across organizational boundaries occurs regularly and easily," and development of executive talent is accepted "as a line responsibility." Such companies recognize that "'growing' a general manager" takes time, and there are no shortcuts" (9).

Nowhere is this better appreciated than in Japan. As Handy et al. (1988) point out, on-the-job training (OJT) "is a Japanese maxim." Managing, the Japanese believe, can "only be learnt by watching, listening to, and practicing under one's older and more experienced colleagues." Accordingly, "Japan has elevated the mentoring role into a formal requirement of every manager," aided by open office seating that "allows potential managers to observe their superiors, especially under stress" (5, 14, 33). More important still is the whole practice by which people commonly grow into managers in Japan. The "Japanese firm hires people right out of school, trains all of them in various jobs through a carefully worked out system of job rotation, supplementing this on-the-job training with short in-firm or extra-mural courses" (Locke 1996a:140).

Okazaki-Ward (1993) has specified this practice in great detail in *Management Education and Training in Japan.* "Systematic in-company management training" really became prominent after 1945. The great *zaibatsu* firms had in fact been recruiting their key managers straight from the university into lifetime employment since the late nineteenth century, but aside from rotation, these people were left to themselves to acquire the necessary skills (18). After the war, however, in-company education for managers became more prominent, while job rotation remained key. "In some large companies employing more than 10,000, as many as 500 of the managers are moved at one time. Apart from the developmental aspect . . . [this rotation] allows individuals to form a wide inter-personal network within the organization" (72). Okazaki-Ward believes that these moves were planned by the personnel department two or three postings ahead. One survey of *katzo* (middle managers) found that 78 percent of firms used "developmental rotation to a firm in a different industry" (140).

From a Western perspective, this may seem excessive, even obsessive. McCall (1988) has written:

> Elegant formal systems do not guarantee effective executive development practice. Rigid career paths, forced mentoring and coaching programs, lock-step rotation plans, catalogs of training programs, and elaborate succession planning tables may actually be counter-productive. Our studies suggest that the development of executive talent is highly individualized. (11)

But the United States is an individual-centered society, and Japan is not. In fact, companies all over the world engage in these practices, even if rarely as systematically and comprehensively as in Japan. Moving, mentoring, and monitoring probably remains the most common form of management development today.

## THE MD BUFFET TABLE

*Off*-the-job are the available courses and programs—opportunities galore to study formally. These are offered by consulting firms, development institutes, public providers, business schools, and companies themselves; they are offered on site, on disk, on the Web, and on screen, big and small. Offerings vary in style, too, from strobe-light courses that flash by some technique, skill, or angle in a few hours to programs running several months that replicate the MBA.

Overall, this constitutes a giant management development buffet table from which managers and their organizations can choose—a little bit of this and a little bit of that, or else a plate piled high with one or two dishes (Meister 1994:19). Some years ago, I looked at the prospectus of the Civil Service College of the British Government. It looked like the telephone book of a small city, running to more than three hundred pages and including hundreds of courses, from "Econometrics" to "Setting the Direction for the Organisation."

Let us take a look at some common practices here, including leadership courses in general and business school offerings in particular. But first some clarification of key terms.

## ENTERTAINING, TEACHING,
## TRAINING, AND LEARNING

Many courses, perhaps more than most people care to admit, do little more than *entertain*. Managers are supposed to sit back passively and be mesmerized by the performances at the front, better still, on a screen. From this they may walk away dazzled, only to wonder the next day what that was all about. Vail (1989) suggests in eloquent words that there is an element of such superficial entertainment in too much management development:

> The "entertainment factor" has skyrocketed in the world of work over the course of my career, but I don't think it has enhanced the quality of what is being presented very much. In fact, I would say that as we have sought to make our graphics more "professional" and our "platform skills" more stylish, we have had to trivialize content. I wonder if participants realize the shallowness of the content they're getting in the midst of all this glitzy instrumentation. Or let me put it a little more fairly: the trouble with some carefully crafted slide presentation, or an elaborate computer-based interactive exercise, or a book that is really an indoctrination machine even though it looks like a book, is that participants can't have a conversation about it or with it. They can't modify it. They can't affect it, teach IT anything. All they can do is experience it from the outside as a closed system . . . they are no longer participants—they are passive consumers *even if the system is interactive!*

By this token, most management development programs, even when based on live lectures or case discussions rather than fancy technologies, amount to entertainment, because the "participants" can't teach them anything. Since the designs are predetermined, the managers must simply consume them. And because the half-life of learning tends to be short (Whetten and Clark 1996:162), they must keep coming back for more, like drug addicts in search of another high.[4]

Entertainment is often the chief criterion by which programs are evaluated. Because the important questions—"What did you learn?"

---

[4]Worse than courses as entertainment, perhaps, but increasingly popular are what might be called "corporate revival meetings," in which hundreds of employees are herded into some large room where they are supposed to be reborn by executives performing on a stage, singing (sometimes literally) the praises of the company. Much of this tells us about the dismal state of corporate leadership.

and "Will it make a difference?"—are difficult to answer, instead people are often asked, in effect, "Were you impressed?" The result can be a confounding of teaching with preaching.

Not much better is a confounding of *teaching* with learning. This happens when students and managers are treated as vessels to be filled. Pour it in, and they have learned it. Using another metaphor, Sue Purves, who headed up executive development at Zeneca, has described this approach to management development as "spray and pray": "We expose people to all sorts of things and hope for the best." Thus the President of the World Bank said in 1997 that he was sending three hundred of his best managers to business school to get a customer orientation (reported in *The Economist*, June 7, 1997). Hopefully they focused on what the faculty said rather than what the school did.

*Training* gets closer to the individual, specifically to his or her competencies. Training courses can be intensive and therefore expensive: for few people, over a number of days, on one subject, such as project management, negotiation, or the management of time.

Last but certainly not least comes *learning*, where the focus is on what the recipient learns, not what the "instructors" teach. That means he or she is involved, in deciding what is to be learned as well as how. The difference between learning and teaching can be rather subtle, and I know of hardly any teacher, no matter how directive, who does not believe that he or she is stimulating learning. But I do know many of their students who are not so sure. (More on teaching versus learning in the next chapter.)

Robert Fulmer, in a 1997 paper entitled "The Evolving Paradigm of Leadership Development," describes leadership programs in the "old days" (60). Participants arrived not knowing what to expect and were handed a series of books and an agenda, specifying hour by hour what was to be learned. Lots of blank paper suggested that the person should listen and take notes. Later came another program, appropriate to the next stage of development. All these programs, in his view, constituted a kind of "slalom course" (62)—in effect, more teaching than learning. But these old days are "passé" (60), writes Fulmer; in "the new world, participants listen occasionally, interact frequently in simulated situations to test their skills or understanding, and frequently spend a significant portion of time demonstrating their ability to apply concepts to real challenges" (60).

But how passé do these old days seem to the many people who still arrive to agendas and schedules and blank sheets of paper? And how much better is a good deal of this new world? Uninformed sharing, for example, is hardly an improvement over passive listening. There is one program that restricted invited experts to seven minutes on their given topic, so that the senior executives could get on with their own comments. The fact that some professors are inclined to talk too much does not excuse the fact that some executives are not inclined to listen enough. At least on complex issues, as, for example, in this program "the evolution of the world economy," the purpose of getting people together for development is neither to fill them full of concepts nor to provide them with an opportunity to talk; it is to stimulate learning at the interface of these two: where concepts, seriously presented, meet experiences, deeply lived.

## CUSTOMIZATION

*Customization* is another term that requires clarification. There are courses that are offered individually, for example, through cassettes, CD-ROMs, and on the Web. Most of the rest bring people together in groups. That does not necessarily mean that they learn together, only that they sit together. Many such courses still treat learning as a personal activity.

Courses that one does alone, at home—so-called "distance learning" ones—are usually designed to be *generic*: the design, the material, and the delivery have all been predetermined, regardless of who happens to be sitting in front of the book or the screen. That suits their very nature. But so, too, is the design of many classroom courses, and it doesn't suit their nature—indeed, it forgoes immense opportunity.

The generic approach has been called "plug and play," whether literally in the case of a cassette or figuratively for a live instructor doing a canned lecture, case, or exercise. This often happens even when a course has been designed for a particular group—for example, sales managers or aerospace managers. They all sit there passively getting the same thing. Think of these courses as equivalent to the market segmentation of cereals: you choose your box, but what you get inside is standardized.

The opposite of this is *customization,* which in its true sense means that the contents of the box adjust to your particular needs *then and there*. This may not be practical for cereals, but it makes a lot of sense in management development, for two reasons.

One is that needs vary, not only across industries, companies, and jobs, but also across individuals and time. In other words, everyone settling in a management development classroom has his or her own needs at that particular point in time. Sure, there are general needs across groups, even across all managers, and these deserve a prominent place in every management classroom. But not alone: the material also has to be tailored to needs that only the individual can appreciate, and therefore incorporate into his or her own learning.

The second reason for customization relates to the point made at the outset of this book, that deep managing and deep learning depend on personal engagement, not just on a detached expertise that "knows better." So managers learn most profoundly when they have significant responsibility for all aspects of the learning process, including its design.

"We have stopped sending our executives to business school. It is frustrating to learn about the marketing of Listerine mouthwash and have what is of primary interest to us treated as an aside," one executive told *Strategy & Business* magazine (Crainer and Dearlove 1999:38). Accordingly, there is now a big demand for customized offerings—programs for the "critical few," as Nancy Badore has put it, instead of the "critical mass."

Business schools long resisted this. As Porter and McKibbin pointed out in their 1988 report, a few of the schools they interviewed claimed to be "quite willing to attempt to accommodate any reasonable request of this nature"—hardly an enthusiastic embracement of customization—while "some other schools" replied that they would not "tailor-make courses" to single companies but instead "offer an array of predetermined programs and leave it up to individual firms to decide whether or not to send their managers" (332). No school would dare make such a claim today. But most do just that. Indeed, even much of the "customization" they offer turns out to be another form of standardization, where standard components are assembled to order. This is like putting together a stereo system: The company gets these lectures and those cases plus an outdoor exercise or two. Even courses customized for a single company—for example, by using cases written about itself—do not go far enough because everyone gets the same thing. To repeat, it is only when the dynamic of the classroom responds to the people present that customization becomes a reality. Think of a house designed by the architect for the family in question or an advertising campaign developed by an agency for one company at one point in time.

But full customization has to go further than that architecturally designed house; it has to respond to the wishes and ideas of these who live in it. So think not of the design of the frame but of its interior decorating. There is continual adapting as it goes along, according to its inhabitants' needs. In a similar way, the truly customized program taps the collective consciousness in the classroom, to stimulate an atmosphere of shared learning. The participants help define the learning agenda; they raise new issues as the learning progresses (*so that* the learning can progress), and they share each others' experiences extensively. This takes them from the passive world of teaching to the active world of learning, which means that "instructors" have to cede a good deal of the control over the classroom to people who are not "students." The accompanying box offers an example of this.

## A CUSTOMIZED EXPERIENCE

I decided some years ago that when asked to do an in-house program, I would suggest a workshop on actual issues faced by the organization. I found that everyone, myself included, learned better that way. When I made the request of David Frances, who was working with Don Young at the Thorn-EMI group in the United Kingdom, I got more than I expected.

The participants were a group of practitioners in organizational development from various divisions of the company. They had been using my book on organizational structuring, so there was a common base of conceptual material. Three division managers, from Computer Software, Lighting, and Music and Distribution Services, each drew up a kind of live case, essentially a collection of materials on structural issues they were facing. The participants read this material in advance, and then, to begin each of three half-day sessions, the division manager outlined the issue, finishing with a series of questions. The class then split into smaller groups to discuss them, after which they presented their recommendations to the division manager and me. The two of us then engaged in a discussion, the division manager drawing on his understanding of the issue and I on concepts that could be used to deal with it. What emerged was an intriguing combination of learning and fishbowl consulting, which helped drive home the conceptual materials, showing how they might be applied, while making some progress on the issues themselves.

Generic programs are designed to give "the word"—the latest technique, current thinking. They are "managerially correct" in that they offer the established views. This can impart information, but it does not stimulate deep learning. Customized programs, in contrast, shake people up, to unfreeze established views and promote reflection. Of course, managers need both in their development. The problem is that they get plenty of the current thinking, but much less chance to "suspend their disbeliefs," to put under scrutiny so much of that managerial correctness, in order to become more thoughtful.

## LEADERSHIP PROGRAMS

Let us take a closer look at some specific kinds of programs, beginning with the highly popular offerings in leadership. I should note that few, even of the most interesting programs discussed here, are customized in the way I have described.

Leadership is a tricky business. Perhaps that is because no one is quite sure what it is, also because successful leadership practice can vary so much from one situation to another. But that has hardly discouraged courses and programs—even back in 1994, *Fortune* found them offered by six hundred outfits in the United States alone, ranging from a $29 book to a $65,000 speech (Huey 1994:54).

Jay Conger (1992, 1996) has provided a useful review of the formal programs by taking several of them himself and interviewing 150 fellow participants along the way. He discusses four types:

- *Personal growth.* "Profoundly influenced by the ideas of the humanistic psychologies of the 1960s and the 1970s, these programs argue that most managers are ignoring an inner call to realize their potential to become leaders. If they could get in touch with their innermost desires and abilities, more managers could transform themselves into leaders" (1992:46). So off they go to engage in outdoor physical activities and indoor psychological exercises. "What does jumping off a cliff have to do with leadership?" Conger asked. It empowers you to take risks and responsibilities, he was told, puts you in touch with your passions. "'If you can leap from this cliff, imagine what you can do back at the office' goes this thinking" (1996:53). Mostly Conger was not impressed. He concludes that "personal growth programs tended to improve participants' personal lives far more than their work lives" (55).

- *Feedback.* The premise in these programs is that "through effective feedback processes, we can learn about our [latent] strengths and weaknesses in a number of leadership skills" (1992:52). Experimental exercises are used and feedback given, informally by peers or through formal instruments; psychologists may also observe behaviors and comment. Conger found that such programs "can indeed produce very positive outcomes for some participants." But people can also be "overwhelmed" with information and may "gravitate to changes that require little or no fundamental shift in our character." To Conger the "greatest shortcoming" of these programs is "the lack of opportunity to shore up weaker skills" and also that sincere desires to change ineffective behaviors "dissipated soon after the program ended," in many cases due to "lack of support and coaching back on the job" (1996:58).

- *Conceptual understanding.* These courses have tended to be the domain of the business schools, offering leadership theories and models—or, more commonly, one model in each program— through lectures and case discussions. Such courses create some awareness of leadership skills and behaviors, in Conger's view, but they hardly encourage deep reflection on the process of leadership or the testing of leadership abilities.

- *Skill building.* Conger found skill-building courses to be the most common yet the least up-to-date on leadership. Here some skill believed to be teachable (e.g., shaping vision, communicating, etc.) is identified in the classroom, perhaps through a case study, and then practiced with feedback. This approach is practical and fast; the question is whether the skill in question can really be taught. For example, "visioning is learned largely through important work experiences, not through a day's exposure in a workshop" (1996:56). Conger argues that people need considerable time to learn a skill, in management as in sports— time to study it, experience it, experiment with it, get coached, and then make improvements. In other words, the setting has to be authentic, tied to the practice of managing. Conger calls these skills-building programs "the nouvelle cuisine of learning"—a little taste of this and that.

Conger concludes overall that the four approaches should be brought together: a conceptual part to understand leadership; skill building to practice teachable skills and awareness building for others; feedback to understand personal strengths and weaknesses; personal growth to bring out emotions and stimulate imagination. This suggests the need for ongoing development and not the "one-shot" course, preferably at key transition points in a manager's career, reinforced with coaching or mentoring.

What Conger does not conclude—although his findings suggest it— is that courses may not usually be an effective way to develop leaders. To my mind, the real development of leaders, in their key beliefs and values, happens in early life. After that, we can certainly *foster* leadership, by developing the *conditions* that bring it out in people—as in the job challenges described by McCall. And I do believe that certain kinds of courses develop people's *managerial* capabilities and understandings—from networking to reading a balance sheet—and also influence their attitudes, which can enhance their potential for leadership. But increasingly I have come to believe that setting out to create leaders in a classroom, whether in short programs or full degrees, too often creates hubris. People leave believing they have been anointed.

## BUSINESS SCHOOL PROGRAMS

With the exception of the conceptual ones, most of the leadership programs Conger discusses are offered by special training and development institutes. The business schools, even under the label of *management* development, tend to favor programs in business. That is how they are organized, how their faculty has been trained, what they are geared up to do. For example, "Financial Management for Nonfinancial Managers" is probably the most common short program business schools offer. As *Business Week* noted in a 1991 report on executive education, which may be no less true today, companies that expected their student-executives to be "steeped in leading-edge thinking" were "often getting instead . . . mere overviews of disciplines such as marketing, taught by narrowly trained academicians" (Byrne 1991:103).

And with much the same lack of integration. A memo circulated a few years ago by a business school well known for its management development programs contained the following guideline. As the "owners" of the program, "It is . . . essential that the [program director] be present on campus during the course of the [program], interact with the faculty to monitor the evolution of the [program], and be available on short notice for the participants. . . . During the [program, the director] should not be absent for more than 48 hours." This meant absent from the school, not the classroom! Introducing the speaker for the day and then disappearing was apparently fine. Except in the evenings: the program director "should be present for each social event"! Leaving aside the social events, a program is apparently the sum total of all the teachers who come and go. Somehow it will all get magically integrated. Why in the world does any company tolerate this?

AMPs    Most prominent of all the business school offerings are the so-called "Advanced Management Programs" (AMPs). Harvard and Chicago introduced ones in the early 1940s (although MIT had a similar program dating back to 1931); by 1958, there were forty such programs (Gordon and Howell 1959:294).

Plato may have needed fifty years to train a good leader, but Harvard promises on its Web site that "you will leave the program as a global visionary" after nine weeks. Of course, Plato did not expect anyone to take off fifty years, but Harvard does require managers to be off the job for the nine weeks. That certainly concentrates attention, but does being away for so long facilitate linking with the managers' experience, and does it fit in with the pace of business activities these days?

Many of these AMP programs look like shortened MBA programs. Their components have similar titles and use the same methods of teaching. Thus, the Harvard AMP "opens with a case series in which the participants take a holistic view of a multinational company as it evolves into a powerful international competitor over two decades." After participants assess their own managerial challenges and objectives, there follows "an intensive four-day module [that] focuses on the fundamentals of accounting and finance." Then comes the core of the program, weeks 3 through 7, which immerse the participants "in the study of key management topics," including "Competitive and Corporate Strategy," "Financial Management," and "Marketing Leadership," as well as "Elective Seminars." The last two weeks focus on the "broad, integrative role of corporate leadership."

As for pedagogy, at the Harvard AMP in particular, cases abound. Encouraged to make changes in the AMP, one new director told *Fortune* that he was "rethinking Harvard's approach . . . he is considering cutting the number of cases from three a day to two" (O'Reilly 1993:54). The 1996 catalog had a passing reference to cases being supplemented by methods applied to "each participant's own situation" but by him- or herself: "Through the use of a daily diary, participants are invited to capture the 'take home' value of each session and apply the new perspectives and skills they've acquired to meet their own particular objectives." One can thus understand Fulmer's (1997) description of the conventional AMP as a "rite of passage," with "little relationship to other developmental activities taking place in a progressive career" (61–62):

> [P]articipants were expected to engage in case discussions, debate recommendations or alternatives, and sometimes make presentations based on their conclusions about class assignments. These assignments often involved a business case that had little direct relevance to the participants' situations back at the office; however, it

was hoped that they would be able to make applications when and if similar situations presented themselves. (60)

NOT VERY DEVELOPED    Management development programs in the business schools thus appear to be not very developed or advanced. As *Business Week* reported in a 1997 survey of "Executive Development Trends" in forty-four companies, "fewer than 25% of the respondents indicated that universities were generally effective at meeting [their] criteria." The article concluded that "the halo of credibility" was gone from the business schools, whose place at the center of the development universe was being taken over by the companies themselves (Vicere 1998:538, 539, 541). And by consultant firms: *Business Week* reported in 1999 that 53 percent of the companies surveyed said that consultants were "the most effective providers of executive education"; only 39 percent said that of the business schools (Reingold 1999:77).

Yet here and there, in the business schools and elsewhere, are some rather intriguing developments.

## SOME NOVEL PROGRAMS

There is a great wall in many of the prestigious business schools. On one side are the crown jewels, the degree programs, carefully guarded by the faculty. On the other side are the managerial development programs, paid little attention by the faculty since others take responsibility for them.

The common result is the standardized offerings just described, convenient enough to attract busy faculty. But another result is the occasional interesting innovation, because any professor who cares to do something novel can have remarkable freedom. Anything goes, so long as the market responds favorably—no pedantic committees to get past, just budgets. The same tends to be true, of course, for providers outside the business schools. Here I review briefly, for illustrative purposes, some interesting examples. Many more can be found; these are mostly programs that I have personally seen in operation.

GHOSHAL'S PROGRAMS    Sumantra Ghoshal is a good example of a professor working on the other side of that wall, first at Insead, then at the London Business School. In the early 1990s, he led the creation of a program for Digital Equipment Corporation (DEC), to "develop the international capabilities needed to support" the company's move into a new business (Ghoshal, Arnzen, and Brownfield 1992:54).

The program ran in three phases over the course of a year. The first, consisting of two weeks at Insead, identified the forces of going into the new business and established projects and their research plans for the second phase. This ran through the year and consisted of on-site research in a number of Digital's large customer accounts, to identify the specific challenges and constraints of the new business. The third phase brought these groups back to Insead, for two weeks "to analyze the research data . . . and compare and contrast the different cases so as to formulate a conceptual model and some general conclusions" (56).

Ghoshal et al. describe the program as not so much designed and implemented as "evolved" by Insead and DEC people together (59). They claim that the program built bridges "between executive development and organizational change . . . between action research and action learning . . . and between business school faculty and a group of educational professionals within the company" (65). (As the program ran, DEC "began to feel the effects of the worst earnings decline in its history." Costs were cut, but it was decided to maintain the program.)

Ghoshal went on to develop an equally unusual consortium program at Insead called the Executive Forum. I was involved in the second of these and was struck by two of its activities in particular.

To open the program, a one-day visit to EuroDisney was arranged, during which the participants were released in groups to roam around as observers/researchers and report back to Disney managers in the afternoon. Called "The Organizational Scavenger Hunt," its designer and facilitator, Richard Pascale, described the assignment on the bus ride to the site. Participants were challenged to apply their powers of observation and induction "to learn as much as possible of what makes EuroDisney tick"—its strategy, market position, staff morale, management philosophy, values, and so forth. Participants were "free to do anything, repeat anything, that a EuroDisney guest might do," and more: "e.g., devise clever experiments that 'test' the system to its limit and observe how it responds," so long as it was legal and inoffensive to the host and Insead's relationship with EuroDisney. The scavenger hunt turned out to be a great success, both in opening the participants up to the pathbreaking design of the course and in sharpening their powers of observation and insight.

The second activity was to divide the class in the middle of this five-day program and fly everyone to the participating companies located in Europe (Daimler-Benz, Royal Dutch Shell, Smith Klein Beecham). There they spent a day interviewing and observing and returned to class the next morning to report. I wondered what they could find out in a day. A great deal, I discovered, much like a chess master sizing up a board at a glance. In their feedback on what part of the program the participants appreciated most, they dwelled overwhelmingly on these visits. As in the DEC program, these experiences were woven around concepts introduced formally by the faculty.

Ghoshal later moved to the London Business School, where he and Lynda Gratton established the Global Business Consortium, which brings together six senior managers from each of six companies for three modules of five days each, in Asia Pacific on "Global Strategy and Organization," in North America on "Growth and Business Development," and in Europe on "Leading Transformation." Again, "the program combines leading-edge academic research and analytical tools with opportunity to share experiences." Each company team has a CEO challenge, a project set by the chief executive to whom the findings are presented at the final module. One day is also devoted to "consortium cases"—"in-depth analysis of how each consortium company sustains competitive advantage in the region being visited."

AVIRA AND ASPEN SEMINARS    AVIRA (for Awareness, Vision, Imagination, Responsibility, and Action) is offered several times a year, over five days, by Henri-Claude de Bettignies at Insead for up to twenty senior managers. This is run mostly as a discussion of broad issues around a table. "There are no lectures or case studies. The issues discussed are the current concerns of today's business leaders and specific problems brought by participants" (Web site, 2003). The aim, which seems especially suited to managers at this level, is not to transfer knowledge or develop skills so much as develop self-awareness and explore alternate logics, especially about leadership—also to "unlearn," which de Bettignies has described to me as a "painful process."

Similar to AVIRA, at least in intentions, are the Aspen Institute's one-week Executive Seminars, in which managers learn "from the great thinkers of the past" (Aristotle, Jefferson, Locke, etc.) and discuss around tables, again in Socratic style. The 2000 brochure describes this as "the seeking, the finding, and the releasing of wisdom through the process of dialogue."

THE U.S. ARMY PROGRAM    Richard Pascale (1997) has written about a fascinating simulation on a massive scale run by the United States Army National Training Center (NTC) for leadership development and organizational change. "Over a grueling two-week period, an entire organizational unit of 3,000 to 4,000 people [at all levels] go head-to-head with a competitor of like size in a simulation so realistic to life that no participant remains unscathed" (134). I visited the site with

Pascale and saw simulated tank battles taking place in the desert with aircraft support.

One brigadier general reported learning more in the NTC than he had learned in the previous fourteen years of his career. "Day after day, you are confronted with the hard evidence of discrepancies between intentions and faulty execution, between what you wanted the enemy to do and what he actually did" (135).

Six hundred instructors were involved, one for each person with managerial responsibility; they shadowed them through the eighteen-hour days. The debrief event, called "After Action Reviews," could be harassing; we saw seasoned commanders cowering under the criticism (hardly discouraged by their sleep deprivation). Such a review, according to the commander of the NTC, "has instilled a discipline of relentlessly questioning everything we do. Above all, it has resocialized three generations of officers to move away from a command-and-control style of leadership to one that takes advantage of distributed intelligence" (136).

CCMD PROGRAM    One of the best management development activities I have witnessed was created by the Canadian government Centre for Management Development (CCMD), for the country's most promising senior civil servants. It entailed fifty-six working days in all, half in Ottawa, half in field studies elsewhere, spread over six months.

A precourse phase began with a personal executive and physical assessment and concluded with the identification of a personal development strategy. The first module of four weeks followed soon after, focusing on "long-term trends" and "global challenges facing Canada," with field studies across the country and abroad, as well as action learning in small groups. The next module, two months later, also of four weeks, focused on management and "Canada's political, social and economic traditions and experiences," again with field studies. Leadership was the focus of the third module, of three weeks, together with "key short term policy and management issues facing Canada," including a concluding report to the heads of the Canadian civil service.

The CCMD program emphasized "self-directed learning," "small group interaction," and "an emphasis on . . . intellectual renewal and professional 're-tooling.'" These were the words on paper, but I saw them brought to life on several occasions in a remarkably enthusiastic classroom.

In a presentation of the program at a conference in June 1993, co-director Ralph Heinzman articulated the "large trends" for CCMD and management development in general: first to create deep experiences of personal transformation, second to develop a global awareness, and third to establish a closer link between learning and work. He saw the purpose of the CCMD program as no less than to develop the wisdom of the participants.

Emphasized throughout the management development literature is the importance of getting the support of top management. But rarely is there recognition of the other edge of that sword: that programs dependent on the support of particular godfathers become vulnerable when they leave. Time and again I have seen wonderful initiatives, like that of the CCMD, ended because of a changing of the managerial guard, or because of the departure of the program's own directors: "It's not *my* program" is the all-too-common attitude of those who follow, rather than "Is this a worthwhile program?" The management development landscape is littered with the remains of wonderful programs that new people simply did not bother to continue. We don't lack for good ideas in management development so much as people open enough to use them.

# LEARNING IN ACTION

Action Learning, so called, has long been used in management development. But that was mostly in Europe, especially by people connected with Reg Revans in England and then Belgium.[5] Then Jack Welch introduced "Work-Out" at General Electric, with a not dissimilar philosophy, and much of America became hooked on this form of management development. "Action Learning: Executive Development of Choice for the 1990s," headlined one journal article (Keys 1994), decades after Revans's initial efforts.

And so, in the trendy world of management, every self-respecting program now seems to have its mandatory action component. Busy managers are made that much busier doing projects with their colleagues, partly to learn, partly to network, and largely, it seems increasingly, to accomplish something for their employers.

Where to position Action Learning? When a project is simply added to a program, this can be considered coursework—and appeared as

---

[5]Actually, back in 1915, John Dewey wrote about the need to connect thinking to action and how students must have "a genuine situation of experience" in which a "genuine problem develops . . . as a stimulus to thought" (in Burgoyne and Mumford 2001:25).

such in many of the programs already described in this chapter (as well as in many revised MBA programs, as described in Chapter 7). Looked upon as a philosophy for developing managers, however, as Revans and his followers did, it belongs here as a distinct form of management development, somewhere between the less formal moving and mentoring connected to the work and the more formal courses disconnected from it. Field activity combined with serious reflection creates a kind of laboratory to learn—a course in the world of work, if you like. But treated as an excuse to get things done, where action takes precedence over reflection, this is not management development at all, just more business as usual. I shall consider Action Learning here as a form of management development and return to it briefly as a pedagogy in the next chapter.

## ACTION LEARNING, REVANS-STYLE

In *The A.B.C. of Action Learning,* Revans (1983) criticized learning in the abstract and argued for learning by doing. "There can be no action without learning and no learning without action" (16). He had a particular kind of action in mind: "the posing of questions by the simple device of setting [managers] to tackle real problems that have so far defied solution" (11). This they were to do in a "program," which "allocate[ed] to each participant . . . a real-life exercise," carried out on a full- or part-time basis (16, 19). So while the problem may have been real, the experience was not—not natural but added on (i.e., imposed unnaturally).

In these programs, Revans did not reject "formal instruction" so much as consider it an aid in tackling these problems—a stimulant to "exploratory insight" (12). And key here was reflection on the experience: "Lasting behavioral change is more likely to follow the reinterpretation of past experiences than the acquisition of fresh knowledge," especially when it comes "through exchanges with other managers themselves anxious to learn by reordering their own perceptions."

On the other hand, for Revans, "the intervention of experts, is, at best, ambiguous; in general, opinionative; and, at worst, reactionary" (14). So the "responsibility of the management teachers" is to create the "conditions in which managers may learn with and from each other" (15; Revans was harsh in his criticism of "non-involved facilitators, including case study teachers" [16]). Key to such learning is the tutorial group, or "action learning set" in Revans's terminology. Here "students learn to reflect on their experiences, uncover the assumptions brought to bear on their actions, reframe these assumptions on the basis of theory and practice, and then test out new actions with their associated skills" (Raelin 1993a:6).

All of this makes a great deal of sense and in fact forms one basis for the approach described in the following chapters: learning related to doing, in an inductive and even exploratory manner.

Yet Revans then turned around and embedded the whole thing in a rather inflexible "scientific method." He described the "successful stages" of the Action Learning process as observation or survey; provisional hypothesis or theory; trial, test, or experiment; audit; and review (16, 17–18). He claimed that "the sequential notion is important," (31) "forcing upon [managers] the planning of their time" (33), even though creative problem solving has been shown to be an iterative process, in which doing informs thinking as much as thinking informs doing (Weick 1979). Once again, managing was reduced to analyzing. More curious still was Revans's attitude toward senior management. He described projects imposed by it as perhaps "already clearly identified by several powerful factions within the organization," to deal with "some embarrassment that can no longer be ignored." For him, "Action learning has nothing to do with such diversions, but is concerned with encouraging *real* persons to tackle *real* problems in *real* time" (62), as if there is something *unreal* about the concerns of senior management, while Action Learning itself can be free of power struggles.

## MiL

As mentioned earlier, this kind of Action Learning spread mostly through Revans's efforts in Europe, including into some MBA programs (see Gosling and Ashton 1994). The MiL (Management in Lund) institute in Sweden, an independent foundation created in 1977, has used a version it calls "Action Reflection Learning" (see Figure 8.2) with its network of about 150 member companies and 100 professional associates. In its "open," "partner," and "internal company programs," small teams of mixed participants conduct change projects in other parts of their own companies or other companies, supported by a learning coach. This is reinforced by a series of residential workshops in which the learning is shared and experts make presentations.

MiL's problem-solving approach sounds more flexible than that of Revans. According to Lennart Rohlin (1999), MiL's founder and president, participants are encouraged to "create their own . . . perspectives and theories through facilitated reflection." MiL, he claims, likes to

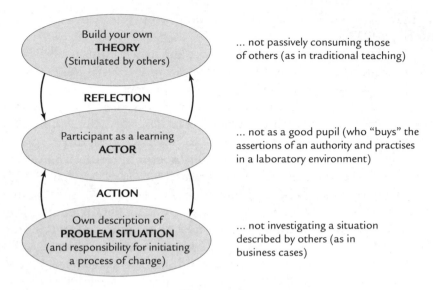

FIGURE 8.2

MiL Learning Philosophy (from Rohlin 1999:8)

work with "'paradoxes of management': between action and reflection, order and chaos, the hard factors of human relations and the soft dimensions of business processes" (ii). But perhaps reflecting Revans's sentiments about senior management, although more constructively, MiL states its wish to move organizations from "Employees in hierarchies" to "Partners in networks," and from "Authority and control" to "Empowerment and trust" (9). This suggests that the kind of management development an organization uses can influence its very assumptions about managing (as we saw in Chapter 5 and will see in the following chapters).

## WORK-OUT AT GENERAL ELECTRIC

Perhaps Revans might have been delighted that Work-Out became so popular in the United States in the 1990s, to spread a philosophy he so long espoused. Or perhaps he would have been disconcerted that it was driven by a chief executive and focused on action more than reflection.

After he took over the chief executive position at General Electric in 1982, Jack Welch wanted to attack its bureaucratic procedures and break down the walls between its functions and its levels of management. Like many CEOs who followed his lead, Welch began by slashing—selling businesses, cutting levels of management, reducing staff groups, and the like—to the point where be became known as "Neutron Jack," for eliminating the people while leaving the buildings intact.

But like few other CEOs, Welch followed that with something quite different. He wanted improvements in productivity and thought that the people closest to the operations had a key role to play in this, given a chance to speak up. So in 1988 he and Jim Baughman, who headed GE's Crotonville management development center, created Work-Out, "to convey the idea of getting the nonsense 'worked-out' of General Electric, of the 'workout' people engaged in to make themselves lean and agile, and of the problems that needed to be 'worked out'" (Slater and Welch 1993:214).

Over the years, various ideas seem to have been mixed and matched under this label, at least according to the reports and articles about it. In effect, Work-Out had its initial, specific usage, but has also been used as an "umbrella concept" for other GE initiatives (Dave Ulrich, in personal correspondence), of which two are discussed here.

THE EVOLUTION OF WORK-OUT    In its original form, conceived as a kind of "New England town meeting" where citizens dialogued with the town fathers, managers came together with workers of a business in groups of forty or fifty. They divided into three or four subgroups, which were facilitated by outside consultants and academics. Over the course of three days, they figured out how to streamline the business— "getting rid of the bureaucratic red tape and minutia," in the words of Steve Kerr (interviewed in Hodgetts 1996:70), who also ran Crotonville. They started with "the low hanging fruit," those things easy to change, such as "How can the number of reports be reduced?"

> After each group identified its list of improvements, action plans would be developed and a champion assigned for each plan. Then, on the last half day of the session, the manager of the business would come in with four or six lieutenants, and they would listen for three hours to these ideas. They would then have to say yes or no on the spot regarding each proposed change. As a result of these sessions, GE was able to downsize and increase productivity at the same time. (70)

In their book on Work-Out—a kind of handbook as to how to do it—Ulrich, Kerr, and Ashkenas (2002) describe it as more than problem solving and bureaucracy reducing: "It is also a catalyst for creating an empowered workforce" to challenge bureaucratic growth, and it "can help create a culture that is fast-moving, innovative, and without boundaries." Work-Out can also "become a vehicle for developing managers and leaders who make quick decisions in an energizing dialogue with employees—instead of hiding in their office making decisions by fiat" (xiv).

A report in *Fortune* five years after the start of Work-Out, however, refers to something quite different, a second approach: "giving teams of executives real live business problems to solve . . . identified by top management of a division or the whole company." Baughman offered as examples "What is the market for GE financial services in India? How can GE serve the automobile industry better?" In this version, a group of 40 GE executives, culled from the company's senior 3,500, were divided into six teams that worked for a month, "rac[ing] around the world, interviewing and researching," after having been prepared by consultants and business school professors who taught them "new ways of organizing, thinking and deciding." Each team presented its findings to Welch and other senior managers (O'Reilly 1993:54). GE also engaged in what was called "Best Practices," another "segment of Work-Out," according to Slater, in which its people visited other companies to benefit from their ways to improve productivity. This was later extended, according to Kerr, to visits among various GE businesses. This seems like a third approach.[6]

Kerr talked in his interview about early resistance to the original Work-Out: Because of Welch's championing of it, "people had to feign an interest, even if they didn't have one. At the present time, participation continues to be a problem" (Hodgetts 1996:72–73). Kerr elaborated as follows:

> [Work-Out is] still being used, but it's gone through a series of changes. In Stage 1, it was done in a formal, conscious way. We used to call these "unnatural acts in unnatural places" . . . because the action was outside the normal realm of business; and we used to take it off site. . . . In Stage 2, we would train the trainers to do it inside their own businesses. We called this stage "unnatural acts in natural places." . . . When a transition is done correctly, the initiative should eventually move to Stage 3: "natural acts in natural places." People doing it naturally as a way of life. We

---

[6]In his 1996 interview with Hodgetts, Kerr distinguished the three approaches, referring to the second as CAP—"Change Acceleration Process"—which he said replaced Work-Out (rather quickly, it would seem, just as all kinds of other companies were copying it!). And the third, "Best Practices," he described as something else again. Kerr claimed that the original Work-Out had by the time of the interview become so internalized in the company that no one was bothering to track it.

seldom do workouts in a formal, explicit, centrally driven way any-
more. Most of the businesses do use it on a regular basis. . . . And
if someone up top were to ask me how many workouts got done at
GE, I would say I'm delighted to tell you I have no idea. It's un-
orchestrated. It's now all natural acts. . . . Today, it's politically acceptable not to do workout, or at least it's not politically risky not
to do it because no one's tracking it. *I think* people are now doing
it for the payoff. (72, 73; italics added)

An interesting comment on America's most famous management development program!

And an interesting evolution for this as a form of management development. Of the CAP version, Kerr said, "[Y]ou have to come in with
a project . . . a 'need to do,' not a 'nice to do.'" The focus was clearly on
the acting, not the reflecting, likewise on getting results more than developing managers per se. Of course, that may be how GE developed its
managers, by using these processes to imbibe a culture of change: learn
by doing and replicate it in other settings. If so, then perhaps Work-Out
really belongs under Moving and Mentoring (if not Monitoring),
strobe-light-style!

## ENOUGH ACTION?

Where does Action Learning leave us? Personally I am left to wonder.
Managers are busy people—in fact, after all the downsizing and such,
busier than ever. Their jobs are loaded with action, or at least should be,
and they usually have no shortage of projects.

Of course, different kinds of projects—projects that take managers
to new places, with new problems—can be beneficial. Work gets done
while new learning can occur, as McCall made clear. And a culture can be
shifted, as at GE to promote innovation. But that, too, is action oriented,
and I return to Revans's plea for reflection connected to action. Welch was
worried about bureaucracy at GE—the reluctance to take action—and
his programs addressed that. But for their development, do managers
today need more action, or greater opportunity to reflect on the more-
than-enough action they already live? Put differently, do they need to enhance their capacity to take action or their capacity to reflect on the
action they already take? I pose these questions rhetorically, because while
the purpose of organizations may be to take action, the purpose of management development is to improve the quality of those actions. And that, I
shall argue in the next chapter, requires managers to step back from action.

At the height of the popularity of Work-Out, *Training and Development* magazine ran an article entitled "Strategic Shifts in Executive Development." Companies were looking for help in attaining their objectives, so "executive development professionals responded by focusing on customized, strategic and results-oriented development programs driven by top management" (Mann and Staudenmier 1991:37). These "must be designed so that participants are convinced that attendance is integral to getting their real work accomplished, rather than simply an escape or time off for reflection" (40). *Simply time off for reflection.* What a curious statement! It is dead wrong, and antithetical to learning, no matter how fashionable it may be in management development practice today. That is because learning is not doing; it is reflecting on doing. And reflecting is not an escape but an essential part of the management process—and probably its weakest component in today's hyper world.

Of course, doing for the purpose of reflecting—exemplified by that U.S. Army exercise—can be a powerful way to learn. But only so long as the end is kept in mind: to learn, not just to act. As Joe Raelin (1994), an enthusiast of Action Learning, has noted, its "detractors feel that most AL programs privilege practice at the expense of theory" (305).

One paper on Action Learning (Pedler 1997) reproduces a cartoon of a hot air balloon with weights hanging down labeled "task" and "self-development." The line below reads, "If we want to keep going, one of them will have to go." Revans reportedly saw this and commented, "Don't [they] know [they] have to do both!" But can organizations have their action cake and eat the learning, too? Does what MiL calls "Earning while learning" work as easily as they would like to believe? Or does earning eventually drive out learning, and results eventually co-opt reflection? Pedler's reply is that "[i]n practice, it is often difficult to hold the two priorities simultaneously" (256). Maybe, therefore, it is time to recognize that learning should not be mixed up with acting. Maybe, instead, management development should simply make use of the acting managers already do.

# CORPORATE ACADEMIES

Management development perhaps reached its most elaborate state in the staff colleges of old. These were units dedicated to the intensive development of managers associated with particular institutions. As such, their activities were customized to those institutions, if not to their own personal needs. Thus, alongside training in concepts and competencies came a good dose of indoctrination, to strengthen the bond between the individual and the institution, and so ensure full acceptance of its values, norms, and strategies.

The best-known staff colleges (e.g., West Point, Sandhurst) have, of course, been military, to form their officer corps. Conger (1992:39–40) in fact notes that "ancient and medieval armies . . . had various programs to teach their young officers the arts of war," although the focus was primarily on physical skills. Similar institutions existed for civil services, most famously, perhaps, to develop the mandarins of ancient China.

While staff colleges continue to exist in the military, elsewhere the concept seems dated. Yet recent developments in the corporate sector, especially in the United States, suggest a resurgence of the idea. During the 1990s, many corporations created extensive inside units to focus on the development of their managers and other personnel. They used a variety of labels for these, the most fashionable of which became "corporate university."

To my mind, this has been an encouraging development, not only because it recognizes management development as a complex process in need of care and customization, but also because it has countered the trend in courses of distancing managers from their companies, including the belief that managers are responsible for their own development. (Less encouraging, however, is the label "university," which only serves to camouflage interesting ideas that have nothing to do with universities. These units are intended to develop people, not to do research and grant degrees.[7] How sad, then, that corporate units are pretending to be universities just as business schools are pretending to serve customers— both to the distraction of their basic purposes. The label "academy," "institute," or "center," used, respectively, by LG, GE, and Boeing, would seem to be more appropriate.[8])

---

[7]In fact, those corporate training units established earlier that moved to grant degrees, such as the Arthur D. Little School of Management and General Motors Institute, eventually became independent and even changed their names.

[8]Meister's (1994) book on corporate universities lists thirty units, only half of which used the label "University" (and one "U"). Four are called "Institute"; four, "Center"; and three, "College." It is worth bearing in mind that this first use of the term *university* was meant as a joke. McDonald's created "Hamburger University" in the 1960s and offered a bachelor's degree in "Hamburgerology" (Web site, 2003). And the corporate unit that later popularized the serious use of the term, namely Motorola University, has almost disappeared at the time of this writing. In a 1990 article in the *Harvard Business Review*, its founder, Bill Wiggenhorn, was quite candid

In her book *Corporate Quality Universities,* Meister (1994) describes this new trend in management development as based on lifelong learning for employees at all levels, from hourly workers to senior executives and beyond, into the supplier/customer chain. Attention is placed on the development of job-related competencies and the instilling of a sense of the corporate culture, linked to the strategic needs of the business. And so, like those old staff colleges, the programs tend to be developed for the corporation. "Corporate classrooms are moving away from offering a cafeteria curriculum of hundreds of courses to concentrate on" programs to develop "the organization's core competencies" (21). Some, for example, make "deliberate and consistent use of storytelling within the training function" to communicate "aspects of the company's history, traditions, successes, and failures" (110). Centuries ago, minstrels walked from town to town singing the songs that knitted communities together. Today corporate minstrels are accomplishing the same thing in these classrooms.

The Boeing Leadership Center offers a good example of the interesting things that these institutions can do.[9] It has a large campus near St. Louis, which can house 120 guests. Between February 28, 1999, and May 1, 2000, the Center graduated 2,920 people in its core programs and received 17,143 day guests. The Boeing people consider the Center a "crossroads," where managers of all levels of the company come together for purposes of "strategic alignment, company-wide cultural integration, networking, and best practices sharing."

---

about the use of the term, noting that "I was afraid the name university was too pretentious. This wasn't to be a seat of free and open inquiry. This was to be training and education for work force and managers" (80). But the "chief executive liked the label; he thought it would create an expectation we'd grow into" (81). Wiggenhorn made clear how his unit differed from a university—for example, that the teachers tended to be "recently retired Motorola employees" and "married women with college degrees whose children have left home" (82). Nonetheless, the label stuck, and there followed the Ford Heavy Truck University and many others (Meister 1994). "Peter Huston, the director of Hart Schaffner & Marx University, believes the university theme has been successful . . . because the target audience . . is not [the company's] employees, but rather the retail salespeople who sell . . . [the] suits in retail stores . . . [and get] a status and cachet they do not have in their current jobs on the sales floor of Macys's or Dillard's" (46).

[9]This description is based on a presentation I attended by Carol Yamada, a senior manager at the center, on May 31, 2000, at the Executive Development Spring Conference, held in southern France, organized by Bob Mountain. The proceeding day, Harry Stonecipher, the president of the company, made an initial presentation on the Center.

In 2000, the center was offering seven programs, systematically laid out along managerial levels, from entry to executive, in the domains of business leadership, operational leadership, people leadership, and personal leadership. Mostly, these programs were tailor-made for Boeing's needs and offered at the Center, although the design and/or delivery of some were done with the help of outside experts.

These programs were intended to come at transition points in a manager's career, to focus on the competencies needed then. The program for new middle managers enabled them to practice "new roles as steward of the business, leader of change, and bridge between strategy and executive," while a program for executives gave them a "whole system" perspective. The elaborate program for new first-line supervisors (not common, as noted in this chapter's introduction), called "Transition to Management," included three components: "basics," about topics such as compensation, union relations, and ethics; "working effectively with people" and "managing the business"; and "leadership," to define "the role of the manager" and "link leadership behavior to business results." In 2000, the Center was giving this program to groups of twenty-four people sixty times annually!

More customized, and less, are corporate academies that focus development on the individual manager. Assessment centers are sometimes used to determine specific needs, and then courses as well as career counseling and job rotations are arranged accordingly. Here customization is for the individual but not for the corporation. And then there are companies that let particular business schools take the lead in developing and delivering their programs, but under contract and according to their own specifications.

## THE FUTURE OF THE ACADEMIES

Has this aspect of management development run its course? As noted in an earlier footnote, the place that gave rise to the flurry of these activities, Motorola University (see Wiggenhorn 1990), has almost disappeared as I write this. And a recent article in the *Financial Times* claims, "Our corporate survey shows that most big companies are now lukewarm on the subject of corporate universities" (Bradshaw 2003a). If so, that would be a shame—a throwing out of the baby with the bathwater—because while corporations may not need "universities," the message of this chapter is that they do need comprehensively thought-out activities to develop their managers.

# JAPANESE VERSUS
# AMERICAN PRACTICE

We can pull much of the discussion in this chapter together by contrasting management development practices in Japan with those in the United States, since they seem to sit at the two ends of the management development spectrum. Of course, a whole range of practices can be found in both countries, and while some of the traditional Japanese companies may be cutting back on their extensive practices, as we have just seen some of the American companies have been extending theirs. But overall, attitudes in these two countries toward management development differ enormously.

Large Japanese corporations have not relied on external degree programs to prepare their managers, only to educate the people they hire, thoroughly and basically—and not in management. They have then done their own management development, which can be thorough indeed.

According to Okazaki-Ward, at least as of 1993, the process typically begins with concerted induction: "On 1 April most firms hold a special ceremony to welcome new recruits. The President gives a welcoming speech outlining the corporate vision and the philosophy and ideals of the company." There follows "an initial course of training, to engender . . . a sense of group identity," which can be very extensive (244). This can last up to a year or more and generally includes hands-on experience (OJT) and other temporary assignments, such as working on the floor of a factory, supported by the mentoring of an "older brother" assigned to work closely with the recruit (246–47).

The "solid middle" period of the career follows, with more serious supervisory postings as these people gradually rise in the organization over about ten years, while "they cultivate a problem-seeking habit of mind" (248). An article in *The Economist* (1991:23) noted that "[f]ormal assessments take place as often as three times a year."

Alongside this come "development exercises"—for example, working out a plan for achieving some objective in consultation with a superior—as well as projects requiring more initiative, all to develop a holistic point of view. This is supplemented by specific training in functional skills, such as accounting, with attendance at outside courses on the rise (313).

The sum total of all this is rather remarkable in its extensiveness, also for how it combines the various practices of management development discussed in this chapter: extensive moving, mentoring, and monitoring; courses along the way; some equivalent of action learning (long before it became fashionable in the West); all integrated into careful management of the career (as in the corporate academies). Only "sink or swim" seems absent—perhaps!

I do not know whether Japanese corporations have used the term "staff college" or even thought about the concept, yet theirs may well be the ultimate example of it, at least in business. A manager from Toshiba who was visiting the London Business School, upon being told that most of the students had quit their jobs to do the MBA, exclaimed, "Toshiba is the school, then!"

Contrast this with the American reliance on courses—for example, the claim in a 1997 Harvard brochure that its Program for Management Development "teaches executives in eleven intensive weeks what could otherwise take years of experience to attain, even with the best on-the-job training." It continued: "Learn how to gain sustainable competitive advantage through building and nurturing critical capabilities," how to "create a learning organization," and how to "re-engineer the supply chain." All in eleven weeks in a classroom!

The newer corporate academies notwithstanding, the conclusion reached by Handy et al. (1988) in their report on management development practices probably still stands: "formal education forms the backbone of America's approach to the development of her managers" (52). Likewise in England: "Certainly a functional career, an appraisal scheme and a three-week management course are a poor substitute for the Japanese way, yet most British organizations currently do little else" (183).

## An "Unnatural" Act

Boyatzis (1995) takes this American perspective further, in a way much further. Because he believes management to be "an unnatural act," "development and preparation for becoming a manager must be intentional," not based on "the 'life-experience' 'sink-or-swim' approach" most organizations have used. The key word here seems to be "preparation," not "development," because Boyatzis highlights the "role of graduate management education (namely, the MBA) . . . to help people explicitly begin that process" (50). Managers, in other words, like surgeons, must be prepared in school to perform acts that are unnatural. Thereafter, although surgeons have to be further trained on the job, managers can apparently move right in. In America, if not Japan!

Here, most sharply, we find the concern that led to the writing of this book. If management is an unnatural act, then the MBA has had it right all along. A couple of years in a classroom and off you go to practice it, generically, "professionally." But if management is a natural act, then artificial education renders it unnatural, and so distorts its practice.

Obviously, not everyone in America shares Boyatzis's view. Indeed, not everyone at the Harvard Business School would agree with the quoted claims about how much can be learned in a management development program. For example, Harvard professor John Kotter commented on how "growing a general manager takes 10 to 20 years and there are no shortcuts" (McGill 1988). If so, the holistic approaches of some of the corporate academies have it right, not to mention the more extensive processes used in Japan. What a shame, then, that so much real management development has had to happen beyond the universities rather than in conjunction with them.

# DEVELOPING MANAGERS
# BEYOND THE CATEGORIES

My conclusion to this chapter should now be evident. Some approaches to management development focus on experience and the job, others on education and the person, still others on results and the corporation. Each has advantages and limitations. They make the most sense when taken together—not added together, but combined judiciously, according to specific need.

Short courses can provide key inputs; they convey articulated knowledge and can develop certain competencies. Degree courses for practicing managers are described in the following chapters as powerful boosts to management development. Systematic career movements, reinforced by coaching and periodic assessing of progress, foster learning from experience. Action Learning, with adequate reflection, strengthens the capacity to do this. And bringing much of this together in a corporate academy, better still in the kind of practice common in Japan, offers powerful possibilities for integration. Even sink or swim has its place: it is sometimes good to sink, just a little, in order to better appreciate swimming.

Figure 8.3 repeats the initial diagram of this chapter with the elements of our discussion laid on. To the left is the zone of *educating,* the domain of the business schools, with their conventional MBA programs

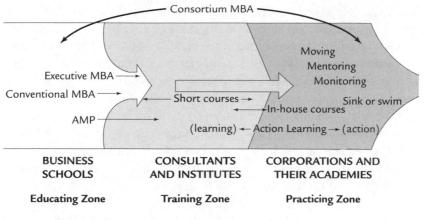

Consortium MBA

Executive MBA

Conventional MBA

AMP

Short courses →

In-house courses

(learning) ← Action Learning → (action)

Moving
Mentoring
Monitoring

Sink or swim

**BUSINESS
SCHOOLS**

**CONSULTANTS
AND INSTITUTES**

**CORPORATIONS AND
THEIR ACADEMIES**

**Educating Zone**

**Training Zone**

**Practicing Zone**

Personal development

Manager development

Management development

Organization development

Social development

FIGURE 8.3

Forms of Development and Education in Management

removed from practice as well as their Executive MBA and short AMP programs connected to practitioners, if not to their practice. This is *personal* development.

In the middle is the zone of *training*, the domain of consultants and institutes that offer mostly short courses, often focused on managerial skills. These courses can be connected to practice or to theory, ideally to both. This is the realm of *manager development* and *management development*.

And on the right side is the zone of *practicing*, the domain of the corporations and their academies. Some activities, such as moving, mentoring, and monitoring, take place exclusively here, while others can stretch back into the other zones—consortium programs, for example, all the way back to the universities. (The action of Action Learning takes place here, while the *learning* can stretch back to the left.) This is the realm especially of *organization development* but also, looking to the right, of *social development* and, to the left, of *management and manager development*.

As noted earlier, Americans lean to the left, with an emphasis on outside education and training to develop the individual independent of his or her context. Here exists the prevailing attitude that "it is primarily

an *individual's* responsibility to acquire this grounding, although benev-
olent corporations should do what they can to help" (Handy et al.
1988:59). And the Japanese lean to the right, especially in favor of moving
and mentoring. This side treats management as more of a natural practice rooted in context, while the other sees it as more of a "profession,"
even an unnatural act, and so relatively context-free.

Of course, the growth of the corporate academies has shifted American practice toward the right, but perhaps not so far as might be expected, given the residual reliance on courses. Systematic moving is not
all that common, although mentoring in the form of coaching is becoming
more popular in the United States. Telling, however, is that this is being
done increasingly by consultants engaged by the managers themselves.

But culture should not be the determining factor here. Specific needs
within countries vary by industries and companies. For example, mass
producers may have greater need for educating in the conventional business functions, since that is how they tend to be organized, whereas
high-technology firms, with more fluidity in their structures, may benefit from more flexible educating as well as more on-the-job mentoring
and moving. As Raelin (2000:11) has pointed out, in these more volatile
contexts, "learning how to learn" may have to replace learning specific
skills, for managers and workers alike.

Likewise, the most appropriate form of development will vary with
the stage of a manager's career. Hill (1992) writes in her book *Becoming
a Manager* that the "current emphasis on the acquisition of managerial
competencies (especially managerial knowledge as distinguished from
skill) and on classroom learning may be misplaced" for new managers
(265). They need to learn "how to seek information and solve problems
in semi-structured situations," "how to observe and diagnose interpersonal problems," "what it means to be and what it feels like to be a
manager," and to deal with the anxiety that managing entails (266).
True enough, but they also need some grounding in the basic business
functions—the language of business—without this giving a false impression of managing. Hill also notes that new managers "crave . . . feedback
on performance"; they need to "learn their strengths and weaknesses"
(269), which suggests the importance of on-the-job development, especially through mentoring.

As people become more experienced and confident in their managing, and may be ready to move toward general management, the time
may be best for intensive *management* education, to open them up to
the full breadth of practice. Ways to do this are discussed in Chapters 10
through 14.

Later in the career, for those who have moved into senior management positions, short courses on broader social and economic issues, more concerned with wisdom than technique, may make the most sense. Management, always a craft that uses some science, may become more of an art as a manager progresses in his or her career.

In any event, the different approaches discussed in this chapter have to be seen as a portfolio on which to draw for the development of managers at various stages of their careers. To conclude this chapter together with those that preceded it, the object is not to find the one best way to educate and develop managers. It is to combine the many good ways, not to blur their distinctions but to combine their strengths.

# 9

# DEVELOPING MANAGEMENT EDUCATION

*It's all so simple, Anjin-san. Just change*
*your concept of the world.*

—JAMES CLAVELL, *SHOGUN*

The conclusions reached in the previous chapters suggest a wholly different approach to developing managers, at least in intensive educational programs. This is the subject to which we now turn.

The ideas presented in this chapter may be very different from prevailing educational practice. But our own experience with them (discussed in the following chapters) suggests that they can be rather easily realized, once we get back to fundamental notions of learning. These notions are wonderfully well illustrated in the best article I have seen on education for management development, even if it was written about children in grade school. Excerpts from it are worth the space and time taken by the following box. Change the learners in the story to managers, and you need change hardly another word to appreciate precisely what is needed in management education.

As the article suggests, in the spirit of the quotation that opens this chapter, it is really all so simple: We just need to change our concept of the world of management education.

## A Curious Plan: Managing on the Twelfth

*(extracted from an article by Patricia Clifford and Sharon L. Friesen [1993] in the* Harvard Educational Review, *reprinted with permission)*

*The Mock Turtle went on:*
    *"We had the best of educations—in fact, we went to school every day."*
    *"And how many hours a day did you do lessons?" said Alice, in a hurry to change the subject.*
    *"Ten hours the first day," said the Mock Turtle, "Nine the next, and so on."*
    *"What a curious plan!" exclaimed Alice.*
    *"That's the reason they're called lessons," the Gryphon remarked, "because they lessen from day to day."*
    *This was quite a new idea to Alice, and she thought it over a little before she made her next remark. "Then the eleventh day must have been a holiday?"*
    *"Of course it was," said the Mock Turtle.*
    *"And how did you manage on the twelfth?" (from Lewis Carroll,* Alice's Adventures in Wonderland)

Every September, teachers and students gather together in our classroom to learn. Each of us, teacher and child alike, walks through the door bringing experiences and understandings that are ours alone. Yet, each person is also embarking on a journey that he or she will come to share with others. This journey is made anew every year with every class. . . . We are committed to developing a classroom where teachers and children are passionate, robust learners. . . . We are searching for school curriculum that acknowledges the importance of the lived experience of children and teachers; that understands growth as more than an interior, private, individual matter of unfolding development. . . .

We met David and his parents on the first day of school. They had just returned to Canada after spending seven years in Africa, where they had lived and worked among the Masai. Although he was of European descent, David had been born in Africa. He went to a village kindergarten, and played and tended cattle with the Masai children. . . . [A]s we watched David take his first tentative steps in school, we often forgot that the life David had been living until the end of August was radically different from the one he now had to negotiate in our large, complicated, noisy Canadian classroom.

Throughout September and into October, David spoke very little. . . . One day in early October, [he] arrived at school with a huge book about the Masai and asked if he could show his book to the other children. This was the first time David had ever offered to share part of his life experiences with the whole class, to teach us all what he knew best—life among the Masai. David stood in front of the class with his book. He flipped to a few pages and spoke softly . . . the children were entranced. They had so many questions to ask David, so much they wanted to know. . . . Here was the perfect chance to bring David into the full life of the classroom.

That afternoon, David's mother came to volunteer in the class-room. We asked her if she would speak to us about the Masai. She agreed, took her place in a small chair at the front of the group, and opened David's book. As she spoke, David stood quietly at her shoulder, gently stroking her long hair. He seemed to relax into the memories of that safe, familiar place. . . . As our eyes met above the heads of the children, we knew we had been waiting for this all along, without knowing it: waiting for David's life in Africa to come alive for us. . . . Up to now, David had blended in too readily with all the other children. . . .

Our efforts to see all children as contributing members of our classroom community is a kind of standing invitation, but we never know who will take it up, or how they will do it. It appeared that David had decided that *now* was his time, and he made the first es-sential move. . . . The class was filled with curiosity, and questions overflowed the hour we spent together. . . . The next day David brought us *Bringing the Rain to Kapiti Plain*. . . . This book was just the beginning of the stories about Africa. . . . David brought in other [books and] things to share with us, such as elaborate beaded collars and knives used to bleed cattle. . . .

We continually ask ourselves: How much of the life that is lived com-pletely outside of school is welcomed into the classroom as knowl-edge and experience that can enrich us all? How much of each child gets to come to school? When a child says, "This is me, and I am ready for you to know it," we feel we must try to honor this offering, not shut it out, control it, or hurry to get on with the curriculum. . . .

David bringing into the class in this way opened up new possibilities for him, but it did something just as important for the whole class. All of the children lived the experience of a standing invitation. By observing how we attended to David and to others who also offered *their* stories, the children came to understand the importance of what each of them might bring to the journey our class had embarked on together. [This means] that each child's voice can be heard, and that their speaking can make a difference to our curriculum decision making. . . . At the beginning of the year we could not plan for these moments, but we were prepared for them because we knew that they would inevitably arise. . . .

It is our belief that when curriculum is divorced from real life, children often lose connections with their own memories and histories. They lose touch with who they are. They may exist in our eyes more as students than as emerging selves, and we wonder if they continue to learn in any passionate sense of that word.

. . . [W]hen the children see their own questions returned to them as the basis for subsequent work and study, they come to know curriculum as a living, deeply connected experience. Curriculum is not delivered to them through activities made up by others; it is created with them, inspired by the work of the community of which each of them is a valued member. . . .

What [came as] a surprise to us was to see, in our relationships with the children, the power of imagination to build connections that were not only personally gratifying, but also educationally profound. . . . Perhaps what is most unexpected . . . is the extent to which [the children] learned more than we had ever imagined possible. . . .

Lessons need *not* lessen from day to day, month to month, year to year. Children and teachers *can* find new and powerful ways to come to know each other through real work that engages their minds, hearts, and spirits.

We can all, in fact, manage quite nicely on the twelfth.

## BEGINNING IN A DIFFERENT PLACE

Porter and McKibbin introduce their 1988 assessment of the state of management education and development with a call to "transcend the narrow interests of particular groups":

How, as a nation can we best educate and develop those individuals who now have—and will have in the future—responsibility for managing, leading, and directing our organizations . . . ? How, in short, can we make the best use of available—and clearly limited—educational and developmental resources to enhance the quality of management? That, in essence, is the overriding question of the Project being reported here. (3)

That is the overriding question of this chapter, too. But it begins in a very different place: that it is not "individuals" who should be developed, but members of a social system in which leadership is embedded; that only those who *already* have managerial responsibility can be educated and developed as managers; and that *international* and *global* are empty words when the purpose is to educate "as a nation."

Later Porter and McKibbin write about the curriculum "as a useful and logical starting point." It "specifies what is taught to students [later referred to as 'the cream of . . . youth'] in what order and sequence" and also "provides the structure for the educational delivery system. If the faculty can be thought of as the 'senders' and the students as the 'receivers,' then the curriculum, along with teaching, can be considered as an essential part (the structure) of the 'transmission' process" (47).

All of this may have been fine to modify MBA programs as conceived. But it has stood in the way of reconceiving management education. So our logical starting point here is a replacement of what is "taught" by what is learned and of "students" and "youth," "cream" or otherwise, by experienced adults. We question the very notion of "curriculum," certainly with its order and sequence; most management education has too much structure already. The logical starting point is the needs of managers and their organizations, which can never be fully known in advance of meeting a particular class, as well as the nature of the learning process itself, which has to adapt flexibly to that class. "Transmission" is but one part of this process—and by no means the most important part: Learning does not flow like electricity. And learners should no more be seen as "recipients" than faculty should be seen as "senders." Both have to be seen as participants in a learning process.

This, I hope, sets the tone for where we are going—namely, away from so much conventional education and toward that classroom in Calgary. Conventional educating has mostly impeded serious learning. From grade school to graduate school, we need something very different, just as does managing itself—less controlling and more engaging—to take us not away from basic academic values but more seriously into them.

Eight points are presented, as basic propositions for management education. These describe what I believe to be the right people for management education followed by the right ways for developing them. The right consequences are blended into the discussion.

## PROPOSITION 1. MANAGEMENT EDUCATION SHOULD BE RESTRICTED TO PRACTICING MANAGERS.

I have argued that managers cannot be created in a classroom but that existing managers can further develop there. Their experiences can turn the classroom into a rich arena for learning, even in the use of conventional methods. Cases, for example, can help managers see their experiences in other contexts, while theory can help them generalize from their experience. One is like travelers' tales, the other like maps. Both are appreciated best by people already familiar with the territory (after Gosling, in personal correspondence).

WHO TO SELECT, AND BY WHOM?     Who should get into that classroom? Who can best judge leadership potential? Certainly not the person him- or herself, and hardly some disconnected selection committee in a university. The obvious answer is those who have witnessed that potential in action—namely, people who have worked with particular candidates.

Certainly managers must be intelligent, and test scores provide one basis for measuring that. But demonstrated performance on the managerial job provides a far more effective basis for selection—and far more appropriate for a society in need of leadership. Management education, in other words, should be a privilege earned by performance as a manager, not a right granted by the score on a test.

As noted earlier, MBA programs rely initially on self-selection: the candidates apply; the schools select. Then the graduates emerge on a "fast track." Shouldn't we be reversing this order by requiring that people who have proven themselves, in an industry and an organization, be selected accordingly? That would also help ensure that people come to the classroom with a certain humility—an appreciation of what they don't know and need to know. Are these not, after all, the prerequisites for serious learning? In response to that old question about leaders being made or born, MBA programs are designed to make them. Proposed here is to enhance the making of those who are born and made.

The most effective way I know for such selection is to have organizations suggest their candidates and support them, by paying for the education, including the cost of their people being off the job. This gives them the incentive to choose carefully, sending people in whom they have a great deal of faith.

Test scores, essay questions, grade point averages, and the like, can never get close to the effectiveness of such a selection process. Let me illustrate. My own university, McGill, has always insisted on an undergraduate degree for graduate studies. It made its first exceptions in our masters program for practicing managers (discussed in the following chapters), because of the rich experience of the people sent by their companies. Someone asked me after the program had been running for six years whether this posed any problem in the classroom. No, I said; in fact, no participant who lacked an undergraduate degree came to my mind as problematic. Indeed, several came to mind as among our very best participants. There are several reasons for this. First, the lack of a degree motivated them to work harder: They were deeply appreciative of having a second chance. Second, having made it without the degree meant these people were among the very best. There had been no fast track for them. And third, lacking the earlier education, they were especially ready to learn. But so were the other managers who have come on our program: People in midcareer don't invest such time casually.

MBA programs make all kinds of mistakes in their selection processes, not about basic intelligence so much as about managerial ability, plus that will to manage discussed in Chapter 1. Many MBA graduates are smart people who should never be allowed to manage anything. Our experience, in contrast, suggests that selection by the sponsoring organizations leads to few mistakes about the will to manage, the ability to manage, *and* basic intelligence.

Of course, selection in the workplace raises other problems. For one, organizations may make limited choices. They may, for example, preclude mavericks, and authoritarian organizations may choose authoritarian managers. But these are problems within the organizations themselves, beyond the educational process; they have to be solved where they arise. Educating mavericks or nonauthoritarian managers independently will not solve that problem. I should also add that there is nothing in the educational proposals here that makes such people problematic in the classroom. We have also accepted some entrepreneurs in our program, as well as senior managers from small businesses, some of these certainly mavericks, and they have worked out fine.

Another problem with this kind of selection, especially in the current climate of easy come, easy go, is that many organizations may balk at the cost of sending managers to such programs. Why invest in people who might leave? I reverse this: If that is the organization's attitude, then its people will be inclined to leave! In other words, this attitude, too, should be seen as a problem in the organization, not in the educational process proposed here. Any organization that balks at investing less than half a year's salary to improve the practice of its managers through education deserves the turnover of managers it probably gets. My advice to good managers in such situations is to find an employer who respects their talent.

WHEN TO SELECT? If the answer to "Who to select?" is practicing managers, and to "By whom?" is those who work with these managers, then the next question is "When to select?" Three points in the managerial career suggest themselves: entry to the job of managing, midcareer, and senior-level managing.

As shown in Figure 9.1, there is a trade-off here. As managers progress in their careers, they can bring greater experience to bear on their education. Their employer is also more likely to invest in that education, having come to know their capabilities and the likelihood of retaining these people. On the other hand, new managers can benefit more from such learning: their habits have yet to form, they have their full careers ahead of them, and they may more energy and inclination to study. The diagram suggests that midcareer may be best: late enough to select effectively yet early enough to benefit from the learning. Young managers may lack the necessary experience; older ones may have too much of it.

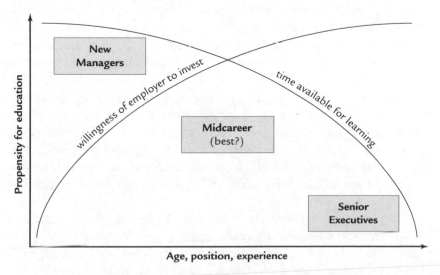

FIGURE 9.1
When Is Best for Management Education?

But there can also be significant benefits to intensive education for younger managers. "[W]e know surprisingly little about the transition to management," Hill (1992:2) writes in *Becoming a Manager*. But we do know that new managers need help: The ones she studied felt that whatever initial training they received "did not go far enough. . . . [T]hey were ill-prepared to handle the many dilemmas they encountered" (239). Indeed, when executives were asked to identify key events in their careers, the things that made a difference in the way they managed, they pointed to their first managerial job, when they were perhaps most open to learning from experience (242).

Perhaps, then, there is a need for two levels of programs (as shall be discussed later), one mostly managerial for people in midcareer, the other strongly managerial but with significant need-to-know functional material for newer managers. In both cases, however, the education should be combined with other forms of management development, especially the moving, mentoring, and monitoring discussed in the last chapter. Junior managers can particularly benefit from mentoring alongside educating.

## Proposition 2. The classroom should leverage the managers' experience in their education.

It makes no sense to select people steeped in practice and then ignore it in the process of educating them. This just denies use of the most powerful tool we have: their own natural experience. Critical to the learning, therefore, is the leveraging of this experience, as described in "Managing on the Twelfth," so that the learning revolves around what the learners know best. By allowing managers to stay on the job, coming into the classroom periodically, their experiences can be woven throughout the educational process, which can extend back to the workplace.

Doing this, of course, creates the tension of having to do a job and trying to learn at the same time. But that is just one of several tensions that have to be faced rather than circumvented if the learning is to take deep roots.

THE CONNECTED CLASSROOM    In their 1959 report, Gordon and Howell referred to part-time programs as "a great opportunity," given the maturity, experience, and motivation of the students—"an approximation to the ideal case we have been describing in the report" (286). But they felt such programs presented "a serious problem" because of the limited time to study and fatigue after a full day's work. Gordon and Howell had evening programs in mind. But other formats, with more extended time in the classroom, can work effectively.

Of course, too much time away from work can be stressful back at work. But too little time can interfere with serious learning. The short programs, like strobe lights, can be artificial, while the long ones, like floodlights, can blind managers to the experiences left behind. We have found, like others discussed in Chapter 7, that classroom modules of one to two weeks every few months allow for deep learning without undue disruption of the practice.

NATURAL AND CREATED EXPERIENCE    The key ingredient for management education is *natural* experience, that has been lived in everyday life, on the job and off. As Whitehead put it in 1932, "There is only one subject matter for education, and that is Life in all its manifestations" (10). He wrote his book as "a protest against dead knowledge" (v) that is "merely received into the mind without being utilized, or tested, or thrown into fresh combinations" (1–2).

This is not to deny the usefulness of *created* experience during study, such as engaging in a drama workshop to bring out concerns or visiting a cottage industry to gain another perspective on business. When such activities are authentic, they can be powerful, adding something visual and visceral to so much of educating that is verbal. In my opinion, however, created experience, including action learning and other project work, should be viewed as supplementary, not central, to the educational process. The most powerful learning comes from reflecting on experiences that have been lived naturally. Indeed, because every practicing manager is loaded with such experiences, a classroom full of such managers makes for a most remarkable learning situation.

THE CUSTOMIZED CLASSROOM    In his article on the myth of the well-educated manager, Sterling Livingston (1971) cited evidence that the best managers think for themselves—they display a certain individuality in their behavior, appropriate to the context: "Every manager must discover for himself . . . what works and what does not work for him in different situations" (83). The important implication of this is that management education itself has to be fundamentally customized, to the individual. This means designing into the curriculum the flexibility to respond to the people at hand.

It would obviously be prohibitively expensive to design a program for a particular manager the way an architect designs a house for a particular family. That is not what I am suggesting—not quite. The metaphor is inappropriate in two respects: first, the architect does the designing, albeit in consultation with the family; second, the house is completed before the family moves in.

Extend the metaphor to what happens afterward and it gets closer. When the house is completed, the family moves in, and, as mentioned in the last chapter, furnishes it. In other words, it customizes the interior to its own needs. In fact, that process often stretches over a considerable period of time—in a sense, it never stops. This is the case even with families that move into perfectly standardized houses. That standardization reduces the cost of construction, yet it allows the inhabitants to customize the interior. The interior of programs that truly develop managers needs to be customized in the same way.

The classroom equivalent of the house, therefore, is an overall structure provided by subject matter that is filled in by the needs and experiences of the managers who inhabit it. In such a classroom, it is not just a question of when the class will be studying marketing with what cases and so forth but how Alan can engage the class with his concerns about the tunnel vision he finds in his company's marketing channels.

The case study method was quoted in Chapter 2 as "probably as close to practical experience as one can get in a classroom" (Aaronson 1992:179), and, while lacking "some realism . . . seems to convey more of the essential nature of business administrative problems than any other method" (quoted in McNair 1954:86). This may be true when the students have no experience of their own. But the point of this book is that management education is wasted on people who have no experience of their own. As for people who do, the closest the classroom can get to practical experience *is* their practical experience! Published cases are fine for exposure to the experience of others. But they can never get close to the experience that has been lived by the learner—his or her own "live cases."

Put differently, there is too much teaching and not enough learning in management education—too much control of the classroom by "instructors." Professors certainly have much formalized knowledge to convey (as will be discussed in the next point) and other experience to diffuse through cases, but this has to meet what the participants bring to the classroom. In other words, learning takes place where the *push* of the teacher meets the *pull* of the learners. The push of theory and cases dominates the full-time programs; the pull of practice dominates many of the short courses. Management education belongs where the two meet.

## Proposition 3. Insightful theories help managers make sense of their experience.

Porter and McKibbin (1988) note in their study that the company people they surveyed wanted management education to be "more 'realistic,' 'practical,' 'hands on'" (303). We have heard all these demands often enough. They are wrong. Managers who are doing their job live practice every day. They hardly need the educational setting to get them more practical. (As for the inexperienced students who make such demands, the Holy Grail of the "real world" is readily and realistically available in the real world. Get a job!)

Education is hands-*off*; otherwise it is not education. It has to provide something different—conceptual ideas that are quite literally *un*realistic and *im*practical, at least seemingly so in conventional terms. People learn when they *suspend their disbeliefs*, to entertain provocative ideas that can reshape their thinking. That is what education is all about.

Certainly managers have to be "practical"—they have to get things done. But they also have to be thoughtful. The best of them think for themselves—express that individuality Livingston wrote about. The worst copy others—not learn from others, just copy them, mindlessly. They look for some external secret to managerial success, some formula or technique, without realizing that this itself is a formula for failure. Put differently, a central purpose of management education is to encourage the development of wisdom. This requires a thoughtful atmosphere in the classroom, where individuals can probe into their own experience, primed by interesting ideas, concepts, theories.

*Theory* is a dirty word in some managerial quarters. That is rather curious, because all of us, managers especially, can no more get along without theories than libraries can get along without catalogs—and for the same reason: theories help us make sense of incoming information. "[E]xperience is not enough. People may learn little from their experience, unless they have a means for classifying and analyzing it" (Sims et al. 1994:284).

It would be nice if we could carry reality around in our heads and use it to make our decisions. Unfortunately, no head is that big. So we carry around theories, or models, instead: conceptual frameworks that simplify the reality to help us understand it. Hence, these theories better be good! The university is society's instrument for developing and disseminating good theories.

John Maynard Keynes once quipped, "Practical men, who believe themselves to be quite exempt from any intellectual influences, are usually the slaves of some defunct economist." In other words, we use theory whether we realize it or not. So our choice is not between theory and practice so much as between different theories that can inform our practice. For managers, that is where serious education comes in.

What kinds of theories best inform practice? I believe that five characteristics are key:

- *Surprising theories.* Theory is insightful when it allows people to see deeply, imaginatively, and unconventionally, into practice, to open their eyes to new perspectives. Theory that reinforces conventional beliefs—banal theory, of which there is no shortage—doesn't much help because it doesn't much change behavior. Helpful theory tends to surprise, not for its own sake but because it provides insight to a reality people thought they understood, for example, that there is not one but various models of capitalism at work in different countries. Such theory is quite literally subversive: it undermines conventional beliefs and thereby promotes deeper thinking. Imagine, for example, a course called "Leadership by Asking Questions"![1]

- *False theories.* Theory itself is neutral. But the promotion of any one theory as truth is dogma; it turns learning into indoctrination. That is because no theory can ever be true. Every one consists of a set of symbols, usually words on pieces of paper. This is not reality, but the simplification of reality, and so cannot be true. A simple example will explain: The round Earth theory. We discovered "truth" in 1492: The world is round, not flat. Well, think again. The world bulges at the equator. And it has bumps called mountains. So the world is no more perfectly round than it is perfectly flat. Round, of course, has proved better for sailing ships. But not for building them—does any shipbuilder correct for the curvature of the sea? For building ships, the flat Earth theory works fine, just as does Newtonian physics for all kinds of applications, Einstein's insight about relativity notwithstanding.

- *Alternate theories.* The implication of this for the practice of management is profound: that theories are used, not because they are true but because they are useful—*under particular*

---

[1]Discussed by Carlo Bramat, the dean of the Duxx Graduate School of Business Leadership in Mexico, at an Aspen Institute Conference (April 11, 1999).

*circumstances.* And so we have no business promoting single theories in our classrooms—no "one best way," thank you, no trendy managerial correctness. Situations vary enormously. What we should be doing in our management classrooms, therefore, is drawing out the implicit theories that managers have in their minds—what Argyris and Schön (1996) have called their "theories-in-use"—and offering alternate theories, competing explanations of the same phenomena, so that the managers can interpret their experience from different perspectives. When it comes to theory, in other words, managers need choices, not dogmas. (See the box on page 253.) Table 9.1 on the next page lists some of the phenomena about which alternate theories can be useful to managers.[2]

- *Discomforting theories.* Having to consider conflicting theories may not be comfortable. It is much easier to be given "the word," especially when it confirms our existing prejudices. That may be entertainment, but it is not education, and it encourages bad management. As F. Scott Fitzgerald put it, "The test of a first-rate intellect is the ability to hold two opposed ideas in the mind at the same time and still retain the ability to function." If only managers could keep it to two! Perhaps the best advice for managers comes from Whitehead: "Seek simplicity and distrust it." Karl Weick captures this sentiment perfectly in his claim that education can simplify or it can complicate, in order to make people comfortable or uncomfortable. Worst of all for managers, and sadly probably most common, are programs that simplify to make them comfortable. Of course, programs that complicate for discomfort may not be much better. Weick (1996) argues instead in management development for "simplicities that discomfort or complications that comfort" (252).

- *Descriptive theories.* Finally, notice something important about the theories, models, and concepts that I have been discussing: They describe more than prescribe; they try to explain how the world works, not how it should work. Crainer and Dearlove (1999:xx) discuss with relish a high-powered conference of academic gurus embarrassed by the question: "Were business schools reporters of best practice or leaders in best practice?"

---

[2]Examples of well-known books written to open up managers to alternate theories are Morgan's (1986) *Images of Organization* and Hampden-Turner and Trompenaars' (1993) *The Seven Cultures of Capitalism.* My own books in this spirit include two about various forms of organizations (Mintzberg 1979, 1983) and a third on ten schools of thought on the strategy process (Mintzberg, Ahlstrand, and Lampel 1998).

They needn't have been embarrassed: it was the wrong question. Professors have no business doing, either. Their role is to explain practice. "People [in executive education] do want to know what to do, but even more, they want to know what things mean, how to make sense of events" (Weick 1996:257–58).

Managers these days are inundated with prescriptions. These are the problem in management, not the solution, because situations vary so widely. Who would go to a drugstore that dispenses one kind of pill? So why do managers go to courses that prescribe one kind of technique, the solution for every company, whether strategic planning or shareholder value? What managers need is descriptive insight to help them choose or develop prescriptions for their own particular needs. The fact is that better description in the mind of the intelligent practitioner is the most powerful prescriptive tool we have, for no manager can be better than the conceptual frameworks he or she uses. That is the basis of wisdom.

### Table 9.1 ALTERNATE MODELS FOR MANAGERS

#### Models of the Individual

- As a rational actor (economic model)
- As an emotional actor (psychological model, creative model)
- As an social actor (political model, sociological model, administrative model)

#### Models of the Organization

- As a machine
- As a brain
- As an individual (the entrepreneur)
- As a network
- As a set of experts, etc.

#### Models of the Organizational Processes

- As systematic
- As directed
- As organic

#### Models of Society

- Economic
- Sociological/anthropoligical
- Ethical, etc.
- Political/legal
- Historical

## ONE MODEL OF PEOPLE, OR MANY?

Mentioned earlier in the book was Jensen and Meckling's (1994) article on "The Nature of Man." It introduces five models of human behavior, only to dismiss four in favor of their "Resourceful, Evaluative, Maximizing Model"—a narrow and ultimately rather demeaning view of human behavior.

Kunal Basu was asked to do a session on models of human behavior in our masters program for practicing managers. He started in the same place, asking the managers to read Jensen and Meckling's article before the class. But instead of using four of the models as straw men to support a fifth, he used the whole paper as a straw man to support the idea of alternate models, by focusing attention on all of these models, and others.

To reinforce this, Basu showed a classic Japanese film called *Rashomon*, about a couple who are attacked by a bandit in a forest near Kyoto. The film tells the story several times—by the husband, wife, bandit, and a witness. Each describes that one reality in a different way, to put themselves in the best possible light.

The class used all of this material to engage in lively debate about the nature of human behavior, the need for multiple perspectives on it, and whether it can be modeled at all. One group of managers in the class, on their own initiative, later drew a map depicting all the models, and asked their colleagues to locate their own companies on it. That took the discussion further.

## PROPOSITION 4. THOUGHTFUL REFLECTION ON EXPERIENCE IN THE LIGHT OF CONCEPTUAL IDEAS IS THE KEY TO MANAGERIAL LEARNING.

Many management programs promise "boot camp": Be prepared to work hard, they warn—this is no country club. Managers certainly don't need a country club atmosphere for their development, but neither do they need boot camp. Not more boot camp, thank you; too many live it every day! Boot camps train soldiers to march and obey, not to stop and think. Managers today desperately need to stop and think. They need to step back from the action and reflect thoughtfully on the experience they live all too pervasively.

A point made in the last chapter bears repeating here: Learning is not doing; it is reflecting on doing. T. S. Eliot writes in one of his poems, "We had the experience but missed the meaning." Reflection is about getting the meaning. Indeed, in his book *Rules for Radicals*, Saul Alinsky (1971) argues that an activity becomes "experience" only *after* it has been reflected on thoughtfully:

> Most people do not accumulate a body of experience. Most people go through life undergoing a series of happenings, which pass through their systems undigested. Happenings become experiences when they are digested, when they are reflected on, related to general patterns, and synthesized. (68–69)

Sure, we need doers in high places. But we need doers capable of reflecting-in-action, as Schön (1983:60) has put it, to overcome "a parochial narrowness of vision."

Every manager today is forced to carry around a great deal of conceptual baggage. There are all those theories and models, most of them subconscious, and all those heavily promoted techniques—all that managerial correctness to which everyone is supposed to subscribe. In addition, every industry has what Spender (1989) calls its own "recipes"—the accepted beliefs and procedures about how things are supposed to work there. Put all this and a great deal more together, and you can appreciate why thoughtful reflection is so important in the development of managers.

On the Nature of Reflection    Reflecting does not mean musing, and it is not casual. It means wondering, probing, analyzing, synthesizing, connecting—"to ponder carefully and persistently [the] meaning [of an experience] to the self." And not just about *what* you think happened but "*why* do you think it happened?" and "*how* is this situation similar and different from other problems?" (Daudelin 1996:41).

All of this requires struggling. As noted earlier, implicit theories or models have to be surfaced and disbeliefs suspended so they can be put under scrutiny—not an easy thing to do. Then alternate models have to be considered. For all this to happen, people need to be curious, alert, engaged—there has to be a vibrancy in the classroom. This requires, not the popular new educational technologies (Internet learning and CD-ROMs, etc.), which can take the learners in precisely the opposite direction, but good old-fashioned low technology, personal and intense—educators working with students on a log. There is, in other words, no shortcut to the true development of managers. Such development may seem expensive, but management itself is more expensive. And failed management is far more expensive.

REFLECTING ALONE AND TOGETHER    All reflection is ultimately personal. But managers learn personally by reflecting collectively, too.

Managers need time to reflect alone on what they have been through (McCall 1988:8). In the classroom, they can just be allowed quiet time to think, perhaps supported by writing in a journal. Beyond the classroom, they can write reports to connect what they learned there with their experiences on the job. (Examples of doing both will be described later.)

It is critical that this reflection alone be allowed to happen on the manager's own terms. The faculty may introduce the concepts and theories, but each manager has to link them to his or her own experience, as he or she sees fit. Ultimately, the "cases" have to be his or her very own.

Beyond this, managers can benefit from sharing their experiences and reflections with each other in small groups, to stimulate deeper interpretation. "Managerial learning is a social exchange," according to Revans (1983); "the job [is] the syllabus and the colleague [is] the teacher" (15, 53).

From these group discussions can come learning on a third level of reflection, in the overall classroom, where the best insights can be shared. The idea, of course, is to get all three levels working together, depicted in Figure 9.2 as the meshing of gears, with that of the individual turning the small group which turns the full class.

The learners may come from a particular "community of practice," such as a company or an industry; that makes it easier for them to communicate. But sometimes too easy, because together they may be blind to broader meanings. So there are benefits to a community of *learning* that involves people from different practices. Ideal, perhaps, is a combination of the two communities, so that people can go into and out of affinity groups—sometimes reflecting on practice with like-minded colleagues, other times with different colleagues across practices. (Later I shall discuss a classroom architecture to facilitate this approach.)

Of course, experience is shared at every management development program. Speak to managers coming back from one, and they will tell you about all the interesting discussions that took place at meals, coffee breaks, after hours. These discussions are often what they have appreciated most. So why can't they be the center of attention in the classroom itself? Why, in other words, can't the class time be as engaging as the time out of class—by allowing the managers to reflect collectively on their own experience? Indeed, doing so in the classroom allows that

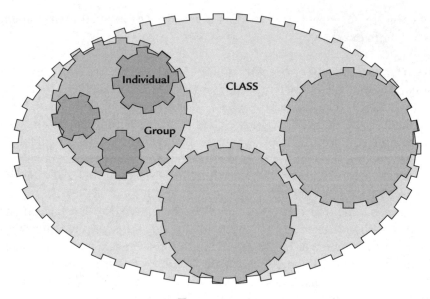

FIGURE 9.2
Reflecting Meshed on Three Levels

sharing to be stimulated by interesting theories, concepts, cases, and other materials that the faculty can introduce. The most important point that management academics have to learn is that experienced managers have at least as much to learn from each other as they do from the faculty. Given half a chance, managers can teach each other in ways that can be startlingly effective.

Likewise, the faculty have to appreciate that they have at least as much to learn from practicing managers as from their own research. This does not relegate their role to observers on the sidelines, although they can certainly do more of that. It means getting involved in the learning brew that is every interesting classroom, by dropping in interesting conceptual materials and helping to stir occasionally. It never ceases to amaze me how much insight can be generated by a classroom of engaged experienced managers. (The first time we ran our program, one of the managers, Alan Whelan of BT, came up to me during the third module and announced, "This program is a failure." Things seemed to be going very well; Alan, in particular, was so enthusiastic. What did he mean? Alan explained: "There are so many interesting ideas coming up in class, but they are not getting beyond the class. The learning is lost on others." I told him I would have to write several articles a day to keep up!)

## Proposition 5. "Sharing" their competencies raises the managers' consciousness about their practice.

Beside concepts are competencies, or skills—the hows alongside the whats and whys. (Despite efforts to distinguish skills from competencies in the literature,[3] in practice they are often used interchangeably, as I shall do here.) These are obviously critical to the practice of managing: Competencies exercised in the managerial job turn thoughts into actions. But they are difficult to deal with in an educational classroom. Moreover, acquiring various competencies does not necessarily make a manager competent.

Competencies in Management Education?    Teaching concepts is a relatively straightforward business. But developing competencies—*training* for skills—is not. It can be difficult and time-consuming, requiring "learning the basic ideas, experimenting, being coached, receiving feedback" and carrying that learning on (Conger 1992:178). One short management development course I knew, on presentation skills, ran in two sessions of several days each with just a handful of managers. Do just a few skills likes this, and you will break the budget of almost any degree program.

Moreover, most of the talent for skill development is not found among academics so much as with professional trainers, whether self-employed, company employed, or in consulting firms. Sure, there are professors adept at inculcating soft skills, and courses that allow them to do so, a common one being negotiations. And there are interesting textbooks (e.g., *Developing Management Skills* by Whetten and Cameron [2001 in its fifth edition]).[4] But professors get hired into

---

[3]My colleagues Kanungo and Misra (1992), for example, have described competencies as "required for non-routine and unprogrammed tasks" (referring "to intelligent functioning and the abilities to engage in cognitive activities"), while skills as more routine and programmed, context and task specific ("triggered by the demands of specific tasks") (1321). These two would, however, seem to constitute a continuum along these dimensions more than two distinct categories. I should add that the *Random House Dictionary* uses each term in defining the other.

[4]A vigorous debate has, however, arisen about mixing up the training for skills with the teaching of concepts. McKnight (1991), for example, argues that skills are "a product of the human subconscious" and so cannot come "from conceptual learning." He faults the Whetten and Cameron text, which he considers the best available, as falling into the trap of trying to make skill development too conceptual (207). Instead, it "must be student-centered," with the professor playing the role of "coach" who watches closely while a student practices a skill (212, 213). That might be reasonable were there not such limited inclination to do such coaching in business schools.

"tenure-track" positions because of their ability to think and do research, not teach skills.[5] So none of this has ever become mainstream in the business schools, despite repeated calls for it.[6]

COMPETENCIES IN MANAGEMENT DEVELOPMENT    Competencies have received far greater attention in management development. There are all kinds of courses devoted to particular ones, such as those of leadership discussed in the last chapter. Yet compare these with a list of many of the competencies that managers seem to exhibit in their jobs (see Table 9.2), and you realize how limited and even haphazard training for competencies can be. And how much do we really know about developing some of the most prominent competencies, such as strategic thinking, even leadership (as discussed in the last chapter), and designing (discussed in the accompanying box)? Perhaps like that old tale from the Middle East, we look for the keys to managerial competencies under the light, where we can see clearly, instead of in the darkness where they are lost.

---

### THE COMPETENCY OF DESIGNING IN MANAGEMENT EDUCATION

In an intriguing little book called *The Sciences of the Artificial*, Herbert Simon (1969) made the point that designing is central to what he calls the "artificial sciences"—his label for people practices such as medicine, engineering, architecture, even music, as well as management. Designing is human intervention to create or change something: build a bridge, write a symphony, cure a disease. Managers design structures and strategies, and they oversee processes by which these as well as products, buildings, and processes get designed.

---

[5]This is not necessarily true of other parts of the university. As Serey and Verderber (1991) point out, skill teaching is hardly uncommon in everything from language training and scientific laboratory technique to art, music, and medicine.

[6]Including my own: "The management school will significantly influence management practice only when it becomes capable of teaching a specific set of 'skills' associated with the job of managing" (Mintzberg 1973:188). We took this seriously at McGill and ran a "Skill Development" course in our MBA program for some years (see Waters 1980). It was handed from one faculty member to another until no one could be found to do it, and then it died. There is, by the way, an interesting irony here, because here is one area where the lack of managerial experience in the MBA does not get in the way. For certain skills, such as conducting negotiations, most students do have natural experience. Here, then, it is the inexperience of the faculty that gets in the way!

For Simon, design is the key to training in these fields. Yet attention to it varies enormously: Architecture teaches it centrally and formally; medicine focuses attention on a narrow form of it called diagnosis; and business schools, despite Simon's towering presence in the field, have not explicitly recognized designing skills, although they certainly make prominent use of expressions such as "organization design."

Yet without so designating it, or perhaps even recognizing it as such, business schools do teach a form of designing: as analysis. In effect, designing reduces to analyzing.

Simon's own position on this is instructive, because on one hand he promoted it, and on the other hand he decried it. In a sense, he got what he wished, but was not happy about the result.

*The professional schools will reassume their professional responsibilities just to the degree that they can discover a* science *of design, a body of intellectually tough,* analytic, *partly formalizable, partly empirical, teachable doctrine about the design process. (58; italics added)*

Simon was quite serious about this, commenting that "there is no question . . . of the design process hiding behind the cloak of 'judgment' or 'experience'" (156). His book contains a lengthy example from a doctoral thesis of a highly programmed method for highway design (145–46), and at one point he even celebrated the role of the computer in the composition of music (158).

Recall (from Chapter 2) that Simon also championed the role of the basic disciplines (economics, psychology, mathematics) in business education, with its resulting emphasis on analysis. Ironic, therefore, is his concern that

*the natural sciences have almost driven the sciences of the artificial from professional school curricula. Engineering schools have become schools of physics and mathematics; medical schools have become schools of biological science; business schools have become schools of finite mathematics. The use of adjectives like 'applied' conceals, but does not change, the fact. . . . It does not mean that design is taught, as distinguished from analysis. (56)*

But design *is* taught in the business schools, *as* analysis. And so they have not "nearly abdicated responsibility for training in the core professional skill" of designing, as Simon claimed (57), so much as deflected that responsibility to analysis.

Management, as discussed in Chapter 1, and the other "artificial" fields, are *practices* that combine art, craft, and science. Medicine, for example, may lean toward science, management toward craft, architecture toward art,[7] but all require all three. Allow too much science in designing, as is common in medicine and management, and technology becomes the designer, with a resulting decrease in creativity, insight, and experience.

So let us accept Simon's important point about the role of designing, if not his approach to exercising it, and conclude that in management, we really need to come to terms with this key competency.

_____

[7]It is interesting in this regard to compare Schön's (1983, 1987) description of the practice and teaching of design in architecture with Simon's views.

### TABLE 9.2 A LIST OF MANAGERIAL COMPETENCIES

**A. PERSONAL COMPETENCIES**

1. Managing self, internally (reflection, strategic thinking +)
2. Managing self, externally (time, information, stress, career +)

**B. INTERPERSONAL COMPETENCIES**

1. Leading individuals (selecting, teaching/mentoring/coaching, inspiring, dealing with experts +)
2. Leading groups (team building, resolving conflict/mediating, facilitating processes, running meetings +)
3. Leading the organization/unit (organizing, merging, building culture, managing change +)
4. Linking the organization/unit (networking, representing, collaborating, promoting/lobbying, negotiating/dealing, politicking, protecting/buffering +)

**C. INFORMATIONAL COMPETENCIES**

1. Communicating verbally (listening, interviewing, speaking/presenting/briefing, writing, information gathering, information disseminating +)
2. Communicating nonverbally (seeing [visual literacy], sensing [visceral literacy] +)
3. Analyzing (data processing, modeling, measuring, evaluating +)

**D. ACTIONAL COMPETENCIES**

1. Scheduling (chunking, prioritizing, agenda setting, juggling, timing +)
2. Administering (resource allocating, delegating, authorizing, systematizing, goal setting, performance appraising +)
3. Designing (planning, crafting, visioning +)
4. Mobilizing (firefighting, project managing +)

_Note._ This table derives from a model I developed of managerial work (Mintzberg 1994), together with a review of many other lists from published and company sources. Many of them—I hope not mine as well—mix skills, values, traits, and even wishes, in strange ways (e.g., from one company list: coaching, customer focus, commitment; or in a prominent textbook: financial management, hard work, clear thinking, respect).

COMPETENCY SHARING    Charles Lindblom (1968) has pointed out that training is most suitable for practices that have been "codified." Yet these, I have been arguing from the outset, are few in the practice of managing. Should we, therefore, give up on skill development in management education altogether, and accept what a colleague once told me—that "You train dogs, not managers"? Must we, in other words, leave this kind of development to moving and mentoring on the job, where it happens anyway, however informally, and to those formal short courses that deal with at least a few competencies?

Not quite. I believe that in management education we can do more than we think even if less than some believe. Beyond the notion of training lies a role well suited to the academic classroom: We can call it *competency sharing*.

Identify a managerial competency, such as negotiating or managing projects—better still, a particular application of one, such as negotiating with partners in a joint venture or dealing with a time delay on a project—and you can usually find enormous experience about it in a classroom of practicing managers. (There can be almost half a millennium of managerial experience in a class of forty middle managers.) Give them a chance to share it in an atmosphere of thoughtful reflection, and watch what happens. The first time we tried this in our program, asking the participants, "How do you reflect in a busy job?" the ideas poured out spontaneously for about forty minutes, filling up several flip chart sheets. Managers love the opportunity to share their experience and to be opened up to the experiences of others. And they can learn a great deal in the process.

Competency sharing is not about how a particular competency *might* be practiced, according to some general theory, or *should* be practiced, according to some popular article, but how it *has* been practiced by those managers in the room—what has worked and not worked for them. They simply got a chance to air and compare their practices.

All kinds of things can come up in such sessions—good and bad practices, trivial and profound ones. Getting them out exposes the managers to alternate ways of behaving, just as getting out different conceptual models exposes them to alternate ways of thinking. The reason this is important is that it increases the managers' awareness of their own practices, so that they can continue to learn from their ongoing experience. Think of this, in the spirit of reflection, as a kind of "consciousness-raising" about competencies.[8]

---

[8]A number of management writers have advocated much the same approach, including McKnight (1991:205), Kotter (1990:4), Conger (1992:49), and Lee (1989), who distinguishes an "awareness training" school for leadership from a "skill building"

This approach can work even for the many competencies that don't lend themselves to formal training. Consider strategic thinking. It is difficult to imagine any adult being turned into a strategic thinker in a classroom. But competency sharing can certainly make a manager more aware of strategic thinking—what it is, how it works, who does it, when it is necessary—and so improve his or her use of it.

## PROPOSITION 6. BEYOND REFLECTION IN THE CLASSROOM COMES LEARNING FROM IMPACT ON THE ORGANIZATION.

Most organizations are happy to send their people away on programs to get back more fully developed managers. They shouldn't be. Stopping at that disconnects the learning process from the learning context. It also renders it indulgent—for the benefit of the isolated individual. And saddest of all, it foregoes enormous potential.

The MBA is personal learning, with the intention of offering better talent at a higher price. This has helped breed a culture of self-serving managers. But the result is much the same from many management development programs, even though the organizations send the managers and pay the fees. In his book *Evaluating Management Education,* Robin Hogarth (1979) assessed the learning of 246 participants in the CEDEP consortium program. A summary from his book is reproduced in Table 9.3. Notice the wording, repeatedly: "enabled *me*," "*I* much appreciated," "for *me*," "helped *me*." Every single statement in the table has that tone except one, which reads, rather lamely, "The acquisition of new techniques helps relations within the company." Management education has to get beyond *me* and *I*, at the very least to encourage managers to get beyond themselves—in other words, to approach leadership.

The first point in this chapter called for the selection of managers from within their own organizations. This implies a strong commitment between the individual and the sponsoring organization, which should work two ways: The organization commits to the individual, and the individual has an obligation to spread his or her learning back into the organization.

In our program, we call this *impact,* and we work it into the design. Its intention is to extend management development into organization development.

---

one and quotes the director of a program at the Center of Creative Leadership that "[o]nce [managers'] consciousness is raised, they have a pretty good idea of what to do" (23, 24).

TABLE 9.3  ASSESSMENT OF THE LEARNING AT CEDEP
(from Hogarth 1979:93; italics added)

| ITEM | PERCENTAGE AGREEMENT ($n = 246$) |
|---|---|
| *Human relations and increased contacts* | |
| • CEDEP enabled *me* to be in contact with people who work in other fields. | 98 |
| • *I* much appreciated the contact with managers from different companies and nationalities. | 97 |
| • The human relations aspects have been particularly valuable for *me*. | 86 |
| • Above all, CEDEP has been an intellectual enrichment *for me*. | 84 |
| *Knowledge* | |
| • It was very helpful for *me* to have to do mental exercises again. | 89 |
| • CEDEP has enabled *me* to acquire knowledge about subjects *I* previously knew nothing about. | 85 |
| • The acquisition of new techniques helps relations within the company. | 73 |
| • It was particularly helpful *for me* to acquire quantitative techniques. | 68 |
| • CEDEP mainly helped *me* to understand my company better. | 50 |
| • *I* have above all brought *myself* up-to-date in *my own* field. | 23 |
| • *I* mainly acquired practical recipes. | 19 |

With the popularity of Action Learning and Work-Out, one aspect of impact has become a big thing: You learn something and then use it to make your organization function more effectively. Let's call this *action impact*. But there is another aspect that should become a bigger thing. Let's call it *teaching impact*.

All managers have to be teachers. As coaches or mentors, they have to develop their own people and aid their colleagues by sharing ideas and experiences. This should be especially true of managers granted the privilege of formal education: The learners away should be teachers back home. Impacts of this kind can range from sharing readings the managers found interesting to briefing colleagues on particular classroom sessions, even running miniature replications of whole modules, as some of the managers in our program have done. Every aspect of the educational process can be carried back for teaching impact (as we shall see in Chapter 13).

Impacts of both kinds require a radical departure on the part of both the schools and the sponsoring organizations. The schools have to open up—they have to become more responsive to the needs of the managers and their organization—and the organizations have to raise their expectations about the programs on which they send their managers and do something about this.

Managers usually go away to programs alone, so they come back feeling isolated. They have learned new things and wish to make changes. But no one seems to care. So they get frustrated. This is a widely recognized problem, addressed in programs as well as in print. But rarely does it get addressed in practice.

With a little effort, sponsoring organizations can turn the problem into an opportunity. While schools should be managing the educational process less, organizations should be managing the consequences of it more. For example, they can send people to programs in cohorts so that they can work together during the program. Back at work, arrangements can be set up to enable them to share their learning, and encourage natural changes that grow out of it. In Chapter 13, I shall describe what some of the companies we work with have been doing in this regard, supported by efforts in our classrooms.

The benefits of both action and teaching impact should be evident. Less evident, but also important, is the fact that with corporations these days so obsessed with "deliverables," such impacts can help justify the costs of management education and so support its main purpose, which is less easy to pin down—namely, the development of more effective managers.

## PROPOSITION 7. ALL OF THE ABOVE SHOULD BE BLENDED INTO A PROCESS OF "EXPERIENCED REFLECTION."

Blend together all the elements discussed in this chapter, and you get a rather new process of management education, which we can call *experienced reflection*. As illustrated in Figure 9.3, the managers bring their experience to the classroom, where the faculty introduce various concepts, theories, models. We can say that the managers live in the territory while the faculty provide the maps. Reflection takes place where these meet: experience considered in the light of conceptual ideas. The resultant learning is carried back to the job, where it impacts behavior, providing further experience for reflection on the job and back to the classroom. This constitutes a recurring cycle, from tacit understanding on the job to explicit learning in the classroom back to tacit application on the job, and on to the next educational module.

Experienced reflection in the classroom confronts new ideas with established beliefs, individually, in small groups, and across a whole class. Because this is a pedagogy of sharing and adapting, the learners have to

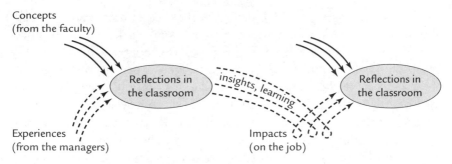

FIGURE 9.3

Experienced Reflection in Management Education

be significantly self-organizing, with considerable time free, sometimes spontaneously, to follow the natural patterns of discovery.

All of this, it should be repeated, is decidedly low-tech, because the human brain is a low-tech device. It absorbs and processes information exactly as it always has, no matter how fancy the input device. Once those inputs hit the eyes and the ears, that's it: The same old human processes take over. So the bottleneck is in the human brain, as it is in all true education. But so is the power—to synthesize and to create. No computer comes close. That is what can make this kind of management education so powerful.

Blending the Business Pedagogies    Experienced reflection can also blend the pedagogies of business education—lectures, cases, exercises, projects—but around the learning of the manager rather than the teaching of the professor. Each approach, in other words, can be used to provide inputs on which managers can reflect, according to their own personal experience.

Consider these different pedagogies in terms of four basic dimensions of learning, from shallow to deep: absorption (internalizing knowledge), application (using it in some limited way—for example, to solve a problem), execution (gaining experience with the knowledge, as in role playing), and reflection (finding the meaning in experience).

Lecturing, alongside reading, is probably the most common pedagogy in the business schools today. (For some years, I have been doing a little study: Every time I pass a classroom, I note who is talking. Guess the result!) It is about absorption or, to repeat an earlier metaphor, about filling up that vessel called student. Tip it, as is done in examinations, and much of the learning spills out. Perhaps little has really been absorbed.

Case study discussions are probably the second most common pedagogy, alongside other simulations of managerial work (such as business games). While case studies have been portrayed as execution—to develop managerial skills and gain a managerial perspective—as concluded in Chapter 2, they look more like application, even absorption (at least where the case is used to illustrate or convey some message). If lecturing is about filling the vessel, then case discussions are about leading the student to water in the hope that he or she will drink.

Action Learning, in the form of fieldwork and other projects, involves execution in a new situation and so offers greater potential for reflection. But because the experience is added on, and therefore also artificial (see Figure 9.4), the opportunities for reflection get limited.

Experienced reflection, as a fourth pedagogy, can make beneficial use of these others as sources of inputs for reflection: concepts through lecturing, the experiences of others through cases, new experiences through field studies and projects. But its real power lies in blending these with the natural experiences of the managers (illustrated in Figure 9.5), which should take central place in the learning process.

Of course, each manager in such a classroom has lived only his or her own experiences. Context, ultimately, is personal—totally customized. In a case discussion, in contrast, everyone shares a single expe-

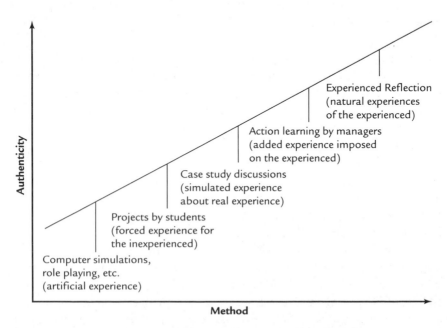

FIGURE 9.4
Management Pedagogies on a Scale of Authenticity

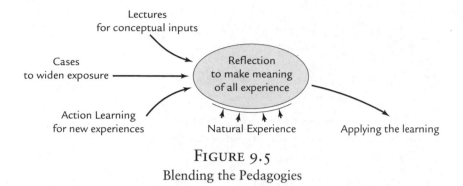

**FIGURE 9.5**
Blending the Pedagogies

rience. But that is a secondhand experience. And in project work, each group lives one experience. But that is forced experience. The advantage of natural experience is that it is robust, deeply felt by the person who has lived it yet easily shared with colleagues who have lived similar experiences. For example, all managers share the experiences of having negotiated contracts or having had to make key decisions under stress. In some respects, all the managers in a classroom have lived each others' experiences; they are all protagonists, seeing in the stories of colleagues their own stories reflected back. How the different managers have lived their experiences and responded to them can be compared to encourage rather sophisticated learning. Moreover, in a modular program the managers return repeatedly and so get to know their colleagues' contexts rather well. The collective experiences of such a classroom become a set of ongoing living cases.

Stories, it should be emphasized, can be key learning devices. Sims et al. (1994:281) have pointed out that "managers prefer the analogue" to the digital. So do all sophisticated learners, including schoolchildren in Calgary. That is why stories are so powerful: They "convey analogue knowledge," blending experiences with ideas.

BLENDING THE LEARNING    To get from there to here, we need to shift the classroom focus from teaching to learning. Sure, the two are linked, and there is need for both. But which has the focus of attention makes a great difference, as suggested by the quotations in the box on page 268.

Teaching is "instructor driven"—it transmits material, usually in neat packages. Accordingly, it tends to be controlled, convergent, and categorical. That can be important for conveying information about concepts, and even competencies—things to be "covered." But to repeat a point introduced in Chapter 1, teachers who always "know better" undermine learning.

## ON TEACHING VERSUS LEARNING

- *"I am always ready to learn, although I do not always like to be taught."* (Winston Churchill)

- *"I was watching how learning happens when people aren't meddling with it."* (Nancy Badore, commenting on a management development experience)

- *"I need the fix of talking in front of a group of people about something I enjoy."* (a professor quoted in a *Business Week* article [Bongiorno 1994:45] about the best business school teachers in the United States)

- *"By its very nature, teaching homogenizes both its subjects and its objects. Learning, on the other hand, liberates."* (Bennis 1989:70)

- *"Learning is a process of construction. In other words, what is learned is put together by the learner."* (Gaskins and Elliot 1991:41)

- *"We hate teaching; we love learning."* (feedback to the faculty in our International Masters Program in Practicing Management)

Learning focuses on the student and how he or she develops. Ultimately, therefore, it has to be responsive and customized, blended into a stream of discovery—much like managing itself, where experiences, concepts, and reflections blend together as the manager goes along. And so should this be true of management education, back and forth between the classroom and the job.

## PROPOSITION 8. THE CURRICULUM, THE ARCHITECTURE, AND THE FACULTY SHOULD ACCORDINGLY BE SHIFTED FROM CONTROLLED DESIGNING TO FLEXIBLE FACILITATING.

All of the preceding points call for a reconsideration of much that has become sacred in business education. And not a moment too soon! If the ideas in this chapter have merit, then they should be subversive, undermining much current practice. So much that is now directive—the design of the curriculum, the layout of the classroom, the role of the faculty—has to become facilitative. In other words, it has to support the learning, not drive the teaching.

CURRICULA TO COLLABORATE     Management programs, whether long term for education or short term for development, are almost always chopped into neat "courses" and "classes," each with its own box of disassociated knowledge, skills, cases, and so forth, all packaged together in a "curriculum." That is teaching. "If this is Tuesday, or the second semester, it must be Ethics." Back to that old machine assumption: If the planners do their job in advance, the parts will magically add up to a whole, just like automobiles coming off an assembly line. Think of this as intrusion—everything gets stuck in. Marketing gets stuck in. Ethics gets stuck in. Even that "capstone" course on strategy gets stuck in after all the others.

Courses and classes do not add up to an education. If in their own work "[m]anagers cannot focus on isolated, separated problems for long," if they "need to develop an ability to synthesize information from a wide variety of sources and appreciate the interconnectedness of phenomena and decisions" (Whitley 1989:220), then shouldn't education for management be designed to deal with this?

For example, if ethics is truly important for a company, then it has to infuse all of a company's behavior. Appointing a vice president for ethics, as if one person can be responsible on behalf of everyone else, is silly. Everyone has to behave ethically. Likewise, if ethics is important for educating managers, then designating a course to "cover" ethics is likewise silly. It has to infuse the classroom, across all kinds of issues, whenever they arise, from expanding a business to pricing a pharmaceutical. In the same way, strategy and people are not isolated disciplines, but phenomena linked to everything organizations do. To extend that old story, because management is not an elephant made up of disassociated parts, management education cannot be a butcher that hacks it up for the convenience of the curriculum.

Imagine, therefore, a program woven together of values and attitudes, blending stories with ideas, using engaging methods of learning to hold the participants responsible for reflecting together on their experiences. Imagine a faculty with an ongoing presence, who help blend the ideas that come up from one day and one module to the next. This is an integration that flows, rather than having been designated.

None of this renders the faculty passive. Quite the opposite: It engages them more deeply by involving them, like the students, in the unfolding dynamic. "No surprises" in the classroom means no learning for the professor—and not much for the students either. We need less control in management education and more collaboration.

A PLACE TO REFLECT    The university is an ideal place to reflect. It is a magnet for people who like to be *critical*, in the two meanings of the word: "Inclined to find fault" and the "art or act of judging the quality" of something (*Random House Dictionary*). Many academics are certainly inclined to find fault. But that becomes useful when it is combined with the art of judging quality: to see beneath, above, and beyond the obvious, to the deeper and higher meaning of important things. This is what can make the university such a powerful setting for the development of managers. And it is what makes so unfortunate current trends in the business schools toward hype and "businesslike" behavior.

If managers need to step back, suspend disbeliefs, and reflect on interesting ideas, then what better place than the safety and seriousness of the academic setting, where "the adventure of action meets the adventure of thought," without pressure or interruption, "to weld together imagination and experience" (Whitehead 1932:143, 140). Academia is a good place to escape from the easy answers in order to reflect on the difficult questions.

A SPACE TO REFLECT    Whitehead (1932) also wrote that "the combination of imagination and learning normally requires some leisure, freedom from restraint, freedom from harassing worry" (146). This point can only be true of the university if it is true of its classrooms. Boot camps, intense examinations, and classrooms designed to put pressure on the student get in the way of learning.

The classrooms common in business schools today line up students in neat rows so that they can all see the professor. That setup may be fine for conveying information from the front, but it hardly facilitates sharing among everyone else. Arching these rows in the shape of a U so that the students can also see each other for case discussions may be an improvement, but that puts attention on the individual, not the group, especially that individual at the front, in the so-called pit. These are classrooms designed more for competition than collaboration, for making points more than for sharing experiences. They speed things up; they do not slow them down.

Take a look at the photographs of teachers in the business school brochures. I collected several from executive programs at Harvard: the professor always making a point (with a finger in the air!), while all the managers look on obediently, out of focus! Does this look like a setting for managers?

We know from all kinds of research that managers work mostly face-to-face, whether one-on-one or in small groups. They rarely line up in large groups. We know further that they spend a great deal of time with their peers. Yet here they all are gazing down on the authority figure in the front. It looks like a caricature of hierarchy! We also know that despite the advent of fancy information technology, managers still favor physical presence. They practice a people job. Why move them out of the classroom, away from each other—just to use that technology?

The classroom may not be the workplace, but it should at least be compatible with it. A flat classroom with round tables facilitates natural discussion in small groups alongside formal presentations. There is no need to "break out." Managers can go in and out of reflective discussions on a moment's notice. Each table becomes a little learning community in its own right, within the larger learning community that is the whole classroom. And by varying how people sit—in company groups, by job concerns, cross-culturally, and so on—the focus of discussion around the tables can be varied. While the conventional classroom clearly shows itself to be designed for the faculty, this kind of seating allows the managers to assume co-ownership of the space. In Chapter 10, I will discuss how this architecture has proved critical in shifting management education from teaching to learning.

A FACULTY TO FACILITATE    Adaptable educating in a flexible space requires an adaptable and facilitating faculty. This has to begin with the design of the curriculum, as already discussed. The faculty certainly have to be designers—architects of the learning experience—but as architecture was discussed earlier: not by designing and drawing, to create rigid structures, but by establishing flexible superstructures that can adapt to the people inside. The faculty, in other words, have to be the designers of an ongoing social process as much as the conveyers of conceptual knowledge. And unlike most architects today, they have to remain on site while their designs become reality. Bloom (1987:20) has likened this role to midwifery, in that the faculty help facilitate a perfectly natural process. Just because people are called professors does not mean they have to spend so much time professing.

It is nice to have star teachers who convey interesting material in enticing ways. But we need people who can introduce interesting material and then engage the class with it—by stimulating, listening, integrating. This means not only going with the flow but also introducing new concepts "just in time," as they become relevant to the discussion at hand. More to the point, it means that the faculty have to encourage the managers to get involved in that process. So considerable control has to be ceded to the learners, to help set the agenda as key issues arise.

We have a 50-50 rule in our classrooms, which calls for half the time over to the participants *on their agenda*. We struggle to achieve it and rarely overdo it. But we do seek that delicate balance between directing and facilitating.

In one of our modules, class time was mistakenly scheduled to end too early in the afternoon. So at the last minute some of the sessions were extended. Faculty members arrived carefully prepared, only to be told they had an extra hour. The timing proved perfect! They loosened up and allowed lots of time for reflections on their inputs. Hence, rule 4 was added to the set guidelines we prepared for "professors who wish to educate real managers," reproduced in the accompanying box.

---

### TEN RULES FOR PROFESSORS WHO WISH TO EDUCATE REAL MANAGERS

---

1, 2, 3. Don't pack it. Don't pack it. Don't pack it.

4. Schedule an extra hour for each session, but don't tell the "instructors" until they arrive.

5. Profess less: the participants have at least as much to learn from each other as from the professors. (This is about what they learn, not about what we teach.)

6. Let the participants run with the concepts on their agenda.

7. Be flexible; let good discussion go: If necessary, cut what is supposed to be "covered."

8, 9, 10. Listen. Listen. Listen.

---

All of this, we have found, requires not trained facilitators, let alone star entertainers, so much as smart people with facilitating skills. We cannot do much for good facilitators who are not terribly good with the concepts, or with star professors who need to control the discussion, or just plain listen to themselves. But we have had remarkable success with smart people and decent lecturers willing to facilitate a good discussion. In all of the locations of our program, including Japan and India where we were warned about traditional approaches to teaching (not that Western locations are ultimately different), we have been able to coax good academics—meaning open learners—over to this pedagogy. This success stems from the fact that truly able professors enjoy learning a lot more than teaching. They may have been used to lecturing in the classroom, but they have also been used to learning in research. So why not in the classroom? They can, after all, think on their feet, and that is a very valuable skill in facilitating experienced reflection.

I recall an economist in India who made a perfectly good presentation in an early morning session in our program, followed by some questions, before taking a break. I looked at the schedule and found that he was to do much the same thing after the break. Uh-oh, I thought, the participants will protest. They need a chance to run with the material.

He returned, put a facilitating question on the board, and asked them to discuss it at their tables. The class got active. Later he drew out their findings in a plenary session.

"How did that happen?" I asked a colleague after the session. "Easy," he answered. "I took him aside and suggested it. He said, 'Sure, why not?!'"

My greatest delight has been to watch people who never gave much thought to teaching method (myself included) come alive with the energy of such a class, seeing their concepts come alive in the context of experience. In this kind of architecture, with these kinds of students, many have been willing to loosen up and give it a try. Of course, hitherto creative teachers get especially enthusiastic in such a classroom too, because it is so sympathetic to their skills. They no longer need to struggle against the current. Many are less enthusiastic about returning to conventional programs.

## Toward Engaging Management

Chapter 4 discussed styles of managing labeled calculating and heroic, to make the point that they are undermining management practice. Another style was introduced there but not discussed, labeled *engaging*. It is time to discuss it, because I believe it is a style encouraged by the approach to management education that has been described here.

Chapter 1 made the distinction between those fields populated by experts who have to know better, as in surgery, and those in which knowing better is the problem, because it preempts the engagement of the recipients. Managing and educating were described as examples of the latter—both require facilitating more than controlling. But traditional management education has favored professors who believe they know better, and that, in turn, has produced managers who believe they know better, too.

Yet over the course of the last century, our perceptions of managing has been moving in the opposite direction. Compare Henri Fayol's famous words of 1916—managerial work as planning, organizing, coordinating, and controlling (four labels for controlling)—with the more recent writings about organizations as flexible networks of knowledge workers. Shouldn't we be educating managers in ways consistent with how we believe it should be practiced? In other words, shouldn't we be engaging managers in the classroom so that they can be encouraged to engage other people in their organizations?

Described here in ideal terms, closest to craft, engaging managers connect on the floor; they are less inclined to deem from detached offices. They dig out impressions beyond reading facts, by listening more than talking, seeing and feeling more than sitting and figuring. They are inclined to inspire more than empower, to collaborate more than control. The idea is to ensure other people are in control. So these managers do not see themselves as the allocators of resources, including those human resources, so much as the strengtheners of the bonds among human beings.

Overall, such managers favor care over cure; they do not act as surgeons who slice left and right so much as caregivers intent on avoiding surgery in the first place. They see their organizations as networks, not hierarchies, with themselves operating throughout, not on top. And that means strategies look to them more like trees to be planted, by many people, than as lightning bolts thrust down from above. If "I deem so that you do" is the implicit motto of the heroic manager, then "We dream so that we do" is that of the engaging manager. These people engage themselves to engage others—namely, to bring out the positive energy that exists naturally within people. This takes that old leadership adage about people thinking that they did it themselves one important step further, to the realization that people *do* do it themselves.

Table 9.4 contrasts the two main styles of management that we have been discussing. The description of heroic management is reminiscent of the tables at the end of Chapter 2, on the impression left by MBA education, and near the end of Chapter 4, on "Rules for Being a Heroic Leader." That of engaging management draws on comments made in various places in our discussion. MBA education tilts to one side of this table; I believe management education should be tilting to the other.

A farmer lying on his deathbed tells his children that there is a fortune buried in the field. All they need do is dig it up. After his death, they dig and they dig. They never find the fortune. But their digging improves the field, and so they live comfortable lives. We need to do a lot of digging in the field of management education.

## TABLE 9.4 TWO WAYS TO MANAGE

| HEROIC MANAGEMENT | ENGAGING MANAGEMENT |
|---|---|
| 1. Managers are important people, quite apart from others who develop products and deliver services. | 1. Managers are important to the extent that they help other people who develop products and deliver services to be important. |
| 2. The higher "up" these managers go, the more important they become. At the "top," the chief executive *is* the corporation. | 2. An organization is an interacting network, not a vertical hierarchy. Effective leaders work throughout; they do not sit on top. |
| 3. Down the hierarchy comes the strategy—clear, deliberate, and bold—emanating from the chief who takes the dramatic acts. Everyone else "implements." | 3. Out of the network emerge strategies, as engaged people solve little problems that grow into big initiatives. |
| 4. Implementation is the problem because while the chief embraces change, most others resist it. That is why outsiders must be favored over insiders. | 4. Implementation is the problem because it cannot be separated from formulation. That is why committed insiders are necessary to resist ill-considered changes imposed from above and without. |
| 5. To manage is to make decisions and allocate resources—including those human resources. Managing thus means analyzing, often calculating, based on facts from reports. | 5. To manage is to bring out the positive energy that exists naturally within people. Managing thus means engaging, based on judgment, rooted in context. |
| 6. Rewards for increased performance go to the leadership. What matters is what's measured. | 6. Rewards for making the organization a better place go to everyone. Human values matter, few of which can be measured. |
| 7. Leadership is thrust upon those who thrust their will on others. | 7. Leadership is a sacred trust earned from the respect of others. |

# 10

# DEVELOPING MANAGERS I
## *The IMPM Program*

*Do not go where the path may lead; go instead
where there is no path and leave a trail.*
—RALPH WALDO EMERSON

What should Vladěna do? She has a good education—a bachelors degree in philosophy from a reputable Czech university and a masters in international affairs from a well-known American one. She has excellent experience, having worked for an international consulting firm and then an Internet startup before becoming a manager with a Czech telecom company. There she practices management using her experience and her wits. That is all she has, beside the mentoring of an experienced colleague. Vladěna is smart and personable. She wants to go to business school.

What will it do to her? Increase her bargaining power in the international job market, to be sure. Give her a better understanding of business, too, including the vocabulary to face other managers with MBAs. But will it make her a better manager?

Through several chapters, I have argued no, quite the opposite. Now I would like to describe perhaps not what Vladěna is able to do right now but what I hope all Vladěnas will be able to do in the near future.

## THE INTERNATIONAL MASTERS
## IN PRACTICING MANAGEMENT

A group of colleagues and myself, from Canada, England, France, India, and Japan, have spent the better part of the last decade bringing the intentions of the previous chapter to life. We did not wish to create just another program or even just a novel one. We set out to change the course of management education: to showcase an approach suited to the serious education and development of practicing managers. The attainment of knowledge and the enhancement of competences are important, but we wanted our program to go beyond these, to help people become not just more effective managers but wiser human beings—more thoughtful, more worldly, more engaging.

The result is the International Masters in Practicing Management (IMPM), which we believe is true to the tenets of the last chapter. We still have a long way to go, but we have come a long way too—enough—I believe, to present our experience as indicative of what is possible. My intention in this and the next four chapters is to convince you of that, by describing the IMPM's design, functioning, results, and offshoots.

I make no pretence of objectivity here. My colleagues and I have put our hearts and souls into this activity, so you will have to accept a certain degree of enthusiasm instead. Besides, objectivity is boring, while we have created something exciting. What we have done and learned requires some space to be appreciated, so this discussion has been divided into several chapters: on the IMPM setting (Chapter 10); on mindsets as an organizing framework for management education (Chapter 11); on learning back on the job (Chapter 12); on the impact of such education on the sponsoring organizations, including its costs and benefits (Chapter 13); and on the diffusion of this innovation into other programs, short and long (Chapter 14).

In developing the IMPM, we borrowed the best innovations we could find from other programs for practicing managers (many of them, as noted in Chapter 7, in England), added a number of our own, and wove all this into a comprehensive model that we think of as a single innovation. Thus, while parts of the IMPM can be found in other programs, the package cannot, although these chapters have been written to change that.

Sprinkled throughout are anecdotes, stories, and comments from those involved in the program—participants, company people, faculty, observers. (Some of these come from papers written by these people for a conference held on the program in England in 2000. They can be seen,

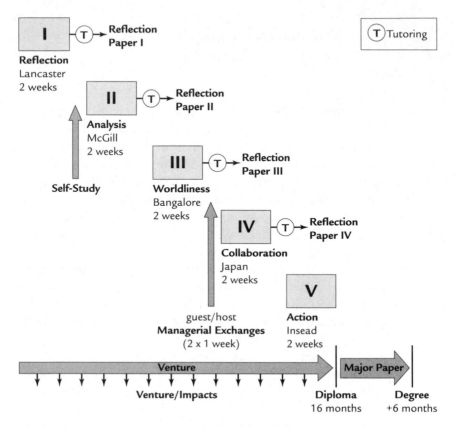

FIGURE 10.1
Structure of the IMPM

and will be referenced, at www.impm.org.) All of this is offered in the hope that others will borrow from our experience, as we have borrowed from others, so that we can all get on with the long-overdue job of developing management education.

OVERVIEW    Figure 10.1 shows the outline of the IMPM as five two-week modules at our five locations, each devoted to a different managerial *mindset* (called reflection, analysis, worldliness, collaboration, and action). Around these are the program's other activities, many of which happen back at work. *Reflection Papers* are written to link the learning of each module to the participants' context. These, especially, are supported by *Tutoring* (shown with a *T*). What we call *Self-Study* develops the "language of business" in marketing, finance, and accounting, in preparation for Module II. *Managerial Exchanges* takes place between Modules II and IV, in which the participants pair up and spend a week at each other's workplace. A *Venture*, as well as *Impacts*, focus on change activities back at work. All of this spreads over almost a year and a half, so that the IMPM becomes ten weeks of classroom activity embedded in a sixteen-month educational journey. Following this, those who wish to receive the Masters of Practicing Management degree write a *Major Paper* as a kind of small thesis.

Middle to senior managers, mostly in the age range of thirty-five to forty-five, are sent and sponsored by their companies. (I will use the word *company* for convenience, although one prominent NGO has been active in the IMPM, and a sister program has been developed for social sector organizations.) A given class, which we call *cycle*, of which there has been one each year since the spring of 1996, usually has about thirty-five to forty participants. We request that the companies send them in groups so that they can work together on company issues and also that the class can be seen as several working clusters and not just a collection of individuals.

## Geographic Setting: Authentically International

We set out to create an authentically international experience in the IMPM—not a domestic program with foreign activities but one truly balanced across different parts of the world, centered in none, so that each location feels both local and foreign. The companies that have sent participants are headquartered in all five of our locations and sometimes beyond. While they have been asked to commit to only one cycle at a time, most have participated in most or all of the cycles, including (up to Cycle 8, started in 2003), Fujitsu and Matsushita from Japan, LG from Korea, Électricité de France (EDF)/Gaz de France, the International Federation of Red Cross and Red Crescent Societies headquartered in Geneva, BT from Britain, Lufthansa from Germany, and Alcan and the Royal Bank from Canada. From India, we have had mostly senior managers from small companies, which has worked fine (although some larger companies there, including Hewlett-Packard, Coca-Cola, and Bharati Telecom, have sent managers more recently). Typical of our balanced attendance was Cycle 3, with fifteen Asians, fifteen Europeans, six North Americans, two Africans, and one South American.

MULTICULTURAL, NOT "GLOBAL"    Our program may sound rather international, but it is not meant to be "global." Like most managers of even the most "global" corporations, our participants have mostly been

## TABLE 10.1 GLOBAL OR CROSS-CULTURAL
### (adapted from Costea and Watson 1998)

| AN AMERICAN MBA PROGRAM IN BUDAPEST | THE IMPM |
|---|---|
| • Participants are similar in East and West. | • Participants' identities are as diverse as their cultures. |
| • Teaching materials and methods are transferable because business practices are universal and management is "global"—hence the focus on teaching as transmission. | • Teaching materials and methods have to adapt to different needs because managerial practices are contextual—hence the focus on learning as personal and shared reflection. |
| • Manager is seen as an abstracted, individual self with behavior mainly ordered by economic rationality. | • Human self is seen as a dynamic combination of processes and events happening in relation to other selves. |
| • Learning is seen as cognitive and decontextualized. | • Learning is seen as interactive, in relationships. |

rooted in their home cultures.[1] Our intention has been not to rip them out of these cultures but to leave those roots intact while extending their reach to other cultures. Why impose conformity when we can benefit from diversity, to explore different perspectives? In this spirit, our intention has been to create *worldly* managers, not global ones. (See Table 10.1.)

The IMPM has thus become a meeting ground of different cultures—across countries and companies—in a safe and relaxed setting, on each other's home territories. That opens up the learning, including putting into question the very notions of global and local. Stereotypes fade quickly in such a classroom, as people find commonality where they expected diversity and diversity where they expected commonality. This, of course, happens in every program with international participation, but the fact that the IMPM is as Japanese as it is British, as Canadian as it is Indian, and so forth, makes all the difference. Moreover, because the participants are locals in one of the modules, and can therefore host their colleagues, experiences abroad become less voyeuristic and more engaging.

---

[1] A poll in one of the cycles, as to who in the class carried a passport different from the location of head office, was rather revealing, about this group and probably "globalization" in general. Only the Alcan and Red Cross people put up their hands in any numbers. Almost all the other participants, despite in some cases widespread international experience and even current location abroad, were nationals of the headquarters country.

With this has come something quite novel for the partner schools: an expectation that they embed their modules in the local culture—to discover their managerial roots, so to speak. Some schools embraced this challenge more than others, most notably in Japan and India (about the context of development if not about an Indian style of managing).

## STRUCTURAL SETTING:
## A BALANCED PARTNERSHIP

The IMPM has been set up as a balanced partnership, of the Indian Institute of Management at Bangalore (IIMB); Insead in Fontainebleau, France; the Lancaster University Management School in England; the McGill University Faculty of Management in Montreal, Canada; and in Japan a group of faculty drawn from three schools, at Hitsosubashi University, Kobe University, and the Japanese Advanced Institute of Science and Technology (later including the Korean Development Institute in Seoul).

The program has a small central administration independent of any school, which includes a program director and a program administrator. A cycle director, usually from one of the schools, oversees and coordinates the activities of a particular cycle and attends all of its modules. Each school names a module director for each cycle, who heads up the local design and delivery team and attends the entire module. These module directors, plus the cycle director (who often heads up the module in his or her own school), do most of the tutoring.

All of these people together also form the Organizing Committee concerned with programwide issues. This has worked well because people represent schools, not departments. So they do not lobby for their particular functions (nor need they lobby for their schools, since each has its own module). But they have not been shy to lobby for their views of what the programs need (to the point where we have come to call this committee the "Mob of Six").

Finally, the deans or directors of the various schools form the Governing Committee of the program, which meets annually, usually in conjunction with the annual meeting we hold for representatives of the participating companies, where we share our learning and practices.

All of this adds up to a most unusual partnership. I have been asked repeatedly by academic colleagues, especially in the United States, how we have managed to sustain such a partnership. At first the question puzzled me. We manage it like any alliance, I answered, with a good deal of attention. Then I realized what was driving the question. In many collaborations, a prestigious school, usually American, takes the lead, and others follow. The IMPM partnership works because it *is* a partnership; there is no lead school.

The partnership extends to the companies that send the participants, but more de facto than de jure. These companies do not form a "consortium" that owns the program, but the fact that so many have remained with the program over the years, and meet with us annually to share experiences, has produced a rather strong partnership. (More on company activities later.)

## CONCEPTUAL SETTING: MANAGERIAL MINDSETS

A major challenge for us was to come up with a framework to get past the functional structure that has so dominated business education. Criticizing it is easy enough, but we needed a structure to replace it. So we gave a good deal of thought to developing one that would be managerial.

The traditional business functions see the world as made up of problems out there, to be slotted into the bodies of specialized knowledge in the schools—marketing, finance, human resources, and so forth. The world is seen as objective, amenable to the application of systematic knowledge. Give managers the tools, and they will solve the problems.

Managers, unfortunately, do not live in such a world. Their world is messy and confusing. Those problems that can be slotted into the conventional functions can be delegated to functional specialists, leaving behind the difficult problems. These are managerial precisely because they don't fit into the neat categories.

As noted in Chapter 8, some programs have used thematic structures, around issues such as globalization and supply chain management. This is better, since it approaches concerns as they can appear on the managerial agenda. But such themes can be narrow and temporary. Managers need a framework that is more stable and broadly conceptual.

DERIVING THE MINDSETS[2]    As suggested in Figure 10.2, everything an effective manager does is sandwiched between *action* on the ground and *reflection* in the mind. Reflection without action is passive; action with-

---

[2]The framework described here was influenced by a model of managerial work that I developed a few years earlier (see Mintzberg 1994).

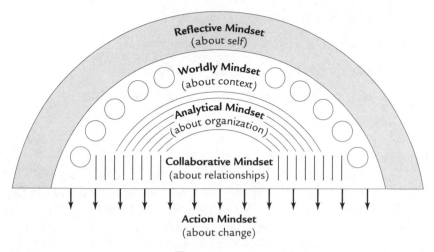

FIGURE 10.2
A Framework for Management Education

out reflection is thoughtless. Effective managers thus function at the interface of these two *mindsets*: where reflective thinking meets practical doing. We thus sandwich our program in the same way, beginning with a module on reflection and ending with one on action.

But reflecting and acting about what? We see the whats on three levels: about people and their *relationships*, about the *organization* being managed, and about the world around that organization—namely, its *context*. This gives us two mindsets and three subjects.

But each of these three subjects has another mindset most closely related to itself. For people and relationships, we take that to be *collaboration*—getting things done cooperatively with other people, in negotiations, for example. About the organization, we take the predominant mindset to be *analysis*. Organizations depend on the systematic decomposition and combination of activities that analysis is all about. And about context, we take the most important mindset to be, not global, but *worldly*, which the *Oxford Dictionary* defines as "experienced in life, sophisticated, practical," suggesting a deep appreciation of reality in its many forms.

Likewise, the two initial mindsets also have subjects of their own. For reflection, that is *self*: Managers reflect ultimately as individuals. And for action, the subject is *change*, across all the other subjects—self, relationships, organization, and context.

Put this all together and you have five perspectives that have to be combined in the practice of managing:

- Managing Self: the reflective mindset
- Managing Organizations: the analytic mindset
- Managing Context: the worldly mindset
- Managing Relationships: the collaborative mindset
- Managing Change: the action mindset

If you are a manager, this is your world!

We mapped these on to our five locations, so that each partner could develop its module based on one of the mindsets—not exclusively, but essentially. Much of this has in fact proved fortuitous: We do reflection in England, home to people who can be rather thoughtful; analysis at McGill, in North America, where the analytical approach to management has had its fullest development; worldliness in India, a very different place where so many worlds collide; collaboration in Japan, which gives great attention to that mindset; and action at the France-based Insead, which has great strengths in the teaching of change. It has, in fact, been fascinating to see how the modules have taken on these five different flavors—for example, a rather inquisitive flavor about reflection in England compared with a more hard-nosed flavor about action at Insead.

We make no claim to this framework being scientific or comprehensive, only that it has proved particularly useful in our program (see Gosling and Mintzberg 2003). Managers relate to it easily and naturally; they can see themselves and their work in it. Also, we do not use the label "mindset" to set anyone's mind. We have all had more than enough of that! Rather, we see these as attitudes—turns or frames of mind that set activity in motion. Think of them too as mind*sights*—namely, perspectives. Just bear in mind that, improperly used, they can also be *minesites*: too much of any, in the absence of others, can blow up in a manager's face, whether it is obsessive analyzing or compulsive collaborating, etc.

## PEDAGOGICAL SETTING:
## THE REFLECTIVE CLASSROOM

How to bring these mindsets to life? Our purpose has been not simply to teach these frames but to give them life in the learning process. That is where our approach of experienced reflection comes in: to leverage the extensive and varied experience of managers around the perspectives of reflection, action, collaboration, analysis, and worldliness.

We do not want "students" in our classroom—vessels sitting there waiting to be filled—any more than we want "customers"—buyers lined up to receive our "services." We want *participants*, who take responsibility for their learning by bringing their own experience to bear on it. "The fox knows many things, but the hedgehog knows one big thing" is an ancient Greek expression. Reflecting on experience is the IMPM's one big thing.

For deep reflection to occur, the participants—and the faculty— have to relax their everyday assumptions and open their minds to new and sometimes seemingly strange ideas. In Samuel Coleridge's famous phrase, already used several times, they must willingly suspend their disbeliefs; in a related phrase of one of our cycle directors, Ramnath Narayanswamy, they have to "institutionalize doubt."

Reflection takes place inside and outside our classrooms. I shall discuss the outside activities later, concentrating here on reflection inside.

APOSTROPHE TABLES    We use what we call "apostrophe tables" for seating. After spending time in the class, Jeanne Liedtka, of the Darden School at Virginia, referred to this architecture as "a kind of breeding ground for subversive student democracy!"

This idea came about after a question from Nancy Badore, who became well known for setting up an ambitious executive development program at the Ford Motor Company (see Helgesen 1990). "How do you intend to sit people?" she asked me before we began. "I suppose in one of those U-shaped classrooms," I replied. "Not those obstetrics stirrups!" Nancy shot back. That became one of the more important moments for our development. We sat down with an architect and came up with another design, which has become absolutely critical to our whole approach.

We call them apostrophe tables because participants sit around circular tables spread out in a flat classroom, and in some places we add extra little tables (the apostrophes) for those who have to swivel around to see a presentation. We do not want people sitting there as individuals in tiered rows, all facing an "instructor" who directs the proceedings. Nor do we wish to disrupt the class in order to "break out" for small-group discussions—which should happen frequently. This seating, as noted in Chapter 9, creates a set of communities around the tables and a sense of community in the whole flat room. It feels very different from the assembly of individuals in a traditional classroom. Because the participants can face in to share experiences as well as out to hear presentations, they own the space as much as the faculty do. In a sense, the classroom has no obvious front, other than a wall where presentations are made. This architecture may restrict class size—we find it works well with up to about forty people—but much beyond that, any class-room risks shifting from learning to teaching.

Most important, this seating allows the class to go into and out of group discussions, sometimes for a few minutes at a time. We can, for example, ask whether there are any "table" questions—questions considered by the groups around the tables instead of just coming from the first individual who raises a hand.

Our seating arrangement is certainly convenient, and round tables have certainly been used elsewhere, but I believe that, compared with the usual arrangement of business school classrooms, it is revolutionary—as suggested by the story in the accompanying box.

---

### "I *SEE* WHAT YOU MEAN!"

Tomo Noda of Insead wanted to get involved in IMPM-style education, but had never been in one of the classrooms. So we invited him to the opening of a new cycle at Lancaster—the first day of a new class.

As program director, Jonathan Gosling began by outlining briefly what was to come. After about ten minutes, he called for questions. There were none—everyone was new, too shy to start. So Jonathan talked for another five minutes and then said, "Why don't you discuss this around your tables and see if there are any questions." There was an immediate buzz in the room, as all took up the request.

Tomo walked over to me with a gleam in his eye. "I *see* what you mean!" We had explained the IMPM approach to him in advance, and he understood everything we said. But a few minutes in that classroom, even with a brand-new group, and he *saw* the difference!

---

We have sat people in all kinds of ways around the tables: in company groups to consider different models of organization; by country of residence to compare consumer behaviors; according to job titles to consider the pressures of managing; and so on. Other times they sit randomly or explicitly mixed ("No one from the same company or country at any one table"). Once, after one intensive session on "Managing Selves," the women in the class decided that—for once—they wished to sit together.

IN AND OUT OF WORKSHOPS    This architecture can encourage the faculty to rethink their approach. That is because the class they face consists of communities, not just individuals, who face into their own concerns as much as out to the faculty's ideas. Nothing, of course, stops faculty members from making their own inputs; indeed, introducing interesting material is a critical part of the process, whether by lecture, case discussion, or prior reading, etc., to stimulate the learning. But this happens best when the material is turned over to the participants around the tables *on their agendas*. They have to run with it—see how it can be made insightful in their own contexts. That is what opens up profound possibilities for learning.

Here, especially is where our "50:50 rule" comes in: Half the time, we try to turn the classroom over to the participants on their agendas. After I do a session on forms of organizations in the second module, for example, I ask the participants, sitting in company groups, to discuss how they can use this material to better understand the structural problems in their companies.

Workshops can run short and long. Table questions need take only a few minutes, as can some other discussions. In one session on morality, the professor stopped his presentation repeatedly for ten-minute discussions around the tables—for example, on "Does a manager have to be 'good' to be good?" This worked well. I asked afterward whether he usually does this sort of thing. "Never before," he answered. "I read your 'Instructions to Instructors' [about our approach] and decided to give it a try!"

More commonly, the groups around the tables get into the issues for the better part of an hour—to get to the meaning of their experiences. As this happens repeatedly, over the course of five modules, the participants get to know each other's context rather well. The classroom thus becomes a kind of running set of live cases.

MORNING REFLECTIONS    Absolutely central to the whole learning process is what we call "morning reflections," an idea introduced by Ramesh Mehta, the director of the Cycle 1 Module in Bangalore. (I will use numbers to designate the year of the cycle—e.g., Cycle 6 means our sixth class—and Roman numerals to designate the modules—e.g., Module IV is the one on collaboration in Japan.) First thing in the morning, when the mind is fresh, often after thoughts have come up since the previous day, everyone is asked to reflect. The key here is to capture, share, reinforce, and extend the learning in this especially relaxed time of the day.

We start with a few minutes of personal time for everyone to write thoughts in the "Insight Books" they are given. (One graduate held it up at a meeting in her company to welcome new participants to the program and said, "This is the best management book I ever read!") It is rather remarkable to see a classroom full of normally very busy managers sitting in absorbed silence.

Discussion follows around each table, to share these thoughts. Ten to fifteen minutes of this serves both to surface and to screen individual ideas. Open-ended plenary discussion then follows, primed by the small-group exchanges (usually led by the module or cycle director, sometimes by participants). Needless to say, these discussions can run long—while a professor anxiously waits to begin the scheduled morning session. The solution to this problem is simple. Let him or her wait (and learn, too). Sure, this can affect the day's schedule. But, to repeat, we are there to learn, not to cover ground, and much of our best learning happens during these morning reflections. Even—especially—when they run long, often the better part of an hour. Frank McCauley, who headed up executive development at the Royal Bank of Canada, visited our class in India and attended a morning reflections. He later told a *Fast Company* journalist, "That was the most fascinating conversation in an academic setting that I have ever seen. We zoomed around the room discussing everything from political to economic issues, and then got into ethics and business" (Reingold 2000:286).

As this suggests, anything can come up in these sessions: thoughts about yesterday's issues, happenings in the companies, items in the news, concerns from earlier days and earlier modules. So these morning reflections become a running commentary—a main thread—across the entire program, to blend all the learning.

SHARING COMPETENCIES     One form of reflection that seems to work well, although we have not used it nearly enough, is the competency sharing discussed in Chapter 9. The object here is rather modest: not to present best practice, or even to propose good practice, but simply to share actual practice—how the managers in the room have used certain competencies.

It is interesting how many ideas come out when you ask a group of experienced managers to share some competency experience. Everybody loves to tell a favorite story, and in competency sharing lots of stories get told, about what worked and what didn't. As noted in Chapter 9, when we asked in the very first module, "How do you reflect in a busy job?" the ideas poured out. Almost everyone in the room had something to say—at one point eight people were trying to get in. Such discussions are not dramatic. They are quiet and low-key, yet enthusiastic.

Competency questions for other modules can include "How do you manage around formal structure?" (Module II), "How do you get close to customers?" (Module III), "How have you managed a big shift through little changes?" (Module V). The list is endless and highly relevant. Such questions come up naturally in a classroom of managers; the trick is to stop what is being done and allow time to consider them.

Experienced reflection in all these aspects does not just mean using more workshops and engendering greater participation. It is much more than that: It is about reconceiving the classroom to put the focus on the experience of the learners. And that changes everything.

THE FACULTY ROLE IN A REFLECTIVE CLASSROOM    As faculty in this program, we teach; our job, as noted, is to introduce interesting materials to the classroom. So we lecture, assign readings, lead case discussions, design exercises, run simulations. We do what all proper management professors do. (We even grade papers.)

But beyond that, our role is to stimulate deep and insightful reflection, which as noted earlier requires a shift in orientation. We have to help draw out the participants' experience and work with them to make key connections among the conceptual inputs and their personal experiences.

This requires some designing, for content and especially for process, but mostly it requires engaging: The faculty have to be involved, physically by their presence, intellectually by their thoughts, emotionally by their energy. It looks easier than, say, lecturing, but it is far more demanding. If I had to identify one skill most critical to all this, it would be the one in shortest supply in so much contemporary education: listening.

Kentaro Nobeoka, as codirector of Module IV in Japan, commented that to manage a class interactively, the professor needs to get 95 percent of what is said. With English as his second language, he figured he got about 75 percent. Maybe that is because he tried harder, because I doubt that most English-language faculty in our program get that much. (Of course, they really get far less, because so much of the discussion happens among the participants around the tables.)

The faculty set the tone, which has to be one of openness, flexibility, and suspended disbelief—a high level of thoughtfulness where everyone is prepared to listen more than talk, and then talk based on what has been said. All the best intentions, manifested in the most wonderful curriculum, are necessary but far from sufficient conditions. The learning is hugely dependent on the tone set in the classroom—of trust all around, earned by respect of everyone present for each other.

In most programs, the faculty come and go; they fly over, drop a message, and fly on. We do not favor this pigeon view of teaching. We have faculty who come and go, too, but in between we expect them to land and engage the class, particularly in workshops that link their material to the participants' experience.

There may be a place for a few "stars" who can mesmerize the class with their ideas. The trouble with more than a few of them, however, is that the mesmerizing interferes with the learning. I have watched too many stars who, while quick to take questions, will not be diverted from their own agendas, and whose ideas in the classroom seem to have a half-life of a few hours.

A key distinguishing feature of the IMPM classroom is the faculty who stay and facilitate, notably the module director for each module and the cycle director for all modules. By remaining on site, meaning in the classroom, they become a key part of the glue that holds the whole learning experience together. They get to know the participants, their experiences, and their concerns, while working with them as a cohesive class.

Over time, we have strengthened the role of the cycle director, providing that person with more time in the classroom to discuss program activities that happen outside the classroom—notably the reflection papers, managerial exchanges, ventures, and impacts. (Having these two people in class may seem expensive, but it should be realized that they take sole responsibility for much of the class time—perhaps up to one-third in all—including discussion of the above activities, morning reflections, and field studies [discussed later], most involving little preparation time.)

But the faculty cannot facilitate alone. The participants have to take up that role, too. Learning does not happen as long as people sit back waiting to be facilitated. So a measure of our success is the extent to which the participants grow into the role of facilitators. The spirit of this was expressed by a faculty observer who commented after a particularly satisfying session: "They felt *he* [the professor] brought closure. *They* brought closure!" A related story is told in the accompanying box—a nice way to close this chapter on the IMPM setting.

## SPIRITUALITY IN THE CLASSROOM

He was a senior professor of religious studies who had never faced a classroom of managers before. He was to talk to them about "Spirituality and the Practice of Management," in Module I on Reflection, and then do a drama workshop with them. This whole activity was scheduled for a full day plus some of the following morning.

As he began to talk, with what seemed to me about three words in every sentence that I had never heard before, I thought, "Uh-oh." Amid references to "grand narratives" (like Genesis) and "little narratives" (personal stories), his own grand narrative was falling on the deaf ears of people concerned about their own little narratives. But the class listened politely. For a while. Then a hand went up, followed by a comment to the effect of "Could you, uh, maybe clarify that last point?" Similar questions followed, and he started to get defensive. The class and the speaker started to go their separate ways. Some tense moments followed. How are we going to get through a day of this, I thought.

Then someone said, "I'm struggling to understand what you are trying to say." It was the perfect sentiment: not that she had tuned out, but that she was trying to connect. He had obviously worked awfully hard to prepare his presentation—too hard—and obviously had interesting things to say. This comment acknowledged it and expressed goodwill. The professor relaxed and took on a more pragmatic tone, and the morning finished with some useful learning.

The afternoon was very different. The professor led an exercise, a "feeling" for spirituality, and then organized the class into groups that presented skits on the reactions to the module. That worked fine.

Following this, we all sat in a big circle to reflect on the day. There was good discussion, with relaxed warmth. Then one of the Japanese participants, not yet comfortable in English (this was the first few days of the first module), spoke up, saying, in effect, "You know, to be honest, I have not understood anything of the morning materials." The class, very sensitive to a colleague, picked up on this in terms of what might be done in the remaining hour the following morning. A mention was made of focusing on Western religion alone, specifically Christianity, but the professor misunderstood this comment to mean a request for something on comparative religion. No, everyone said. At this point I suggested, motioning to the professor, "You should present a description of Christianity, as you set out to do this morning, so that you [motioning to the Japanese participant] will understand it. And if you do, then we shall all understand it. But [turning back to the professor] you must do no preparation." (Images of him being up to 4 A.M.) Everyone agreed.

There followed the next morning one of the most impressive presentations that any of us had ever heard.

The class had empowered the speaker. Great managing is not about making just something out of what you get but something wonderful. These managers suspended their disbelief and through honest struggle learned about spirituality—in religion and in that classroom.

# 11

## Developing Managers II
### *Five Mindsets*

*This is the course in advanced physics. That means
the instructor finds the subject confusing. If he didn't,
the course would be called elementary physics.*

—Luis Alvarez, Nobel laureate, 1964

Let us turn now to the core of the IMPM, the classroom activities
built around the five mindsets. The distinctive nature of each, combined with our particular pedagogy, posed quite a challenge to each of
the module teams, forcing them to think afresh. In this chapter, I describe the five results, after introducing the basic issues we had to face in
designing all of the modules. Our intention has been to create five
unique experiences that blend into a single integrated program.

## Designing the Modules

Our modules had to be designed but not overdesigned; in other words,
they had to be designed for flexibility in the classroom. This is a bit like

cooking: Get the right pot, drop in good ingredients, heat carefully, stir periodically, and then let the process take over.

Four goals have driven us in the design of each of the modules:

- We have to *cover* the subject matter of each mindset—for example, in Module III, various aspects of managing context (e.g., consumer behavior, financial markets, stakeholder relationships), ideally as alternate descriptive models (e.g., various forms of capitalism), and related competencies (e.g., networking and negotiating). But that has been the easy part; academics are used for "covering ground," at least conceptual ground.

- Beyond coverage, we had to develop a *theme* for each module, to encourage a natural synthesis as it flows along. In the fourth module (Managing Relationships), for example, the theme became "Management is not about controlling people but about facilitating human collaboration." The themes, of course, have developed and shifted as new faculty became involved. The mindsets have proved to be rich canvases on which to paint interesting ideas.

- As module director at McGill, Kunal Basu emphasized that we need to get beneath the obvious interpretations of each mindset, into its *deeper meaning* in the practice of managing. We have to get to the inner truths, he said, to tell the deeper stories. What is the essence of analysis in organizations? What is the real meaning of development to participants from developing and developed countries? All themes simplify; in the words of Karl Weick (1996), we had to get to the "profound simplicity"—beyond the "conspicuous" regularities to the "hard-won simplifications which capture the lessons of . . . more complex experience" (252).

- Trickiest of all was to bring each mindset to life—not just to present material about it but to *live* it during the module. In some modules, that proved easy: If you are not Indian, to feel context in India you need only take a walk. Likewise, reflection has been built into the very notion of the module in Lancaster. But how to feel change in Fontainebleau or analysis in Montreal? It is easy to teach analysis in a business school. But how do you experience analysis? How, in other words, do you get fish—participants and faculty alike—to appreciate water?

I do not include integration in this list of goals, because we have discovered that it has to be woven into all the components, rather than being formally designed. In other words, this kind of education is not about taking steps up to the top of some mountain, where everything can finally be seen, so much as about working together to create a fine cloth. Integration has to take place as we combine individual and collective efforts, interconnecting the fibers of different ideas. The resulting cloth is certainly woven, but by no particular thread so much as by every single one—by every single idea and experience discussed in that classroom.

## GENERAL MODULE DESIGN

To proceed from these lofty goals, we had to fill in the spaces on those damnable sheets called schedules. Everyone is supposed to know what is happening all the time. In theory at least. If this is Tuesday, at Chicago, it must be Shareholder Value. We fill in those sheets in the IMPM, too, but hopefully with some white spaces that keep parts of them empty.

Figure 11.1 depicts the overall module design. This is to suggest not that the modules mimic each other—a visit to our five classrooms would quickly dispel that notion—but that a common framework helps blend them into a single experience.

We begin most of the modules with "reflecting back," to review thoughts and experiences since the last module, and we end most with reflecting forward, to consider the return to work and on to the next module. Between the two come mostly the content sessions of a half or

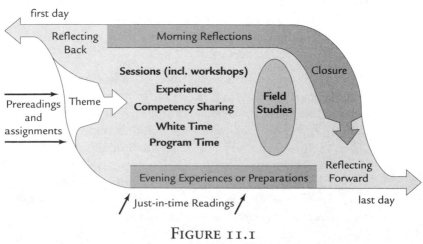

FIGURE 11.1
General Module Design

full day on topics related to the particular mindset, introduced by lectures, exercises, cases, etc., followed by workshops at the tables.

Educational programs are generally designed around courses that run periodically for weeks or months; developmental programs tend to have sessions of a few hours each. Our modules are like courses that run for two weeks, while our classes are like sessions that run for a few hours.

While it is important to make the greatest possible use of the experiences that the participants bring to the classroom, we also create some experiences on site—visits of various kinds, exposure to the local culture, and so forth. Here what matters is not the fancy events that impress, so much as the interesting experience that gets people thinking. For example, a canned speech by a local dignitary may add nothing substantial, while having a well-briefed class question that person can be enlightening. And, of course, with the emphasis on the verbal in the classroom, there is much to gain from attention to the visual outside it. Thus, near Lancaster, the class regularly visits original sites of the industrial revolution, to appreciate the challenges of managing in another time.

Another important component of all modules, increasingly so as the program has developed, is labeled *program time*. Here the cycle director deals with issues related to the program at large. Every program, of course, has some of this, but it takes on special significance in the IMPM, with special sessions that consider the impact of the learning back at work, share insights from the Reflection Papers, and brief and debrief the Managerial Exchanges and Ventures. Figure 11.1 also shows time for Competency Sharing and Morning Reflections, already discussed, and White Time and Field Studies, discussed next.

WHITE TIME    The best way to beat those damnable sheets is to fill in some of the blanks with blanks. I call this *white time*—no black ink in those white spaces. ("I'm sorry; that time is taken. We're doing nothing then.") Unexpectedly interesting things inevitably arise in management programs. What a shame when they cannot be accommodated in the classroom. White time provides the chance to return to them.

Program designers often live in mortal fear of what radio announcers call "dead air." What if no one has something to say? I can hardly recall any such silence in our classrooms; the managers don't lack for interesting things to discuss, only for the time, and freedom, to discuss them. In spite of our good intentions, including Morning Reflections and our 50-50 rule (violated when things run behind schedule), the IMPM participants have one unrelenting complaint: not enough time to share among themselves. White time can fix that, by allowing us to design *out*, not just design in. (See the accompanying box on IMPM Forums.)

## IMPM FORUMS

In the second module, on the analytical mindset, we schedule a day each on a number of the business functions—marketing, finance, accounting, information technology. The mornings are dedicated to "cutting-edge" material in these fields, and one year (Cycle 4), we decided to block out the afternoons for open-ended *Forums*—in effect, everything you always wanted to know about marketing one day, finance another, and so forth. Participants were able to list on a flip chart topics they wished to discuss (e.g., in marketing: "How can you brand a new company?"; in finance: "Has any company implemented the 'balanced scorecard'?"), and other topics came up in the morning sessions. Several of the specialized faculty, sitting among the participants at the tables, took part in the general discussion; no one was at the front.

The first day we tried this, in finance, the Forum was scheduled from 2 to 5 P.M.—three open-ended hours. The discussion ran to 5:45! In the middle of the afternoon, someone asked for a primer on Economic Value Added. One of the Alcan participants, highly experienced in this area, went up to the board and gave a well-received account. Later the group quizzed their Red Cross colleagues about how it finances its campaigns. The next day, in accounting, the Forum started later but ran to 6:30. No dead air!

In Cycle 7, I was to lead a full day on forms of organizations, to compare Machine, Professional, Entrepreneurial, and Project types (Mintzberg 1989:Pt. II). I introduced the conceptual material in the morning, with a couple of workshops for the groups to consider it in their own companies. Things went faster than expected, so we decided to hold a forum in the afternoon; Brenda Zimmerman, who was the module director and has a creative flair for designing workshops, joined me. We drew on a number of issues that had come up in the morning, "just in time," so to speak, but with a little more structure than in earlier forums.

- One person had asked about alternate ways to organize the same activity in the different kinds of organizations. We chose new product development as the activity and asked who had extensive experience in it. There were four volunteers, and happily they came from organizations that leaned to different forms. The four sat on stools at the front of the class and answered questions about how they were organized for new product development. A lively discussion ensued.

- Another issue concerned control in project-type "adhocracies"—how they do it, compared with more conventional organizations. People had been sitting at the tables in company groups, and we asked them, based on the morning workshops, which form best described their companies. Each of the four types was represented, so we designated one corner of the room for each and asked people from companies favoring that form to huddle there and discuss how their control systems reflected their form. They then presented their findings, which made clear, using the experience in the classroom, the extent to which control systems differ in the different forms.

- A manager of a Canadian company had asked how *kaizen*, or continuous improvement, can become a regular activity instead of a sporadic one. We called on the participants from Fujitsu, a company with extensive experience in this area. Out of their comments and the discussion that followed came the conclusion that treating this as a technique, with formal meetings, is quite different from instilling it as a philosophy, in regular work.

This was just one afternoon, but rich with learning from experience, related to concepts. It took just three ingredients: (1) appropriate raw material—namely, experienced participants and applicable concepts; (2) a classroom culture that prizes reflecting on experience; and (3) a few simple ideas to organize the discussions.

FIELD STUDIES   We use *field studies* in all our modules, but in a particular way: Participants visit the local operations of the companies represented in the class. These are not passive tours, but active investigations, on a subject related to the module, for example, a "cultural audit" at BT in the first module or probing into change processes at Lufthansa in the last one.

Except for the first module, the participants from the company are responsible for setting up the studies (but not for accompanying their colleagues; they go to another company); they decide the issue to be studied, associated with the mindset of the module, divide the class into groups of about five to investigate the issue in various parts of the company (preferably what we call high and low, from senior management to ground operations), organize these investigations, and brief the class on all this.

The groups go out for one full day. The next morning, all those that have been to a particular company get together to consolidate their findings, which are presented to the class in the afternoon, followed by open discussion, including reactions of the participants from those companies.

These presentations seem to work best when they are not too polished. We don't need PowerPoint any more than executive summaries. We need to get the interesting findings out, to stimulate free-wheeling discussion. The intention here is not to prescribe change but to offer descriptive insights. In other words, these should be seen as thoughtful inquiries, not consulting studies, that add to the weaving together of the module's activities. Besides, how often can a manager get comments from trusted colleagues on his or her situation, with no axes to grind, nothing to sell, no authority figure to impress?

I mentioned in Chapter 8 my surprise at how well the one-day visits to colleagues' companies worked in the short courses developed by Sumantra Ghoshal at Insead. This is what inspired our field studies, and, again, I find it quite remarkable how well they work. Participants from the companies frequently praise the insightfulness of their colleagues' comments, while people interviewed back in the companies often comment on how much they learned simply from the questions they were asked. "Why don't we ask each other those simple questions?" one Matsushita manager remarked.

These field studies may seem like case studies, but they have several key differences: The experiences are visual and can be visceral, not just verbal—the participants are out there, on site; they have already come to know the companies through their colleagues; and these colleagues, who have lived these "cases," can take them to a deeper level. I recall one BT manager who visited a call center at the Royal Bank of Canada telling the class that his own job was to help set up such centers for BT clients, but never had he seen one that had been designed around the behavioral factors first, followed by the technological factors. He was impressed! The manager of that call center, a participant in the class, sat there beaming! To repeat a point that bears repeating, experienced managers have a great deal to learn from each other's experiences.

PUTTING THIS TOGETHER   Add together all of the components discussed here, and you end up with quite a range of activities in our modules—from reflective sessions to content sessions to visits to forum to field studies, etc., linking every which way. But that is what helps sustain the interest.

Bill Van Buskirk, a creative management educator (see, e.g., Van Buskirk 1996), visited our classroom and remarked on "how self-organizing the whole thing is." Maybe that is the best measure of success: the extent to which the participants take charge of the learning, become partners, or citizens, of the program. We have examples of this from the participants of one cycle who asked to run the Morning Reflections, and from those of another cycle who took the initiative to meet with and brief faculty presenters ahead of time.

Let me turn now to the specific modules. Developing them has been quite a challenge—five challenges, in fact. But this is what has attracted an interesting and enthusiastic faculty. How do you take all the characteristics just described and develop two weeks of class time around a mindset that has never been addressed before, to have its own special character yet blend into a cohesive overall program?

Richard Rumelt of UCLA once quipped that if two professors have the same idea, one of them is redundant. That has not been our problem! Everyone involved in this program has had his or her own ideas. And they continue to. So described next is not necessarily our current or best practice—as I write this, something is being changed, even improved—but the essence of some of our practice as we went along.[1]

# Module I: Managing Self— The Reflective Mindset

The IMPM opens in Lancaster by setting its own tone. The purpose is *reflection*: to appreciate it, do it, live it. There is an ancient Chinese expression attributed to Lao Tzsu that "knowing others is intelligence; knowing yourself is true wisdom." Our intention in this module is to encourage some true wisdom.

Of course, a module on reflection represents quite a change from the pressures of daily work, but no less from most management education and development. Yet *what* we do in this module is perhaps less unusual than *how* it gets done—and *how much* of it gets done. For here we have two solid weeks of activities related in one way or another to reflection. Figure 11.2 shows a conceptual overview, or map, of this module.

---

[1] I should say that as program director, I was in attendance at the first twenty-two modules of the IMPM—that is, all of the first four cycles plus the first two modules of the fifth. Since then I have taught in three of the modules regularly and have been most involved in the second module at McGill, where I am codirector in Cycle 8, 2003.

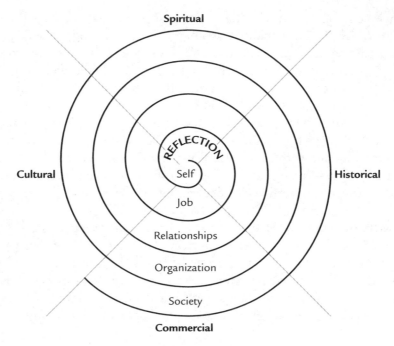

FIGURE 11.2
Map of the Reflection Module

To develop a reflective turn of mind, the participants focus on themselves, their work, and their world, to appreciate how they think, act, and manage; how they cope with the stresses of being a manager; and how they learn from experience to become more discerning—more "critical" in the constructive sense of this word. In the metaphor of Jonathan Gosling, who ran this module for the first two cycles, reflecting is like peeling an onion, to reveal successively deeper layers:

- society (history, economy, ethics, spirituality)
- organization (culture, structure, knowledge)
- relationships (with others, with groups)
- job (managerial work, managing self, managing time)
- self (experience, style)

The first three mirror the next three modules of the program, which indicates another intention of this module: to provide an overture to the entire program. Module I launches the program by introducing all of its elements and also by bonding the class into a tightly knit learning community. The participants don't lose their national identities here but reinforce them, by learning how to use them to deepen their appreciation of the world. One participant claimed she discovered her Americanness here in northern England!

*Reflect* in Latin means to refold, which suggests that attention be turned inward so that it can then turn outward, to see a familiar thing in a different way. This is much of what happens in this module.

The details of the activities in this and the other modules are described in a companion volume (accessible on www.impm.org), so I shall just provide overviews here. As shown in Figure 11.2, four content dimensions—spiritual, historical, cultural, and commercial (or economic)—are woven through the sessions on self, job, relationships, organization, and society. There are sessions on managerial work and management thought; on the learning organization and appreciative inquiry; on morality and the role of religion; on the meaning of work and the nature of self. All of these are combined with reflective workshops. The theme of the module, as it has evolved, is to appreciate how context shapes self, through work and culture.

The module is also interwoven with a set of experiences: out-of-door exercises at the outset to encourage bonding; a theater workshop to appreciate the nature of spontaneous interaction; a session on spirituality that has taken the class on a "pilgrimage" to a pagan site, a Buddhist monastery, and a Christian church (discussed in Roberts 1999); and a trip into economic history that visits a cotton mill and the "new economy." There is also that "culture audit" of the British companies represented in the class.

A surprising number of the participants have told us over the years that this module turned out to be a life-changing experience. Initially, this effect took me by surprise, but it should not have. Managers are terribly harassed these days. They rarely stop, even in their so-called free time. Suddenly they find themselves in a relaxed setting, free for hours on end to engage in all kinds of unexpected reflective activities, and the results can be profound. Near the end of the second cycle, a participant polled her classmates as to whether the IMPM had been a life-changing experience. All but one said yes (the one was not *yet* sure!), and most pointed to the opening module at Lancaster.

We were nervous the first time we ran this module, not only because the program was so new but also because we had no precedent for running two weeks of reflection for managers. Now, with several years' experience behind us, we can only wonder why that should have been. Contemporary managers have a great deal of time *not* to reflect. By beginning with reflection, the IMPM sets a tone for developing more thoughtful, more balanced, and wiser managers.

# Module II: Managing Organizations— The Analytical Mindset

From reflection at Lancaster, we go to analysis at McGill. Quite a shift in mindset! And the source of untold hours of reflection at McGill, I can assure you, about how to teach a module about analysis.

As noted earlier, the obvious answers were all too easy. In business schools, we specialize in teaching analysis; at work, the participants specialize in using it. So the module could have just taught about technique and been done with it. That way at least we would have "covered" the language of business. But we had to do much more than that—for example, put analysis under the scrutiny that it puts everything else. This was our charge at McGill: to get the fish, professors and managers alike, to appreciate water, and land. This meant stepping far enough away from analysis to be able to go more deeply into it. In other words, we had to get inside the analytical mindset: Who really does analysis, why, how, and to what effect?

Key to module design was coming up with an insightful frame. Indeed, the whole notion of choosing and applying a frame can be seen as the essence of analysis. Figure 11.3 shows a map of this module, similar to the generic module map shown in Figure 11.1, but with straight lines, to convey the structured nature of analysis as the decomposition of a whole into its component parts.

The module itself decomposes into three parts, a first called *framing*, which introduces it; a second called *functional frames*, which considers the specific business functions; and a third called *fusion*, which seeks to bring these frames together.

We frame analysis at the outset by offering different perspectives on the nature of analysis—for example (in Cycle 8), sessions by a well-known philosopher on the role of science (Bunge 1998) and by a researcher on how the game of analysis is played out in business (Langley 1995). Another session contrasts analytic, artistic, and craft approaches to strategy making.

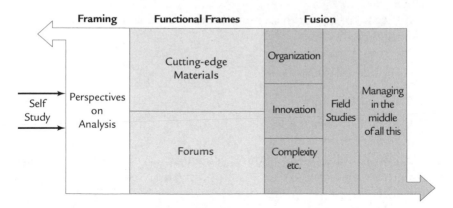

FIGURE 11.3

Map of the Analytical Module

The overall frame having been set, we move to specific frames—namely, how analysis is commonly applied in business organizations, in the functions of marketing, finance, accounting, and information technology. As noted in the earlier box on IMPM Forums, a day is devoted to each, typically in two parts. The morning offers "cutting-edge" materials (sometimes as electives), for example, about options in finance. Here in some cases we have successfully used junior faculty, whose limited experience with management groups is compensated for by the currency of their ideas. We have even used graduates of our own program, such a banker who taught one elective in options. And in the afternoons, we have run some of those open-ended forums discussed earlier, where everyone could raise issues about the function in question, including competency sharing as it came up (e.g., in a marketing forum, "How do I get close to my customers?").

One difficulty with organizing these functional frame days is that the level of knowledge can vary enormously in such a class, from people who have spent a career in a function to others who have barely worked with it. That is where our Self-Study comes in—preparatory work in advance of the module to bring people up to a certain level, in marketing, accounting, and finance (discussed later).

The third part of the module concerns fusion. Here we seek to override the functional decomposition by looking at the organization as a whole, from various perspectives: different forms of organizations; complexity theory; the role of "designing" in management; and innovation. The field studies also serve as fusion, by allowing the managers to probe into how analysis is used in the North American organizations represented in the class (e.g., in strategic planning or financial reporting).

At the end of one of these modules that he directed, Kunal Basu put up the following:

- Reflection. Analysis
- Reflection, Analysis
- Reflection ↔ Analysis

In other words, are these separate, sequential, or interactive mindsets? Clearly, we wish to get to the bottom of this list.


# MODULE III: MANAGING CONTEXT— THE WORLDLY MINDSET


The third module of the IMPM changes many of the participants, too. Partly this is India, which has a habit of doing such things to people; partly it is the module itself; mostly it is the symbiosis of the two. This module is *about* context, but the participants live context here as well. As suggested earlier, for all but the Indian participants, India hits people like a wave from the ocean: It is not only another world, but in a sense, otherworldly. As illustrated in Figure 11.4, a map of this module, it has been designed on the assumption that being exposed to other people's worlds brings insight to one's own world, and thus helps to make a person more worldly-wise.

We live on a globe that from a distance looks uniformly round. Correspondingly, "globalization" sees the world from a distance that encourages homogenization of behavior. Is that what we want from our managers?

A closer look, however, reveals something quite different: This globe is made up of all kinds of worlds. Should we not, therefore, be encouraging our managers to become more worldly, defined earlier as experienced in life, in both a sophisticated and practical way? Managers need to get into worlds beyond their own—other people's worlds, their habits and cultures—so that they can better know their own world. To paraphrase T. S. Eliot's famous words, they should be exploring ceaselessly in order to return home and know the place for the first time. That is the worldly mindset.

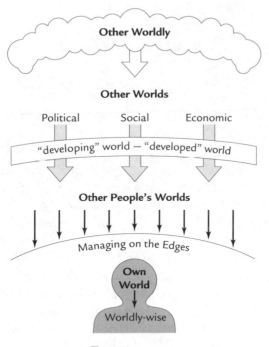

FIGURE 11.4
Map of the Worldly Module

Of course, to do all this in two weeks is obviously a tall order. But it is surprising how far we can get, how powerful simple experiences in a new context can be. In our feedback from Cycle 1, a participant described this as "the total immersion module," while another wrote, "Most revealing, even shocking. . . . Bangalore changed the way I viewed the world." India is a thoroughly different place yet ideal for the international development of managers—a truly developing country with widespread facility in English and a strong academic infrastructure.

Porter and McKibbin (1988), in their assessment of management education, call for greater "attention to the external environment—governmental relations, societal trends, legal climate, international developments, among other areas—for the obvious reason that these events 'outside' the organization are increasingly penetrating into the internal operations of the firm and affecting its core efficiency and effectiveness" (318). This is precisely the intention of this third module of the IMPM, but with a focus on encouraging worldliness. (See the box on page 306.)

Against the backdrop of developing society in general and India in particular, this module seeks to weave the various components of external context into an appreciation of worlds beyond one's own. That comes

## Worldliness at Fujitsu

*(from the Reflection Paper by Amane Inoue, Cycle 5, 2000)*

Japanese people sometimes confuse the meanings of "Global" and "Worldly," compared to the term "Local." However, the term "Global" actually means "affecting or including the whole world" whereas "Worldly" means "having a lot of experience and knowledge about people and life." In the McGill module, we studied in an attempt to find new concepts by asking provocative questions. This provided us with a means of drawing out key points or issues concerning the company. At that time I tried to form some provocative questions according to the company policy, which was "Fujitsu pursues the status of a Global solution provider company." However, how can Fujitsu be a Global solution provider company when the solutions are of a localized nature? That is, the solution for Fujitsu Europe will be different to that of Fujitsu India. [Instead] if you were to say that "Fujitsu pursues a Worldly solution provider company status," then the whole of Fujitsu and its employees can understand this concept more clearly. In fact, the term "Worldly" best describes Fujitsu's aims because of its connotation with experience; "global," albeit meaning "Worldwide," does not convey the necessary experience or knowledge required for a company of Fujitsu's standing. Employees can therefore identify better with the "Worldly" solutions status.

alive in a number of specific experiences, such as yoga early each morning (on a voluntary basis) and evening entertainment in theater, music, and dance. But for the non-Indians, just being there, especially among fellow Indian managers, brings this other world alive. It takes them past the nice abstractions of economic, political, and social differences in the classroom, down onto the streets where the differences come alive. "How can you possibly drive in this traffic?" asked an American participant, shaken up on her drive in from the airport, of the module director. He said, "I just join the flow." Worldly learning can begin! There is order on those streets of Bangalore, but you have to get inside another world to appreciate it. The module opens with visits to the diversity that is India, from a food market to a software campus, a few kilometers and several centuries apart. This may have shock effect. But after the participants are asked to reflect on this from the outside comes the real shock that such a tour is possible in New York City, too.

The core of the module focuses on political, social, and economic dimensions, in "developing" as well as "developed" worlds. For example, the political context is conveyed as both controlling and conflictive, manifested in issues such as regulation, privatization, and governance. The social context can be seen as cultural and collaborative, concerned with networks and alliances as well as organizations that are neither public nor private—cooperatives and developmental NGOs, for example. The economic context considers competition and consumption; here is where globalism comes, in the form of financial markets, consumer behaviors, and industry analyses.[2]

Shown in Figure 11.4 between one's own world and other people's worlds is the managerial theme of this module: "Managing on the Edges," between the organization and its context. As Raphael (1986) has commented in his book *Edges*, biologists have found that many of the most interesting things happen at these interfaces, for example, in the narrow zone between land and sea, where "living organisms encounter dynamic conditions that give rise to untold variety." And to tension as well: "The flora of the meadows," for example, "as they approach the woodlands find themselves coping with increasingly unfavorable conditions"—different soil, less sunlight, competition from alien species of trees and shrubs. "The Edges, in short, might abound with life, but each living form must fight for its own" (5–6). And so it is for managers who must likewise function on the edges: chief executives and sales managers most evidently, but all managers, who must connect their units to the broader world around them. Here managing becomes linking more than leading, convincing more than controlling, dealing more than doing. And so this third module addresses the related competencies of networking, negotiating, working with different stakeholders, and managing across cultural divides.

If Lancaster is about looking inward and McGill is about looking outward, then Bangalore is about looking outward to see inward. In a sense, this module marries internalized reflection with externalized analysis. One might say that worldliness puts analysis and reflection into context.

---

[2]There may appear to be some overlap here with material of other modules, but the focus in the different modules actually brings out the uniqueness of the mindsets. For example, marketing and finance are discussed in Module II with regard to doing analysis and applying technique and in Module III with regard to understanding the behavior of consumers and financial markets in different contexts.

# MODULE IV: MANAGING RELATIONSHIPS — THE COLLABORATIVE MINDSET

The Japanese term *ba* describes a shared space for emerging relationships, especially to create meaning (Nonaka and Konno 1998). This has been a popular theme for the fourth module: There are lectures and readings on ba, a great deal of discussion about it, and the term gets used in many of the follow-up Reflection Papers (sometimes for the IMPM itself).

Not just the content but also the mood and tone of this fourth module is very different from the others. For one thing, it conveys the Japanese worldview unequivocally. As noted earlier, here is one place on the globe that has not been inclined to go with the "global" view of management. So while India opens up perspectives on other worlds in general, Japan opens up perspectives on another world of management in particular. And not just from the faculty: The real power of the module comes from the fact that this world is brought to life by those who live it—the Japanese managers in the class—and where it lives—in the field visits to their companies. Observing people at Fujitsu sitting in a big open space, with the manager's desk at one end, a Canadian banker reacted with horror at the idea of the boss being able to watch everyone all the time. But maybe he isn't bossing, one of her Japanese colleagues suggested; maybe he's helping!

Hiro Itami, the module director for Cycles 1 and 2, described this module as follows: "Management is not to control people. Rather, it is to let them collaborate." This module is thus about "managing human networks." As for shareholder value, Itami liked to tell the class, on behalf of Japanese business, "Let's go out and hire ourselves some shareholders!" For years, I tried to encourage him to include something on leadership. We have to pay some attention to it, I kept saying; Module IV is the obvious place. Then I suggested "styles of leading" instead. "We could do that!" he replied. "Leadership" itself, I learned from my colleague, is part of the Western style of managing!

Kaz Mishina, who took on the directorship of the module later, followed suit. He conceived the Japanese style as "leadership in the background," being about "letting as many ordinary people as possible lead." As one of the participants quipped, the manager becomes a "ba-tender"!

Key to appreciating this is tacit knowledge, another idea that has infused this module—the sense that we use far more knowledge than we can formally articulate. Ikujiro Nonaka, dean of Japanese management academics, teaches the subject in the module (see Nonaka and Takeuchi 1995).

All of this is conveyed in the experiences as well as the content of the module. "Breathing the local air," as Itami puts it, has included visits to numerous Japanese sites, including the massive Tokyo fish market, the offices of Fujitsu, reconstruction sites after the Kobe earthquake, and a Japanese primary school to observe the roots of cooperation. Particularly well received has been a session where Fujitsu workers come into the classroom to talk about how they engage in kaizen. With the involvement of LG, part of the module is now run in Korea, with its own experiences.

A map of this module (Figure 11.5; compare this with the more linear map of Module II) comes from Kentaro Nobeoka, co-module director of Cycle 3. He laid out the content around the coordinates of (1) the nature of collaboration, being either implicit/social/informal (namely tacit) or explicit/rational/formal; and (2) the scope of collaboration, from the individual level to the intrafirm, interfirm, and national/societal levels.

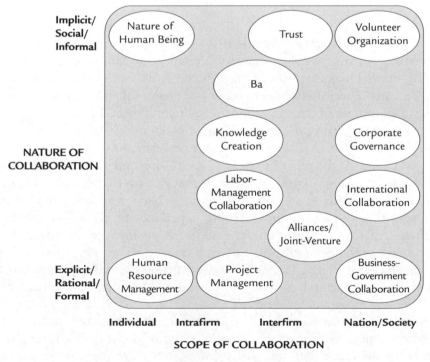

FIGURE 11.5

Map of the Collaboration Module (modified from Nobeoka)

So, for example, there have been sessions on the nature of the human being (implicit and individual, such as Basu's session on models of people, described in a box in Chapter 9), on alliances and joint ventures (interfirm, explicit), and on business–government collaboration (national, explicit).

Competency sharing in this module can include sessions on team-working, culture building, mentoring and apprenticing, and the art of nonverbal communication, plus the various skills of collaborating. A lengthy closing workshop has been used to turn the module over to the class for an afternoon, to self-organize and consider their learning of the two weeks around the theme question of "How do you motivate first-line employees?" Following presentation of their conclusions to the faculty on the next day, the group in Cycle 1 sang, "There is a kind of 'ba' . . . all over the world!"

# MODULE V: MANAGING CHANGE— THE ACTION MINDSET

After the experiences of Module III in India and Module IV in Japan, the class returns to a more conventional management topic in a more conventional management setting, at least for the Europeans and North Americans. This is the action mindset (originally called catalytic), about the management of change, at Insead in Fontainbleau, France.

Insead specializes in teaching change; it has all kinds of people who do this very well. That has not been our problem; moving away from it has (in some of the other modules as well)—beyond good teaching, to active learning, too. Beyond presenting change, covering it, discussing it, the class has to live it, and also live their members' experiences of it, and so turn this into a profound learning experience by getting under the label of the module and into its essence. A problem with calling the module "catalytic" originally was that a catalyst remains the same while changing other things. The world needs managers who change others by first changing themselves. And that has meant changing how we as faculty design a curriculum about change.

Module V has developed in two respects: in format and in the uses of experience. In format, the module has moved closer to courses, or blocks—sustained focus on particular aspects of change, as shown in the map of Figure 11.6. After an opening session designed to debunk

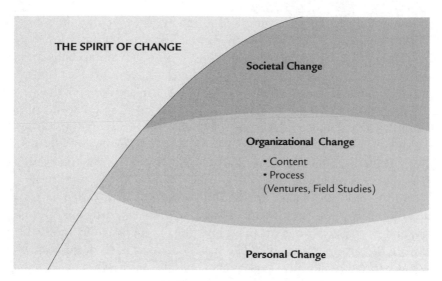

THE SPIRIT OF CHANGE

Societal Change

Organizational Change
• Content
• Process
(Ventures, Field Studies)

Personal Change

FIGURE 11.6
Map of the Action Module

standard notions of change (e.g., that changing is good and resisting change is bad), there are three blocks.

One block focuses on macro change—more dramatic and discontinuous, usually top-down, leader-driven, deliberately strategic. Cases and examples are used to show how such change has taken place successfully in different organizations.

Another block concerns micro change, especially from a middle management perspective, where most of the participants can be found. Venturing and the use of projects is especially important here, compared with restructuring and broad strategy for the macro block.

The third block is about personal change, to allow the participants to focus on issues such as their own styles of rendering change and their own biases in action. For obvious reasons, this tends to be the most experiential of the three blocks and has included setting personal agendas for future action. (There are also several sessions on societal change.)

Change experiences are woven into the module in various ways. Of course, workshops builds on the participants' own experiences linked to the various conceptual inputs. The field studies are also particularly important here. As might be imagined, after a year and a half with colleagues from companies such as Lufthansa and Életricité de France, visits to those companies to investigate change activities can be highly revealing. One group, for example, found in part of a company more of a "sense of urgency" to change among the first-line employees they met than among the managers. Particularly revealing have been field studies to Red Cross disaster relief sites, including refugee camps in Tanzania and operations in Kosovo (before the module, on a voluntary basis).

A significant part of this module is dedicated to presentations of the Ventures—the change projects in their own companies that all the participants have been conducting throughout the program (discussed later). These become case studies, if you like, by the protagonists about changing their organizations.

Additional experiences during the module have included a visit to the Louvre for a presentation on changes in painting, driven by technology, and exercise sessions dropped into the class at various intervals to activate the group physically. (The instructor had been doing this with Insead people for several years at the exercise center; this was the first time she ever stepped foot in an Insead class!)

This is a tricky module, for the same reason that Module II is tricky: It is too easy to do what academics do best—that is, teach *about* change, providing examples through cases and driving them home through concepts. We have moved beyond this approach, to use experiences—including that developed during the sixteen months of the program. But we have to take this much further, as we must in all of the modules, to bring their mindsets more to life in the classroom.

To conclude this discussion, Table 11.1 lists various dimensions of the five modules.

TABLE 11.1 DIMENSIONS OF THE MODULES

| MODULE | MINDSET | SUBJECT | SCHOOL | MANAGING |
|--------|---------|---------|--------|----------|
| I | Reflective | Self | Lancaster (England) | Itself |
| II | Analytical | Organization | McGill (Canada) | In the middle |
| III | Worldly | Context | Bangalore (India) | On the edges |
| IV | Collaborative | Relationships | Japan and Korea | Human networks |
| V | Action | Change | Insead (France) | Comprehensively |

# 12

## DEVELOPING MANAGERS III
### *Learning on the Job*

*Experience is not what happens to you.*
*It is what you do with what happens to you.*
—ALDOUS HUXLEY

A great deal can be done in the classroom, as I hope has been demonstrated in the preceding chapter. But the essential philosophy of the IMPM—the very notion of learning connected to experience—means that much of it has to happen back on the job, albeit stimulated by what took place in that classroom. The participants may lack free, or at least uninterrupted, time on the job, but that is where their experience occurs, so that is where many of the connections have to be made. Accordingly, we sought, and continue to seek, ways to encourage this in accord as much as possible with our credo of using work rather than making work—to design the activities between modules to connect to the work already being done. A tall order perhaps, but we believe we have made considerable progress.

As can be seen back in Figure 10.1 on page 278, these intermodular activities include Reflection Papers written after the modules, Self-Study between Modules I and II, the Managerial Exchanges between Modules II and IV, the Ventures that run throughout the program, and the Major Paper after the last module. Each is discussed here in turn.

## REFLECTION PAPERS

While we seek to create a reflective atmosphere at our modules, these last only two weeks, five times, in a program that runs a lot longer than that. And during those two weeks, the participants are bombarded with all kinds of new thoughts, in no small measure from each other. All of this takes time to digest. We run many workshops at the modules to help the participants link this material to their experience. But these happen away from that experience. And returning to the site of the experience can prompt important new thoughts. So we introduced Reflection Papers to encourage this kind of learning back at work. For an indication of how interesting such reflective learning can be, and how central this is to the whole philosophy of the IMPM and what distinguishes it from so much other management development, see the accompanying box, excerpted from a discussion about the spirituality session discussed in a box in Chapter 10.

### REFLECTING ON SPIRITUALITY

*(excerpts from the Reflection Paper for Module I
by Kerry Chandler, Motorola, Cycle 2, July 1997)*

*Worlds Apart?* "Spirituality and the Practice of Management" was a session which taught me more about the process of human behavior and its link to the experience of learning than it did about the topics of religion and management. I found a profound sense of satisfaction as I experienced the day unfolding. Allowing myself to participate in a journey which started with a highly intellectual theologian lecturing in a style most were unaccustomed to, matched with the faculty, designers, and in fact the birth fathers of IMPM witnessing a virtual rebellion by the participants, to a conscious decision by the theologian to quickly adapt a different style, to actual learning about the link, and often lack thereof, of spirituality and management, to finally, a self-discovery of self found, of all places, in two tracts from a Sinead O'Connor compact disc entitled *Universal Mother* [used by the professor].

It took no less than ten minutes into his lecture for me to realize that [the professor] put a great deal of effort into preparing to deliver a semester long lecture to a group of mid- to senior-level corporate professionals, an audience which was in fact, worlds apart from that to which he was accustomed. It took no less than eleven minutes into

the lecture for me to feel discomfort with my fellow module participants for challenging [him], in fact halting him midsentence to almost
demand a different delivery style. It took no less than twelve minutes
for me to witness a man who had spent so much time in preparation
hurt by this demand for something different, thirteen minutes for me
to see him muster up the courage and the drive to change, in spite of
his hurt feelings, and perhaps fifteen minutes for me to be thankful
for being a witness, and silent participant in the process.

In many respects, I can relate to the place where [he] found himself the day of his presentation. I, too, have found myself in situations where I was profoundly aware of my knowledge, experience
and often, intuition, that I could contribute in my world of work at
Motorola. I have sometimes struggled with both the method of expression of my thoughts, ideas and facts, as well as the timing of
such. As a member of the Human Resources function, I have felt that
my contributions though important, were too "soft" to be valued in
the technical world of Motorola. I coped with these perceptions by
sometimes holding back, but more often, by forcing my thoughts and
ideas into a process-driven, measurable, and therefore, presentable
concept. Upon reflection, many of these ideas may have lost their
meaning and value to the organization by my forcing them into a
mold where they didn't belong. While it was important for [the pro-
fessor] to communicate to us in a style with which we could understand, it was equally important that we did not force him to simply
"be like us" to the extent that our learning and opportunity for
growth for having experienced [this] experience, was hampered.

When [the professor] closed one segment of his session with the
track "Famine" from the Sinead O'Connor compact disc, I was
struck with a deep sense of communality and ability to relate to
an artist, who up until this point, was worlds apart from me. In
"Famine," Sinead "raps" about the impact of the historical famine
in Ireland, from her perspective as an Irish woman. She has become
aware of a different perspective, the Irish rather than British perspective, of what this historical event was all about, and how it has been
a struggle to be educated on this alternate view frequently discussed,
and often denied. She points out that to move from the place of hurt
to a place of peace, there has to be a certain level of recognition, then
a time to grieve, then forgiveness.

As an African American woman, born and reared in the United
States, I felt that I could have simply changed a few words in the

song, and the track would represent feelings I have dealt with too often to count. I am constantly reminded of my "blackness" in America, typically with some subtle, yet distasteful form of treatment. Very few people are willing or even able to hear an account of what these experiences feel like. I have often been told by white men in America "I am not responsible for the actions of my great-grandfathers." They don't want to dialogue about racial issues in America that occurred two hundred years ago, twenty years ago, or even twenty days ago. For me, this form of denial is personally damaging in the sense that it sometimes makes it difficult for me to get to a point of forgiveness and understanding. . . .

Upon my return [to work], I found myself with slightly different perspectives in both the business operations and the human resources settings in which I am a part. Typically, I fulfilled, perhaps even exceeded the expectations of both my internal customers, as well as my Human Resources colleagues. I challenged where appropriate. I set Human Resources goals and metrics for my team, and took a leadership role in driving toward their completion. I challenged myself to search for ways to make the business more productive by looking for ways to accelerate the performance and enhance the contributions of the people in the organization—after all, as we frequently state, "people are our most valuable asset."

After Module I, I still see myself doing these things, but with a different spirit and perhaps even, a different motivation. The different spirit is one of creating space for creativity, allowing time for the answer, being comfortable with the idea that sometimes there is no answer, and most importantly, finding peace in the space that allows for reflection. The different motivation I am experiencing is one which is now more personal, than perhaps driven by the business in which I operate. While there is certainly a link, I find myself driven more by the spirit of the Human Resources function, than by what the business demands that Human Resources professionals become.

Many of the participants report working on their ideas for the Reflective Papers during the airplane ride home. But not once it lands. The worlds of Lancaster, Bangalore, and the other locales quickly recede into the background as they encounter their family and workplace for the first time in two weeks. But several weeks later, once some kind of normality has returned, we ask them to revisit all the material of the module and write a paper that links whatever of it seems most relevant to themselves, their job, their organizations, their world.[1]

Revisiting the material of the module is easy enough. The readings, handouts, overheads, personal notes, and so forth, spring back to life upon review. And being back on the job, with experience at hand, facilitates the making of connections. Indeed, it allows the conceptual materials to be seen in a new light. Earlier I mentioned a session at Lancaster that was rated poorly yet then used extensively in the first Reflection Papers. As one participant from a later cycle commented in a similar vein:

> During the time at Lancaster, there were a number of occasions where I found myself thinking, "What possible relevance could this have to my working practice?" Within the spirit of the course and maintaining an open mind, I persevered. On reflection I was often surprised by the very real relationship that some of these areas have to my practice as a manager and the linkages between different areas which appeared to be superficially discrete. (Rob Sanders, of BT, Reflection Paper for Module I of Cycle 5)

We knew that the managers attending the IMPM were busy people, made that much busier by the program. So we did not expect long Reflection Papers. We were, however, pleasantly surprised and remain so after almost a thousand of these papers. The managers really get into this. Twenty pages, single-spaced, are not uncommon, although on average they probably run closer to ten or fifteen, double-spaced. We have been pleasantly surprised by the content, too. These are not the reports managers are used to doing—not those terse analytical arguments preceded by executive summaries. "A Reflection Paper is not what we are trained to do in business," one participant commented, where everyone expects "four or five bullet points." Nor is it like any academic assignment the participants may have done in earlier studies, where they had to go into a library or dig out data in some other way. The raw materials are there: conceptual inputs from the classroom and experiences from work. We ask the managers to combine them in a reflective way, a rather unusual request in this world—not to muse, but to let go and make creative links between the world of ideas and the world of practice. We

---

[1]Because of the logistics of the program, which winds down at Module V except for the Major Paper, it has not been appropriate to ask for a Reflection Paper on this last module. But the Insead faculty have successfully instituted an activity whereby the participants write a brief Reflection Paper about the module near the end of it.

don't want academic treatises any more than executive reports. We want thoughtful reflections.

And that we get. Not always right away. Some people are puzzled by the request, at least at the outset, and struggle with it. Others get into it immediately. But both groups have often characterized the experience as "intensive." One manager told of going to his office on a Sunday morning to spend a few hours on the paper, expecting to be home by noon. He worked until 4 a.m.! Another told us that when faced with a case to analyze, you just do it—maybe not creatively, but you get it done. Faced with a blank sheet of paper, however, you have to make your own statement. There is no template, no model (although we do provide examples of good ones at the first module, and the tutors, as will be discussed later, work closely with the participants on their early papers).

For many of us on the faculty, the best of the Reflection Papers have been among the most interesting writings we have seen from colleagues or students. And from the managers' perspective, as Nancy Badore put it after tutoring, writing a think piece connecting issues to experience can create "astonishing commitment." One participant reported that he "was amazed at how much I actually ended up reading and reflecting *after the module*." A new faculty tutor was heartened at how much his group had taken away from the module yet "only realized it somewhat later." Another participant claimed that ideas in one of his Reflection Papers paid for the program several times over. Another reaction bears quotation at length because it gives a good idea of how this process can work:

> When I returned from Module 1, I knew more about myself and
> through the Reflections Paper identified a few key changes I
> wanted to make in the way I approached things. I believe today
> I act differently as a result of the session. I re-read the Reflection
> Paper regularly to revive the learning and make sure I continue
> to internalize it.
>
> During Module 2, I looked for similar personal revelations
> during the course of [the] weeks; however, they didn't evolve. After
> leaving Montreal, I felt I had some new concepts and technical
> skills; however, I wasn't sure how they would impact my day-to-
> day work. The concepts seemed to be more applicable to running
> a large organization as opposed to running a portion of it.
>
> It wasn't until I sat down to do the Reflection Paper from the
> module that I began to understand how relevant the key learnings
> were. Immersed in the daily activity and priorities associated with
> my work while going back over the material from the classroom
> sessions at night made the connection clear. This wasn't an awak-

ening-type experience like Module 1; however, gradually the pieces fell into place and the resulting paper will act as an action plan for me once I am placed as an Area Regional Manager. (Vince Isber, Royal Bank of Canada, Cycle 1)

There was a proposal from a faculty member in Cycle 2 to focus some of these papers on specific topics—for example, to analyze the organization's balance sheet for the Module II paper. There were howls of protest from the class; keep them "flexible," "open-ended," "creative," "or else we'll just knock them off," people said. Accordingly, the assignment for all of these papers has maintained the following wording:

> Revisit your notes and insights, the readings and experiences of the [. . .] Module. Then, in the spirit of the [. . .] mindset, prepare a paper on the implications of this learning for yourself and/or your job and/or your organization. Please probe beyond description: Try to analyze, interpret, synthesize, etc.

There is something awfully significant—and therapeutic—about the simple act of looking inside oneself, stimulated by interesting ideas on one side and rich experiences on the other. That, we have concluded, is what management education should be about.

## TUTORING

We use tutoring in the IMPM, old British-style tutoring and its more recent manifestation in Action Learning (not to mention how professors work with doctoral students). Members of the faculty (mostly module directors) work with small groups of participants located in a common geographical area (to minimize travel). The groups meet at the first module and then four times more between each of the modules.

Tutoring personalizes and sustains the learning process, providing a connection for each participant with several colleagues and a member of faculty. This allows for ongoing support for all the assignments of the program and links to all the learning, in class and at work. The members of the tutorial group share experiences with each other, while the tutor acts as a learning coach to help anchor people in this new and sometimes strange environment. That can be especially important for the early Reflection Papers. (These papers are submitted to the tutor first and when considered acceptable go to the cycle director and university for final assessment.)

A tutorial meeting can be just a get-together in some common place to discuss the assignments, the program, and the learning. But increasingly they have grown beyond that, to all-day—and sometimes several-day—experiences at the workplace of a participant, to include visits, meetings with colleagues, and brainstorming sessions about issues there. Red Cross participants have been particularly creative about setting up tutoring meetings at some of their relief sites, which have had profound influence on their classmates and tutor, as can be seen in the accompanying box.

---

### A TUTOR'S DIARY IN AFRICA

*(by Oliver Westall, published in* The Times Higher Education Supplement, *August 17, 2001)*

Wednesday

A second day of tutorials with International Red Cross managers in Nairobi. We look at their assignments: cultural diversity within the Red Cross, humanitarian advocacy in the information age, and bilateralism within the Red Cross. Later, we relax in the tropical night watching startlingly beautiful dancers dressed in white silk at an Ethiopian restaurant.

Thursday

Up early to see Red Cross work in Kisumu on Lake Victoria. I need to see the work to be a helpful tutor. I am met by the Red Cross branch. They explain the local challenge: a 30 percent HIV/AIDS infection rate.

Jacqueline, a nurse caring for 600 sufferers in their village homes with basic medication and nutrition, answers questions with informed authority.

We make courtesy calls on a dynamic Asian mayor . . . and a concerned provincial commissioner. From there we go to Kabuor, a tiny village. We meet an HIV/AIDS self-help group who explain their problems: no health, no energy, no work, no food, no family. Frederick, the meeting's organizer, died yesterday. Will we pay our respects? Esther, a pretty eight-year old, runs in: Her parents are dead and she is HIV-positive.

We meet the Village Council and Parent Teacher Association. Kabuor Primary School has 300 children; 105 are orphans. Grandmothers take the strain. These dignified people are straightforward: "We are sorry to have to say this, but please help us."

> The children demonstrate their HIV/AIDS learning with stunning chants and dances. A local puts some money in the shirt of the lead dancer. We take the hint and follow, joining in the dance—everyone laughs. It is the best shake-down I have ever enjoyed. We see Esther spying through a hedge. Her grandmother cannot afford the school fee. We call her across. A colleague later sorts out the fees.
>
> We go to Frederick's parents' home. We walk past the skeleton of branches that were as far as he got in building a new home. Frederick's elderly parents and two daughters stand in silence by his wasted body. Jacqueline leads us in prayer and commemoration. I kiss his mother and the children and leave something with his father. There are tears as Red Cross staff recognize the grim eye of the storm in this silent, devastated hut.
>
> Friday/Saturday
>
> I pack up and fly home.

Tutoring may be a time-consuming and expensive business, but the tutor provides a key connection between the participants and the program. (Imagine a Japanese participant being able to work with a Japanese tutor after attending the first module in England.) In a sense, by connecting locally, it helps to customize the program at the edges. Quy Huy of Insead, who is now program director, has claimed that those IMPM participants got the most out of the program "who faced challenging and critical tutors" (memo to IMPM faculty, April 28, 2002). The tutors also provide personal connections into the participating companies, becoming the point of contact for the program. So the time and cost of tutoring can be well spent.

## SELF-STUDY

*Self-Study* refers to the work participants do in preparation for the analytical mindset of Module II, to bring themselves up to a basic need-to-know level in the business functions of marketing, accounting, and finance. (We have also considered adding material in economics before Module III.)

We first called this "close learning," to make the point that the usual label, "distance learning," is distant from the provider but close to the user. We now prefer Self-Study, which better describes the actual activity.

We also think of this as language training. The IMPM is not an MBA, but its graduates from business should have some basic literacy in the language of business. Many, in midcareer, arrive with that literacy and could even teach the material. (As noted earlier, they sometimes do.) But others do not. So we provide help on the basics, to be studied at home, through programmed instruction, workbooks, textbooks, screen, or paper—whatever works best. (Our experience to date is that a workbook works best in accounting, a textbook in marketing, and both in finance.)

Of course, we do not pretend to compress the MBA courses on these subjects into what we recommend to be about forty hours of Self-Study (depending on the participant's background). Rather, we provide what we believe to be an appropriate level of exposure for those not so exposed, much as do the major consulting firms (discussed in Chapter 4) that put their new recruits without business education through three weeks of courses. As discussed later, an IMPM for new managers would likely augment this Self-Study, bringing the program a little closer to the MBA.

## Managerial Exchange

A hugely successful part of the IMPM, the Managerial Exchange, was introduced almost inadvertently. Before the start of the program, we had come across a magazine reference to something similar that took place at Hewlett-Packard.[2] But an initial attempt to track it down failed, and we did not pursue it. Initially, our second module, on the analytical mindset, ran three weeks. That proved to be too long away from work and home, and we decided we could do it in two weeks. But since we had committed to the universities for a certain amount of work to earn the degree, we had to add a component for that week. Why not visits by the managers to each other's workplaces, Jonathan Gosling suggested at a meeting, and everyone agreed—sure, why not? Don't the participants learn so much from each other?

That is how the most popular, and next to Reflection Papers, perhaps most powerful, component of the IMPM came to be. As we found out, working in a common classroom of people from around the world is

---

[2] "'The best two days of my career.' That's how George Sparks, a general manager of Hewlett-Packard's measuring-equipment business, describes the time he spent following Frances Hesselbein around. As a learning experience, H-P sometimes assigns one executive to 'shadow' another with qualities worth emulating" (*Fortune*, November 27, 1995:68).

one thing; leaving your banking office in Toronto to enter the high-tech world of Osaka is quite another.

SIMPLE EXECUTION     The Managerial Exchange is almost as simple in execution as it was in conception. Think of it as an anthropological experience—time spent in a different culture, simply to live its life for a while. The managerial exchange has also been described as being on the individual level what the field studies are on the organizational level—but more intensive and directly focused on the nature of managerial work. The class members pair up, across companies and countries, and some time after the second module each person spends a week with his or her partner at work, back and forth, as guest and as host.

As faculty, we need do little more than ensure the organization of this component in class, with some briefing before and debriefing after. The briefing has taken the form of a half-day session on the nature of observation, how to keep a journal to record notes, and how to give constructive feedback to the host. At the visit, on the fourth day, the guest drafts feedback comments, and on the last day, he or she shares them with the host. After the return visit has been completed, a Reflection Paper is written on the whole experience, as host and guest. "What was happening to you? What was happening around you? . . . . [T]ry and deduce patterns in your management style, clues as to how corporate and national culture affect you" (from an IMPM briefing document by Simon Western). These reports, and the experiences themselves, are debriefed in Module IV.

Referring back to the window people and mirror people discussed in Chapter 9, it might be concluded that the window people prefer the guest role, as observers, while the mirror people like to play host, to see their behavior reflected back in the eyes of their visitor. What helps to make these exchanges so successful is that everyone has to play both roles. The guest learns by asking questions, however naive ("Why are you doing that?"); the host learns by the questions being asked. "There is someone looking in the whites of the eye and asking 'Why? Why? Why?' And you have to respond," one participant remarked.

PARTICIPANT REACTIONS     While we have developed various guidelines for these exchanges, one of the most interesting of all—bearing in mind that to date there have been almost five hundred weeks of exchanges—was the very first one, which took place before there were any guidelines at all.

The Cycle 2 exchanges were supposed to take place after Module IV, but Mayur Vora, an entrepreneur in food products from India, and

Françoise LeGoff, a manager on the Africa desk at the Red Cross Federation in Geneva, got a head start: Mayur visited Françoise on his way to Module IV. He came with his wife, who works with him, and they stayed in a free apartment just above where Françoise lived, so they also had time together away from work.

When Mayur saw Françoise typing on her PC at work, he expressed surprise. Couldn't a secretary do that? Differences in pay scales between India and Switzerland suddenly became evident, and so did their consequences. When, on the last day, Mayur proposed to Françoise that he would be happy to speak with any of her people who were interested, they all lined up, secretaries included, to convey through him their thoughts on her style of managing.

Françoise was so enthusiastic about the experience that at the module a few days later, she sat me down to provide her reactions at length. I knew then we were onto something special.

He kept asking her, "Why are you doing that?" and by the end of the week, she was asking it of herself, too. "He was like a mirror for me," Françoise said. The experience "was not comfortable for me at the beginning," but it turned out to be "very powerful." Mayur told her that she took too much responsibility on her shoulders and had to learn to say no more often and delegate more. He also commented on the body language he saw in the Red Cross headquarters. The whole experience was much more than Françoise thought it would be: "I was totally exhausted at the end!" The following Monday morning, two of her assistants came in with specific proposals for change.

GUEST ROLES    This was only one experience—indeed, only the first one—but indicative of what can happen in such an exercise. Guests can tour; they can attend meetings; they can be asked for advice; they can do whatever people in such a setting find valuable. A Toronto banker accompanied his Red Cross host to a refugee camp in West Africa, and he was deeply moved by the experience. Asked later whether he could apply this learning to his workplace, he replied, "Yes! All of the time!" When she submitted her report as his guest in Toronto, he circulated it to the people around him and included it as part of his 360-degree assessment.

Some guests choose to play the waif, making those simple observations that can be so insightful. "Declare yourself to be naive," a faculty member advised. "Do your homework and be willing to sound stupid." Others play the role of coach, or confessor, or alter ego, or consultant. But about the latter, one participant suggested that the guest should engage in a "shadowing" assignment, not a consulting one, expressing the sentiment of other colleagues that managers don't need more expert advice; they need honest comments on what they do. "You don't get much feedback, especially on the way up," one participant remarked, rarely from a friendly colleague with no ax to grind. A "friendly audit" is how one person characterized the experience.

UNEXPECTED LEARNING    The best learning from these exchanges is often the most unexpected. One BT manager commented on a visit to Japan where "they spent a half day talking about *one* word. We never do that!" Before another exchange, Takeshi ("Terry") Yukitake of Fujitsu briefed Philippe Thirion of EDF:

> We have the famous *oo-beya* (big one-room) office. The circumstance will be quite different from yours but this is our culture. Please enjoy it. I am trying to find your desk near my desk; however, if not, we will share my desk or you will have a desk in ten-desks block. (Do you remember, ten desks makes one block and my desk is in front of the block.) I apologize for your inconvenience, but again this is our culture.

Philippe, of course, did not speak Japanese. Yet that situation can lead to another, even richer kind of learning. Not knowing the language forces the guest to observe more intensely, taking in nonverbal behaviors and so developing a skill that can be most beneficial to any manager. "I'm glad I chose a country where I did not understand the language," one guest wrote.

The Managerial Exchange is, in a sense, a full week of "white time." Managers are usually energetic and resourceful people, so give them free time and they find something useful to do with it. Developing the skill of observation is a very useful thing to do. One guest commented on a two-hour meeting, "I had to find a new way to learn." She observed the flow and later gave her host impressions on the role he played there.

This learning extends beyond the host, much as in the field studies. The host's colleagues learn from the unexpected questions and observations of an outsider looking in. "For your information, let me ask you a few questions," reportedly quipped movie mogul Sam Goldwyn. In his briefing document to Terry, Philippe listed as a goal of the visit: to "express your astonishment [by] questioning us in order to help progress." Another host, Mark Jones of Zeneca, commented on the experience: "When Ron [Foss, of the Royal Bank of Canada] came in, he was asking questions from a completely different direction—people found this very interesting and useful. As a result, one of my managers spent a week with him later on." From his perspective, Ron wrote a memo to the faculty:

> I will admit that in the weeks and days prior to going to Zeneca to see Mark Jones I was kicking and screaming a little because of the new job and the demands at work. . . . However, having now experienced the opportunity I have no regrets and would not trade it in at all. How many times in your career can you take what you know, what you are trying to learn and apply some or all in a business and industry that you know little about? It is like taking your toys and playing in someone else's sandbox. . . .
>
> Mark was at Royal Bank just this last week and I think he too found it to be a good experience. His observations were accurate and his ideas and points of view very refreshing. He has given us a few very good things to consider as we move forward. . . . I was grateful for the candidness and different perspective.

Participants sometimes have trouble writing about the experience: "the exchange had an element of 'you had to be there' which just cannot be written about in any sort of satisfactory way," wrote one participant. This, however, seems to represent, not an absence of learning, but a different kind of learning. If action learning is visceral, about doing, then Managerial Exchanges are visual, about "seeing"—about being there and observing. This kind of learning is more tacit than explicit and so cannot easily be expressed in words. Yet the participants are insistent in their claims about the profundity of the experience. "I have a thought and can't express it," goes an old poem, followed by "You have no thought and have expressed it." This is a basic tenet of formal education, but our experiences in the Managerial Exchanges suggests it can sometimes be dead wrong!

In these Managerial Exchanges, we push the essence of the IMPM to its limit, with great success. This activity is highly personal, engagingly collaborative, thoroughly customized, fundamentally reflective, and authentically international.[3]

---

[3]For more detail on the exchanges, see www.impm.org/westerngosling. Needless to say, the potential for managerial exchanges is enormous, within existing management development programs and as freestanding management development activities. Under the auspices of Lancaster University, Western and Gosling established a dedicated organization (see www.lead2lead.net) that extends these services to other organizations.

## VENTURES

With respect to currently popular practice, especially in management development, the Ventures in our program are not unusual. This is a kind of action learning, in which the participants undertake projects to effect some kind of change in their organizations. Alongside the reflective character of the rest of the program, however, the execution can come out differently.

We ask that the Ventures address what would not otherwise have been done, or else be done differently as a result of being part of the IMPM. Of course, over the sixteen months of the program, many of these Ventures are bound to change course. As Kerry Chandler of Motorola reported, "Every model, everything was changing. My job was changing. My life was changing. So was my Venture." Accordingly, we make it quite clear that the object of the Venture is to learn, not to carry out plans—indeed, especially to learn from the changes to the Venture made along the way. Kerry ended up doing her Venture on personal change in the IMPM! (Some of her results are presented in Chapter 13.)

The participants may do their Venture singly or in groups. Although we encourage the latter, in the early years most chose to work alone, usually on issues close to their own workplace. But the IMPM is supposed to help generate a company-wide perspective, and so a rise in the number of group Ventures over the years, in a few cases specified by the company, is welcome. (In Chapter 14, I will describe a broader use of Ventures in a companion program.)

Ventures topics have included the following:

- "Creativity, Learning, and Innovation" at Zeneca (Cycle 2 group), which included interviewing other IMPM company groups at length, (the Fujitsu participants, for five hours).

- Developing a course called "Web Monitoring" to teach Lufthansa senior managers about the Internet (Oliver Sellnick, Cycle 4); 120 senior managers, including four members of the executive board, subsequently took the course from sixty young people who "mentored" them; this activity won the prestigious German Human Resource Management Award for 2000.

- "Establishment of a New Silk Road for Software and Service Business," from Europe through the Middle East, India, and China, to Japan (Roy Sugimura, Matsushita Cycle 1); the board of the company subsequently assigned him to pursue this topic.

The Ventures are guided by the tutors and overseen by the cycle director, who receive periodic reports as well as the final one. As noted earlier, there is a full debriefing of the Ventures at the final module, including presentation of them to their colleagues. The participants are also asked to reflect on their ability to achieve change and their organization's ability to accept it.

Some companies have been quite enthusiastic about the Ventures. Like all such projects, they provide a tangible "take away." Zeneca, which assigned Venture topics to each group, had them report the final conclusions to the senior management, while Lufthansa extended the activity internally by assigning an "executive sponsor" to each Venture. Some other companies, however, have expressed the belief that the IMPM does well at developing their managers, and that is sufficient. (More on this later.)

Alexei Gartinski of the Red Cross (Cycle 2) wrote that his Venture provided the "'missing link' between 'doing' and 'thinking.'" He himself worked in management development, and he did his Venture on "Changing the Focus of the [Red Cross] Federation Training Programs," an example of doing differently a project that he was doing anyway (i.e., using work). He commented afterward:

> Without putting [this project] into a venture frame, we would
> have probably moved in the same direction but more as a trial
> and error process, having less of an overall long-term perspective.
> I think because of the venture we worked on the project in a
> more "conscious" way: . . . we introduced additional elements of
> analysis and structure in our thinking, which in a unit like ours
> doesn't do any harm! One of the main lessons learnt in the ven-
> ture process was simple enough: *making sense of what you are
> doing helps.*

The questions that remain are how commonly this happens and how to respond to the learning needs of the various participants while accommodating the practical needs of their companies.

## MAJOR PAPER AND DEGREE

One of the best decisions we ever made was to offer the IMPM as a masters degree. My own feelings on this were initially mixed. Why bother? It's the learning that matters, not the credential. True enough, but we have found that the credential increases the learning. Not because of some childish "If you don't do the assignment, you won't graduate" threat but, in practice, quite the opposite: The degree becomes a natural quid pro quo that establishes a mature relationship between the participants and the faculty. Various activities come with the degree, so the participants, serious managers who understand a commitment, do them. And so they learn more. This is in contrast to the notorious problem of getting managers to do outside assignments in non-degree programs. I recall the head of one prominent program, with a format but not content much like the IMPM (company groups in two-week modules, etc.), boasting to me that he saw no need to offer a degree. Yet he had great difficulty getting the participants to do work between the modules.

Interestingly, the degree causes others to take the program more seriously, too. For the companies, the degree helps the management development staff attract good candidates and also stands the program higher in the perception of senior management. As for the schools, as noted earlier, degree programs are like the crown jewels: The faculty take notice when the school's name is embossed on those certificates. That can bring about closer scrutiny, and therefore more conservatism, but it can also replace an "anything goes" attitude in nondegree programs with one of "We better make this good." And it can draw the best faculty into the program. The people who ran the early modules in Japan were both deans of major business schools; at Insead, two ex-deans ran the early modules.

In our initial design, we struggled with a tricky problem: how to keep the program attuned to the needs of practicing managers while justifying the granting of a masters degree. There was a key meeting in Japan when five of us sitting around a table in a restaurant faced two agenda items: this, and the need to set a date for our next meeting. Typical of a great deal of our deliberation, we resolved the critical former item in a few minutes with one key idea, while giving up on the scheduling after an hour of discussion.

The key idea was to institute a "Major Paper" as a kind of mini-thesis after completion of all the other activities of the program. That way, we could enhance other, less traditionally academic activities with a more conventional one. (See Figure 10.1 on p. 278, which shows the other activities terminating after sixteen months, followed by the Major Paper for about six months.)

Besides anchoring the IMPM as a degree program, the Major Paper is also the most intensive and most personal requirement of the program. Participants are expected to do it on their own and to go deeply into an issue.

We hold a Major Paper workshop adjacent to the fifth module, which has presentations on research methods and provides opportunities for the participants to discuss their proposals with each other and a faculty member. Then each participant is assigned a faculty adviser who works with him or her and evaluates the result.

In our guidelines on the Major Paper, we define it as neither a formal thesis[4] nor a simple report but a substantial assignment normally carried out through a review of serious literature supported by in-depth study. Key to this is substantiation, compared with the Reflection Papers, which are based more on personal opinion and reflection. The guidelines make clear, however, that "[t]his is not just an academic requirement but a key part of your development as a manager: to deal with the investigation of a significant issue. It is the ability to take the broad view based on in-depth understanding that often distinguishes the great senior executive. . . . The major paper can be designed to have an important impact on your organization; or need not—that is your choice. . . . [But] it has to go beyond this . . . as a contribution to the understanding of some issue."

An obvious question is: What relevance does such an academic requirement have for practicing managers? And the answer, provided by our experience, is: a great deal more than might be imagined. These papers generally turn out to be of considerable relevance to the people who do them.

A good example is a paper on federalism done by Luc De Wever of the legal office of the Federation of Red Cross and Red Crescent Societies (Cycle 1). He had an assignment to rethink the organization's constitution and used the Major Paper to advance that. Near completion, Luc wrote to his adviser about "a huge task . . . which turned out to be an exciting one." The paper considered federalism across a broad range of experiences, from the U.S. Federalist Papers on the division of powers between the federal government and the states, to the divisional form of structure used in business, including Charles Handy's (1992) article linking this to the federal concept. In Luc's terms, this study was used to draw conclusions about "how federal the Federation is and could be." He presented his conclusions to a committee of the board on the Constitution.

Listed here are other examples of these Major Papers, which can be seen to vary widely. Indeed, a listing of all the topics addressed in a

---

[4]McGill offers masters' degrees with and without thesis; the IMPM is officially without thesis.

given cycle provides an interesting picture of what is of concern to managers at that point in time. (I have in fact offered such a list to doctoral students in search of thesis topics.) We can also see in these topics, as in much else of the IMPM, a coming together of the concepts of scholarship with the concerns of practice.

- "Channel Tunnel Vision," Alan Whelan (BT, Cycle 1): not about some vision of the Channel Tunnel but about tunnel vision in marketing channels

- "The Role of Japanese Technology in Emerging Markets," Bunji Mizuno (Matsushita, Cycle 3)

- "Banking Industry Collaboration in Canada: From Reluctant Bedfellows to Strategic Partners," Shari Austin (Royal Bank of Canada, Cycle 4)

The format of the IMPM—sixteen months of the other activities followed by six months on the Major Paper—has allowed us to do something else that proved fortuitous: making the degree optional. Participants can stop after the fifth module and get a certificate of attendance (the only document that can legally carry the names of the various schools) as well as an Insead diploma. Or they may continue with the Major Paper, registering at either McGill or Lancaster, which offer the degree and assign a member of faculty to supervise the paper.

The degree may be optional, but telling is the fact that to date almost all the participants have chosen to register for the degree, and most of those have completed it (in all, about 80 percent of the participants get degrees). So we have been able to keep our cake and eat it, too: we can sustain a design suitable to the development of managers yet get the discipline that comes with the degree. I conclude from this that serious educational programs have an important role to play in the development of practicing managers. Hence these chapters—and this book!

WHY AN MPM?    One final word on our label for the degree. We could have saved a lot of effort and just called this an MBA. (At one point, we even considered "Managerial MBA," but the dean at McGill wasn't too keen on this!) Establishing a new label, especially in the face of one so firmly entrenched, is no easy matter. But we had to do so for this very reason. The label MBA sends all sorts of signals that we wished to counter: that the education is steeped in analytical technique; that the attendees have been trained generically, out of context; that the degree makes people more marketable; and so on. We decided on the new label *Masters of Practicing Management* to signal that this is a new initiative, to be understood in its own terms.

In fact, the obscurity of the label helps in a way, because the MPM is designed to make its graduates *less* marketable: It seeks to strengthen the bond between manager and organization. By developing people in context, it is designed to help them *do* a better job, not *get* a better job. You don't shift such long-standing habits with old labels. As suggested earlier, after a century, it is time for a new degree!

# 13

## DEVELOPING MANAGERS IV
### *Impact of the Learning*

*You see things as they are, and you ask "Why?" But
I dream things that never were, and I ask "Why not?"*
—GEORGE BERNARD SHAW

We turn now to the impact of this new kind of management education, in various respects. We begin by considering the costs—in particular, does the IMPM pay? Then we look at IMPact, our label for the influence of IMPM learning back at work. This leads us into a broader discussion of results—does the IMPM benefit? The answer, discussed last, really lies in the assessments of those who have been involved in the program—participants, especially, but also company people, faculty, and observers.

## DOES THE IMPM PAY?

There seems little doubt that the IMPM offers something special for the development of managers. But it costs the companies in terms of money and the participant in terms of time, since so much of it is based on personal, face-to-face contact. If, however, as I have argued, there are no shortcuts to true management development, then the question becomes: Who will pay for it?

SHOULD THE COMPANIES PAY?   MBA programs can cost a small fortune. But this is usually paid by individuals who expect to enhance their earnings. In the IMPM, however, almost all the participants are sent by their employers, who pay.

There are two contemporary reasons why companies should not pay for this. First is the "easy come, easy go" nature of the corporate scene today, at least in the United States. People are now so mobile, goes the argument, that it makes little sense to invest in them. Let them look after their own development. The second argument, not unrelated, is that even those who stay in the company move so fast that they just don't have the time for intensive development.

I find both arguments misguided. For one thing, companies are not casual collections of independent agents; they are systems of people united in social networks. Investing in this kind of education strengthens those bonds and thus the company.

For another, especially in a world with so much hype, confusion, and angst, people need to stop and take stock; they need to consider the broader perspective. Short, easy, strobe-light courses, and even longer ones fashioned as boot camps, may only reinforce some of the worst tendencies in current practices of management. We don't need to replicate the problems of management in the classroom, but to correct them. In a world of superficiality, there is the need for substance; in a world of pressure, there is the need for reflection.

But should companies pay for this? Yes, without any doubt—if they consider leadership as important as they claim. Leaders do not appear immaculately conceived, ready to be plugged in, from MBA programs or anywhere else, including the IMPM. No classroom can do that. Leaders arise in context. But serious management education can enhance the potential for leadership by improving people's understanding of context and capacity for managing.

THE BARGAIN OF EXPENSIVE MANAGEMENT EDUCATION   This kind of development costs money. The IMPM fee for 2003 was $45,000, plus an additional $6,750 for those taking the degree. (Companies can reasonably expect participants to pay the latter. Participants from India and the Red Cross pay about one-third of these rates. The lower cost of the module in India balances this out.) Living costs run at about $12,000 (less for those who accept cheaper accommodations), plus there are travel costs (expensive in business class, cheap when prebooked). Multiply this by several people sent on a given cycle, and you end up with a rather substantial expenditure for a company.

So is this expensive? Yes, indeed, when assessed against many management development budgets. But should it be so assessed? Managers cost a lot more than that, and failed management is hugely expensive.

The manager going on the IMPM from a developed country can be costing his or her company in salary and benefits during its two years of duration four or more times the cost of the program. Put the other way, for two years the company has incurred an increase of 25 percent in the cost of that manager. How much improvement would it take to justify that investment? Not much at all—and the evidence (discussed later) suggests that companies are getting a lot more than that. So the problem is not costs so much as budgets; the accounting in most firms charges this kind of development as expense to a staff department instead of investment in the operations.

But what if some of these people leave the company, carrying the investment with them? These figures suggest that a company would have to lose quite a few of its participants before this investment becomes negative. But again, that may be the wrong question. Is this a matter of wasting money on people who leave or saving money on people who stay? In other words, beside the obvious loss of some people is the less obvious retention of others. The IMPM is designed to strengthen the bond between manager and company. This alone could justify the costs. On September 20, 1999, *Business Week* ran a cover story on the "brain drain—what smart companies are doing to keep senior stars on the job." Sending them on programs like the IMPM could be one of them. (Later I shall present figures on company retention rates.)

Frank McCauley, who brought the Royal Bank of Canada into the IMPM, has made another argument about its cost: that this can broaden a manager's international perspective far more cheaply, and perhaps even more effectively, than a temporary assignment abroad. Counting incentive compensation, housing, health care, tax equalization payments, and other costs, he estimated the typical expatriate compensation package at two and a half times that for the same person in Canada. "The economics of the IMPM looks much different in that light!" he wrote in a memo. In fact, many of the companies participating in the IMPM use it to prepare their managers for international assignments.

Put all this together, and company support for management education begins to make a great deal of sense—as soon as it gets past the budgets of management development. For those companies that see beyond share price in the next few quarters, this is not disconnected managerial education but integrated organization development.

Of course, there is another side to the equation, beside the costs—namely, the benefits, to the participants and to their companies. Does the IMPM make that much difference? Two aspects of this are considered in this chapter: the direct impact of the education and the assessments of benefits by those involved.

# IMPact

Another factor key to this discussion was introduced in Chapter 9 as *impact*, although here it can be called IMPact (or anchoring, as in another program discussed later). To develop better managers is one thing; to develop better organizations *in the process* of developing better managers, rather than *as a consequence* of developing them, is quite another. In other words, programs like the IMPM should be designed so that *organization* development results directly from management development, as the participants carry the learning into their companies.

Impact can take two different forms, as introduced in Chapter 9. One, *action impact*, improves something in the organization. That is the purpose of the IMPM Ventures, as well as much management development today, including Action Learning and Work-Out. My concern with this, expressed earlier, is that while the purpose of an organization is to take action, the purpose of development is to improve its *capacity* to take action. And that often requires stepping back from action.

The second form, *teaching impact*, transmits the learning of those in the program to others. As discussed in Chapter 9, all managers have to be teachers—helping develop their own people and their colleagues by sharing what they have learned. That is what mentoring is all about. And who better to teach than managers who are themselves in a learning program?

One of the participants of our program commented, "There is nothing but a string of opportunities here." True enough, but along with them come a string of challenges. People may learn in groups, but it is assumed that they carry it away as individuals. So along with the management program comes the syndrome of the lonely learner, felt especially at reentry: "I came back changed, and nobody cared." It would be nice to believe that we avoid this in our program by having several people learn together from the same company. But when the modules end, most of them disappear into different parts of the company. "How do I carry all this back to my job?" one participant asked. "I get off the escalator, meet my colleagues, and they are all in the same place I left them."

One company representative described the same problem in their in-house programs, where *everybody* is from the same company!

It has been said that you should never send a changed person back to an unchanged environment (Raelin 2000:21). But you *always* do. Programs are designed to change the participants, not the environment. So maybe that has to be changed. We are working on it, with the participating companies.

THE RANGE OF IMPACTS    As we began to think about this issue, we realized that the program was already having all kinds of impacts, in both actions and teaching. Many of these have been small, but they add up. With a little encouragement from our side, even just to make the participants aware of each other's impacts, there could be many more.

Impact occurs when a participant returns from a module and shares a reading with a colleague; when he or she changes a process based on some learning; also when a host group is jolted by a question from a guest on a Managerial Exchange; and when that group is so impressed that it picks up and does an exchange of its own. Other impacts result more directly from the Field Studies, the Ventures, and the Major Papers.

To appreciate the possibilities, Figure 13.1 maps IMPacts on three dimensions. One is the source of impact—the *what*. As indicated, using the symbols of the figure, this can be any activity of the program, from a Reflection Paper to an event at a module to a Field Study. A second dimension concerns the recipient of the impact—the *where*. This may be the unit managed by the participant, another unit or the whole com-

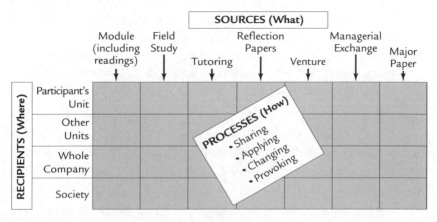

FIGURE 13.1
A Map of IMPacts

pany, also into the broader society (including the participant's family). The third dimension is the process of impacting—the *how*—which can be thought of as:

- sharing materials,

- applying methods,

- changing behaviors,

- provoking new frames.

I mean these to be in ascending order of impact. Sharing materials leaves the initiative to the recipient, whereas applying methods alters established procedures, and changing behaviors alters other people. Most impactful of all is provoking a reframing of perceptions, since this encourages other people to see things differently and so possibly stimulating a major shift. Notice that while the second and third are largely action impacts, the first and fourth are more teaching impacts. The implication of this is that transmitting the learning of the program can be more impactful than using it to render direct change. The following examples give a sense of the variety of impacts that have resulted from the IMPM:

- Jack Donner, a Motorola participant in Cycle 2, involved his colleagues in the modules by sending home a regular stream of electronic postcards about what he was learning. (Sharing)

- Francine Dyksterhuis and Wendy Youzwyshyn of the Royal Bank of Canada (Cycle 2) hosted "open houses" for members of their staff to share experiences of the modules. More formally, Matsushita has held "Friday Forums" to enable participants to discuss with colleagues issues that came up at the modules. (Sharing)

- Jeff Guthrie of the Royal Bank (Cycle 3) took an idea he read in an assigned book by Jay Galbraith (1995) and for his Venture created a "distributed organization," allocating responsibility for various central staff functions to particular line units across Canada. (Applying)

- A Motorola group, impressed with a Managerial Exchange visit from a Lufthansa participant, picked up and went on their own exchange to Lufthansa. (Applying)

- Gorur Gopinath, an entrepreneur who had developed various businesses before the IMPM, conceived India's first helicopter charter service as his Venture, which he has subsequently grown into a discount airline. (Changing)

- Simon Cooper of BT (Cycle 3) wrote his Module III Reflection Paper in the form of a speech he had to deliver to a division of the company. He used it "to illustrate how we must become more worldly and have global intentions. . . . It took directly a series of inputs from India in particular and fed them in to my normal day job, adding real value" (e-mail, May 5, 1999). (Provoking)

An interesting account of the impacts of one participant, and his reflections on them, are presented in the accompanying box.

---

## ONE IMPACT ACCOUNT

*(letter to two IMPM faculty members from Simon Herriott, Avecia [which was part of Zeneca], Cycle 4, May 3, 2001)*

Gentlemen,

The last "i" is dotted and the "t" crossed on my final paper, and thus short of graduating, the IMPM journey is now truly over. Shame! If we could justify everything in life on the basis of pure enjoyment and the pleasure of good company and intellectual stimulation, I would be starting all over again now. . . . I thought I would briefly reflect, as others have before, on the vexed question of "back home impact."

**Real Changes**

If we accept for a minute, that in this world of "bottom lines," my personal development due to IMPM has no value until it has real economic impact, I think that I can still substantiate a growing list of real changes that I have been able to make as a direct consequence of the learning gained. Here's my stock take:

*Our business strategy emphasizes a vision of the type of business that we wish to be and of the competencies that we wish to develop, alongside the usual financial aspirations. It encompasses a flexibility in the "what's" and "how's" that my previous attempts have tried to eradicate rather than encourage.*

*We continue to report financial outputs, but our business team spends its time looking at input and activity measures, lifted directly from my McGill reflection paper. We have changed the reward systems for our sales team and have incorporated 360-degree feedback for the management team; both based largely on learning that I gleaned from fellow participants.*

*My own 360-degree feedback carried some messages which chimed strongly with Jean-François Manzoni's [of Insead] exhortations to managers to be even-handed with their employees, whether respected performers or not. I think I'm winning, though time and the next round of feedback will tell.*

*We have re-designed our customer service office space, taken away walls and introduced open, "collaborative" spaces; a move that was rather more radical here in the U.S. than it might appear elsewhere.*

*My Indian paper identified a market opportunity that remains on the "drawing board" but is under serious consideration, and the interest that I showed in innovation for my final paper has landed me a role in steering strategic research for the company.*

Design and implementation of all these changes has ultimately been a team effort, but in each of them, the IMPM experience has been the source of inspiration.

### Implications

There are two broad patterns that emerge: first (perhaps rather obviously), that greatest success can be achieved where the individual has the authority to implement. Two years ago, the impact that I would have been able to make would have been much less.

Second, that I didn't set out to use the knowledge gained from the IMPM in this way, it just happened. In other words, as I faced a (normal) set of managerial and strategic challenges, I found myself far better equipped to deal with them. This may reflect a "reactive" personal style, but I would prefer to think that it is the inevitable and proper response to emerging changes in our environment, and that the business would, conversely, be poorly served by selective implementation of techniques drawn from a menu. You have told us often enough that you have little sympathy for the teaching of a manual of business techniques and that the IMPM is the "anti-MBA." However, it is therefore axiomatic that if, as you intend, IMPM graduates leave with a deep well of tacit knowledge (rather than a neatly parceled manual), that it will be much harder to "prove" back home impact, as you have consistently tried to do.

I am afraid that you will have to continue to try, as will we, the students; hence my list. But, ask me where the next contribution of the IMPM will be made to my business and personal life, and I will respond that I have no idea! I am confident, however, that it will.

I suspect I am not alone in grieving the end of a searching and stimulating two years. Thank you both; it was a lot of fun!

Sincerely yours
Simon Herriott

We have made one advance in impact that I find especially important. Taizoon Chinwalla, of Motorola, wrote to the faculty after completing Cycle 2 that Impact should become a formal part of the program, for example, by changing the Venture into a series of reports on impacts attempted and achieved, and what was learned. (A participant in Cycle 3 dubbed such reports "Refl'Action"!) We have not so changed the Ventures, but Taizoon's enthusiasm landed him the position of codirector of Cycle 5 (while doing his job at Motorola), where he held regular sessions with the class on their impacts. This is now a regular part of the program.

Figure 13.2 shows a range of postures for impacts, from simple individual learning at one end (Work-In) to aggressive action changing at the other (Work-Out)—in other words, from conventional business education to action learning management development. The two postures shown between these extremes are perhaps where attention should now be focused. One is labeled *shared learning*, where the learner of the classroom becomes the teacher on the job. The other is labeled *induced changing*, where attention is not on carrying out change projects so much as using the learning to provoke change. Formally assigned "big hit" change projects should probably be left to processes that arise naturally within the organization.

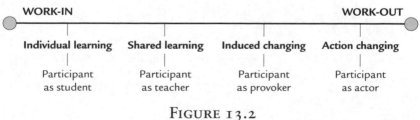

FIGURE 13.2
Impact Postures

THE COMPANY ROLE IN AND BEYOND IMPACTS    So far, I have discussed impacts as they come from the participants themselves, whether by conscious design or just happenstance, as Simon Herriott described. As managers return to their old contexts with new ideas, it is natural for them to try to make things different. But this can also be encouraged, and efforts to do so in the classroom have already been discussed. Now let us turn to efforts by the companies. The experiences of the IMPM suggest that management education and development will become profoundly more effective when the companies participate actively with their managers. This applies especially to impacts but also to activities before and beyond them.

Figure 13.3 shows the possible company roles in a program such as the IMPM: They select the participants, prepare them for the program, deal with reentry after each module, encourage impacts of all the program activities, and manage the final reentry as well as subsequent career development. The companies vary enormously in how they manage these processes. Some, for example, hand-pick candidates for the program from among their "high-potential" managers, while another once sent out information on the program to its ten thousand managers and then dealt with the five hundred inquiries that came back. Similarly, preparation for the program varies, from handing out a few of our documents to full-fledged briefing sessions with graduates from the company. (The Matsushita participants on the first cycle introduced themselves by proudly displaying a picture with their "teachers." They attended English-language training for two weeks; Module I ran four weeks for them!)

With regard to company management of reentries and impacts during management programs in general, one practice dominates: Do nothing. Our own experience is that companies tend to give careful attention

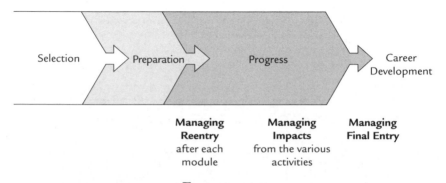

FIGURE 13.3
Company Roles around the Educational Process

to the selection and preparation of candidates at the start and/or to the management of their career after, but they are less inclined to help with reentry and impact during. Happily, however, this situation has begun to change in the IMPM, partly encouraged at our annual meeting with company representatives.

One thing companies can do is provide support for the participants. If the program assigns tutors, then the companies can assign mentors. That way the participants get supported on each end. Zeneca, for example, had each participant link laterally with a member of the executive committee. The company can also designate a group of learning partners—junior managers—with whom each participant can share his or her learning; they can even do a kind of "shadow IMPM" with the participant. In a similar vein, but going senior instead of junior, some companies have named a kind of Venture Board to oversee that activity. Some companies, as noted, have also assigned Venture topics.

Of all the IMPM companies, Lufthansa has perhaps been most active in seeking to extend program learning into the company. It has assigned a member of its School of Business (LHSB) to work with its participants and, in Cycles 5 and 6, also designated a senior manager as sponsor of each Venture and arranged to circulate the results. Lufthansa has also held several special meetings. One before the start of the program brings the new participants together with their managers, LHSB people, and IMPM graduates. After each module, a meeting has also been held to discuss the lessons learned as well as progress on the Ventures, Managerial Exchanges, and other activities. And a final meeting celebrates completion of the program.

Following a discussion at LHSB in October 2000, I wrote an e-mail to the IMPM faculty about these meetings, suggesting that they could provide a wonderful forum for impacts—a place for participants to share the ideas and consequences of the program. These managers would be learning with the appreciation that a group of colleagues at work are listening, systematically. That could encourage them to keep notes in class, an "IMPact diary," to record possibilities for impacts, and to prepare reports on actual impacts achieved, big and small, to share at these company meetings. The cohort in a cycle could also report after each module on how it sees the company differently. Indeed, why not feed forward, and use these meetings to suggest relevant topics for workshops at the modules?

Initiatives of all these kinds could make management development programs profoundly more effective. But that will take a radical departure from so much current practice, including recognition that parallel efforts have to happen inside the companies. We talk a lot about "learning organizations" these days. Extending management development into organization development can bring these words alive. Not by having managers running around doing projects, but by leveraging their learning in all sorts of ways. There *really is* nothing but a string of opportunities here. If the schools could find ways to work effectively with the companies, then programs for practicing managers, degree ones in particular, could become their most important educational activity.

## DOES THE IMPM BENEFIT?

The IMPM may pay, compared with the alternatives, but does it benefit? Does it render serious, sustained, useful changes? After he had read a paragraph I had written on "Does the IMPM Pay?" Frank McCauley of the Royal Bank wrote to me: "What you want the reader to take away from this paragraph is an impression of the richness of IMPM, not its cost." I agree. But how do I do that? Frank could make such a comment because he visited the class and watched the participants he sent develop over the whole program. He *saw* the richness. What about the reader who cannot?

I address first the most common answer to such a question—prove it with numbers—because I believe it to be the wrong answer. You can't prove anything with numbers. You can sometimes provide an indication, which I shall do. But beyond that, the best I can probably do in a book like this is allow those who were there to speak for themselves. That will not prove anything, either, but it may encourage some readers to get closer to the richness of the experience and find out for themselves.

FAITH IN MEASUREMENT? Numbers, to repeat, prove nothing. They give reasonable indications of some phenomena, but learning is not one of them, nor is leadership. Everyone might make a big fuss these days about "performance," "payback," "deliverables," and "results," but the fact is that when it comes to learning and leadership, the benefits, unlike the costs, cannot be quantified.

You are reading this book. You know what it cost you, in money and in time. So what are the benefits? If you think the learning is wonderful (I hope so), can you put a figure on that? Can you know how the learning will pay off? Or maybe you think this book is nonsense— you have come a long way for that!—but then, months from now, without even realizing it, you do something useful because of what you read. So let me suggest that you be suspicious about numbers when it comes to processes like learning. (This advice alone should recoup the cost of the book!)

Of course, the modern way is to get rid of what can't be measured. Rely on the numbers. If we can't measure it, so the saying goes, then we can't manage it. Well, then, we shall have to get rid of most startups, because few generate reliable numbers in advance. Likewise, we shall have to get rid of truly new product development, because rarely does anyone get the potential markets right. (Pampers were introduced for the travel market; they never believed people would use disposable diapers at home.) And, by the way, we shall also have to get rid of senior management, sometimes the most enthusiastic measurers of them all, because we can't measure their effects either. (If you think share value does it, then I suggest you read the newspapers.) All of these are acts of faith. Indeed, what is more an act of faith than measurement itself? Who ever measured the benefits of measuring?

According to a *Business Week* report on October 18, 1999 (Reingold 1999:80), "Already, 30% of the companies surveyed by *Business Week* have tried to quantify their programs' success, though few report solid results." Do they ever? "Verified knowledge in this area is discouragingly slim," wrote Gordon and Howell back in 1959, citing a claim from a decade earlier and adding that the "situation is not a great deal better today" (75). Nor today, almost a half century after that.[1]

The head of executive development at one prominent business school said that "in the end, the real private-sector measure of executive education will be the effect it has on the company share price" (*Canadian Business Magazine*, advertising supplement, December 31, 1999). That is just plain nonsense. I defy this person to make that connection. Believe instead Jack Welch, who "always refused to measure Work-Out, saying it'd die if they started to measure and track the results it was producing. Instead, he'd know in his gut when it was working and when it was not" (Ulrich, Kerr, and Ashkenas 2002:23).

Certainly we should measure what we can—so long it does not bias what we can't. The trouble is that it so often does. It drives out judgment, without which all measurement is useless.[2]

---

[1]For one particularly sophisticated effort to assess systematically the results of an overall program, that of CEDEP in France, see *Evaluating Management Education*, by Robin Hogarth (1979).

[2]See Devons (1950: chap. 7), summarized in Mintzberg (1994a:205–66) for a brilliant exposition on this; see also *Impediments to the Use of Management Information* (Mintzberg 1975), summarized as "The Soft Underbelly of Hard Data" (Mintzberg 1994a: 257–66), and the discussion of efficiency reported in full in Mintzberg (1989: chap. 16).

Like other programs, we assess responses to individual sessions as well as whole modules. But sometimes, at least, we have gotten away from those tyrannical numbers and asked simply, "What is the first word that comes to mind to describe this session [or module]?" On one session, for example, we received these responses: "enlightening, foundation, insightful, creative, more fun!, interesting, uncertain, artistic, useful, different, etc." The words can get the reader to think; they are a lot more informative than 4.2.

But any assessment can be tricky. Earlier I mentioned a session in the first module of the IMPM that was terribly downrated, and then used extensively in the Reflection Papers. Had we done the evaluations two months later, we would have received an entirely different result. "You leave thinking, 'Why did I spend the day there?'" wrote one participant about such an experience, "and a month later it's the first thing on your mind!" Education is more than a popularity contest.

Moreover, all too often, we measure the parts and forget the whole. Gosling and Westall (www.impm.org/goslingwestall.pdf) found a "striking" result in the evaluation of Module I of the IMPM: "While individual sessions usually obtain a more than adequate response, and some are exceptionally highly rated, this in no way approaches the response to the module as a whole." That the whole is valued as "considerably greater than the sum of its parts" has to be a significant sign of success.

With this in mind, let us look at the results of the IMPM, mostly in words, some woven into stories, even a few numbers to begin. Of course, gestures, inflections, facial expressions, and the like—namely, being there—tell it much better. But if you cannot be there, comments and stories are the next best thing, at least when they come from those who were there. Happily, we have many of these comments and stories from a wide variety of people involved every which way, because with something as novel as the IMPM, everyone is assessing it all the time, not numerically but judgmentally.

RETENTION RATES    Let's begin with the judgments of the participating companies. They vote with their budgets: They pay the bills, which, as already noted, can be substantial. The IMPM is not a consortium, so the companies are not required to commit to more than one cycle at a time. So a good indication of how we have done is how often the companies came back. Table 13.1 provides the answer: overwhelmingly. Across the eight cycles to date, of a total of sixty-one times that companies sending several participants had to decide to return, they did so fifty-one times in the next year, and fifty-six times counting those that came back after

## TABLE 13.1 COMPANY PARTICIPATION IN THE IMPM CYCLES

| Company | CYCLE 1 1996– 1998 | CYCLE 2 1997– 1999 | CYCLE 3 1998– 2000 | CYCLE 4 1999– 2001 | CYCLE 5 2000– 2002 | CYCLE 6 2001– 2003 | CYCLE 7 2002– 2004 | CYCLE 8 2003– 2005 |
|---|---|---|---|---|---|---|---|---|
| Alcan | 3 | | 3 | 4 | | | 4 | 3 |
| BT | 5[1] | 4 | 3 | 4 | 3 | 6 | | |
| EDF/GDF | 3 | 2 | 2 | 4 | 3 | 1 | 3 | 2 |
| Fujitsu | 1 | 3 | 3 | 2 | 3 | 3 | 3 | 3 |
| Lufthansa | 4 | 5 | 4 | 4 | 4 | 4 | | 5 |
| Matsushita | 5 | 3 | 4 | 4 | 4 | 4 | 2 | 2 |
| Red Cross | 3 | 3 | 4 | 3 | 2 | 4 | 2 | 2 |
| Royal Bank of Canada | 5 | 4 | 4 | 3 | | 4 | | |
| Motorola | | 5 | | | 3 | | | 1 |
| Zeneca | | 4 | 4 | 4 | | | | |
| LG | | | 4 | 5 | 4 | 3 | 3 | 3 |
| Marconi | | | | | 5 | 4 | | |
| India[2] | 2 | 3 | 5 (1 Alcan affiliate) | | 1 (1 BT affiliate) | 6 | 9 | 3 |
| Other[3] | 1 | | | | | 2 | 3 | 7 (4 from Via Rail) |
| Total | 32 | 36 | 40 | 37 | 33 | 41 | 29 | 31[4] |

[1]Includes two from Telenor partner.

[2]Indian participants are counted together because, for the most part, especially up to Cycle 5, they have been entrepreneurs and single senior managers from small companies. (We did have one BT affiliate in Cycle 5 and one Alcan affiliate in Cycle 3, counted here.) In Cycle 6, we began to attract participation from larger companies: Sasken Communication Technologies joined with two people in Cycle 6 and one in Cycle 7, Hewlett-Packard India sent two people in Cycle 7, and Coca-Cola India sent one in Cycle 8.

[3]Others include one Bombardier participant in Cycle 1 and another in Cycle 7, two members of the Aga Khan Foundation from Canada in Cycle 6, and one person each from 3Com, Lendlease, Siemens, and Swiss Re. Via Rail of Canada joined Cycle 8 with four people.

[4]The drop in Cycles 7 and 8 reflect the events of September 11, 2001, and subsequent reluctance to fly, as well as a worsening economic situation, which has affected attendance at most company-sponsored programs.

skipping one or more cycles in between.[3] That has to be a rather re-markable retention rate—better, we suspect, than many consortium pro-grams.

Most of the companies have stayed with us through most of the cy-cles, many through all eight, and some missing a cycle or two and then coming back. Our dropout rate of participants themselves has likewise been very low, probably well below most degree programs for experi-enced managers—about two people per cycle, on average.

As for company retention of the managers sent on the IMPM, these figures seem rather good, too. Matsushita used to send its managers to American MBA programs. About 9 percent subsequently left the com-pany, a figure that Matsushita (if not American companies) found unac-ceptable. It joined the IMPM at the outset and has sent managers to all of the cycles—twenty-eight people in all. Not a single one has so far left the company. In other cases, particularly companies in the English-speaking world, the figures are higher, but not excessively so. At the Royal Bank of Canada, on the higher end, six of the twenty participants sent on the program left the company. Overall, of our first three groups that began the program in 1996 to 1998, 18 of the 108 participants have left their companies as of 2003. Figures for more recent years are lower. I have no comparable data from other programs, but I imagine that our figures must be very low—lower, perhaps, than regular turnover of managers from many companies today.

At the welcoming meeting for the Cycle 8 Lufthansa participants, data were presented on all twenty-five Lufthansa graduates (to the end of Cycle 6): Ten had significant "vertical career development," nine "significant horizontal development," and three had not yet moved. Two left Lufthansa—one to a friendly (i.e., partner) company, the other to a company owned by Lufthansa—and a third was on paternity leave. This record was described by Herr Schollmeyer, the head of executive personnel and human resource development, as "an extraordinary im-pact" compared with other programs.

COMPANY COMMENTS   Why do the companies keep coming back? For our conference held with all the groups involved with the IMPM, in the spring of 2000, just before the start of Cycle 5, Sue Purves of (then) Zeneca solicited comments from representatives of the companies in-volved in the program, which she pulled into a paper (at www.impm.

---

[3]For example, Motorola was in Cycle 2 with five people and came back in Cycle 5 with three people. I did not count the fact that one person from Motorola came in Cycle 8, because that was more of a personal decision supported by the company.

org/purves). She noted on behalf of her colleagues that "[t]he companies which joined the IMPM program were all actively engaged in looking for leadership development opportunities which differed from traditional courses on offer in many business schools." They wanted programs that would have a strong impact on their people, in terms of "depth of thinking, the ability to synthesize and learn quickly, and the courage and judgment to act," development aspects they felt were not readily available in conventional programs. The IMPM also attracted companies for its cross-cultural dimension and the fact that this program came within a business school "knowledge framework . . . yet tempered with the reality of the business world"—even though the "outcomes were rather less prescribed than in other programs."

Comments from the company representatives suggest that the retention rate has much to do with the program's "intense influence" (to quote from Fujitsu) on the participants. Frank McCauley of the Royal Bank of Canada told a *Fast Company* reporter (Reingold 2000) that the IMPM "changes people more than any program I have ever seen— ever. It brings them to a different place." He elaborated in the Purves paper: "To learn about a mindset and then literally walk in that mindset along the streets of Bangalore is invaluable. . . . [People] become more reflective, more open, more understanding of change. It turns down their volume but increases the richness of their music." Sue Purves herself described such changes in the Zeneca participants as "profound and subtle." The paper concluded: "All the organizations and individuals recognized the enormous personal growth that was achieved during this program." The IMPM "represents a giant step forward in executive education."

PARTICIPANTS' COMMENTS    We have no shortage of comments from the participants themselves. Earlier I referred to Kerry Chandler's Venture in which she found that all but one of her Cycle 2 classmates found the IMPM to be a "life-changing" experience. This is reflected in many written comments submitted several years after graduation—for example, "It made me a different person" (participant in Cycle 3), and "This is one of these weird programs where, it's not so dramatic, something just changes inside." This second comment comes from Taizoon Chinwalla of Motorola (Cycle 2), who went before Motorola University's board of directors to lobby for its continued participation in the program:

> My pitch was purely soft. I told them how I had changed as an individual. I talked a lot about how I had been able to bring balance into my life, which I had been trying to do for the last fifteen years.

There was some very deep things within me which I didn't understand which this program helped surface.

I took a gamble. I am sitting in front of these guys who are all analytical guys and I'm saying all this soft stuff and they were actually very impressed with that. They didn't want to hear the hard stuff because they've heard it all before. Here was somebody standing in front of them, opening up, and saying, "Look, I have a deep sense of insecurity about myself, I realize that, and that has changed my management style." That was a breath of fresh air for them.

What we hear especially—or at least remember best—are stories from participants about their experiences related to the program. Several are told in the following box. While they are obviously selective, they do give a flavor for the program at its best. (Note that the learning about a particular mindset does not come exclusively in the module by that name.)

---

## STORIES FROM THE MINDSETS

### A Couple of Reflective Stories

- During the good-byes at the end of the first module of the first cycle, after someone said, "It was great meeting you," Alan Whelan of BT retorted, "It was great meeting myself!"

- A Lufthansa participant from Cycle 6 told company colleagues starting Cycle 8 how much he had learned at the start of the program and of sharing this experience with his wife. She told him she was relieved that at last he was beginning to see what had been so obvious to her and subsequently became very supportive of his commitment to the program.

### A Couple of Analytical Stories

- "It took Lancaster for me to understand Marx after five years at a Soviet University!" (Evgeni Parfenov, Red Cross, Cycle 2)

- Two accounts from different places and times—a Japanese and Indian participant, on different cycles—were remarkably similar. Both were being forced into obvious decisions by shallow analyses in their companies: Close the plant; speed up a slow project. After the analytical mindset in Montreal, they each went back and analyzed more deeply; for example, they analyzed the analyses of others—where people were coming from, what data and assumptions they were using; they dug out other sorts of information that didn't make it into the conventional analyses; they found limitations in the techniques used; most important, they recognized biases in their own thinking. As a result, they saw things differently, changed course, and helped resolve the problems.

## A Worldly Story

- For the 2000 conference (www.impm.org/williams.pdf), David Williams, who interviewed the IMPM graduates, described an outdoor exercise at the very beginning of the program, when a Korean moved in quietly to solve a puzzle after an American and German colleague had failed. The American, in her words, "lashed into him" for not letting them know "up front" that he could do it and having them "waste all that time. He just looked at me really calmly and said, 'Actually in my culture we don't do that because that's called bragging.' Ouch. That was a crystal moment for me." What impressed the writer, however, was not the incident so much as the participant's ability to articulate it: "[S]omehow the IMPM makes the abstract knowledge real. . . . [T]his appears to be one of the secrets of the IMPM. It teaches us what we think we already know."

## A Collaborative Story

- In Cycle 1 in India, the class went to an ashram for two days. During a free moment, a number of the participants turned some sticks and a wad of paper into a floor hockey game. They competed viciously; two were slightly injured. At the next module, in Japan, a professor from Insead reviewed the plan for the final module. When he suggested there would be a "competition" for presentation of the Ventures, the class exploded. Speaking for his colleagues, one of the fiercest competitors at the hockey game declared, "We do not compete with each other!"

## A Story from Action

- I received the following in a letter from one of the Royal Bank people, Vince Isber, whom I tutored in Cycle 1. (Recall in reading it the discussion of confidence versus competence in Chapter 3.) "Henry, I'm not sure we spent much time talking about your comment [asking] my opinion on whether IMPM provided confidence to the participants. Speaking strictly from my point of view, there are two separate forces here. I have always been confident . . . with my value and worth within the organization. So my organizational confidence was high. I wasn't as confident or possibly aware of the broader perspective of management and the potential impact we can have on society and the organization. I would call this confidence outside the world of [the Royal Bank]. Now after the first four modules, I feel I am much better prepared to lead and contribute to society through the organization. My awareness of broad management concepts has increased as has my confidence outside the organization. This actually had a unique effect on my level of confidence within the organization."

### A Final Story of How It All Came Together for One Manager

- This comes from Jack Donner, Motorola, Cycle 2: "When I started the IMPM, I was responsible for a global sales team comprising account management teams serving most of the Fortune 500 companies. My career was characterized by continuous overachievement of targets and frequent promotions. I hoped the IMPM would help me to move beyond a pure sales role into general management.

  "However, I soon discovered that my way of thinking about the function of a sales department depended on specific industrial organization and existing technology. My reflective papers gradually revealed to me that I could have a bigger impact on my company by helping to re-define the relationship between sales, marketing and business development (acquisitions and alliances). Luckily my managerial exchange took me to a marketing department in a completely different industry on a different continent. This really helped me to see how differently things can be done, and when my exchange partner visited me I asked him to concentrate on clarifying our assumptions and options for change. This turned out to be useful for him too, and we immediately started the change process by selecting some of our teams to visit each other, much as we had done during the Management Exchange.

  "This was met with a very dynamic and enthusiastic response from our colleagues—including those who did not visit, but acted as 'hosts.' We were able to set up a new organization that re-defined our function and accountability.

"This topic became the main focus of my venture, and my major paper went more deeply into the new sales channels that this opened for us."

FACULTY LEARNING    As I first drafted this section in January 2001, the third module of the fifth cycle was taking place in Bangalore. It was the IMPM's twenty-third module and the first one I missed (Jonathan Gosling having taken over as the director of the program). As I traveled to earlier modules time and again, often on long trips, I often asked myself what in the world I was doing. The answer always came back soon after arrival. A few minutes into that classroom, and my enthusiasm was reignited. Oliver Westall of Lancaster, who has directed two of the cycles, has echoed this sentiment. He also said that the participants' response to his material revived his excitement about economic history. I doubt there is another classroom in any of our universities, whether in physics, medicine, theater, or other subject, where the level of energetic learning, by the faculty too, surpasses what goes on in the IMPM.

Tony Dimnik, a professor of accounting at Queens University and one of the most respected management educators in Canada, made this comment (in Schachter 1998) about his involvement as a professor:

[T]he experiences of the people in the room will be as good as any case studies you get. They are, really, protagonists in their own cases. They know the issues. . . . We just have to draw it out, which is difficult to do sometimes. . . . I've taught many of the cases so many times, I know exactly what people will say at different points. I have my steps planned before I go into class. But in this approach, you're never quite sure what will happen. . . . The faculty is enthusiastic because we're learning as much as the participants.

Earlier I wrote about our success in converting a number of traditional professors to the method of experienced reflection. But why not? Bright faculty, no matter how traditional, relish a good discussion. Why not with experienced managers in a thoughtful setting? These faculty have not lectured out of any love of lecturing; it has just been what professors do. So why not engage the class in the use of their material and learn too!

Of course, I also wrote earlier about those professors who just want to lecture and be left alone, or to guide the class through a preplanned case discussion. Maybe they have already learned enough—they know better—or maybe they just need to be in control. In none of our experiences is this better illustrated, and in none is the contrast between the IMPM and conventional business education brought into sharper juxtaposition, than in the letter reprinted in the accompanying box. Jonathan Gosling wrote it, but did not send it, to a professor who blew up at the class when he felt that some of the participants had not sufficiently prepared the case he was doing. He berated the class for so long that one of the participants later reported, "I thought he was kidding." Jonathan was not.

---

## Getting "Nailed"

Dear Professor . . .

It is a privilege to have seen you teach on the IMPM last week. Your reputation is well deserved.

You had a good deal to say about how MBA students at Harvard behave, and how professors behave toward them. I kept my silence, intrigued to discover your gist, but now let me join the fray by questioning your comparison between the Harvard students and IMPM participants.

Firstly, you were keen to point out how nervous Harvard students are of being nailed. No one likes to be nailed by a professor of Harvard, [your school], or even Lancaster. But to be honest that is the least of the anxieties of people in this group. For example:

- Evgeni, from the Red Cross, must avoid his Iraqi operations being nailed by U.N. [delegates], which would compromise his delegation's readiness for disaster relief. . . .

- Ian, from the Royal Bank of Canada had his family relocated from Toronto to London during the module. His ethical concerns are more to do with the disruption of his children's education and friendships, and of course his responsibility for several $m of RBC funds.

He, like the others, is conscientious and curious. They are not short of opportunities for getting nailed. As a matter of fact, they have all just spent a week in one-to-one visits to each other that we call a Managerial Exchange, in which their managerial practice was open to scrutiny by one of their IMPM colleagues. Many of them were nailed on matters that really count. . . .

- Usha, from Motorola, learned from Hideo that her world-leading reliability testing system is still [a little] behind the elusively simple Matsushita process.

- Srinivas, proprietor and CEO of a bakery in Bangalore, heard from Clive that for all his principled support of his workforce, the shortcomings of some of his most senior managers are threatening the business. . . .

All that being said, it was discourteous of some of them not to have prepared for class. Perhaps their contrition was what motivated them to whole-heartedly enter the case discussion, once it began, and to offer their own experiences of similar ethical dilemmas—even if this was after you had written the answers on the board!

Yours sincerely,
Jonathan Gosling
Cycle 2 Director

Ludo van der Heyden, the module director for Cycles 3 and 4 at Insead, told the IMPM conference of 2000 that "I used to see my role as 'I know what's good for you, what you need to learn, how I can examine you.' Now I see my role as 'How can I help you?'" My own way of putting this is that after twenty-eight years of being a professor of management, I finally became a management professor. The IMPM has been *our* staff college!

We need faculty in this program who are seasoned, attuned to the concern of practitioners, and knowledgeable about management and business issues in general (except for the specialized sessions). They also need to think well on their feet, which means they usually have to be good scholars, willing to go with the flow in the classroom, with the confidence to shift gears when something interesting comes up. All of this may sound like a tall order, but we are delighted with the result. I doubt any of us realized in advance how successful we would be in bringing regular academic faculty into the center of management development.

Some dazzling things go on in management development; few in the IMPM. It is more about the depth of the ordinary things. Come into the classroom and you may find dead silence, as everyone is writing in their reflection books. (These are managers?) Or perhaps there will be discussions around the tables. (These are managers!) Or a participant may be engaging a professor in the application of some concept. (This is a revolution?) Not fancy stuff at all. But beyond the obvious parts is the subtler whole, and it is radically different from almost all the programs for managers that I have seen. Serious management education happens here.

## STILL LEARNING

I am evidently proud of the program. But our job is far from finished, and I would like to discuss a few of my main concerns to conclude this chapter.

First among these has to be Impact, the transfer of the learning from the classroom to the workplace. I have written about extending management development into organization development, especially by spreading the learning. I am pleased that our faculty and some companies have begun to address this issue in a concerted way, but we have a long way to go. Real progress here will depend on a more radical reconception of management development/education than we have made, especially concerning class/work connections.

I have also expressed ambivalence about how much "act" we really want in Impact, and how much action in action learning in general. In this ambivalence I am not alone. Among the participants we have had a few hesitant to act back home so as not to appear privileged, and others who felt obliged to act there precisely because of the privilege of being sent on the program. Views have likewise varied among the faculty and the companies. Kaz Mishina, who has directed Module IV for a number of years, sent an e-mail to the faculty (July 15, 2001) claiming that the IMPM "has been designed right for the Japanese companies," since the two involved have sent participants to all the modules. It is "crucial to run the IMPM even better with a strong focus on inputting (or learning) as opposed to outputting (or showing off learning)."

Others don't agree. John King of BT (Cycle 5) commented about a reorganization he made that was influenced by an Impact session, "Without the thought processes triggered by reflection on the McGill and Lancaster modules, the final look and feel of the service organisation would have been very different. I am . . . convinced that the real key to using the IMPM is the synthesising of all the learning into actual projects."

Sue Purves, for some years responsible for executive development at Zeneca, has herself been ambivalent. She remarked, "You can leverage the people. I am not sure you can leverage the learning." She also wrote in the paper cited earlier, "All of the organizations participating perceived that this program provided personal growth unmatched by other programs but the organizations struggled to develop the capability to bring the ideas in house." On her own behalf, she commented, "The link to be strengthened now is that between individual and organizational learning. This is a major cultural shift which must be achieved to gain the benefits of individuals' profound learning from IMPM."

I remain personally convinced that we can make great progress on this issue if we recognize the distinction between teaching-impact and action-impact and treat them differently: Teaching-impact should be more formally managed and promoted, while action-impact should be allowed to happen naturally, although both should be shared in the classroom as a kind of consciousness-raising of the possibilities.

Another area of concern to me is *competency sharing*. That is not because it is difficult to do—in fact, once started, it is rather easy—but because it can be highly beneficial yet gets lost amid all the other activities. If we had a little bell that went off every time a competency issue came up—"OK, now that someone has mentioned negotiating with government officials, let's stop and share experiences"—the problem would be solved. Perhaps we should embed such bells in the heads of the participants, so they can remind faculty members (happily) paying too much attention to the discussion.

On the whole, *tutoring* works well in the IMPM but poses a logistics problem in our particular situation. It is too expensive to bring the tutors to every module, yet having them tutor near home, close to the participants' workplaces, distances them from other activities of the program (except the module that most of them direct). We have thought about tutoring within the companies, by graduates of the program. That would ensure full knowledge of the activities, but at the expense of the connection to the universities. Of course, the problem would disappear in a similar program run in a single location, as in a sister program described in the next chapter. But that comes at the expense of international exposure.

On another front, stating our 50-50 rule is not the same as achieving it. Rarely do we err—certainly from the participants' perspective—in providing too much time for the participant workshops on their agendas. We are getting better, as we come to realize how much learning these workshops encourage, but we are not there yet. We, too, have to "cover" all sorts of material, as if what professors think about in advance is more important than what comes up in the class. All too often, it is exactly the opposite. Speaking for myself at least as much as some of my colleagues, if we could listen more, we could all learn more and so have to teach less.

We *are* getting better at "self-organization." I have sometimes imagined that the aims of the IMPM would be fully realized when the participants take over the classroom altogether. There is not much danger of that, I assure you, thanks to the participants as well as the faculty. We do need balance. But we began so far from it, and remain so well short of it (compared with our own intentions, if not other programs), that moves in this direction should be welcomed. Michael Heuser, as the head of the Lufthansa School of Business, said of the IMPM that "[t]his is a process, not a program." We have come a long way, but we have a long way to go, too.

We could also do better in some of our modules, especially to bring the mindsets to life in the classroom. Aside from Japan, and India to a lesser extent, we could also do better in portraying the variety of styles of managing found in different parts of the world.

Finally, I come to my greatest concern. For eight years, the IMPM has been running one class for about thirty-five people. Ask these people, and I believe you will find that we have had great success. In quality, not quantity. We can expand the IMPM somewhat—we planned to introduce a second cycle per year until the events of September 11, 2001 put a temporary stop to that. But if the innovation is to be "diffused," as management people say, it has to get beyond our own partnership. That is why I have written these chapters. And that is how I shall close this discussion in the next chapter—on the diffusion of our innovation.

# 14

## DEVELOPING MANAGERS V
### *Diffusing the Innovation*

*Most technologies take twenty years
to become an overnight success.*
—PAUL SAFFO

What exactly is the IMPM? A program? A process? A laboratory?
A template?

It certainly is a program, the term I have been using all along. And
as I quoted Michael Heuser at Lufthansa in the prior chapter, it has certainly been a process, too. But it is more than either of these.

The IMPM has been our laboratory, to develop, test, and integrate a
number of innovations in management education. Some we created ourselves; some we borrowed from others; the most important one combines them all: The IMPM may be *made up* of innovations, but we see it
as *an* innovation.

I believe I speak for my colleagues in claiming that this innovation is
now solid—clearly defined in concept and successfully executed in practice. Into our eighth year, together with related initiatives (described in
this chapter), the innovation works, consistently. So it is time for its own
impact, beyond its own activities. It is time, in other words, to change
management education—or perhaps to begin it in earnest.

In September 2000, at our annual meeting of IMPM company representatives with faculty, there were about fifteen people in the room, sharing experiences. I said I hoped to attend such a meeting in 2010 with five hundred people in the room. If one hundred thousand people can be trained every year in masters programs in business, in the United States alone, then surely there is potential for tens of thousands of people doing a Masters of Practicing Management.

So I believe the IMPM should be seen as a template as well, for the development of other programs. Not to copy it, but to appreciate its essence and build in that spirit.

## POSITIONING THE MASTERS OF PRACTICING MANAGEMENT

Before considering various possible forms of diffusion, it could be useful to consider how true management education differs from conventional business education on one side and much of management development on the other. This is shown in Table 14.1. Most of the table speaks for itself; I just wish to add a few summary words about the bottom line.

The focus of intention in the MBA is better decision making through training in analysis—in general rather than in any particular context. This sees management as some kind of profession or science; hence the learning is *generic*. In contrast, much of management development focuses on specific skills of concern to companies, often to do with leadership in one way or another. Management is seen here as less of a science and more of an art and a craft. The focus of intention of the MPM degree, different from these two, is better judgment in context, to help managers become more thoughtful about their particular situation—issue, job, company, context.

The MPM focuses on managing—not on knowledge in management and the business functions, or on leadership per se, but on the practice of managing in context. For this, it uses its own style of pedagogy, labeled "experienced reflection", which encourages more craft in the practice of managing and somewhat more art, with less reliance on science than conventional business education. It therefore takes managers from the styles labeled "calculating" and "heroic" toward that labeled "engaging". We could say that the MPM favors *managing quietly* (Mintzberg 1999a).

Earlier I quoted the ancient Greek expression that while the fox knows many things, the hedgehog knows one big thing. I see the MBA as a fox program: It develops people who are clever, move fast, and know many things. The MPM is to me a hedgehog program, concerned

### TABLE 14.1 POSITIONING MANAGEMENT EDUCATION

| COMMON CHARACTERISTIC | BUSINESS EDUCATION (MBA) | MANAGEMENT EDUCATION (MPM) | MANAGEMENT DEVELOPMENT |
|---|---|---|---|
| Target audience | Business aspirants, on own | Experienced managers, from companies | Experienced managers, in companies |
| Timing | Full-time study | Sequence of modules | Short blocks |
| Organizing framework | Business functions | Managerial mindsets | Corporate concerns |
| Focus on | Analyzing (models, theories, techniques) | Managing (judgment, "soft skills") | Leading (skills or knowledge) |
| Pedagogy | Absorbing established knowledge via lectures and cases | Reflecting on experience via sharing | Applying ideas via projects and exercises |
| Seating | Tiered rows | Round tables | Varied, with break-out rooms |
| Ultimate intention | Better decisions in general (science) | Better judgment in context (craft) | Better skills in companies (art, craft) |

that its graduates know one big thing. David Williams summarizes his interviews with the IMPM graduates as follows:

> Most business courses take people who know a little about a subject and transform them into people who know a lot. They are intellectual boot camps, and if you stay the course the transformation from civilian to corporate soldier is always the same. It is therefore possible to listen to a single participant talking about the course and to have some sense that the experience . . . will be true for the others. . . . [F]or the IMPM [t]here is no easy way to generalize. . . . [E]ach participant will have learned many different things. Some of these learnings will mirror those of others, some will be unique. But the total transformation will be individual and complex, and not easily described. (www.impm.org/williams.pdf)

To me, that one big thing, made up of all those "many different things," is this "total transformation," usually toward greater thoughtfulness.

Our hope for the graduates, therefore, is not heroic success but just plain better managing, in the same job or a new one. As noted earlier, this program is about doing a better job, not getting a better job. These people will get better jobs if they do better jobs. Both are happening.

If the MBA programs get the analysts, we seem to get the crafts-people. (The artists mostly stay away from school.) We used an instrument several times that assesses personal orientation toward art, craft, and science. Craft always came out way ahead for our group, followed by art, not science. For example, at the second module of Cycle 3, twenty-two out of thirty-eight participants came out with craft first, thirteen with art first, and three with science first. Of the twenty-two with craft first, art was second for thirteen and science for nine. (Incidentally, the four faculty members present scored with the majority, craft first, followed by art. This would likely be in sharp contrast with most of our business school colleagues, suggesting that there is a corresponding self-selection among the faculty.) So the IMPM seems to attract what it reinforces, just as does the MBA.

## Toward Broader Diffusion

If we are to get those five hundred people to that conference in 2010, then we shall have to hurry up and get past the IMPM, to the MPM, and beyond, into management and executive development. Figure 14.1 maps out five paths to this, labeled Expansion, Extension, Differentiation, Infiltration, and Compression.

*Expansion* simply means more cycles offered by a related partnership. The IMPM governing committee has approved this in principle; we have been waiting for better economic conditions. But this is obviously limited.

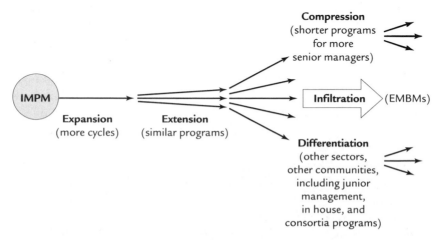

FIGURE 14.1
Broader Diffusion of the IMPM

More hopeful is *extension*. The IMPM is not patented—as noted earlier, academics maximize ego, not profit—and we have always encouraged others to pick up where we leave off. For example, Dean Carlos Arruda of Dom Cabral Foundation, associated with Minas Garais Catholic University in Brazil, wrote to us in May 2002, "We've learned a lot about the IMPM program and applied some of its concepts into our MBA. It worked so well that our program was appointed by a Brazilian business magazine [*Exame*] as the best executive MBA program in Brazil."

Mostly, our experience to date is that these ideas are carried forward by people with hands-on experience in our classrooms—namely, faculty and sometimes guests who have seen the IMPM at work. Thus diffusion within our own partner schools has come easier than diffusion beyond them (as we shall see; note also the Insead Web site on its new EMBA). This is, however, changing as a broader array of people get involved in the IMPM, and others become more attuned to these ideas.

Beyond extension is *infiltration*—concerted effort to change existing programs. As noted several times, there is little here for the conventional MBA but much for the EMBA. Catering to employed people, many of them managers coming in on a part-time basis, there is every reason to make these programs more managerial, and the IMPM points the way. Accordingly, our own partnership has developed an "E Roundtables" initiative for existing EMBA programs, described later in this chapter.

And beyond infiltration is *differentiation*, to apply the learning of the IMPM to other sectors and other communities. A major example of this will also be described here: an MPM for voluntary sector managers in Canada, which has run through its three intended cycles at McGill with enormous success. McGill's Faculties of Management and Medicine are also starting an IMHL (health leadership) for senior managers from all aspects of health (hospitals, community agencies, etc.; see www.imhl.ca).[1]

Particularly useful could be an MPM for more junior managers. A number of companies have raised the idea with us, but nothing has yet jelled. It would likely have to contain more need-to-know business functional material, much of that perhaps taught through self-study (as in the Open University), and thus end up as a hybrid of the IMPM and

---

[1] A public sector program has been discussed, but this idea faces two problems. Doing it internationally would probably not be possible: Even Canadians and Americans would be baffled by each other's practices. Doing it domestically, perhaps combining national, regional, and local governmental officials, would be feasible but perhaps difficult to fund. In health care, in contrast, much of technology and practices are the same around the world; even the systematic differences, from state-run to private, lay themselves out along a continuum, with every system experiencing pressures from both sides.

MBA, including most aspects of the IMPM (mindsets, reflections, exchanges, tutoring, etc.). The benefits of allowing new managers to share their experiences, concerns, and frustrations with each other could be particularly powerful, especially when combined with in-house mentoring. Such a program seems to me a natural, that will soon see the light of day, most likely as a consortium of a few companies that wish to develop many of their new managers together, perhaps focused in specific sectors, such as financial services or high technology.

A number of people familiar with the IMPM have raised broader issues of differentiation: How about managers and entrepreneurs from small companies, or mavericks not sent by their companies, and individualists who wish to go their own way? And what about managers from companies unwilling to spend on the development of their people?

I have one reply to all this. The essential idea behind the IMPM is that managers learn best in their natural contexts. There are better and worse routes to an IMPM classroom, but only those that bring managers able to learn in context are acceptable. Indeed, as noted, from India we have had many single managers and entrepreneurs from small businesses, which has worked fine (although being able to work in class with several colleagues from one's company is preferable). So an IMPM class of, say, entrepreneurs, should work well—indeed, be fascinating—because they would relish sharing their experiences (although my suspicion is that most would prefer something shorter than our degree version).

As for the mavericks and individualists who have to pay the fees themselves, that would be fine so long as they are managers able to learn in context. But could they if the company is unwilling to sponsor them? Maybe they should convince the company to respect and support them, or else find a job in one that does. In any event, the IMPM is for managers, not people who aspire to be managers; indeed, I have argued repeatedly that *no* management program should be.

Finally, *compression* refers to shorter versions of the IMPM, mostly for more senior managers. I describe in this chapter a major initiative of BAE Systems for its most senior managers, a smaller one that McGill ran for the Royal Bank of Canada, and our current plans for a novel Advanced Leadership Program based on specific issues brought in by company groups. One idea that could be intriguing, and in fact is being done in Exeter University's Masters in Leadership, now run by Jonathan Gosling, is a cross between an IMPM-style classroom and personal coaching. Let's call it a *coaching group*, a kind of small support group, whether for new or middle or perhaps even senior managers. They work individually with a coach and get together periodically to discuss experiences and share concerns.

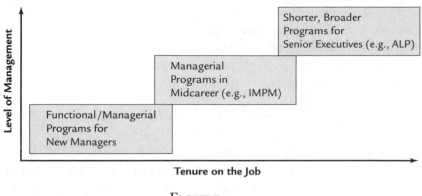

FIGURE 14.2

Programs by Stage of Career

Figure 14.2 maps some of these programs along stages of the managerial career. Let me now turn to the specific examples of diffusion mentioned earlier.

## VOLUNTARY SECTOR MASTERS PROGRAM

Frances Westley, a colleague at McGill and close friend, taught in the IMPM and was impressed by the experience. When a request came from the J. W. McConnell Family Foundation for a program to strengthen the leadership of Canadian "voluntary" organizations (including the arts, environment, youth, health, social services, and poverty reduction), she drew up a proposal inspired by the IMPM.

The result was the McGill-McConnell Master of Management for National Voluntary Sector Leaders, fully funded in development and mostly so in operations by the McConnell Foundation. The program ran for three cycles, as planned, with forty managers each time from organizations operating across Canada, such as the Kidney Foundation, Amnesty International, Canadian Parents for French, and the YMCA. The McConnell Foundation people worked closely with the McGill team, which drew its faculty, including module directors, from across the country.

Frances wrote a paper for our 2000 conference (www.impm.org/westley.pdf) that describes her experience. Most germane for our discussion here is her comment about the "robust nature of the IMPM design," especially the mindsets, which provided "an extremely flexible but stimulating blueprint." The program is built around five similar mindsets with a sixth on values, called the "ethical mindset," woven through the others. (Frances is so enthusiastic about the participants' papers in the program, and their importance for the voluntary sector, that she is preparing a six-volume publication of the best of them, one for each of the mindsets.)

Most other aspects of the IMPM can be found in this program, such as the seating, the various out-of-class activities, and the two-week module schedule. *Anchoring* is this program's label for what the IMPM calls Impact, and it has been carefully managed. Each participant designated an Anchoring Team back at work, composed of "partners" through whom the learning was extended into the organization, beginning with a one-day workshop for all members before the first module.

Because the McConnell Foundation wanted the program to have a major impact on the whole voluntary sector in Canada, use was made of an interesting version of the Venture, called Theme Integrative Projects (TIPs). The participants worked in teams on themes of consequence to the whole voluntary sector and reported their findings at a sector conference or in a sector publication. Examples of TIPs studies include: volunteers in Canada as a force for social change, and the development of partnerships with other sectors.

This initiative, which Frances describes in her paper as "the first, fully developed progeny of the IMPM," suggests how the basic design can be adapted to other contexts, retaining its essence while relaxing some of its specific features (in this case, the international dimension and the clustering of participants by company, since all were clustered by sector). She has also highlighted the synergy of the two programs, referring to the collaboration among the faculty involved in them as having "created an explosion of learning about pedagogy" at McGill:

> As academics, we rarely spend much time watching each other teach and even less time exploring extensively issues of course design. But the IMPM and the MMVS have been team projects, both in design and in implementation. . . . With the two programs co-existing at McGill . . . new ideas move rapidly back and forth between them. Everything from catering coffee breaks, to tutorial sessions, to the right words to use to describe projects, to serendipitous breakthroughs in the classroom are quickly communicated and adapted. This has created a sense of energy and excitement at McGill that is quite novel and certainly, I think, gets communicated to the course participants.

# E ROUNDTABLES

I noted earlier that EMBA programs train the right people in the wrong ways with the wrong consequences. In other words, they take experienced people, many of them managers, and largely replicate regular MBA programs designed for inexperienced people. The opportunities to apply many of the IMPM innovations thus becomes evident: the pedagogy, the mindsets, the reflection papers, the managerial exchanges, and so forth. The format may be different—weekend or evening classes instead of modules of two weeks—but these can easily be worked around.[2]

Our initiative in this regard is called "E Roundtables," now in development. It will bring together the students of existing EMBA programs from around the world in three modules of one week each, a first in England on the reflective mindset, a second in India on the connected mindset (the manager between organization and context), and the third in Canada on the action mindset. The idea is to hold a kind of international EMBA fair, where students from all sorts of places get together and share their experiences as managers, and perhaps also pair up to do managerial exchanges. (We may also introduce a postgraduate certificate version of this, for practicing managers, including MBA graduates.)

Of course, the numbers here will be far greater than in any IMPM class. But the intention is to break the overall group into classes of about forty, as internationally mixed as possible, so that activities can be run on three levels: lectures and guest panels in plenary for the whole group; much of the specific learning in the classes of forty; and within these, small groups sharing their experiences at mixed roundtables. Faculty members from the participating schools will work with these smaller classes, the more experienced ones as facilitators, those more junior as mentees.

In effect, the E Roundtables are designed to be the international component of domestic EMBA programs and perhaps their intensive managerial component as well. This is planned to begin as an option for students in lieu of several elective courses, eventually to become a fully integrated component of these programs. In fact, our real hope is that this will diffuse other aspects of the IMPM design into these programs, as local faculty and students became familiar with the IMPM approach.

---

[2]The success of English schools with one- and two-week modules suggests that American programs could easily be shifted this way. Moreover, clustering could be done in class by industry or job type, for example, and participants need not be sponsored if they at least come with the requisite experience and connection to context.

One last point, not entirely trivial: the *E* in E Roundtables does not stand for *Executive*. It stands for *Experienced*. We shall have succeeded in this "infiltration" when the same can be said for the *E* in EMBA!

## SHORTER MINDSET PROGRAMS
## IN COMPANIES

Companies have adopted the mindsets notion together with the pedagogy in various ways. Described next are two programs that ran for many cycles and were highly successful, one by BAE Systems that has used five mindsets, the other for the Royal Bank of Canada that focused on one.

BAE STRATEGIC LEADERS PROGRAMME    Early in the IMPM, British Aerospace (now BAE Systems), in the midst of integrating a merger, picked up the notion of mindsets and, in partnership with Lancaster and the participation of Bangalore, developed a rather elaborate program for its most senior managers. Called the Strategic Leaders Programme, it has been running annually with fifteen participants since 1996. By the beginning of 2003, all of the most senior managers had been through it.

The program consists of five modules of five to seven days each, spread over thirteen to fifteen months, each in its own location with its own local director. In the February 2000 to May 2001 version (Cycle 3), the modules were as follows:

- In the U.K., the Receptive Mindset ("heightening one's sensitivity and tolerance" to one's own behavior and the world)

- In India, the Reflective Mindset ("to notice the cultural lenses through which we habitually see," which "prompts alternative views of the company")

- In the United States, the Competitive Mindset ("how to lead the reconfigured company in a rapidly metamorphosing industry")

- In China, the Collaborative Mindset ("puts collaboration into global context," including "leadership of cross-cultural alliances, joint-ventures, and mergers")

- In Slovenia, the Catalytic Mindset ("leading in the midst of overwhelming change," concerning "behaviours and temporary organisations that convert chaos into renewal")

ANALYSIS TO ACTION    The Royal Bank of Canada, which joined the IMPM at its inception, was looking in 1998 for a short program to foster a venturing, action-oriented spirit. They were impressed with the second IMPM module, so McGill and the company together designed a three-and-a-half-day program called "From Analysis to Action." It was offered six times over a three-year period to groups of twenty-five bank officers.

Participants were asked to send in a single page on some "burning issue" before they arrived—a key concern about which they wished to take action. These were shared among the group in advance, discussed on the first evening, and then woven into the workshops through the next three days. These workshops were intended to encourage, not drive, action taking, whether by the sponsoring individual or in teams that emerged during the program. Supporting this was conceptual materials to open people up beyond conventional analysis—for example, to strategy as a process of venturing more than planning.

## ADVANCED LEADERSHIP PROGRAM

A number of us with experience in the IMPM took a good look at the so-called Advanced Management Programs (AMPs) offered by many of the prestigious business schools (and discussed in Chapter 8). These have probably been the most successful programs for management development, yet most seem hardly advanced at all:

- They are designed mostly around the business functions for managers leaving these functions on their way into general management.

- They make claims about innovation yet are remarkably alike; they also emphasize "globalization" yet typically run in one Western school.

- They sit people as individuals in rows facing an "instructor" to discuss teamwork, collaboration, and empowerment.

- They promise "boot camp" to people who need to step back and reflect calmly on their experience.

- They rely on practical cases yet ignore the wealth of experience in the classroom.

- They expect the participants to take one or two full months off work to discuss the pressures of working in today's world.

The BAE and Royal Bank programs indicated to us that much of the IMPM approach could work in programs of shorter duration. So we have set out to challenge the AMP with an *ALP*—a truly *advanced* leadership program (see www.alp-impm.com). Its design pushes beyond the IMPM, too, in two respects. First, we sell tables rather than chairs in the ALP: There is only one price, for a table of up to six senior managers, no matter how many the company actually sends. We want teams in this program, not individuals. Second, we ask each team to come with a key issue that it can explore in consultation with the teams from the other companies. The company can construct its team around the issue or else send a natural team that is already working on the issue; merged companies and alliances can also send teams to work on issues related to their collaboration.

Note the one big difference between these issues and the projects in Action Learning: Instead of the program making work back at work, it advances natural issues of work in the classroom. In other words, the only commitment of the participants is the time spent in the classroom, where a thoughtful atmosphere is used to reconsider key company concerns.

Companies generally have two ways to approach a thorny issue: with an internal task force or by hiring external consultants. The ALP combines these in a way that can be far more powerful than both: An internal group addresses the issue with external colleagues acting as friendly consultants in a thoughtful atmosphere. As management development, the cost of this program may seem regular; as consulting, it may be a real bargain!

While the issues can vary widely—stimulating innovation, dealing with a difficult merger, keeping the knowledge from walking out the door in a world of downsizing—executives from all the companies will likely have lived all of them in one way or another. And so they can bring their experiences to bear in helping their colleagues while learning themselves. We have found in the IMPM that addressing each other's concerns can be an awfully powerful way for managers to learn.

Faculty from Bangalore, Insead, Lancaster, and McGill have worked on the ALP design, partly with representatives of interested companies. (Reingold [2000] wrote up one of these early meetings in a *First Company* article.) We have settled on three modules of one week each, spread over several months, as illustrated in Figure 14.3 and described here:

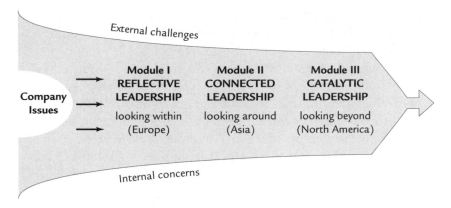

FIGURE 14.3
The ALP Design

- *Reflective Leadership*, in the English Lake District, focuses on self, probing into individual behavior, leadership style, and culture. Each group presents its issue to the class, which is then discussed by the other groups mixed around the tables. They feed back their interpretations and suggestions, and near the end of the module, the company group presents its reframing of the issue.

- *Connected Leadership*, in Singapore and Bangalore, considers organization and environment, with the leader as link between the two, rooted in both. Some of the topics for formal presentation at this module are decided at the first module according to the company issues under consideration; these in turn feed into renewed workshops on the issues.

- *Catalytic Leadership*, in Montreal, looks at the leader as agent in the process of change, bottom-up-emergent as well as top-down-directed, self-organizing as well as formally organized, with leadership as energizing as well as strategizing. Considerable time is devoted at this module to reports on the company issues with regard to achieving change.

The very aspects that make conventional management development unattractive to some managers (the pressures of the job, the disconnection of the classroom, etc.) could be what makes the ALP attractive to them. It connects to work in a way that does not increase the pressures at work. Indeed, by offering profound insights to seemingly intractable issues—as a roomful of like-minded colleagues with similar concerns but no ax to grind could well do—the ALP may be able to reduce some of these pressures. Perhaps most notably, this shift from projects on the job to issues in the classroom could render a significant change in management development, by using the work that managers do naturally. We thus think of this as third-generation management development, beyond the directed lectures and cases of the first, and the make-work Action Learning of the second, to reflective learning from real issues in the third.

## The Essential Characteristics of the IMPM Innovation

The programs just discussed are summarized in Table 14.2, together with their key characteristics. This table shows how the IMPM is beginning to serve as a template for a family of new-generation management development programs, degree and nondegree. By listing the various innovations of the IMPM down the side, with check marks across to show which are found in the various programs, the table captures what is essential in this new approach and what can be modified or dispensed with. As can be seen, all the programs make use of the modules, the mindsets, the pedagogy, and the seating. These are the essence of the IMPM innovation. The Managerial Exchanges, Reflection Papers, Field Studies, Tutoring, and Major Paper appear in the degree programs, but not in the shorter management development ones. Ventures, related projects, or issues appear in most but not all of the programs. And the international dimension of the IMPM appears only in the IMHL (for health), E Roundtables, and the ALP; each of the other programs focus on one company and/or one country, all but the BAE program delivered mostly in one place.

If a new technology really does take twenty years to become an overnight success, then we have twelve years to go! (Hopefully not!)

## Educating Managers on the Edges

I know we are not supposed to mix metaphors, but I would like to use three to close this chapter, about borders, tightropes, and ridges. Besides, all three are related to those "Edges" Raphael wrote about, where life is richer and more varied, more conducive to innovation, but also subject to tension. Exciting and difficult places, these edges.

## TABLE 14.2 DIFFUSION OF THE IMPM INNOVATIONS TO DATE

| | IMPM (FROM 1996) | VOLUNTARY SECTOR MASTERS (1999–2002) | BAE STRATEGIC LEADERS (FROM 1997) | RB OF CANADA ANALYSIS TO ACTION (FROM 1998–2001) | E ROUNDTABLES (IN DEVELOPMENT) | ALP (IN DEVELOPMENT) | IMHL (HEALTH) (IN DEVELOPMENT) |
|---|---|---|---|---|---|---|---|
| Modular delivery | 5 of 2 weeks | 5 of 2 weeks | 5 of 5–7 days | 1 of 3.5 days | 3 of 8 days | 3 of 7 days | 5 of 2 weeks |
| Mindsets | ✓ (5) | ✓ (6) | ✓ (5) | ✓ (1) | ✓ (3) | ✓ (3) | ✓ (5) |
| Pedagogy of Experienced Reflection; Roundtable seating | ✓ | ✓ | ✓ | ✓ | ✓ | ✓ | ✓ |
| Company groups | ✓ | One sector | One company | One company | | ✓ (teams) | possibly |
| International participation | ✓ | One country | One company (with JV partners) | One company and country | ✓ | ✓ | ✓ |
| International delivery | ✓ | | ✓ | | ✓ | ✓ | one module |
| Reflection Papers | ✓ | ✓ | | | Possibly | | ✓ |
| Tutoring | ✓ | ✓ | Coaching | | | | ✓ |
| Self-Study | ✓ | ✓ | | | | | ✓ |
| Field Studies | ✓ | ✓ | ✓ | | | Possibly | ✓ |
| Managerial Exchanges | ✓ | ✓ | | | Possibly | | ✓ (multiple) |
| Ventures | ✓ | ✓ (Theme Integrated Projects) | | ✓ (Burning Issues) | | ✓ (Company Issues) | ✓ |
| Degree and Major Paper | ✓ | ✓ | | | | | ✓ |
| Managed Impact | ✓ | ✓ | | | | | ✓ |

In feedback on the program, one participant wrote that we should keep the IMPM "as a work in progress . . . constantly shifting . . . to remain at the edge." Let's see how that can be done.

EDUCATING BEYOND BORDERS     Borders divide. They keep things apart, for better and for worse.

Such borders abound in management education and development. Borders between teaching and learning. Borders between and among "students" and "instructors." Borders between the business functions. Most significantly, a high border between the process of educating and the practice of managing. All get in the way. We need to build bridges across these borders.

What also get in the way are the most common borders of them all, between countries, but here because there are too many bridges across them. As a result, the business schools are remarkably similar around the world, which stifles their innovation as well as their attention to local context. It is as if we have discovered universal truth and every manager in the world must have it poured into him or her. This represents the "global" agenda at its worst.

Company cultures vary, industry cultures vary; national cultures vary; people vary. Management education must respect these variations, which means it has to be far more eclectic, flexible, and customized than it now is. However collaboratively we work across them, we also need some borders in management education and development.

WALKING ALONG TIGHTROPES     There are often tensions along borders. Focus on these—lift up those borders in your mind—and they begin to feel like tightropes. The MBA may seem firm, solidly planted on the ground. But real management education is necessarily shaky, suspended in space. That is because of what is right with it, not wrong. The real problems of managing are up here, amid the ambiguity, complexity, and nuance, not down there on the ground, with the formulas, techniques, and systems.

Working in a program like the IMPM often feels like walking on a tightrope—in fact, on a whole set of tightropes concurrently. There are the tensions between the global and the local; between participants and their organizations; between time in the program and time on the job, let alone time at home; between the tacit approaches of the East and explicit approaches of the West. These all come to our classrooms. In them, there are the tensions built into the mindsets themselves—for example, between action and reflection (need to do, need to think); the analytical and the worldly (need for the explicit, need for the tacit);

change and organization (need to adapt, need to stabilize). More generally, there are the tensions between theory and practice, between the conceptual and the concrete (the push of knowledge versus the pull of issues); between teaching and learning, also between individual learning and shared learning, and between comfort and challenge. There can also be a tension between management education and management development, not to mention organization development. Particularly disconcerting can be the tension between real learning and learning demonstrated through measured assessments (whether grades for the university or "deliverables" for the company).

To take a prominent one of these, imagine a manager walking along a tightrope, carrying one of those rods with weights at each end: the pressures of work on one side and the requirements of the university degree on the other. The manager in the middle is the learning experience. If either weight is too heavy, or too light, he or she will tumble over. Balance has to ensure that the job doesn't unduly interfere with the learning nor the learning unduly interfere with the managing (or the grading and assessing with the learning).

Stretch out all these tensions and you can appreciate the set of precarious tightropes on which the participants and faculty of such education have to walk. But these are not just the tensions of education; most of them come from the everyday life of managing. Thus they have to appear in any program that is truly managerial. Besides, as Frank McCauley of the Royal Bank of Canada has pointed out, only when a tightrope is tense can you advance along it, to make progress. So we have to walk these tightropes, not avoid them. To do so, perhaps we need to see them a bit differently again.

OUT ON THE RIDGE OF MANAGEMENT EDUCATION    In a sense, a ridge is both border and tightrope. It is a border between the terrain on either side (often, as such, a national border). It can also feel like a tightrope, just more solid, although when it gets narrow, you begin to wonder. So the ridge may be the best metaphor of the three, the best place from which to appreciate management education. Hence I close this discussion with it.

Imagine management education up high on an alpine ridge. On one side is a sheer drop: That is the cliff of academic irrelevance. We cannot allow ourselves to fall over that. On the other side, the terrain falls off sharply: This is the slippery slope of easy practicality. Start down there and you may never stop. We have watched too many programs slide that way, just as we have seen too many others go over that cliff and bust into pieces on the rocks below.

So if you wish to embark on this journey, the only safe place is up on the ridge where management education meets management development. It can be a tricky place, requiring constant surveillance. But it can also be an exhilarating one. After all, the interesting things do happen on the edges. Here is where the future for better management can be experienced. Join us: The outlook is great!

# 15

# Developing True Schools of Management

*All change seems impossible. But once accomplished, it is the state you are no longer in that seems impossible.*

—French philosopher Alain

I t is time to renew the business schools—time for the agents of change to change. They may be at the height of their success, attracting high-paying students who in turn have been getting high-paying jobs. And business schools produce enormous quantities of research. Yet they are failing in their fundamental purpose, which is to enhance the quality of leadership in society.

In a number of respects, the business schools have lost their way. They claim to develop managers, yet turn out staff specialists who promote dysfunctional styles of managing. They are meant to be institutions of thoughtful scholarship yet are increasingly drawn to promotional hype. They should be prized for their mindfulness yet often copy each other mindlessly. Many cannot make up their collective minds whether to tone down their material for "relevance" or ratchet it up for "rigor," when they should be repudiating both. Those areas in which the business schools do excel—the business functions, particularly in research—are embedded in educational programs that treat these as management, which just marginalizes management. To use March's terms, there is too much exploiting going on in the business schools and not enough exploring.

*Business* education has not been seriously reconsidered for almost fifty years, and never has *management* education been seriously considered. So it is time for the schools to heed their own prescription—namely, that change should come while things seem to be going well, before the fall.[1] We have many insights to offer in our schools, so long as they are directed to constructive ends, not convenient means.

"What constitutes an excellent MBA program?" asked a professor (in *Canadian Business* [Johnson 1994:30]). "The short answer [is] . . . one that provides the best career prospects for graduates." It is time for the long answer.

# THE PRIVILEGE OF SCHOLARSHIP

Karl Weick (1995) has referred to academic institutions as "places designed to make meaning" (21); Alfred North Whitehead (1932) wrote with regard to business schools, "The university imparts information, but it imparts it imaginatively. . . . A university which fails in this respect has no reason for existence" (139). Business schools that expand into new "markets," coddle "customers," and get "practical" have no reason for existence.

The purpose of an academic institution is to create and convey insights that help learners see their world in different and deeper ways. There is thus one overriding criterion for determining every single activity carried out in such institutions: that they advance insight, either by creating new knowledge or by conveying it thoughtfully.

The term *slack* may have a negative connotation, but it has to be an important component of academic pursuits, for both faculty and students. This is slack, not to squander resources, but to step back and consider important issues, whether by reflection in the classroom or

---

[1]Philip Whitley has drawn a parallel between U.K. schools in recent years and that country's car manufacturers in the 1950s: "able to sell everything they can produce" and so having little incentive to invest in serious change. "The old maxim that in the long run, nothing fails like success, may yet come to haunt the U.K.'s management educators" (Keep and Westwood 2002).

engagement in research. As life gets more hectic, academic institutions become even more important as havens in which to take stock. "Few other social institutions have this privilege bequeathed them," Robert Chia (1996:417) has written.

In research, if not teaching, academics get paid to do what they like. At worst, this leads to indulgence. But at best, it produces the ideas that change the world. In Eastern Europe in times past, the best scholars of the Jewish communities were married to the daughters of the wealthy, so that they could spend their lives in study and thereby preserve and enhance the community's wealth of knowledge. Academics are the modern-day equivalent. Society supports them, in relatively small numbers, to be its conscience, in a sense. For them to squander that privilege is therefore unconscionable.

I believe the role of the *management* school is management development to promote organization development to attain social development. In other words, *how* we serve our purpose is by developing better managers to improve organizations. *Why* we do this is to create a better society. Take away social development, and we indulge our organizations; take away organization development, and we indulge our students. Both have become common.

The body of this chapter begins with consideration of the delivery side, the programs that I believe management/business (M/B) schools should offer in general, if not every school in particular. These amount to a portfolio of programs discussed in earlier chapters. The chapter next turns to the development side—namely, the area of research and how it might be reconsidered. A final section looks at the nature of the schools themselves and how they might be made more effective for both development and delivery—that is, for learning.

# THE M'S, THE B'S, AND THE A'S

There has been striking convergence in the offerings of business schools, specifically around the prevalent MBA model, which has infiltrated both undergraduate education and programs for management development, even doctoral studies. That this does not work even for MBA programs has been the subject of the first part of this book; that it should never have been allowed to infiltrate these other studies is part of the following discussion.

I believe that the M/B schools should unbundle the MBA, specifically trifurcate its intentions into one set of programs about business, another focusing on administration (management), and a third that are truly about mastering. Ironically, the mastering programs are proposed not at the masters level but above and below it, in doctoral and undergraduate studies.[2]

Business schools today act largely as *starting* schools; mostly they launch young people on their careers (even in doctoral programs). The portfolio proposed here suggests the M/B schools can be more balanced as starting schools, developing schools, and finishing schools; besides educating, they can also be specializing schools and enhancing schools—but each in its own way, for its own particular learners. The portfolio also suggests that there can be a wide range of offerings by schools, to reflect the variety of organizations, sectors, and countries. There is no "one best way" in management, even in any one country, let alone "globally." The needs of developing companies differ from those of developed ones, just as the needs of developing countries differ from those of developed ones. And mass production, whose systems and techniques remain so influential across the whole spectrum of business education and practice, is hardly a model for high technology or knowledge work or even entrepreneurship, in business itself, let alone other sectors of society. By standardizing worldwide, the business schools weaken practice.

The portfolio presented here has five components: specialized masters programs for business, more general masters programs for practicing managers, nondegree development programs for practicing managers, bachelors programs to educate, and doctoral programs for adults.

## Specialized Masters Programs in Business

There is a place for the flagship MBA programs that business schools currently offer, but not as currently conceived. We must end the pretense of training business specialists in the name of developing general managers. The *M* will be appropriate when these programs are recognized for what they are: B, not A.

---

[2]This is not to exclude deeper mastering programs at the master's level, such as the Lancaster masters of philosophy in critical management discussed in chapter 7, only to suggest that the potential for such programs is limited.

There is certainly a symbiosis in the conventional MBA. It is relatively inexpensive mass production education for people whose opportunity costs are mostly rather low (even if the fees they pay are mostly rather high). It suits academics interested in research and deans interested in scale. The trouble is that by pretending to be more than it is, the students end up mastering less than they should. This degree should be valued for what it does best.

The obvious change, discussed in Chapter 7, is to drop the *A* and replace it by various specialized designations: an MBM in marketing, or even MBMR in marketing research, an MBF in finance, and so on. (But please, no MBS in strategy: This is neither a specialized function nor a bundle of analytical techniques.) And what about a more general MBA, true to its own nature: a Masters in Business *Analysis*? I suspect this may be too broad, too much once-over-lightly. Perhaps it might work within an industry—an MBB in banking, MBR in retailing, and so forth.

This proposal offers two obvious benefits. First, it allows for more depth, in precisely what students get most effectively out of MBA studies now. Second, it makes clear to students, and their employers, that they have been educated in a business function, not general management.

Of course, students in such programs would need some exposure to other business material, even some about management and organizations. But that only requires reversing what business schools already do, illustrated in Figure 15.1. Students now commonly do a series of core courses in all the business functions in the first year and then specialize in one of them through electives in the second year. Proposed here is a shift to emphasis on the specialization, supported by courses in the other functions, also in management and organization, but to inform specialists, not to develop managers.

Students with little or no work experience could, therefore, be trained in what they can learn best. Then they can go into specialized jobs in business, as most now do, but better trained. Those who subsequently demonstrate the will to manage could come back, as managers, for management education.

Much of the energy of the business schools now lies within the functional areas, which vie with each other for space and place in the MBA curriculum. So why not leverage that energy by allowing various areas to develop their own programs, suited to specific needs in practice. Specialized faculty could thus work with practitioner groups in its specialty—for example, marketing professors with marketing practitioners and associations—codesigning the curriculum, arranging field activities and internships, and placing graduates after graduation. As discussed in Chapter 7, especially in Europe do we find substantial evidence for the

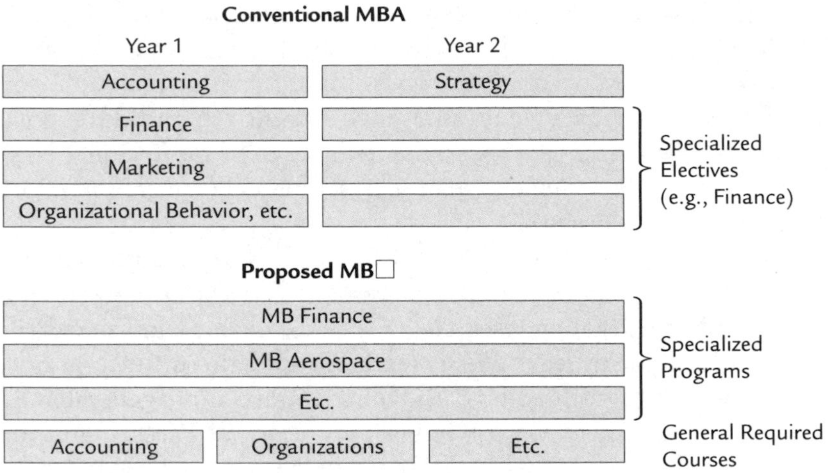

**Conventional MBA**

| Year 1 | Year 2 | |
|---|---|---|
| Accounting | Strategy | |
| Finance | | Specialized |
| Marketing | | Electives |
| Organizational Behavior, etc. | | (e.g., Finance) |

**Proposed MB☐**

| MB Finance | | | Specialized |
|---|---|---|---|
| MB Aerospace | | | Programs |
| Etc. | | | |
| Accounting | Organizations | Etc. | General Required Courses |

FIGURE 15.1
MBA or MB☐

viability of this, including some remarkably creative examples (such as the Bath program in purchasing discussed earlier). Many examples are found in North America, too, especially in accounting: This proposal seeks to extend these initiatives.

## MASTERS PROGRAMS FOR PRACTICING MANAGERS

Obviously business requires managers who understand its specialized functions. But just as obviously must management education goes well beyond these functions. And since the practice of management goes well beyond business, into areas where the *B* of the MBA gets in the way, we really need all kinds of Masters of Practicing Management (MPM) programs. As noted earlier, there should be room for thousands of people in such programs.

I see these programs positioned at two levels. One is for people in midcareer, about thirty-five to forty-five years old with significant managerial experience, generally devoted to an industry or sector as well as an employer that sponsors their studies. This is the IMPM model described in Chapters 10 through 14, and it works. The other is more junior, for people in their first managerial job. This could resemble the

IMPM, but with a heavier dose of the business functions, much of it perhaps in self-study.

I further see these programs as differentiated by sector, with various ones for managers from business, even realms of business such as small enterprises, from health care, from the social sector, and so on. Depending on needs, these might be international, as is the IMPM for business, or local, as has been the McGill-McConnell program for Canadian voluntary sector managers.

As I discussed in Chapter 14 and wish to reiterate here, existing EMBA programs would most logically be reoriented this way because they begin with the right people—namely, practicing managers who stay on the job. I see no justification in such programs continuing to imitate a design that was developed for people without context or experience. Of course, schools hardly have an incentive to change when their current programs are filled to capacity, as these are. But the managers in them have had nowhere else to go. Hopefully we shall soon find out what happens when they do.

As for labeling, the EMBA is almost as well established as the MBA. In principle, it needn't be changed if the *A* takes on real meaning (and the *E* does so by standing for *Experienced*, not *Executive*). But I favor the establishment of the MPM label to convey the message that these studies differ from the MBA. Establishing a new label may be no simple matter, but it has, after all, been a century since the last major label was introduced in M/B schools.

## Development Programs for Practicing Managers

As discussed in Chapter 8, a great wall exists in many business schools, with the degree programs—the crown jewels—on one side, carefully monitored by the faculty, and the nondegree program for managers on the other, mostly ignored by the faculty.

The good news of that chapter was that these latter programs can, as a result, be highly innovative, especially when some imaginative champion gets deeply involved in them. The bad news is that few such people get so involved. The result has been a plethora of standardized programs, often simply to earn easy money. As such, they do not belong in universities. That companies have tolerated them there suggests that they have been mesmerized by the academic credentials. But happily the nonacademic providers, including the companies themselves, have become more active, and sometimes more creative, in providing such courses.

Whitehead (1932) claimed that "universities should be homes for adventure" (147). Imagine treating every management development program as an adventure—as an opportunity to generate ideas and not just cash. Imagine breaking down those unfortunate walls, so that the best ideas of management development can find their way into management education, and vice versa. Hopefully some day, to be a prestigious school of management will mean not to exploit a "brand" but to break new ground.

## BACHELORS PROGRAMS TO EDUCATE

If you want to find the true mastering programs in the business schools today, don't look for them at the masters level. Mastering happens mostly after these programs, at the doctoral level. I believe it should also happen before them, at the bachelors level.

There are business schools—now mostly in Europe, at one time many in the United States—that educated their undergraduate students; they didn't set out to train them. Business schools are, of course, beset with calls for "practical" education. But that term is an oxymoron. Anyone who insists on a practical undergraduate education should be sent to a trade school; he or she has no business in a university. Joseph Wharton saw this correctly at the outset.

Most indicative of the problem now is the confounding of bachelors and masters degree requirements. How often has this been heard: "But I already did 'organizational behavior' in my bachelors program. We even used the same textbook. Why do I have to do it again?" Why indeed: Does it really matter that the person is now twenty-four instead of twenty? Such requests are reasonable because the situation is unreasonable. Contrast this with an organizational behavior course for practicing managers that uses their experience. Would anyone request exemption because he or she did a course by that title as an undergraduate or MBA—even with the same textbook?

There is a simple solution to this problem. Get the applied material out of the undergraduate curriculum. It does not belong there. All too often it makes a farce of the education process. (Recall the discussion in Chapter 2 of "Motivation: That's Maslow, Isn't It?") Read the following e-mail, one of many I regularly receive from undergraduates (and graduates), and ask yourself why anyone, student or professor, should waste his or her time with such "education."

Dear Mr. Mintzberg:

I am writing to you in hope that you could help me with a particular school project of mine. I am trying to elaborate the Strategy Formation argument; unfortunately I am finding it incredibly difficult to discuss this area. Please could you help me? I would be so grateful for your response. Thank you

We can replace the "practical" material of the business functions by solid material from the underlying disciplines in which business and management are rooted (psychology, economics, mathematics, and beyond, into history, anthropology, literature, philosophy, etc.). In other words, let's educate the students. If they have chosen business and deserve to be in a university, then let's provide them with what business needs most: thoughtfulness. "[I]n 1916, the founders of the Graduate School of Business [at Columbia University] . . . believed that a liberal education was the best way to provide businessmen with the 'broad knowledge and special competence beyond that which experience alone can provide'" (Aaronson 1992:163). They were right then, and they remain right now.

Even more important than any particular discipline is the discipline of good thinking, and that can come from a serious grounding in any serious field of inquiry. In the accompanying box, a professor of philosophy makes the case for his own discipline.

## INTERESTED IN BUSINESS?
## STUDY PHILOSOPHY

*(excerpted from a 1990 newspaper article by Thomas Hurka, a professor of philosophy at the University of Calgary)*

How should Canada educate students to compete successfully in the business world? Some provincial governments think it is by teaching them business. . . .

Recent evidence suggests this approach is mistaken. We will produce better managers if we educate them first in traditional subjects in the arts and sciences. We may do best of all if we educate them in philosophy. . . .

Consider the GMAT. . . . Undergraduate business students, whom you would think would be especially well prepared for this test, do badly on it, scoring below average for all test takers. The best results are by math students, followed by philosophy students and engineers. . . .

According to a book by sociologist Michael Useem [1989], [arts and science students] have more difficulty finding beginning managerial jobs than those with business or professional degrees because they lack specific skills in finance or engineering. When they are hired, it is usually lower in the company hierarchy. Once hired, however, they advance more rapidly than their colleagues. . . . An AT&T study showed that, after 20 years with the company, 43 percent of liberal arts graduates had reached upper-middle management, compared with 32 percent of engineers. The Chase Manhattan Bank found that 60 percent of its worst managers had MBAs while 60 percent of its best managers had BAs. At IBM, nine of the company's top 13 executives had liberal arts degrees.

What explains the success of arts and science students? . . . The study of admissions tests found that students do best "who major in a field characterized by formal thought, structural relationships, abstract models, symbolic languages, and deductive reasoning." The more abstract a subject, the more it develops pure reasoning skills; and the stronger a person's reasoning skills, the better he or she will do in any applied field.

This fits the data from business. Corporations report that, though technical skills are most important in low-level managerial jobs, they become less so in middle and top jobs, where the key traits include communications skills, the ability to formulate problems, and reasoning.

Business schools, as meeting grounds of the disciplines, could do a good deal of such educating themselves. Many have economists, statisticians, psychologists, historians, and others on staff who could develop substantial courses that relate disciplinary issues to the nature of the business enterprise. Indeed, such courses done well could stimulate that zest for business far more effectively than ones on the techniques of marketing and strategy.

Joseph Wharton and Alfred North Whitehead (1932:142) made similar calls for undergraduate education in the 1870s and 1930s, respectively. These were echoed in the three major reports on business in 1959 and 1988:

Undergraduate schools . . . should stress the foundation subjects [such as literature and language, mathematics, psychology, and economics] with considerably less attention to the functional specialties and the details of managerial performance. (Pierson 1959:xiv)

*We recommend that not less than half of the four-year undergraduate program be devoted to general education* and believe that considerably more would be desirable. (Gordon and Howell 1959:133; italics in original)

[I]in the course of our investigations we encountered some well-reasoned concern, particularly among senior executives in the business world, that business school students tend to be rather more narrowly educated than they ought to be. . . . [U]ndergraduate education . . . ought . . . [to be concerned] with the education of the whole student. . . . [Indeed,] it is now time for business schools to turn for enrichment to virtually all sectors of the university. (Porter and McKibbin 1988:316, 317).[3]

It is strange that such calls have come regularly from such sources yet have had so little impact.

Many business school professors will tell you that the undergraduate students tend to be more creative and energetic than the MBAs, also more inclined toward entrepreneurship. (Recall the data on this cited in Chapter 5.) This suggests that a broad, idea-based education may serve them and society better than a limited technical one. It also suggests that the designers of undergraduate curricula should relax and let the creative ideas flow.

Robert Chia of the Exeter University business school in England is one professor who has let such ideas flow. Questioning whether the more convergent formal disciplines should form the basis of undergraduate business education at all, he has made the case for more creative study of literature and the arts. Compare his ideas, reprinted in the accompanying box, with those of Thomas Hurka in the previous box, who emphasized "formal thought" and "deductive reasoning," and also with the section in Chapter 3 on the "School of Soft Knocks" for training entrepreneurs in MBA programs.

---

[3]Porter and McKibbin (1988) suggested a reduction of "the business proportion of the [undergraduate] program to as close to 40% as possible, that is, to the lower limit of the amount required for AACSB accreditation" (317). Perhaps they should have questioned that limit.

## CULTIVATING THE ENTREPRENEURIAL IMAGINATION

*by Robert Chia (from 1996:409, 411, 415)*

This paper argues that the cultivation of the "entrepreneurial imagination" is the singular most important contribution university business schools can make to the business community. Instead of the prevalent emphasis on the vocationalizing of business/management programmes in order to make them more "relevant," university business schools should adopt a deliberate educational strategy that privileges the "weakening" of thought processes so as to encourage and stimulate the entrepreneurial imagination. This requires a radical shift in pedagogical priorities away from teaching analytical problem-solving skills to cultivating a "paradigm-shifting" mentality. This, in turn, requires that management academics themselves engage in the practice of what is termed here "intellectual entrepreneurship." ... [This] implies a conscious and deliberate attempt on [their] part ... to explore the world of ideas boldly and without the undue inhibitions of disciplinary restraints, so as to cultivate ... an intimate sense for the power and beauty of ideas. ...

I believe that recourse to literature and the arts provides the best means of stimulating the "powers of association" in young, fertile minds. ... While the traditional scientific mentality emphasizes the *simplification* of the complex multiplicity of our experiences into manageable "principles," "axioms," etc., literature and the arts have persistently emphasized the task of *complexifying* our thinking processes and hence sensitizing us to the subtle nuances of contemporary modern life. ... It is this very act of breaking away from the dominant frames of thought and established conventions that sets the entrepreneur apart from others.

## DOCTORAL PROGRAMS FOR ADULTS

Mastering certainly happens at the doctoral level. But mastering of what?

Doctoral students master the materials—meaning the research literature—and they master research methods, at least the "hard," so-called quantitative ones. What growing numbers of them are not encouraged to master is standing on their own two feet. Too many doctoral programs, particularly in the United States as well as their imitations abroad, fail to treat the students like adults.

THE AMERICAN MODEL   The following sequence of events is not uncommon, particularly in American programs. First, no one is allowed into the program without selecting a predesignated area of study: Choose from the list, like you do at McDonald's. Business schools do not give doctoral degrees for breaking away from the conventional categories or even for combining them; they also do not give many doctoral degrees in business or management—mostly they give them in marketing or finance or strategy and the like, as if all the relevant knowledge about business and management slots neatly into one or other of these silos. It is not a gross distortion to conclude that students who wish to think broadly about business or management need not apply.[4] As a consequence, the thinking of students is not broadened in doctoral studies so much as narrowed.

The new doctoral student, like the new MBA and undergraduate, is greeted with a list of courses, a few required of all, most to be taken according to the specialized area. Once the student has duly completed the required number of courses and written all the required papers, he or she takes the required "general" or "comprehensive" examination, together with the other students in his or her specialized cohort, to be tested on the knowledge contained in a standard reading list.

So to this point, the program of study—for a life of largely independent scholarship—has been designed for the student, who has had little control over the content, perhaps even little opportunity to do anything original.

There is, however, an interesting anomaly here, because along the way the student has been told repeatedly that he or she had better publish or else risk not getting a good job upon graduation—after all, doctoral students at other schools have been so warned as well. Thus, in doctoral studies you are expected to write the overture before undertaking the opera. But how to do that when you have yet to learn about

---

[4] AACSB figures for doctoral degree enrollments in its member schools in the United States in 2002 show 868 in finance, 674 in economics/managerial economics, 657 in accounting, 605 in marketing, 581 in MIS, 337 in behavioral science/organization behavior, 217 in production/operations management, 162 in HR, and 151 in strategic management—for a total of 4,252. In "Management," there were 633; in "General Business," 249; and in "International Business," 143—for a total of 1,025, less than one-quarter of the aforementioned areas.

writing operas, let alone overtures? In many ways, the simple solution is to tuck under the existing research project of a professor. Not a bad idea if this constitutes a true apprenticeship; a bad idea if it constitutes a convenient way for professors to lengthen their publication lists.

The opera is the dissertation, the pinnacle of academic studies, to demonstrate independent insightful scholarship. That so many dissertations these days lack an insightful spark can be traced back to so many programs that offer little room for independence. (Sometimes the dissertation itself is tucked under some professors research agenda.) Not that these dissertations lack rigor; quite the contrary, many contain *only* rigor.

Not all doctoral programs require this whole process, but a remarkable number do, and most go a significant part of the way. They should be redesigned in the opposite direction—to promote creative, independent scholarship. Doctoral students should be selected for their potential to stand on their own feet; they should demonstrate creativity in their work or be asked to leave—the world already has enough pedantic professors; they should codesign *their* programs with their advisers, in the process designating their own specific focus of study, beyond or within the regular categories. In other words, every single student's program should be customized.

Time and again doctoral students are told in their research to address some manageable issue, take a small piece of a big issue. I disagree. The really interesting dissertations address really big issues. Not by trying to study everything, just by focusing attention on something important. These doctoral students are inspired. They go for the jugular. Too many others go for some toenail or other. And they continue to do so as professors. So if you really want to know what is troubling business today, you are literally better off reading Dilbert than most of the academic business journals. (If you are not an academic, I suggest you get hold of one of these journals and read the table of contents.)

THE EUROPEAN TRADITION    Traditionally, doctoral studies in many parts of Europe have stood at the other extreme. At the limit, but again found in some practice, there is no program, no courses, no exams. The student introduces him- or herself to a professor, disappears for years to write a dissertation, and then reappears to reintroduce him- or herself while handing over the document. With the influence of the U.S. business schools, much of this has given way to the approach described earlier. But delightful exceptions do occur, one described in the accompanying box.

## DISSERTATION WITHOUT SOCIALIZATION

A few years ago, out of the blue, I received a letter from a Norwegian consultant named Lars Groth. He wanted some help with his doctoral dissertation. Something about this seemed unusual, so I called Lars and chatted with him. Since I was flying through Oslo's airport a short time later, we agreed to meet. He sent me an excerpt of his dissertation, which I read on the plane. It was about the impact of information systems on organization design. There had been a great deal of dreary publication on this topic since the 1950s, full of promises without facts, but this paper looked interesting. The work was not "quantitative"; indeed, it drew on Lars's considerable consulting experience in the area—a definite no-no in respectable doctoral programs.

Lars explained his problem to me. He had proceeded in classic European doctoral fashion, with a professor in the Sociology Department at Oslo University. Except that just before he was able to return to that desk to hand over his document—a labor of love that took him eight years—the professor died, and none of his colleagues would consider it. Lars explained that there is a rule in Norway that such a dissertation can be defended at one other university, at least if faculty there are willing to consider it. Would I help, he asked.

In fact, he had already approached the well-known Norwegian School of Economics and Business Administration in Bergen. I called Torge Reve, whom I knew there, to support Lars's request. They were already favorable. To the credit of that school, Lars was allowed to defend his thesis in Bergen. It was a memorable event!

I was asked to be the outside examiner. Wiley eventually published the work, as *Future Organizational Design* (Groth 1999), and I got further roped into doing the preface. There I wrote:

*In my comments [at the defense], I explained why this thesis should be unacceptable: The subject is too broad, the topic is too vacuous, no systematic empirical work was done, the document is too long. All of which is to say that there is no formula for writing a thesis, any more than for applying [information technology]. Don't trust the professors when it comes to these things. In fact, this is an extraordinary piece of work on all fronts: depth, creativity, language, structure, historical perspective. It is a testimonial to scholarship without socialization: Few of the highly indoctrinated doctoral students do this well. I disagree with the author in places, but adore the way his labour of love glows from beginning to end. This is what scholarship should be about.*

European-style doctoral dissertations may not always work as well as the one described in the box, just as American-style ones sometimes turn out to be wonderfully creative. But there has to be a middle ground that provides some guidance while leaving responsibility for program design as well as execution significantly in the hands of the doctoral student. I believe we have that in Montreal.

THE JOINT DOCTORAL PROGRAM IN ADMINISTRATION    Thanks to a government university committee, the business schools at the four Montreal universities were forced to offer a joint doctoral program. What looked like a formula for disaster became an opportunity for collaboration. We were able to pool our resources, including several hundred professors, and do something truly interesting, between the European and American models (much like life in Montreal itself). We designed the initial program (a few changes have been made since) with the following characteristics:

- The program is offered in no designated area or, more to the point, precludes no area. Applicants apply with a description of the area in which they wish to study, and the review committees (at the university to which they apply and then a joint committee of the four) accept the strong ones with support from faculty members willing to work with them. Most apply in standard areas. But not all.

- There are no standard paths through the program. Each "program" is customized to the individual student, who works with his or her own faculty committee. Of course, a committee can impose a standard path in its area as a condition of working with it. But most do not.

- After the first stage of *preparation* (demonstration of basic knowledge, in core business subjects) follow the stages of *specialization* and *dissertation,* for each of which the supervising committee is formed. The student invites several faculty members to serve, at least one of whom must be from one of the other three schools.

- The program of study for the specialization phase is developed by the student with his or her committee. It contains appropriate elective courses (about fifty are available each year), two courses in a support area (often in an underlying discipline), and two theory papers (subsequently reduced) in which the student probes deeply into some aspect of the literature. In addition, all students in the entire program take a sequence of three common core seminars: "Fundamentals of Administrative Thought" (since made an elective), "Research Methodology in Management," and "Pedagogy in Management."

- The comprehensive examination at the end of the specialization phase is fully customized: Each student is examined by his or her own committee based on a reading list that they draw up together.

- The supervisory committee is formally reconstituted at the dissertation stage (although the membership often remains the same). As in most other programs, this committee accepts the proposal for the research as well as the final result, both of which are defended publicly. (A paper by Jean-Marie Toulouse and me, detailing the original design of the program, is available from santa.rodrigues@mcgill.ca.)

The Joint Doctoral Program in Administration has been running since 1976 (and has grown considerably in recent years). As of December 2002, it had graduated 234 people, a number of whose dissertations have won prestigious awards. (I should add a personal note here: I have worked mostly with older students in this program, in their thirties, and it has been a delight. They usually bring fascinating work experience and, having left it for the life of the poor doctoral student, generally demonstrate intense and authentic dedication to scholarship.)

# The Role of Research

Since the changes of the 1960s, business schools have become energetic centers of scholarship, eclectic meeting places for a wide variety of researchers. Indeed, a decade had not even passed when *Fortune* magazine published the Zalaznick (1968) article with the subheadline "The business graduates may be prized too much, but the graduate schools are often undervalued" (p. 168):

[L]ittle noticed and surely undervalued is a new and enormously promising dimension to the graduate business schools. In recent years a number of them have worked very hard to recruit first-rate scholars to their faculties, and thereby greatly improved the quality of research they sponsor. These scholars have been tackling an impressive range of difficult problems. (169)

Business school researchers address two central issues of our time. One concerns business, in its various manifestations; as noted, the progress made in some of the functional areas, such as finance and marketing, has been impressive and influential. The other, less clearly recognized, is organization. Not so much management, but organization.

A number of the social sciences, notably anthropology, sociology, economics, and political science, focus on broad issues of society; a single one, psychology, focuses on the individual. But none gives serious attention to the important level of human activity between the individual and society—namely, organizations, which so influence our daily lives. We live in a world of organizations, from the day we are born in a hospital to the day we are buried by a funeral home, including so much that happens in between. The economy itself contains business organizations of all sorts. Government is as much an interacting network of public organizations as a system of legislative and executive politics. The rest of society, so-called civil society, is itself a wide array of all kinds of organizations, variously called NGOs, not-for-profits, trusts, cooperatives, and so forth. We have a desperate need to understand these phenomena, and it is in the business schools where they get particular attention— from people not just trained in business but a variety of the social sciences, who congregate here to focus on issues of organization.

So the potential is enormous. And I believe the output is impressive—in fact, one of the best-kept secrets in the academic world.

## Panning for Academic Gold

Attend the annual meeting of the Academy of Management, and you will find thousands of scholars addressing all kinds of issues pertaining to organizations. Much of this discussion is pedantic, some of it is awful, but the best of it amounts to a substantial body of insight.

The trouble with the Academy of Management meeting is that the researchers talk mostly to each other, as they do in most of their journals. Some practitioners slip in, but most go elsewhere in search of ideas. Many, in fact, dismiss academic research as irrelevant to their needs. But mention a Michael Porter or a James Brian Quinn or an

Edger Schein, and the reaction is different. For the fact is that many of today's most influential management writers—serious thinkers widely read—have made their careers in academia.[5]

EFFICIENT DOES NOT MEAN EFFECTIVE    Academic research on organizations and management suffers from two big problems. First, it is not very efficient. Second, it is not very accessible.

Finding good insights from academic research is like panning for gold. The searcher has to go through a lot of silt and stone before a nugget appears. It is tedious work that most practicing managers avoid. Understandable but unfortunate, because the nuggets can be valuable.

It would be nice if business school research were more efficient. It would be nice, too, if research in physics was more efficient, also research in pharmaceuticals. Get rid of all the useless work and concentrate on the really breakthrough stuff. If only we could tell the difference—even after, let alone before. (A professor of mine once said that theories go through three stages: First they are wrong; then they are subversive; finally, they are obvious.) In fact, making research more efficient is easy—administrators and accountants do that all the time. The hard part is making it effective.

We just can't tell who is going to produce those nuggets or where. The people and places that seem so right—the individuals who speak well, get high grades, the prestigious schools where such people seem so sure of themselves—often turn out to be so wrong, while many of the interesting ideas come from quirky sources. Research is insightful when it produces something unexpected—in other words, when it violates conventional wisdom. So the expected people and places, the seats of

---

[5]A *Financial Times* Web site called FTdynamo.com (now defunct) in January 2001 published a list of the fifty "top thinkers" in management. Of the first ten, four were academics, and another three (Peter Drucker, Charles Handy, and Gary Hamel) have long had academic affiliations. The next nine were all academics. The FTdynamo cast its net wide, to include businesspeople and consultants (Jack Welch and Bill Gates were among the first ten). But "an initial surprise was the poor showing of mainstream consultants." Similarly, the Accenture consulting firm's magazine, *Outlook*, in its January 2003 issue published rankings of "the 50 top gurus." More than half of the first fifteen were academics, and many followed. Consultants hardly figured among these fifteen, and businesspeople, such as Bill Gates and Jack Welch, followed (numbers 19 and 34, respectively). A huge organization of practitioners, the American Society for Training and Development, with seventy thousand members, gives an award for contributions to workplace learning and performance—an applied field if ever there were one. Of the six winners to date, five are lifelong academics, well published in the learned journals; the other is Peter Drucker.

conventional wisdom, often prove less successful than those that seem irrelevant, and often irreverent, too. My idea of a good researcher is the little boy in the Hans Christian Andersen story who pointed out that the emperor wore no clothes.

DOING RESEARCH FOR BILL AND BARBARA    The second problem is accessibility. We academics speak to each other in places like the Academy of Management and write to each other in journals like *Administrative Science Quarterly*. Mostly our researching is a closed shop, decided, conducted, judged, and controlled by ourselves, and therefore often impenetrable to all but the most determined practitioners. We insist on the exclusive right to screen each other's work yet expect society to pay the bill. It is an extraordinary display of arrogance matched only by the acquiescence of those who pay those bills. Of course, we insist on this as a shield to protect our delicate ideas, never admitting that it can also be a smokescreen to obscure bad work.

Researchers in business and management do not study nuclear fission. Theirs are the subjects of everyday life. So any findings of interest should be easily conveyable to intelligent practitioners. And any findings that cannot are probably no good. True, the jargon can get in the way, but that is often another smokescreen for bad work.

Some years ago, Bill, a good friend, asked me to join him for dinner with his colleague Barbara. Here were two smart, articulate managers. Bill ran the distribution (marketing) department of the National Film Board of Canada, with three hundred people, most of whom reported first to Barbara, who was in charge for Canada. She wanted to meet me to discuss leadership.

At the time, I was preparing to attend an academic conference on leadership, as commentator on the papers to be discussed. As I read them, I wondered how Bill and Barbara might have reacted. I decided to make my comments in this regard. "Would that grab Bill and Barbara?" I asked about the conclusion of one paper. Many of the researchers were displeased with my comments. So in preparing them for publication, I decided to solicit the actual reactions of Bill and Barbara to each of the papers, which I published alongside my own (in Mintzberg 1982). Mine turned out to be gentle! A number of them are worth quoting to show the level of thinking of some managers who have never been to a business school:

> This is beyond navel-gazing—it is solipsism. . . . The whole thing is like a Russian matrioska doll—doubtful studies enveloping doubtful studies enveloping studies that were banal, superficial, and un-

interesting in the first place. To make matters worse, much of the presentation is written in a style that can only be described as excruciating. (Bill, p. 245)

Such an awful lot of work to establish that "there is a great amount of dissimilarity and complexity in how leaders carry out their interpersonal contacts." Eureka! (Barbara, p. 243)

[This study] is trying to measure things which are intrinsically non-quantifiable—at least on neat scales. It is like an art critic saying that if the ceiling of the Sistine Chapel were one foot higher and the index fingers of God and Adam one inch further apart, the impact would be 2 percent less. Such an approach is devoid of imagination and misses the point in a truly monumental way. (Bill, p. 246)

The problem with "how to" guides to interpersonal skills is that good leaders do not need them (that's how they got to be leaders!) and bad ones cannot really be taught to use them. (Barbara, p. 247)

Overall, Bill concluded, "Many presentations go to incredible and convoluted lengths and explanations, only to finish by stating the obvious," while from Barbara came "What bothered me most, as I read the presentations, was the gnawing suspicion that all the research was being carried out as an end in itself" (p. 243).

Researchers may have a valid complaint that, judging by the level and tone of so many best-selling business books, the readers have no business passing judgment on their work. Fair enough. But these researchers have no more business writing for themselves. The fact is that there are lots of Bills and Barbaras out there, thoughtful practitioners who do not read those kinds of books and who would be delighted to receive interesting ideas from research (that is why Barbara wanted to have dinner in the first place), just as there are the Porters and Quinns and Scheins happy to supply them. We meet such managers in our IMPM program all the time. Accordingly, I concluded my paper by proposing a "Bill and Barbara test":

Announce that any request for research funding or any submission to a journal will have to undergo screening by an intelligent practitioner. A member of that constituency will have to find it relevant before it is approved. Then watch what happens. . . . If you cannot serve leaders, then how can you hope to serve leadership? (pp. 258–59)

OUT OF THE ARCHIVES, INTO THE GALLERIES    The problem is not only in the doing of research but in its dissemination. Few outsiders know about some of the most interesting findings, at least in organization theory.

Put differently, the archives of organization research are busy places, full of scholars beavering away. Upstairs, however, the museums are rather empty. Many of the most interesting pieces are not displayed, or else they are displayed badly. Beyond the museums, the galleries are certainly full, but of too many people looking for simple tableaus to explain complex problems. Managing is mostly about nuances, while the popular works mostly provide formulas—painting by numbers, so to speak.

We thus seem to be left with a choice between superficial "relevance" in the galleries and artificial "rigor" in the archives. It is time we declared a pox on both these houses. We need to connect serious needs with interesting ideas—bring together the pull of practice with the push of scholarship, thoughtful demand with insightful supply.

Expecting serious scholars to respond to practitioner needs is not proposed here as a way to weaken scholarship but to strengthen it. Having to struggle with the interesting problems of the world carries the challenge to dig deeper, to understand better. It also forces the scholar to communicate more clearly. That is what has driven the works of people like Porter, Quinn, and Schein and made it so successful—and, incidentally, not only among practitioners: The academics need material for their classrooms, too, and they don't find most of it in the "rigorous" research.

There are important journals—*Harvard Business Review, Sloan Management Review, California Management Review*, among others—that can intelligently and successfully bridge the gap between research and practice. But these are few in a sea of much else, and only one has a really wide circulation. Moreover, the tendency of late to veer toward "practical" application does not help. While getting the insightful scholars out of the archives, we also need to get the intelligent practitioners into the galleries.

## ON THE NATURE OF
## INSIGHTFUL SCHOLARSHIP

Rigor versus relevance has been the great research debate of the business schools. Both get in the way of insightful scholarship.

NOT THAT KIND OF "RIGOR," THANK YOU    In the *Strategic Management Journal* some years ago, its editor wrote in an editorial that "if our field is to continue its growth, and develop important linkages between research and practice, as it must, then we need to improve our research and understand that relevance comes from rigor" (Schendel 1995:1). This claim itself was not so rigorous, since no evidence was presented in support of it. As usual, it was taken as an article of faith.

Read the "rigorous" literature, and you may come to the opposite conclusion: that this kind of rigor—methodological rigor—gets in the way of relevance. People too concerned about doing their research correctly often fail to do it insightfully.

Of course, intellectual rigor—namely, clear thinking—does not get in the way of relevance. The editor referred to this too in his editorial (as "careful logic"), but what he meant was the following: "Research in this field should not be speculation, opinion, or clever journalism; it should be about producing replicable work from which conclusions can be drawn independently of whoever does the work or applies the work results" (1).

I think of this as bureaucratic research, because it seeks to factor out the human dimension—imagination, insight, discovery. If I study a phenomenon and come up with an interesting theory, is that not rigorous because someone else would not have come up with the same theory? Accept that and you must reject every theory that has ever been developed, every discovery that has ever been made, from physics to philosophy, because all were idiosyncratic efforts, the inventions of creative minds. ("I'm sorry, Mr. Einstein, but your theory of relativity is speculative, not proven, so we cannot publish it.") Sumantra Ghoshal wrote to the same editor about an article he published that Ghoshal had earlier reviewed:

> I have seen the article three times. . . . The reviewing process, over these iterations, has changed the flavor of the article significantly. I believe that the new argument . . . is interesting but unavoidably superficial. . . . Citations and literature linkages have driven out most of the richness and almost all of the speculation that I liked so much in the first draft. While the article perhaps looks more "scholarly," I am not sure who exactly gains from this look. . . . I cannot get over the regret of description, insight and speculation losing out to citation, definition and tightness.

INDUCTIVE, NOT "QUALITATIVE"   In formal terms, what we have here is a dispute between inductive and deductive research. Induction is about coming up with ideas or concepts or theories from investigation in the first place. It requires probing, sometimes systematically, sometimes not, to generate description rich enough to stimulate the creative mind. Induction is what cannot be replicated because its findings are the inventions of particular brains, like the designing of a new product or the writing of a novel. Deduction, in contrast, involves the testing of such findings to find out how explanatory they are. That is what can be replicated.

Business school researchers usually express this distinction differently, and mistakenly. They contrast "qualitative" with "quantitative" research, as if all inductive research is qualitative and all deductive research is quantitative. For example, some of my own inductive research that has been considered "qualitative" (e.g., Mintzberg 1973; Mintzberg and McHugh 1985) is loaded with numbers.

The problem is the prevalent belief among many of the researchers who dominate the academic journals that "quantitative" research is proper research, while "qualitative" research is something, at most, to be indulged in occasionally. Using these other labels, however, makes clear that deductive research cannot happen without inductive research. In other words, we can only test what we have invented. Therefore, no induction, no new ideas. As Karl Weick (1969) quoted Somerset Maugham, "She plunged into a sea of platitudes, and with the powerful breast stroke of a channel swimmer made her confident way toward the white cliff of the obvious" (63). Sure, theories should be tested. But only when they are interesting.[6]

This dysfunctional prejudice manifests itself most destructively in doctoral courses that teach quantitative methods (mostly statistics) as rites of passages. Those who cannot handle them simply cannot get doctoral degrees, even though there is all kinds of wonderful research with no numbers. Why not preclude from doctoral programs students incapable of coming up with interesting ideas?

MEANWHILE, BACK AT RELEVANCE    On the other side of this debate is relevance. We should no more sympathize with the simplistic calls for relevance than with the snobbish calls for rigor. This notion of being handed "relevance" on some sort of silver platter, with no obligation to think, probe, work, has been the cause of enormous amounts of managerial malpractice.

To repeat, it is not relevance we need, but insight. As discussed in Chapter 9, quoting Keynes, we are prisoners of the theories we carry around in our heads. What we need, therefore, are better theories, alter-

---

[6]"The first rigorous field verification of Darwin's model for rapid evolution of visible traits (such as bill sizes in birds) was in the 1980s El Niño events" (Quinn 2002:96).

nate ways by which to better understand the world. And these come from struggling to incorporate new insights into our own experience. *Struggle* is key: We learn by being puzzled, then suspending disbelief, and finally incorporating the new insight through hard work. That we must struggle to achieve this suggests that whatever is too obviously "relevant" may often be irrelevant.

DESCRIPTION, NOT PRESCRIPTION    There is an important implication from this discussion: that the role of research is to describe, not prescribe. Prescription is the responsibility of the manager faced with an issue. Only he or she can prescribe, in context. Even consultants can only *advise*. The job of the researcher is to help practitioners deepen their *descriptive* understanding—to offer fresh insights so that these actors in context can see the world more clearly and thus act more effectively. When I hear inexperienced students demanding easy prescriptions in the classroom, my response is, "You could not have entered this room without understanding how the door handle works. What makes you think you can get anything done in an organization without understanding how it works?"

Part of the blame for this has to be laid on the functional structure of the business school, which slices up the complicated reality of business so that each professor can trumpet his or her own view of truth. (Recall discussion of Jensen and Meckling's REMM model in Chapter 6.) This has helped turn the educational process into a collection of contradictory prescriptions: the glories of shareholder value in finance, the wonders of social responsibility in ethics, and so on.

These comments apply equally to business publications that push prescriptive answers on all their readers. Again, there is never any "one best way in management," no "practical" solution to everyone's problems. It is fine to present techniques, but descriptively, "critically": how they work, where they have been found to work, when they fail. That way managers can decide for themselves, as they ultimately must, whether, when, and especially how to use them. So let's bring back that skull and crossbones, this time to be stamped on all articles about technique: "Warning: dangerous if taken out of context." Techniques in the hands of wise people can be powerful, but formulas in the minds of the mindless are destructive. That is why M/B education has to focus on helping people become more mindful.

CONNECTING AND DISCONNECTING    Good research is deeply grounded in the phenomenon it seeks to describe. It gets close enough to appreciate the richness and the nuances. Research methods that distance the researcher from the subject, as in many of the questionnaires so easily mailed out, often create confusion more than illumination because the data are too superficial to engender insight. Detachment in the practice of researching is no better than detachment in the practice of managing. Effective researchers often dig their data out, bit by bit, on site.

But after having been close, the researcher has to step back—get far enough from the subject to be able to perceive it differently. In other words, the researcher has to connect and then disconnect.

THEORIES AS LENSES AND HAMMERS    Do we encourage our researchers to connect every which way? Hardly. In the case of doctoral students, we lock them in libraries for years and then tell them to go find a research topic. The library is the worst place to find a research topic. Even students who were once in the world of practice have forgotten what goes on in that world.

The result is that a great deal of research is pushed by some theoretical construct or angle: game theory, networking, corporate social responsibility (yet again), whatever is fashionable in the world of academe. Under the scrutiny of such single lenses, organizations look distorted. Recall the "rule of the tool"—you give a little boy a hammer and everything looks like a nail. Narrow concepts are no better than narrow techniques. Organizations doesn't need to be hit over the head with either.

The most interesting research, to my mind, usually starts from pull, not push; it seeks to address an important concern out there, not to promote an elegant construct in here. It takes its lead from behavior in practice (Lawrence 1992:140). Start with an interesting question, I tell my doctoral students, not a fancy hypothesis. Find some living place where it gets revealed, dig out the data, and bring to bear on it all the potentially relevant theories, concepts, angles, and whatever else you can find in the literature.

I remember years ago the contrast of two small conferences I attended. One was on information technology, full of famous faculty engaged in what I think of "panther research": sitting up in trees waiting to pounce on any correct behavior that went by—in this case, the "proper" use of IT. Push with a vengeance. The other conference was on international business. Why was this one so full of interesting ideas, I wondered? Because these researchers had a constituency: They were being pulled into the interesting concerns of people having to manage in a particular context.

ONE LAST CRITICAL INGREDIENT   There is one final ingredient about research that draws all these others together: passion. Consider these two titles from an Academy of Management conference: "Cognitive Isomorphism in Inter-organizational Evaluative Networks: An Empirical Examination of Image and Identity in Academia," and "Jolted by Gabriel: How Becoming a Father Changed My Career." Which do you think had the passion?

Sure, we need objectivity in research. But we need insight, too, and that comes from deep commitment. Have a look at the accompanying box.

---

### PUTTING THE PASSION BACK IN

*(summary of the author's presentation to the Organization and Management Theory Division of the Academy of Management Conference, 1996)*

- *Screw tenure*. Better to be able to look yourself in the mirror than to hang your head in the faculty club.

- *Publish only when you have something to say*. You will be even happier as a reader.

- *Say it all at once, right, altogether*. Take a chance at becoming famous instead of fractured.

- *Never set out to be the best*. Do *your* best.

- *Create knowledge*. Discover something new; most everyone else is redigesting what is old. Something new is probably staring you in the face right now (like Fleming with that mold). The little boy in the Hans Christian Andersen story did not have the courage to *say* that the emperor wore no clothes; he had the courage to *see* it. After that, saying it was easy.

- *Write for the thoughtful practitioner*. Falling over the vertical cliff of academic irrelevance is no better than sliding down the slippery slope of easy practicality. Stay up on that ridge; it's an exhilarating place to be, less dangerous than either side. Your reasonable colleagues will respect you for it.

- *Get close to action.* Not *"the"* action, just action. Surprise yourself. Then maybe you can surprise others.

- *Be passionate about what you do or get out.*

We have a wonderful opportunity to be passionate in our M/B schools. We address fascinating issues at the center of contemporary society—about business and organizations and managing in general. Psychology and economics get an enormous amount of attention, yet neither explains these strange and important beasts we call organizations. Once we get past rigor and relevance, we shall be filling up our museums and galleries.

## TEACHING FOR RESEARCH

Teaching is now part of the problem in research. Faced with students disconnected from practice, professors have no incentive to connect to it. The calls from such students for "practical" materials only worsens the problem by driving faculty attention to concepts that are too easy, too fashionable. Many faculty have become so conditioned by such students that when faced with practicing managers who do have interesting experience, instead of listening and learning, they just repeat the lectures and cases developed for the others.

What a shameful waste of opportunity. We have seen what can happen when theory meets practice in the classroom, when researchers and managers reflect together on important issues. We saw how that can help managers but also how it can benefit research, by connecting and scrutinizing its ideas, and encouraging the generation of new ones. My own experiences in this kind of classroom never cease to inform and surprise me. So the need is not to disassociate researching from teaching but to connect them for the betterment of both.

Some years ago, *The Economist* (December 14, 1991) quoted a Wharton dean about the school needing to bring "the fruits of Wharton's research into the classroom more swiftly. Like many American companies, Wharton has to shorten its product-development cycle" (74). Nonsense. No one is quicker to talk about his or her latest findings than the academic researcher. As one of my own deans used to quip, "The first thing a new Ph.D. wants to teach is the last thing he or she learned!" The problem is not getting the research ideas into the classroom; it is engaging those ideas with experience so that researchers and managers can learn from each other. Some of the articulate comments about this by Karl Weick of the University of Michigan are reproduced in the accompanying box.

## THE SCHOLARSHIP OF INTEGRATION

*Karl Weick on Executive Education*

[E]xecutive education involves an important form of scholarship. . . . [I]t embodies the scholarship of integration . . . [which is] about making connections, giving meaning to facts [to bear on original research]. . . . [Executives] talk about connections in the world in complete disregard of the disciplinary boundaries they may be violating. Those connections bridge the arbitrary lines we [as academics] draw around disciplines. . . . Their actions of connecting undermine our isolation. . . . I love to make the connections. It's as simple as that. . . .

I think being wedded to a scholarship of integration may be a better platform for executive education than being wedded to a scholarship of application. People do want to know what to do, but even more, they want to know what things mean, how to make sense of events, how their labels may constrain the options they see. . . .

I'm just as interested in connections and integration and patterns that constitute meaning and in sense making, as I am in discovery. And the same holds true for the overloaded executives who sit in my classroom. Thus, it's not surprising that their practice and my scholarship have more in common than you might expect. (1996:12–13)

## THE UNIVERSITY CONNECTION

The preceding discussion has concentrated mostly on the M/B school's connection to practice. Its connection to the university is no less important.

Consider those schools most renowned for their research. They are almost all rooted in strong universities. There are schools such as Insead that maintain an active research agenda without a university connection. But it is usually more of an uphill battle. Even at the Harvard Business School, research may have suffered from the school having been too independent of the rest of the university. Thanks in part perhaps to the ties subsequently forged in its doctoral programs, its research has become much stronger.

Certainly the university connection can be an awful nuisance. (The IMPM had to gain the approval of eleven different McGill committees!) But the other side of this connection is that the university anchors the M/B school in its scholarly pursuits. The pull of practice on one side is balanced by the pull of scholarship on the other. So research at the M/B school also has to walk that ridge between scholarship and practice. Wavering like a drunk between academic irrelevance and easy practicality is hardly desirable.

# REORGANIZING THE M/B SCHOOL

Let me turn finally to the organization of the M/B schools themselves, considering their faculty, course loads, tenure, functions, and disciplines, before I conclude.

## BEYOND 40:40:20

You get to teach in a prestigious school of business by proving yourself adept at research. Thereafter, publication in learned journals qualifies you to continue training the leaders of tomorrow. A curious system indeed!

There is a simple assumption behind this: Being a good researcher magically makes you a good teacher. Its logic is on a par with rigor magically producing relevance. After boasting about the good jobs gained by some recent graduates, the director of the doctoral program at one well-known business school wrote to his colleagues, "These appointments demonstrate the validity of this program's emphasis on solid research as the basis for excellence in teaching." No, they demonstrate how research has trumped teaching. Does the director even know how his graduates teach? For his program, like most others, teaches its doctoral students nothing about teaching.[7]

There are certainly many superb teachers in M/B schools, although sometimes through no fault of the hiring and tenure procedures. (One

---

[7]In our Joint Doctoral Program in Montreal, as noted earlier, we included a course in pedagogy. Some faculty protested. This was not normal. One course in pedagogy—3 percent of the activity—in a program that licenses people to spend as much time teaching as doing research!

famous school became infamous for refusing tenure to the recipient of its best teacher award—three years in succession!) But there are also many bad teachers, some of whom publish.

The claim that you have to do research to be an effective teacher is nonsense; it implies that professors can't read. In other words, they can't teach other people's ideas, or at least cannot understand them if they are not researchers themselves. The facts are often the opposite: There are many cutting-edge researchers who don't want to read or teach beyond their narrow interests. And, as Whitehead (1932) noted, there are great teachers, in fact great scholars, who don't publish:

> For some of the most fertile minds composition in writing, or in a form reducible to writing, seems to be an impossibility. In every faculty you will find that some of the more brilliant teachers are not among those who publish. Their originality requires for its expression direct intercourse with their pupils in the form of lectures, or of personal discussion. (148; Whitehead cited Socrates as an example!)

Why don't we simply assess people on their teaching and their researching independently? And then, why don't we assign workloads accordingly? Isn't it time we unbundled those formulaic approaches that expect the same of all so-called tenure-track faculty, notably that "40:40:20" formula of 40 percent of the time on teaching, 40 percent on research, and 20 percent on administrative work? Given different abilities and inclinations, why not 90:0:10, or 20:60:20? (See Table 15.1.)

True, there are adjunct professorships without demands for research. The trouble is that they are usually treated as adjunct (which my dictionary defines as "subordinate or incidental"). If universities have the two functions of creating and conveying insightful knowledge, why denigrate one?

Good teachers with 80:0:20 loads should be welcomed as respected members of the community, even in regards to tenure. And great researchers who are terrors in the classroom could be relieved of that first 40 percent, or at least restricted to working with doctoral students. Then there are those 40:40:20 professors who de facto retire from the second 40 percent, ceasing to do research after receiving tenure. They should likewise be retired from 40 percent of their salaries, or else be expected to double their teaching (80:0:20). Doing research is not a gift to the university but a requirement of anyone holding a full-time job that requires only part-time teaching.

## Table 15.1 ECLECTICISM IN FACULTY APPOINTMENTS

| POSITION | PERCENTAGE TEACHING | PERCENTAGE RESEARCHING | PERCENTAGE ADMINISTRATING |
|---|---|---|---|
| Conventional tenure track | 40 | 40 | 20 |
| Young Swedish scholars | 10 | 90 | 0 |
| Chaired professors in America | 20 | 60 | 20 |
| Clinical professors in America (part-time) | 40 | 0 | 10 |
| Departmental chairs in Europe | 20 | 30 | 50 |
| Executives-in-residence (part-time) | 40 | 0 | 10 |
| Tenured professors retired from research (part-time) | 40 | 0 | 10 |

Sweden has an interesting system. It offers promising new doctorates a six-year proving period in which they do little teaching but are expected to produce much research (a kind of 10:90:0 formula). After that, they apply to either research or teaching professorships (of the order of 30:50:20 and 70:10:20, respectively), depending on their performance. Of course, chaired professorships in the United States usually come with lighter teaching loads, perhaps 20:60:20. Proven researchers are allowed to teach less. Contrast this with common practice in Europe, where to sit in a chair means to head the department. As a reward for excellence in research, the incumbents get loaded with administration!

I am a big fan of 40:0:10. This is for thoughtful practitioners, often consultants or "executives-in-residence," with academic inclinations and excellent teaching skills. They have much to contribute to the M/B schools, but, by preference, only on a part-time basis, alongside other responsibilities. They are akin to the well-established clinical professorships in medicine, but without the expectations for research.[8] Time and again, especially in Europe, I have seen wonderful examples of rather scholarly people from practice attracted to such positions, many as well read as the most conscientious academics.

From the school's perspective, these people can be strong where regular academics tend to be weak—for example, in skill development and classroom facilitation. They can also provide effective bridges to practice. From their perspective, they get the prestige of a university affilia-

---

[8]The University of Chicago business school uses the term "clinical professorships", but reserves it for a small number of full-time faculty, for terms up to five years, and subject to the affirmative vote of the tenured faculty.

tion, which hardly hurts if their other work is consulting. Indeed, their academic earnings tend to be small in comparison, which means the schools can negotiate rather favorable contracts with them.

None of this is meant to diminish the standing of research. Quite the contrary, it can strengthen it, by taking some of the teaching pressures off the more research-oriented faculty. But it is meant to elevate the standing of teaching, which has to be done in many business schools.[9]

## Beyond Tenure

I wish to add a word here about academic tenure. This practice was introduced to protect the freedom of expression of the professors, particularly from arbitrary dismissal by politicians or university administrators for unpopular views. Today tenure often menaces freedom of expression. That is because the threat to the maverick academic now comes less from the outside than from the inside—namely, his or her own colleagues. Whereas *having* tenure may have protected those who spoke out, today *getting* tenure threatens them. Powerful offended colleagues may be able to deny it to them, whether they are radical economists in one university or conservative sociologists in another, not to mention those whose research is not "rigorous" enough.

I believe tenure can play a useful role when subject to two conditions. First, it should be granted on a balanced assessment of performance, which means ensuring that teaching has a prominent place alongside research, also that the latter is judged by insight to the user (meaning to bring back that Bill-and-Barbara test: intelligent practitioners sitting on tenure committees, too).

The second condition is that tenure be reviewed periodically. The word actually comes from the French, *tenir*, "to hold," but ten does seem like the right number: Tenure could be reviewed every decade or so, not to put people through the whole process again, but simply to ensure that they are meeting their commitments. Otherwise there should be a rearrangement of workloads—for example, an increase in teaching if research has diminished.

---

[9]Opening up the issue of workloads should open up how those workloads get counted. Many schools count by courses; this is the equivalent of trading in camels and goats—you can't negotiate anything smaller. Currency has proved to be a good idea, so many schools can catch up by counting points for various activities, including classes taught, and so on. Insead does this, and so has easily been able to incorporate IMPM teaching in workloads, whereas McGill does not, and so has had to keep IMPM teaching apart from the rest.

## OUT OF THE CHIMNEYS

You also get to teach in an M/B school if you can prove that you are specialized: in marketing, finance, accounting, human resource management, strategic management, and so on—not in business and not in management. Here, too, people interested in the broader issues need not apply; often there is literally no place for them.

Trace the history of the business school, and you find that most of the current functions were in place almost a century ago. Information systems slipped in later, thanks to the computer, and management metamorphosed into the function of strategic management and organization behavior into that of human resource management. Some record of change over the course of a century!

What about innovation? Design? Business History? Plain old management? That the established functions are fonts of important knowledge cannot be disputed. But that they contain all the reverent knowledge certainly can. That these functions have a central role to play in M/B schools is likewise indisputable. But that they deserve a stranglehold over everything these schools do should be accepted nowhere. It is accepted almost everywhere. Programs are designed, courses are allotted, budgets are allocated, slots are designated, and faculty are hired in these terms. Time and time again I have watched some of the most interesting faculty candidates passed over because they did not "fit" in any particular functional department. Everyone agreed they were great. But no department was going to give up one of its "slots"—in other words, dilute its influence.

Herbert Simon questioned this back in 1957, with the claim "Departmental structures must not be allowed to develop within the professional school, or, if they are unavoidable, their importance must be minimized." The schools may have "to give specialized subgroups some particular responsibilities for the recruitment and evaluation of faculty within their specialties—but under no circumstances exclusive responsibility" (351). Today's practice is closer to "under *all* circumstances"!

The dysfunctional effects of this stranglehold have shown up all over this book: in management programs, even *Advanced* Management Programs, that push managers back into the functional silos they are coming out of; in research more inclined to promote narrow angles than address broad issues; in program design as horse trading among the functional areas; and so on. How ironic that businesses are working to break down these functional silos while business schools keep reinforcing them.

I received a memo from a professor who referred to the functions that "dump product" on the MBA. Yet he went on to express concerns about weakening "the feeling of ownership" by these functions, because that could be "fatally damaging" to the MBA. In my opinion, the MBA has already been fatally damaged by such ownership, at least if you believe that running a business involves more than the sum of the functions. Wind (1999) writes, "We need to reshape the faculty and student incentive systems to reward cross-functional achievements. It is only then that we can begin to address the cross-functional questions currently facing businesses" (9; see Porter and McKibbin [1988:323, 332] for almost identical comments). But businesses don't face cross-functional questions; they face questions, period (including no small number *caused* by the separation of functions). We need to reprogram our heads to break out of these narrow categories.

Too often the functions impede serious change in the schools. Propose something new and you typically have to defend it in a committee of functional representatives, each there to protect turf. That is a major reason why the business schools have not gotten past their 1908 degree with its 1950s strategy. We teach our students that established structures can impede necessary change, yet we live with that consequence every day.

As for research, organization of it on a strictly functional basis can discourage what Kuhn (1962) has called "revolutionary" science, as opposed to "normal" science. "The danger is that management research simply takes for granted the management functions that developed with the rise of the large bureaucratic organization, and confines itself to simple 'technical trouble shooting'" (Fox 1992:88). Are the functional areas making the progress they did ten or twenty years ago? If the interesting things happen on the edges, outside the established places, then there are too few edges in the business schools.

I have rarely met a dean who did not decry the functional structure of his or her school. Or one who did anything much to change it. The solutions are easy enough; all we have to do is change our concept of the world. And, what amounts to the same thing, get past the gatekeepers— the faculty in the existing structure. Like getting Swiss movement watchmakers to accept quartz technology. Of course, they eventually did. But it took the outside world to drive that. So wake up, outside world— management education needs you!

For what it's worth, the accompanying box contains my own proposals. But be careful not to get between them and the business schools, or else you risk being run down in the stampede to adopt them.

## Toward Structuring M/B Schools for M and B

- First, never, absolutely never, let any specialized area control budgets, especially concerning slots for hiring.

- Second, subject all hiring decisions to a central committee made up of eclectic people who will act on behalf of the scholarly need of managers and organizations and society. Not just an eclectic mix—eclectic individuals, even if they began in a function. Alongside those you might find within the school, bring in several Bills and Barbaras.

- Third, insist on these kinds of people to design every management program. Bring in the functional specialists only where the design specifies functional activities.

- Fourth, reserve about half the faculty slots for the functions and the other half for people who fit no function but are interested in business and management. Even in the existing functions, favor some people who have strengths across functions—for example, a marketing person with a genuine interest in finance; also ones from the fundamental disciplines, so long as they have genuine enthusiasm for addressing issues of concern to business and management.

- Fifth, a good measure of the robustness of any business school should be the number of people working outside and across the established business functions, including new ones. And a good measure of whether it deserves to be called a management school should be the number of people seasoned enough to reflect thoughtfully with a class of practicing managers.

- Sixth, pay attention to the inside architecture: This is part of the structure that matters. For example, don't place like specialists in nearby offices. They will find each other. Because people talk to their neighbors, mix up the specialists, to help get rid of the ghettos. This is, after all, supposed to be about the "global village."

## A Word on the Disciplines

Part of the great revolution of the business schools after the 1950s was their newfound respect for the underlying academic disciplines, notably economics, psychology, and mathematics. Many of the best schools set out to imitate Carnegie's golden age under Bach, Simon, and the others, by bringing in from the disciplines scholars who focused on broad issues of business and organizations (if not management itself). This made these schools exciting meeting places for ideas—precisely what universities should be about. And that remains the case in many business schools today, to some extent. To *some* extent.

In a chapter of his landmark book *Administrative Behavior*, Herbert Simon (1957) addressed "The Business School" as "A Problem in Organizational Design." He wrote that the three basic disciplines mentioned in the last paragraph "should have an effective beachhead" in these schools (348). For this to happen, the schools would have to convince people in these fields that they "can do significant, fundamental work in the business school environment, and do it *more* effectively there than in the traditional department of economics, psychology, or mathematics" (346). That would involve "some members whose work does not have obvious relevance to business but does command high respect in its discipline," in accordance with their "desire for identification with, and approval by" that discipline (349).

This is what happened in many business schools, for better and for worse. It eventually undermined a number of them, including Simon's own, where economics became dominant (until it eventually separated from the rest).

The M/B schools must certainly draw on the underlying disciplines, including these three and various others, perhaps history, anthropology, even geography. These are the sources of a great deal of knowledge about social behavior, and M/B schools have to draw on every source they can find. But they hardly need to replicate these disciplines to do that. Their professors, too, can read.

Think of the disciplines as roots, as I displayed them in Figure 2.1. They nourish the trunk of business, management, and organizations, and in turn the branches of the applied functions. But as roots, they should remain underground, not push their own theories up.

What the disciplines can do—what they have often done wonderfully well—is produce scholars who belong in the M/B schools because they get their heads around the issues of business, management, and/or organizations. They have helped make these schools much better places. Three of my most cherished colleagues at McGill came out of sociology, political science, and history. They use their grounding to address these kinds of issues, pulled from practice. Frances Westley, for example, who created the masters program for voluntary sector managers discussed in the last chapter, came out of the sociology of religion. But she studies management, not religion (although she has occasionally used that background to advantage, as in Mintzberg and Westley 1992).

As noted in Chapter 2, the business schools don't need self-appointed high priests, such as professors of finance who call themselves "financial economists", or economic game theorists who play at strategy. But they do need eclecticism in their scholarship. In this regard, it is unfortunate that the M/B schools are doing so well in placing their own doctoral students, because that makes the schools less eclectic and so less interesting. We should be refreshing our thinking by hiring significantly across a whole range of underlying disciplines, and beyond.

## CHANGING THE CHANGE AGENTS

It is not easy to be the dean of an M/B school these days, or perhaps any days. Imagine having to be manager of so many people who are supposed to be about management. The M/B schools have tenure, prima donnas galore, the rigidities of departmentalization, entrenched programs and entrenched thinking, all in the name of changing everyone else. Like people who become psychiatrists in vain attempts to feel better, maybe we become teachers of organizational phenomena in vain attempts to get organized.

We talk about new product development while having introduced our last major new degree in 1908; we go on endlessly about strategic change while pursuing a strategy that dates from the 1950s; we teach the world's fanciest models of investment yet in our own decisions rely on one-year payback models. And "No other industry would neglect basic research in an area [curriculum] so central to its mission" (Wind 1999:17), not to mention on the impact of its own graduates on management practice.

There are two evident ways to change a business school: slowly and quickly. I'm not sure either works. Slow change just reinforces the status quo. The structure and the degree programs are too entrenched. Efforts at that kind of change over the past several decades has just dug them in deeper. The business schools have simply enjoyed too much success doing a number of wrong things. So long as society tolerates this—welcomes into positions of leadership people whose education is antithetical to it, supports researchers who talk to each other in closed systems—why should anything change? Besides, real change requires collaborative effort. If the faculty can hardly get together for regular meetings, how is anything supposed to change?

Rapid, dramatic change is, of course, all the rage now. Companies are running around half-cocked redoing everything in sight, at least until disaster strikes, at which point they turn around and change everything back. (More change!) Our M/B schools don't need that kind of sound and fury in the signification of nothing. It is not revolution or re-organization we need, at least for starters, so much as reconception: We need to get our heads around what we do, as compared with what we claim to do. Then we can consider how to do things differently. As this book has sought to express, we need to rethink who we educate, how, and for what purpose; we need to rethink how and why we do research, and for whom; and we need to rethink how we are organized to do both. And, then, if we are honest, we will have no choice but to change.

But will we be able to do this inside our existing structures? Will they be able to take us to the kind of change we need? Will even a revolt by our students, or their employers, or society at large, do it? Or will real change have to come from the rise of competing alternatives—new approaches, new schools, new people, perhaps riding in Trojan horses? Stay tuned.

To return to where we began, will we end up with management schools or business schools? Right now, we have schools of business without much management. Perhaps some will recognize their devotion to business and end the pretense of developing managers. I hope many others will choose to become seriously managerial. We require better managing in this world, and need serious educational institutions to help get us there.

I have never had any desire to become dean of a business or management school. Perhaps I know too much. Besides, I love my day job and would not trade it for anything. But if I did become a dean, my goal would not be to build the best business school in the world. It would be to build the first good management school.

# BIBLIOGRAPHY

Association to Advance Collegiate Schools of Business. "Overview of U.S. Business Schools." St. Louis, Mo., 2002.

———. "A Report of the AACSB Faculty Leadership Task Force." St. Louis, Mo., 1996.

Aaronson, Susan A. "Dinosaurs in the Global Economy?" In *Management Education and Competitiveness: Europe, Japan, and the United States*, ed. Rolv Petter Amdam, xiv. London: Routledge, 1996.

———. "Serving America's Business Graduate Business Schools and American Business." *Business History* 34, no. 1 (1992): 160–82.

Abernathy, William J., and James M. Utterback. "Patterns of Industrial Innovation." *Technology Review* 80, no. 7 (1978): 40–47.

Ackerman, Robert W. *The Social Challenge to Business*. Cambridge, Mass.: Harvard University Press, 1975.

Adweek Magazine's Newswire. "It Sure Did Good Advertising." October 21, 2002.

Alden, Edward. "Inside Track 260 Business Education." *Financial Times*, August 14, 2000.

Alinsky, Saul David. *Rules for Radicals: A Practical Primer for Realistic Radicals*. New York: Random House, 1971.

Amado, Gilles. "A Transitional Design for Management Learning." In *Working with Organizations and Their People: A Guide to Human Resources Practice*, ed. Douglas Weston Bray. New York: Guilford, 1991.

Anderson, Sarah, John Cavanagh, Chris Hartman, and Betsy Leondor-Wright. "Executive Excess 2001." Boston: Institute for Policy Studies, 2001.

Andrade, Gregor, Mark Mitchell, and Erik Stafford. "New Evidence and Perspectives on Mergers." *Journal of Economic Perspectives* 15, no. 2 (2001): 103–20.

Andrews, F. "Management: How a Boss Works in Calculated Chaos." *New York Times*, October 29, 1976.

Andrews, Kenneth Richmond. *The Concept of Corporate Strategy*. 3d ed. Homewood, IL: Irwin, 1987.

Appelbaum, Alec. "Beyond the Bottom Line." *Salon Ivory Tower*, March 1, 1999. (Available on www.salon.com/it/feature/1999/03/olfeature.html)

Argyris, Chris. "Education for Leading-Learning." *Organizational Dynamics* 21, no. 3 (1993): 5–17.

———. "Some Limitations of the Case Method: Experiences in a Management Development Program." *Academy of Management Review* 5, no. 2 (1980): 291–98.

Argyris, Chris, and Donald Schön. *Organizational Learning II: Theory, Method, and Practice*. Reading, Mass.: Addison-Wesley, 1996.

Armstrong, J. S. "The Devil's Advocate Responds to an MBA Student's Claim That Research Harms Learning." *Journal of Marketing* 59 (1995): 101–6.

Aspen Institute. Initiative for Social Innovation through Business. "Where Will They Lead? MBA Student Attitudes about Business and Society." New York, 2002.

Atlas, James. "The Million-Dollar Diploma: Harvard Business School Struggles to Maintain Its Value." *New Yorker*, July 19, 1999, 42–51.

Avery, Simon. "Hewlett-Packard's Profit Falls 66% but Tops Forecast." *Globe and Mail*, May 17, 2001.

Bach, George Leland. "Managerial Decision Making as an Organizing Concept." In *The Education of American Businessmen: A Study of University–College Programs in Business Administration*, ed. Franck Cook Pierson, 319–54. New York: McGraw-Hill, 1959.

Baker, Stephen, and Gary McWilliams. "Now Comes the Corporate Athlete." *Business Week*, January 31, 1994, 71–72.

Balke, W., H. Mintzberg, and J. A. Waters. "Team Teaching General Management: Theoretically, Experientially, Practically." *Exchange: The Organizational Behavior Teaching Journal* 111, no. 2 (1978).

Barnes, Louis B., C. Roland Christensen, and Abby J. Hansen. *Teaching and the Case Method: Text, Cases, and Readings*. 3d ed. Boston: Harvard Business School Press, 1994.

Barsoux, Jean-Louis, and Peter Lawrence. "The Making of a French Manager." *Harvard Business Review* (July–August 1991): 58–67.

Beer, M., R. A. Eisenstat, and B. Spector. "Why Change Programs Don't Produce Change." *Harvard Business Review* (November–December 1990): 158–66.

Beer, Michael, Bert Spector, Paul R. Lawrence, D. Quinn Mills, and Richard E. Walton. *Human Resource Management: A General Manager's Perspective: Text and Cases*. New York: Free Press; Collier Macmillan, 1985.

Beer, Michael, Russell A. Eisenstat, and Bert Spector. *The Critical Path to Corporate Renewal*. Boston: Harvard Business School Press, 1990.

Belson, Ken. "Japan Firms Are Cashing In on Patent Caches." *International Herald Tribune*, March 15, 2002.

Bennett, Roger C., and Robert G. Cooper. "The Misuse of Marketing: An American Tragedy." *Business Horizons* 24 (1981): 51–61.

Bennis, Warren G. *On Becoming a Leader*. Reading, Mass.: Addison-Wesley, 1989.

Berger, C. A. "In Defence of the Case Method: A Reply to Argyris." *Academy of Management Review* 8, no. 2 (1983): 329–33.

Bhidé, Amar. *The Origin and Evolution of New Businesses*. Oxford: Oxford University Press, 2000.

———. "The Road Well-Traveled: A Note on the Journey of HBS Entrepreneurs." Boston: Harvard Business School, 1996.

Bigelow, John D. *Managerial Skills: Explorations in Practical Knowledge*. Newbury Park, Calif.: Sage, 1991.

Bloom, Allan David. *The Closing of the American Mind*. New York: Simon & Schuster, 1987.

Bloomberg, Mary Schlangenstein. "Oryx Gambles on Spar Platform to Help It Repair Fiscal Damage." *Journal Record*, September 20, 1996.

Boettinger, Henry M. "Is Management Really an Art?" *Harvard Business Review* (January–February 1975): 54–60.

Bok, Derek. "Report of the President of Harvard College and Reports of Departments." In *Official Register of Harvard University*. Cambridge, Mass.: Harvard University Press, 1979.

Bolton, Allan. "Joint Architecture by HR Specialists and Business Schools." *Management Development Review* 9, no. 1 (1996): 22–24.

Bongiorno, Lori. "The B-School Profs at the Head of Their Class." *Business Week*, October 24, 1994, 45–46.

Boyatzis, Richard E. "Cornerstones of Change: Building the Path for Self-Directed Learning." In *Innovation in Professional Education*, ed. Richard E. Boyatzis, Scott S. Cowen, David A. Kolb, and Associates. San Francisco: Jossey-Bass, 1995.

Boyatzis, Richard E., Scott S. Cowen, and David A. Kolb. "Conclusion: What If Learning Were the Purpose of Education?" In *Innovation in Professional Education*, ed. Richard E. Boyatzis, Scott S. Cowen, David A. Kolb, and Associates. San Francisco: Jossey-Bass, 1995a.

Boyatzis, Richard E., Scott S. Cowen, David A. Kolb, and Associates, eds. *Innovation in Professional Education*. San Francisco: Jossey-Bass, 1995b.

Bradshaw, Della. "Making Courses Measure Up." *Financial Times*, May 19, 2003a.

———. "Plenty of Room for Naked Gamesmanship." *Financial Times*, January 20, 2003b.

———. "Running a School Like a Business." *Financial Times*, January 20, 2003c.

———. "A Year to Remember." *Financial Times Survey*, October 3, 1996.

Branch, Shelly. "Hunt War on MBA." *Fortune*, March 15, 1999, 79–80.

———. "MBAs Are Hot Again and They Know It." *Fortune*, April 14, 1997, 77–79.

Brickley, Peg. "Foamex Buyout Hits Snags." *Philadelphia Business Journal* 18, no. 34 (October 10, 1999): 1–2.

Brunsson, Nils. "Propensity to Change: An Empirical Study of Decisions on Reorientations." Goteborg: Goteborgs Universitet, 1976.

Buchanan, Phil. "Harvard B-School's E-Mania." *New York Times*, December 12, 2000.

Buell, Barbara. "The Second Comeback of Apple." *Business Week*, January 28, 1991.

Bunge, Mario. *Social Science under Debate*. Toronto: University of Toronto Press, 1998.

Burck, Gilbert. "The Transformation of European Business." *Fortune*, November 1957, 145–52.

Burgoyne, John. "Creating the Managerial Portfolio: Building on Competency Approaches to Management Development." *Management Education and Development* 20, No. 1 (1989): 56–61.

Burgoyne, John, and Alan Mumford. "Learning from the Case Method: A Report to the European Case Clearing House." Lancaster: Lancaster University Management School, 2001.

Burrows, Peter. "Carly's Last Stand? The Inside Story of the Infighting at Hewlett-Packard." *Business Week*, December 24, 2001a.

———. "The Radical: Carly Fiorina's Bold Management Experiment at HP." *Business Week*, February 19, 2001b, 70–80.

The Business Roundtable. "Statement on Corporate Governance." Washington, D.C., 1997.

———. *Statement on Corporate Responsibility*. New York, 1981.

*Business Week*. "The Good CEO." September 23, 2002, 80–81.

———. "How Executives Rate a B-School Education." March 24, 1986, 63.

*Business Week Online*. "The Best Performers." March 25, 2002a.

———. "The Forces That Move Drug Costs." December 10, 2001.

———. "Learning to Put Ethics Last." March 11, 2002b.

Button, Graham. "Marshall Makes Out." *Forbes* 150, No. 12 (November 23, 1992).

Button, Graham, and John R. Haynes. "The Perils of Pearlman." *Forbes* (February 15, 1993).

Byrne, H. S. "FMC Corp." *Barron's*, July 6, 1992, 41.

Byrne, John A. "Back to School: Special Report on Executive Education." *Business Week*, October 28, 1991, 102–7.

———. "The Best B-Schools: Big Changes since 1988 Have Made a Lot of Graduates Happier." *Business Week*, October 29, 1990a, 42–66.

———. "The Best B-Schools: Is Research in the Ivory Tower 'Fuzzy, Irrelevant, Pretentious'?" *Business Week*, October 29, 1990b, 62–64.

Byrne, John A., and Lori Bongiorno. "The Best B-Schools." *Business Week*, October 24, 1994, 62–70.

*Canadian Business*. "Education 2000: Custom Programs for Strategic Training." December 31, 1999.

Cappelli, Peter. "Managing without Commitment." *Organizational Dynamics* 28, no. 4 (2000): 11–24.

Carlton, Jim. "Thinking Different: At Apple, a Fiery Jobs Often Makes Headway and Sometimes a Mess." *Wall Street Journal*, April 14, 1998.

Castro, J., and J. Hannifin. "Gone but Not Forgotten." *Time* 136, no. 8 (August 20, 1990).

Caulkin, Simon. "All Aboard the Gravy Train. But Is an MBA Really the Business?" *The Observer*, November 8, 1998.

Cha, Ariana Eunjung. "Hewletts, Packard vs. HP." *Washington Post*, December 9, 2001.

Charan, Ram, and Geoffrey Colvin. "Why CEOs Fail." *Fortune*, June 21, 1999, 31–40.

Cheit, Earl F. "Business Schools and Their Critics." *California Management Review* 27, no. 3 (1985): 43–62.

———. *The Useful Arts and the Liberal Tradition*. New York: McGraw-Hill, 1975.

Chetkovich, Carol, and David L. Kirp. "Cases and Controversies: How Novitiates Are Trained to Be Masters of the Public Policy Universe." *Journal of Policy Analysis and Management* 20, no. 2 (2001): 283–314.

Chia, Robert. "Teaching Paradigm Shifting in Management Education: University Business Schools and the Entrepreneurial Imagination." *Journal of Management Studies* 33, no. 4 (1996): 409–28.

*Chief Executive*. "B-Schools under Fire." April 1993, 50–64.

Christensen, C. Roland, Kenneth R. Andrews, and M. E. Porter. *Business Policy: Text and Cases*. 5th ed. Homewood, Ill.: Irwin, 1982.

Christensen, C. Roland, and A. Zaleznik. "The Case Method and Its Administrative Environment." In *The Case Method at the Harvard Business School: Papers by Present and Past Members of the Faculty and Staff*, ed. Malcolm P. McNair and Anita C. Hersum. New York: McGraw-Hill, 1954.

Clifford, Patricia, and Sharon L. Friesen. "A Curious Plan: Managing on the Twelfth." *Harvard Educational Review* 63, no. 3 (1993): 339–58. Copyright © 1993 by the President and Fellows of Harvard College. All rights reserved. Reprinted with permission.

Cohen, Peter. *The Gospel According to the Harvard Business School*. Garden City, N.Y.: Doubleday, 1973.

Collins, C., B. Leondor-Wright, L. Thurow, and H. Skal. "Shifting Fortunes: The Perils of the Growing American Wealth Gap." Boston: United for a Fair Economy, March 1999.

Collins, Randall. *The Credential Society: An Historical Sociology of Education and Stratification.* San Diego, Calif.: Academic Press, 1979.

Conger, Jay A. "The Brave New World of Leadership Training." *Organizational Dynamics* 21, no. 3 (1993): 46–58.

———. "Can We Really Train Leadership?" *Strategy and Business* 2 (Winter 1996): 52–65.

———. *Learning to Lead: The Art of Transforming Managers into Leaders.* San Francisco: Jossey-Bass, 1992.

Constable, John and Roger McCormick, *The Making of British Managers,* London, British Institute of Management and Confederation of British Industry, 1987.

Copeland, Melvin T. "The Genesis of the Case Method in Business Instruction." In *The Case Method at the Harvard Business School: Papers by Present and Past Members of the Faculty and Staff,* ed. Malcolm P. McNair and Anita C. Hersum, 25–33. New York: McGraw-Hill, 1954.

Costea, Bogdan. "Executive Education in the Era of the Global: Some Thoughts on Globalism, Diversity, Learning." Bailrigg, Lancaster, U.K.: Lancaster University, 1998.

———. "Representations of Human Diversity in Mainstream Management Education: Critique and Development." Ph.D. diss., Lancaster University, 2000.

Costea, Bogdan, and Stephen Watson. "The Globalisation of Management Education: Differences in International Perspectives." Paper presented at the 1998 Annual International Conference of the Society for Research in Higher Education, Lancaster University, 1998.

Crainer, Stuart, and Des Dearlove. *Gravy Training: Inside the Business of Business Schools.* San Francisco: Jossey-Bass, 1999.

———. "Introduction to Top Fifty Thinkers." Available at www.FTdynamo.com, January 17, 2001.

Cyert, R. M., and J. G. March. *A Behavioral Theory of the Firm.* Englewood Cliffs, N.J.: Prentice Hall, 1963.

Cyert, Richard, and William Dill. "The Future of Business Education." *Journal of Business* 37, no. 3 (1964): 221–37.

Dash, Eric, Ellen Florian, Lisa Munoz, and Jessica Sung. "America's 40 Richest under 40." *Fortune,* September 17, 2001, 193–200.

Daudelin, Marilyn Wood. "Learning from Experience through Reflection." *Organizational Dynamics* 24, no. 3 (1996): 36–48.

Davis, Harry L., and Robin M. Hogarth. "Rethinking Management Education: A View from Chicago." Chicago: University of Chicago Graduate School of Business, ca. 1992.

De Rouffignac, Ann. "Once Great Tyler Now Troubled by Declining Sales." *Houston Business Journal* 27, no. 9 (July 18, 1997).

DeCloet, Derek. "Trolling for Minnows." *Canadian Business* 73, no. 2 (2000): 47–49.

de Meyer, Arnoud, in J. C. Linder and H. J. Smith. "The Complex Case of Management Education." *Harvard Business Review* (September–October 1992).

Deutschman, Alan. "The Second Coming of Steve Jobs." *The National Post,* November 1, 2000.

———. "The Trouble with MBAs." *Fortune,* July 29, 1991, 67–78.

Devons, E. *Planning in Practice: Essays in Aircraft Planning in War-Time*. Cambridge: Cambridge University Press, 1950.

DiNardo, Robert. "No Confidence Vote for Oryx's Changes." *Platt's Oilman News* 73, no. 15 (January 23, 1995).

Dolan, Kerry A. "The Return of Jimmy Three Sticks." *Forbes* 164, no. 7 (September 20, 1999).

Donham, Wallace B. "Business Teaching by the Case System." *American Economic Review* 12, no. 1 (1922): 53–65.

Dooley, Arch R., and Wickham Skinner. "Casing Case-Method Methods." Boston: Harvard Business School, 1975.

Dorfman, Dan. "More Firms Should Bounce Chief Executives." *USA Today*, January 21, 1993.

Dougherty, Thomas W., George F. Dreher, and William Whitely. "The MBA as Careerist: An Analysis of Early-Career Job Change." *Journal of Management* 19, no. 3 (1993): 535–48.

Dreyfuss, Joel. "John Sculley Rises in the West." *Fortune*, July 9, 1984, 180–84.

Drucker, Peter F. *Management: Tasks, Responsibilities, Practices*. New York: Harper & Row, 1974.

———. *The Practice of Management*. New York: Harper, 1954.

———. "Putting More Now into Knowledge." *Forbes*, May 15, 2000, 84–87.

———. "The Theory of the Business." *Harvard Business Review* (September–October 1994): 95–104.

Dunkin, Amy, and Nadav Enbar. "Getting the Most for Your B-School Money." *Business Week*, October 19, 1998, 176–78.

Dyckman, Thomas. "The 1996 Cornell Sponsored MBA-Executive Study: Corporate Leadership: A Survey on Values." Ithaca, N.Y.: the Johnson Graduate School of Management at Cornell University, 1996.

*The Economist*. "Back to the Laboratory." October 7, 1995, 69.

———. "Dons and Dollars." July 20, 1996, 53–54.

———. "The Quiet American." November 8, 1997.

———. "Wharton Business School: A New MBAge." December 14, 1991, 72–74.

*The Economist Global Executive*. "The Scene at Said." November 12, 2001.

Eliot, T. S. *Four Quartets*. London: Faber, 1959.

Eliasson, Gunnar. "The Nature of Economic Change and Management in the Knowledge-Based Information Economy." Stockholm: KTH Stockholm, Department of Industrial Management, 1998.

Enthoven, A. C. Annex A in D. Novick "Long-Range Planning through Program Budgeting." In *Perspectives of Planning*, ed. E. Jantsch. Paris: OECD, 1969.

Ewing, David W. *Inside the Harvard Business School: Strategies and Lessons of America's Leading School of Business*. New York: Times Books, 1990.

Fabrikant, Geraldine. "Executives Tremble as Judge Slaps Hand in Privately Held 'Cookie Jar.'" *New York Times*, June 16, 2003.

Fallows, James. "The Case against Credentialism." *Atlantic Monthly* (December 1985): 49–67.

Fayol, Henri, and Irwin Gray. *General and Industrial Management*. Rev. ed. New York: Institute of Electrical and Electronics Engineers, 1984. (First published in French in 1916.)

Filipczak, R., J. Gordon, M. Hequest, and D. Stamps. "Good Distance Training Looks Like . . . Well, Like Good Training." *Training* 34, no. 1 (January 1997): 13–16.

*Financial Times.* "Concerns Are Raised by Global Thrust." October 22, 2001.

———. *Mastering Management.* London: Financial Times, Prentice-Hall, 1997.

Fitzgerald, Thomas J. "Firms Offer Employees Custom MBA Programs." Available at www.collegejournal.com; cited July 19, 2001.

*Forbes.* "Hard Times for Marshall Cogan." January 26, 1987.

Fox, S. "Debating Management Learning: II." *Management Learning* 25, no. 1 (1994): 83–93.

———. "From Management Education and Development to the Study of Management Learning." In *Management Learning: Integrating Perspectives in Theory and Practice,* ed. J. G. Burgoyne and M. Reynolds, 17–20. London: Sage, 1997.

———. "What Are We?" *International Studies of Management and Organization* 22, no. 3 (1992): 71–93.

Friedman, Milton. *Capitalism and Freedom.* Chicago: University of Chicago Press, 1962.

———. *The Counter-Revolution in Monetary Theory.* London: Published for the Wincott Foundation by the Institute of Economic Affairs, 1970.

Friedrich, Otto. "The Money Chase." *Time,* May 4, 1981.

Fulmer, Robert M. "The Evolving Paradigm of Leadership Development." *Organizational Dynamics* 25, no. 4 (1997): 59–72.

Furnham, Adrian. "Business Schools Should Be Put to the Test." *European Business Forum* 7 (2001): 12–13.

Galbraith, Jay R. *Designing Organizations.* San Francisco: Jossey-Bass, 1995.

Gaskins, I. W., and T. T. Elliot. *Implementing Cognitive Strategy Instruction across the School: The Benchmark Manual for Teachers.* Cambridge, Mass., 1991.

Gendreau, Paul. "What Works in Community Corrections: Promising Approaches in Reducing Criminal Behavior." In *Successful Community Sanctions and Services for Special Offenders,* ed. B. J. Auerbach and T. C. Castellano, 59–74. Lanham, Md.: American Correctional Association, 1998.

———. "Offender Rehabilitation: What We Know and What Needs to Be Done." *Criminal Justice and Behavior* 23, no. 1 (1996): 144–61.

Gerth, H. H., and C. W. Mills, eds. *From Max Weber: Essays in Sociology.* New York: Oxford University Press, 1958.

Ghoshal, Sumantra, Breck Arnzen, and Sharon Brownfield. "Learning Alliance between Business and Business Schools: Executive Education as a Platform for Partnership." *California Management Review* 35, no. 1 (1992): 50–67.

Gilbert, Xavier, and Peter Lorange. "The Difference between Teaching and Learning." *European Business Forum,* no. 7 (2001): 7–8.

Gimein, Mark. "CEOs Who Manage Too Much." *Fortune,* September 4, 2000, 235–42.

Gladwell, Malcolm. "The Talent Myth: Are Smart People Overrated?" *New Yorker* 78, no. 20 (2002): 28–33.

Gleeson, Robert E. "Stalemate at Stanford, 1945–1958: The Long Prelude to the New Look at Stanford Business School." *Selections: The Magazine of the Graduate Management Admission Council* 13, no. 3 (1997): 6–23.

Gleeson, Robert E., and Steven Schlossman. "George Leland Bach and the Rebirth of Graduate Management Education in the United States, 1945–1975." *Selections: The Magazine of the Graduate Management Admission Council,* 11, no. 3 (Spring 1995): 8–46.

————. "The Many Faces of the New Look: The University of Virginia, Carnegie Tech, and the Reform of American Management Education in the Postwar Era." *Selections: The Magazine of the Graduate Management Admission Council* (Winter 1992): 9–27.

Gleeson, Robert E., Steven Schlossman, and David Greyson Allen. "Uncertain Ventures: The Origins of Graduate Management Education at Harvard and Stanford, 1908–1939." *Selections: The Magazine of the Graduate Management Admission Council* (November 3, 1993): 9–.

Godin, Seth. "Change Agent." *Fast Company* (September 2000): 322.

Gordon, Robert Aaron, and James Edwin Howell. *Higher Education for Business.* New York: Columbia University Press, 1959.

Gosling, Jonathan, and David Ashton. "Action Learning and Academic Qualifications." *Management Learning* 25, no. 2 (1994): 263–74.

————. "Educating and Developing the Managers." Paper presented at the International Policy Symposium on Management Education, Lancaster, England 1993.

Gosling, Jonathan, and Henry Mintzberg. "The Five Minds of a Manager." *Harvard Business Review* (November 2003): 54–63.

Graduate Management Admission Council. *The Official Guide for GMAT Review.* Princeton, N.J.: ETS Educational Testing Service.

Greco, Susan. "The Inc. 500 Almanac." *Inc.* (November 2001).

Greenhouse, Steven, *Deflating America's Dream,* New York Times, October 30, 2002.

Griffith, Victoria. "Kellogg in the Media." *Financial Times*, August 18, 2003.

————. "Re-engineering for Business Schools." *Financial Times* (April 1995).

Groth, Lars. *Future Organizational Design: The Scope for the It-Based Enterprise.* Chichester: Wiley, 1999.

Gulick, Luther Halsey, and Lyndall F. Urwick. *Papers on the Science of Administration.* New York: Institute of Public Administration, Columbia University, 1937.

Gupta, Indrajit. "Turning Dream into Reality." *Businessworld*, January 24, 2000, 52–55.

Halberstam, David. *The Best and the Brightest.* New York: Random House, 1972.

Hampden-Turner, Charles, and Alfons Trompenaars. *The Seven Cultures of Capitalism.* New York: Currency/Doubleday, 1993.

Handy, Charles. "Balancing Corporate Power: A New Federalist Paper." *Harvard Business Review* (November–December 1992): 59–75.

Handy, Charles B., Colin Gordon, Ian Gow, and Collin Randlesome. *Making Managers.* London: Pitman, 1988.

Harrington, Ann. "E-Curriculum: Easy Come, Easy Go." *Fortune*, April 16, 2001, 410–11.

Harvard Business School Associates. "The Success of a Strategy: An Assessment of Harvard University Graduate School of Business Administration." Boston, 1979.

Harvard Business School. *HBS Survival Guide.* Boston, 2003.

*Harvard Business School's Enterprise Newsletter.* "Making a Case: The Birth of an HBS Case Study." 2001.

Hayes, Robert H., and William J. Abernathy. "Managing Our Way to Economic Decline." *Harvard Business Review* (July–August 1980): 67–77.

Haynes, Peter. "Management Education: Passport to Prosperity." *The Economist*, March 2, 1991.

Heaton, Herbert. *A Scholar in Action, Edwin F. Gay.* New York: Greenwood, 1968.

Helgesen, Sally. *The Female Advantage: Women's Ways of Leadership.* New York: Doubleday Currency, 1990.

Henry, David. "Mergers: Why Most Big Deals Don't Pay Off." *Business Week Online*, October 14, 2002, 60–70.

Hilgert, Arnie D. "Developmental Outcomes of an Executive MBA Programme." *Journal of Management Development* 14, no. 10 (1995): 64–76.

Hill, Christian G. "Sculley's Shift Was Forced, Suit Argues." *Wall Street Journal*, September 27, 1993.

Hill, Linda A. *Becoming a Manager: Mastery of a New Identity.* Boston: Harvard Business School Press, 1992.

Hilton, Anthony. "Unzipping the Merger Myth." *Management Today* (February 2003): 48–51.

Himelstein, Linda. "New Turbulence in the Jean Pool." *Business Week*, October 12, 1998.

Hitch, Charles Johnston. *Decision-Making for Defense.* Berkeley: University of California Press, 1965.

Hitch, Charles Johnston, and Roland N. McKean. *The Economics of Defense in the Nuclear Age.* Cambridge, Mass.: Harvard University Press, 1960.

Hodgetts, Richard M. "A Conversation with Steve Kerr." *Organizational Dynamics* 24, no. 4 (1996): 68–79.

Hogan, Robert, Robert Raskin, and Dan Fazzini. "The Dark Side of Charisma." In *Measures of Leadership*, ed. Kenneth E. Clark, Miriam B. Clark, Robert R. Albright, Center for Creative Leadership, 343–54. West Orange, N.J.: Leadership Library of America, 1990.

Hogarth, Robin M. *Evaluating Management Education.* Chichester, England: Wiley, 1979.

Horvath, Dezso J. "Horvath Leads the Globalization of York." *The MBA Newsletter* (November 1995).

Huey, John. "The Leadership Industry." *Fortune*, February 21, 1994, 54–56.

Hurka, Thomas. "How to Get to the Top—Study Philosophy." *Globe and Mail*, January 2, 1990.

Huy, Quy Nguyen. "In Praise of Middle Managers." *Harvard Business Review* (September 2001): 72–79.

IMD. "Twenty Years After: MBA International Consulting Projects." Lausanne, 1999.

*Investment Dealers Digest.* "After the Bombshell at Shearson Lehman Brothers." February 1, 1999.

Ioannou, Lori. "Reinventing the MBA." *International Business* (August 1995): 26–33.

Ishida, Hideo. "MBA Education in Japan: The Experience of Management Education at the Graduate School of Business Administration, Keio University, Japan." *Journal of Management* 16, no. 3 (1997): 185–96.

Ives, Blake, and Sirkka L. Jarvenpaa. "Will the Internet Revolutionize Business Education and Research?" *Sloan Management Review* 37, no. 3 (1996): 33–41.

Ivey, Mark, and Michael O'Neal. "Frank Lorenzo: The Final Days." *Business Week*, August 27, 1990.

———. "The Lorenzo Legacy Haunts Continental." *Business Week*, December 17, 1990.

Jampol, J. "New Visions for Executive Education." *Time*, March 30, 1998.

Japsen, Bruce. "You Never Know What's Coming around the Corner." *Chicago Tribune*, December 24, 1998.

Jensen, Michael C., and William H. Meckling. "The Nature of Man." *Journal of Applied Corporate Finance* 7, no. 2 (1994): 4–19.

Johnson, Arthur. "Class Warfare." *Canadian Business* (April 1994): 26–30.

Jones, Del. "Will Business Schools Go out of Business? E-Learning, Corporate Academies Change the Rules." *USA Today*, May 23, 2000.

Kanungo, Rabindra N., and Sasi Misra. "Managerial Resourcefulness: A Reconceptualization of Management Skills." *Human Relations* 45, no. 12 (1992): 1311–32.

Kaplan, Abraham. *The Conduct of Inquiry: Methodology for Behavioral Science.* San Francisco: Chandler, 1964.

Kaplan, Robert S., and David P. Norton. *The Balanced Scorecard: Translating Strategy into Action.* Boston: Harvard Business School Press, 1996.

Kastens, Merritt L. "Cogito, Ergo Sum." *Interfaces* 2, no. 3 (1972): 29–32.

Keep, Ewart, and Andy Westwood. "Can the UK Learn to Manage?" London: Work Foundation, 2002.

Keeton, Ann. "Only 34 Per Cent of Employees Feel Loyal." *The Gazette* (Montreal), October 9, 2000.

Kelly, Francis, and Heather Mayfield Kelly. *What They Really Teach You at the Harvard Business School.* New York: Warner, 1986.

Kelly, Jim, and Julia Davies. "An In-House MBA Programme That Really Took Off." *Personnel Management* 26, no. 9 (1994): 30–33.

Kelly, Marjorie. *The Divine Right of Capital: Dethroning the Corporate Aristocracy.* San Francisco: Berrett-Koehler, 2001.

Keynes, John Maynard. *The General Theory of Employment, Interest and Money.* New York: Harcourt Brace, 1936.

Keys, Louise. "Action Learning: Executive Development of Choice for the 1990s." *Journal of Management Development* 13, no. 8 (1994): 50–56.

Kiechel, Walter, III. "Harvard Business School Restudies Itself." *Fortune* 99, no. 12 (June 18, 1979): 48–58.

Kinsley, Michael. "A Business Soap Opera." *Fortune*, June 25, 1984.

Kotter, John P. *The General Managers.* New York: Free Press, 1982.

———. *Leading Change.* Boston: Harvard Business School Press, 1996.

———. *The New Rules: How to Succeed in Today's Post-Corporate World.* New York: Free Press, 1995.

———. *What Leaders Really Do.* New York: Free Press, 1990.

Koudsi, Suzanne. "MBA Students Want Old-Economy Bosses." *Fortune*, April 16, 2001, 407–8.

Kuhn, Thomas S. *The Structure of Scientific Revolutions.* Chicago: University of Chicago Press, 1962.

Kurb, Milan and Joseph Prokopenko, *Diagnosing Management Training and Development Needs: Concepts and Techniques,* Management Development Series, No. 27, 1989.

Kurtzman, Joel. "Shifting the Focus at B-Schools." *New York Times*, December 31, 1989.

Laing, Jonathan R. "Poor Bill." *Barron's*, October 2, 1995.

Lampel, Joseph, and Henry Mintzberg. "Customizing Customization." *Sloan Management Review* 38, no. 1 (1996): 21–30.

Langley, Ann. "Between 'Paralysis by Analysis' and 'Extinction by Instinct.'" *Sloan Management Review* 36, no. 3 (1995): 63–76.

Lawrence, Paul R. "The Challenge of Problem-Oriented Research." *Journal of Management Inquiry* 1, no. 2 (June 1992): 139–42.

Lazzareschi, Carla. "Apple: Has It Lost Its Bite?" *Los Angeles Times*, February 19, 1989.

———. "Sculley Begins Reshaping Apple Right to the Core Computers." *Los Angeles Times*, February 8, 1990.

Learned, E. P, C. R. Christensen, K. R. Andrews, and W. D. Guth. *Business Policy: Text and Cases*. Homewood, Ill.: Irwin, 1965, revised edition, 1969.

Leavitt, Harold J. "Educating Our MBAs: On Teaching What We Haven't Taught." *California Management Review* 31, no. 3 (1989): 33–42.

———. "Management and Management Education in the West: What's Right and What's Wrong?" *London Business School Journal* 8, no. 1 (1983): 18–23.

———. "Socializing Our MBAs: Total Immersion? Managed Cultures? Brainwashing?" *California Management Review* 33, no. 4 (1991): 127–43.

Lee, Chris. "Can Leadership Be Taught?" *Training* 26, no. 7 (1989): 19–24.

Lenson, Todd. "Directors Beware: Court Decision Applies Public Rules to Private Companies." *Buyouts Magazine*, September 22, 2003.

Leonhardt, David. "California Dreamin': Harvard Business School Adds Silicon Valley to Its Syllabus." *New York Times*, June 18, 2000a.

———. "Harvard Curriculum Adds a Dot-Com Flair." *International Herald Tribune*, June 19, 2000b.

———. "A Matter of Degree? Not for Consultants." *New York Times*, October 1, 2000c.

Levering, Robert, and Milton Moskowitz. "The 100 Best Companies to Work For: The Best in the Worst of Times." *Fortune*, February 4, 2002, 60–61.

Lewin, Douglas. "On the Place of Design in Engineering." *Design Studies* 1, no. 2 (1979): 113–17.

Lewis, Michael. "Boot Camp for Yuppies. The Story of a White House Aide Who Went to Business School and Lived to Write About It." *New York Times Book Review*, May 8, 1994, 6–7.

Lieber, Ron. "Learning and Change—Roger Martin." *Fast Company* 30 (December 1999): 262.

Lindblom, Charles E. *The Policy-Making Process*. Englewood Cliffs, N.J.: Prentice Hall, 1968.

Linder, Jane C., and Jeff H. Smith. "The Complex Case of Management Education." *Harvard Business Review* (September–October 1992): 16–34.

Livingston, J. Sterling. "Myth of the Well-Educated Manager." *Harvard Business Review* (January–February 1971): 79–89.

Locke, Robert R. *The Collapse of the American Management Mystique*. Oxford: Oxford University Press, 1996a.

———. *The End of the Practical Man: Entrepreneurship and Higher Education in Germany, France, and Great Britain, 1880–1940*. Greenwich, Conn.: JAI Press, 1984.

———. "Factoring American Business School Education into the Revolution in Interactive Information Technology." Paper delivered at Retrospective conference on "Educating French Management Professors in North America, 1969–1975," held at FNEGE (The French Management Foundation), Paris, 16 novembre 1998, pp. 1–14.

———. "The Introduction of Business Schools in the United Kingdom: Confusing Historical for Functional Events." Paper presented at the British Academy of Management Conference, Aston University, U.K., September 17, 1996b.

————. *Management and Higher Education since 1940: The Influence of America and Japan on West Germany, Great Britain, and France*. Cambridge: Cambridge University Press, 1989.

Lombardo, Michael M., and Robert W. Eichinger. "Eighty-Eight Assignments for Development in Place: Enhancing the Developmental Challenge of Existing Jobs." Greensboro, N.C.: Center for Creative Leadership, 1989.

Loomis, Carol J. "The 15% Delusion." *Fortune*. February 5, 2001, 102–8.

Lorinc, John. "Class Action." *Canadian Business* 62, no. 9 (1989): 68–76.

Maas, Judith. "Reflections on Discussion Teaching: An Interview with C. Roland Christensen." *Harvard Business School Newsletter* (1991): 1–5.

MacFadyen, Ken. "No Nicks in Remington Exit." *Buyouts Magazine*, September 8, 2003.

Machan, Dyan. "The Strategy Thing (FMC Corp.)." *Forbes*, May 23, 1994.

Main, Jeremy. "B-Schools Get on a Global Vision." *Fortune*, July 17, 1989, 78–86.

Malone, David. "Remember Kofi Who?" *Globe and Mail*, April 10, 2001.

*Management Review*. "Interview with Jonathan Gosling and Henry Mintzberg." Indian Institute of Management, Bangalore (January & June 1998).

Mann, Robert W., and Julie M. Staudenmier. "Strategic Shifts in Executive Development." *Training and Development* 45 (1991): 37–40.

March, James G. "Exploration and Exploitation in Organizational Learning." *Organization Science* 2, no. 1 (1991): 71–87.

March, J. G. "A Scholar's Quest." *Stanford Graduate School of Business Magazine* (1996) (on the school's Web page).

Mark, J. Paul. *The Empire Builders: Inside the Harvard Business School*. New York: Morrow, 1987.

Martin, Justin. "Bashed B-Schools Bite Back." *Fortune*, March 21, 1994, 20–25.

Mast, Carlotta. "The People behind the Rankings." *Selections: The Magazine of the Graduate Management Admission Council* (2001a): 16–25.

————. "Reflections on the Past: Management Education's First Century." Graduate Management Admission Council, 2001b.

*Marketing Week*. "First Blood to Publicis." October 24, 2002.

Maugham, W. Somerset. *A Writer's Notebook*. Garden City, N.Y.: Doubleday, 1949.

Mayon-White, Bill. *Study Skills for Managers*. St. Paul, Minn.: Chapman, 1990.

McCall, Morgan W., Jr. "Developing Executives through Work Experiences." *Human Resources Planning* 11, no. 1 (1988): 1–11.

McCall, Morgan W., Michael M. Lombardo, and Ann M. Morrison. *The Lessons of Experience: How Successful Executives Develop on the Job*. Lexington, Mass.: Lexington Books, 1988.

McCall, M. W., A. Morrison, and R. L. Hannan. *Studies of Managerial Work: Results and Methods*. Greensboro, N.C.: Center for Creative Leadership, 1978.

McCauley, Cynthia D., Russ S. Moxley, and Ellen Van Velsor. *The Center for Creative Leadership Handbook of Leadership Development*. San Francisco: Jossey-Bass, 1998.

McGill, Michael E. "Attack of the Biz Kids." *Business Week* (December 1988): 75–78.

McKnight, M. R. "Management Skill Development: What It Is. What It Is Not." In *Managerial Skills: Explorations in Practical Knowledge*, ed. J. D. Bigelow, 204–18. Newbury Park, Calif.: Sage, 1991.

McNair, Malcolm P. *The Case Method at the Harvard Business School.* New York: McGraw-Hill, 1954.

McNamara, Robert S., and Brian VanDeMark. *In Retrospect: The Tragedy and Lessons of Vietnam.* New York: Times Books, 1995.

McNulty, Nancy G. "Management Education in Eastern Europe: 'Fore and After.'" *Academy of Management Executive* 6, no. 4 (1992): 78–87.

Meister, Jeanne C. *Corporate Quality Universities.* Burr Ridge, Ill.: Irwin, 1994.

Mendoza, Gabino. "The Three Temptations of the Management Teacher." In *The Search for Global Management*, ed. Max Von Zur-Muehlen, Canadian Federation of Deans of Management and Administrative Studies, and INTERMAN, 1990.

*Mergers & Acquisitions.* "Cooper to Exit Auto Business." July–August 1998.

Merritt, Jennifer. "MBA Programs Are Going Back to School." *Business Week*, May 7, 2001, 68–69.

———. "What's an MBA Really Worth." *Business Week*, September 22, 2003, 90–98.

Mintzberg, Henry. "Covert Leadership: The Art of Managing Professionals." *Harvard Business Review* (November–December 1998): 140–47.

———. "Crafting Strategy." *Harvard Business Review* (July–August 1987a): 66–75.

———. "Developing Leaders? Developing Countries?" Working paper, McGill University, 2002.

———. "If You're Not Serving Bill and Barbara, Then You're Not Serving Leadership." In *Leadership: Beyond Established Views*, ed. J. G. Hunt, U. Sekaran, and C. A. Schreisheim, 239–59. Carbondale: Southern Illinois University Press, 1982.

———. "Managing Exceptionally." *Organization Science* 12, no. 6 (2001): 759–71.

———. "Managing Government, Governing Management." *Harvard Business Review* (May–June 1996): 75–83.

———. "Managing Quietly." *Leader to Leader* 12 (Spring 1999a).

———. *Mintzberg on Management: Inside Our Strange World of Organizations.* New York: Free Press, 1989.

———. *The Nature of Managerial Work.* New York: Harper & Row, 1973.

———. *Power in and around Organizations.* Englewood Cliffs, N.J.: Prentice Hall, 1983.

———. "Productivity Is a Time Bomb." *Globe and Mail*, June 13, 2002.

———. *The Rise and Fall of Strategic Planning.* New York: Free Press, 1994a.

———. "Rounding Out the Manager's Job." *Sloan Management Review* 36, no. 1 (1994b): 11–26.

———. *Structure in Fives.* Englewood Cliffs, N.J.: Prentice Hall, 1983.

———. *The Structuring of Organizations: A Synthesis of the Research.* Englewood Cliffs, N.J.: Prentice Hall, 1979.

———. "There's No Compensation for Hypocrisy." *Financial Times*, October 29, 1999b.

Mintzberg, Henry, Bruce W. Ahlstrand, and Joseph Lampel. *Strategy Safari.* New York: Free Press, 1998.

Mintzberg, Henry, and Joseph Lampel. "Do MBAs Make Better CEOs? Sorry, Dubya, It Ain't Necessarily So." *Fortune*, February 19, 2001, 244.

Mintzberg, Henry. *Impediments to the Use of Management Information.* New York: National Association of Accountants, 1975.

Mintzberg, Henry and Alexandra McHugh, *Strategy Formation in Adhocracy,* Administrative Science Quarterly, 1985, pp. 160–197.

Mintzberg, Henry, Robert Simons, and Kunal Basu. "Beyond Selfishness." *Sloan Management Review* 1 (2002): 67–74.

Mintzberg, Henry, and Ludo Van der Heyden. "Organigraphs: Drawing How Companies Really Work." *Harvard Business Review* (September–October 1999): 87–94.

Mintzberg, Henry, and James A. Waters. "Of Strategies, Deliberate and Emergent." *Strategic Management Journal* 6, no. 3 (1985): 257–72.

Mintzberg, Henry, and Frances Westley. "Cycles of Organizational Change." *Strategic Management Journal* 13 (1992): 39–59.

———. "Decision Making: It's Not What You Think." *Sloan Management Review* 42, no. 3 (2001): 89–93.

Mirabella, Roseanne M., and Naomi Bailin Wish. "The 'Best Place' Debate: A Comparison of Graduate Education Programs for Nonprofit Managers." *Public Administration Review* 60, no. 3 (2000): 219–29.

Mishel, L., J. Bernstein and J. Schmitt, *The State of Working America: 2000–2001*, Ithaca, New York, Economic Policy Institute, Cornell University Press, 2001.

Mitchell, Russell. "The Numbers Aren't Crunching Craig Research." *Business Week*, June 1, 1992.

Morgan, Gareth. *Images of Organization*. Beverly Hills: Sage, 1986.

Morrison, Ann M. "Apple Bites Back." *Fortune*, February 20, 1984, 86–100.

Muller, Helen J., James L. Porter, and Robert R. Rehder. "Reinventing the MBA the European Way." *Business Horizons* 34, no. 3 (1991): 83–91.

Munk, Nina. "How Levi's Trashed a Great American Brand." *Fortune* 139, no. 7 (April 12, 1999).

Murray, Charles J. *The Supermen*. New York: Wiley, 1997.

Murray, Hugh. "Management Education and the MBA: It's Time for a Rethink." *Managerial and Decision Economics* 9 (1988): 71–78.

Murray, Sarah. "The Barbarian Who Nearly Flunked Business School." *Financial Times*, January 20, 2003.

Musgrove, Mike. "HP, Posting Profit, Sees a Return on Compaq Deal." *International Herald Tribune*, November 22, 2002.

Nee, Eric. "Open Season on Carly Fiorina." *Fortune*, July 23, 2001, 124–38.

Nonaka, Ikujiro, and Noboru Konno. "The Concept of 'Ba': Building a Foundation for Knowledge Creation." *California Management Review* 40, no. 3 (1998): 40–54.

Nonaka, Ikujiro D., and Hirotaka Takeuchi. *The Knowledge-Creating Company*. New York: Oxford University Press, 1995.

Norman, James R. "The Fallen Angel." *Forbes*, March 28, 1994.

Nudd, Tim. "Partying Like It's 1969: D'Arcy, B&Bers Mourn Alma Mater at Reunion." *Adweek Eastern Edition* 43, no. 45 (November 11, 2002).

Ohlott, Patricia J. "Job Assignments." In *The Center for Creative Leadership Handbook of Leadership Development*, ed. Cynthia D. McCauley, Russ S. Moxley, Ellen Van Velsor. San Francisco: Jossey-Bass, 1998.

Okazaki-Ward, Lola. *Management Education and Training in Japan*. London: Graham & Trotman, 1993.

O'Reilly, Brian. "Agee in Exile." *Fortune*, May 29, 1995, 51–74.

———. "How Execs Learn Now." *Fortune*, April 5, 1993, 52–55.

———. "The Mechanic Who Fixed Continental." *Fortune* 140, no. 12 (December 20, 1999).

————. "Reengineering the MBA." *Fortune*, January 24, 1994, 38–45.

Pascale, Richard, Mark Millenmann, and Linda Gioja. "Changing the Way We Change." *Harvard Business Review* (November/December 1997): 127–39.

Paul, Frederic. "Apple's Scully Hands Off CEO Job, Stays On." *Network World*, July 28, 1993, 22.

Pedler, Mike. "Interpreting Action Learning." In *Management Learning*, ed. John Burgoyne and Michael Raynolds, 248–64. London: Sage, 1997.

Penley, Larry Edward, Paul Fulton, George G. Daly, and Ronald E. Frank. "Has Business School Education Become a Scandal?" *Business and Society Review*, no. 93 (1995): 4–16.

Peterson, Thane. "Zenith Dials Up a New CEO." *Business Week*, March 13, 1995.

Pfeffer, J. L. "A Tip from Harvard MBAs: Their Careers Hint at Where Not to Go." *International Herald Tribune*, January 29–30, 1994.

Pfeffer, Jeffrey. "Mortality, Reproducibility, and the Persistence of Styles of Theory." *Organization Science* 6, no. 6 (1995): 681–86.

Pfeffer, Jeffrey, and Christina T. Fong. "The End of Business Schools? Less Success Than Meets the Eye." *Academy of Management Learning and Education* 1, no. 1 (2002): 78–95.

Pierson, Frank Cook. *The Education of American Businessmen: A Study of University–College Programs in Business Administration*. New York: McGraw-Hill, 1959.

Piper, Thomas R., Mary C. Gentile, and Sharon Daloz Parks. *Can Ethics Be Taught? Perspectives, Challenges, and Approaches at Harvard Business School*. Boston: Harvard Business School Press, 1993.

Pitcher, Patricia C. *Artists, Craftsmen, and Technocrats*. Toronto: Stoddart, 1995.

————. "Balancing Personality Types at the Top." *Business Quarterly* (Winter 1993).

————. *The Drama of Leadership*. New York: Wiley, 1997.

Poletti, Therese. "Meaning of 'HP Way' Defines Fight over Compaq Deal." *Mercury News*, November 25, 2001.

Policano, Andrew J. "Ten Easy Steps to a Top-25 MBA Program." *Selections: The Magazine of the Graduate Management Admission Council*, 1, no. 2 (2001): 39–40.

Porter, Lyman W., and Lawrence E. McKibbin. *Management Education and Development: Drift or Thrust into the 21st Century?* New York: McGraw-Hill, 1988.

Porter, Michael. "Corporate Strategy: The State of Strategic Thinking." *The Economist*, May 23, 1987, 17–22.

Porter, Michael E. *Competitive Advantage*. New York: Free Press, 1985.

————. *Competitive Strategy*. New York: Free Press, 1980.

Pulliam, Susan and Scism, Leslie. "Equitable Companies May Adapt Role as Stock Market's Comeback Kid." *Wall Street Journal Europe*, January 16, 1997.

Quelch, John. "Why Europe Has Some Catching Up to Do." *European Business Forum* 7 (Autumn 2001): 6–7.

Quinn, James Brian. "Strategy, Science and Management." *Sloan Management Review* 43, no. 4 (2002): 96.

Raelin, Joseph A. "Beyond Experiential Learning to Action Learning." *The Organizational Learning Newsletter* (March 1993a): 5–7.

————. "Let's Not Teach Management as If It Were a Profession." *Business Horizons* 33, no. 2 (1990): 23–28.

———. "A Model of Work-Based Learning." *Organizational Science* 8, no. 6 (1997): 563–78.

———. "Theory and Practice: A Theoretical Review of Their Respective Roles, Relationship, and Limitations in Advanced Management Education." *Business Horizons* 36, no. 3 (1993b): 85–89.

———. "Whither Management Education? Professional Education, Action Learning and Beyond." *Management Learning* 25, no. 2 (1994): 301–17.

———. *Work-Based Learning: The New Frontier of Management Development.* Upper Saddle River, N.J.: Prentice Hall, 2000.

Raelin, Joseph A., and John Schermerhorn Jr. "Preface: A New Paradigm for Advanced Management Education: How Knowledge Merges with Experience." *Management Learning* 25, no. 2 (1994): 195–200.

Raphael, Ray. *Edges: Human Ecology of the Backcountry.* Lincoln: University of Nebraska Press, 1986.

Redlich, Fritz. "Academic Education for Business: Its Development and the Contribution of Ignaz Jastrow (1856–1937)." *Business History Review* 31 (1957): 35–91.

Reingold, Jennifer. "The Best B-Schools." *Business Week*, October 19, 1998a.

———. "Corporate America Goes to School." *Business Week*, October 20, 1997, 68–72.

———. "Learning to Lead: Technology Is Driving the Demand for Executive Education—and Creating Lots of New Options for Companies." *Business Week*, October 18, 1999.

———. "The Melting Pot Still Has a Few Lumps." *Business Week*, October 19, 1998b, 104–8.

———. "You Can't Create a Leader in a Classroom." *Fast Company* (November 2000): 286.

Revans, Reginald W. *The A.B.C of Action Learning.* Bromley, England: Chartwell-Bratt, 1983.

Roberts, Richard H. "Performance Learning and Global Pilgrimage: 'World Class Managers' and the Quest for Spiritual Values." Paper presented at the SISR Conference, Louvain, Belgium, 1999.

Robinson, Peter. *Snapshots from Hell: The Making of an MBA.* New York: Warner, 1994.

Roeder, David. "Kraemer to Replace Baxter Boss." *Chicago Sun-Times*, November 17, 1999.

Rohlin, Lennart. "MiL Institute—Concepts and Programmes." Lund, Sweden: MiL Institute, 1999.

Rudnitsky, Howard. "Leverage 101." *Forbes* 150, no. 7 (September 28, 1992).

Samuelson, R. J. "What Good Are B-Schools?" *Newsweek*, May 14, 1990, 49.

Santoli, Michael. "Manhattan Transfer." *Barron's* 80, no. 1 (January 1, 2000).

Saporito, Bill, and Tricia Welsh. "The Toppling of King James III." *Fortune* 127, no. 1 (January 11, 1993).

Sass, Steven A. *The Pragmatic Imagination: A History of the Wharton School, 1881–1981.* Philadelphia: University of Pennsylvania Press, 1982.

Saul, John Ralston. *The Unconscious Civilization.* Concord, Ontario: Anansi, 1995.

———. *Voltaire's Bastards: The Dictatorship of Reason in the West.* Toronto: Viking, 1992.

Sayles, L. R. "Whatever Happened to Management . . . or Why the Dull Stepchild?" *Business Horizons* 13 (April 1970): 25–34.

Scannell, Kara. "Deals & Deal Makers: The Few; the Proud; The . . . M.B.A.S (?!)." *Wall Street Journal*, July 19, 2001.

Schachter, Harvey. "My Way." *Canadian Business*, June 25–July 9, 1999, 49–51.

Schendel, Dan. "Notes from the Editor-in-Chief." *Strategic Management Journal*, 13 (1995): 1–2.

Scherer, F. M. *International High-Technology Competition*. Cambridge, Mass.: Harvard University Press, 1992.

Schlender, Brenton R. "Celebrity Chief: His Shyness, John Sculley Promotes Apple— and Himself." *Wall Street Journal*, August 18, 1988.

Schlossman, Steven L., Robert E. Gleeson, Michael Sedlak, and David Grayson Allen. *The Beginnings of Graduate Management Education in the United States*. *GMAC Occasional Papers*. Santa Monica, Calif.: Graduate Management Admission Council, 1994.

Schlossman, Steven, Michael Sedlak, and Harold Wechsler. "The "New Look": The Ford Foundation and the Revolution in Business Education." *Selections: The Magazine of the Graduate Management Admission Council*, 14, no. 3 (1998): 8–28.

Schmotter, James W. "An Interview with Professor James G. March." *Selections: The Magazine of the Graduate Management Admission Council*, 14, no. 3 (1995): 56–62.

Schneider, Mica. "A New Model for Global EMBAs." *Business Week Online*, October 26, 2001.

Schön, Donald A. *Educating the Reflective Practitioner*. San Francisco: Jossey-Bass, 1987.

———. *The Reflective Practitioner*. New York: Basic Books, 1983.

Schwartz, Nelson D. "Colgate Cleans Up." *Fortune*, April 16, 2001, 179–80.

Sculley, John, with John A. Byrne. *Odyssey: Pepsi to Apple*. New York: Harper & Row, 1987.

Serey, Timothy, and Kathleen S. Verderber. "Beyond the Wall: Resolving Issues of Educational Philosophy and Pedagogy in the Teaching of Managerial Competencies." In *Managerial Skills: Exploration in Practical Knowledge*, ed. John D. Begelow, 3–17. Newbury Park, Calif.: Sage, 1991.

Shapero, Albert. "What Management Says and What Managers Do." *Interfaces* (February 1977).

Sherman, Stratford. "How Tomorrow's Best Leaders Are Learning Their Stuff." *Fortune*, November 27, 1995, 64–70.

Shipler, David. "Robert McNamara and the Ghosts of Vietnam: Robert McNamara Meets the Enemy." *New York Times Magazine*, August 10, 1997.

Simon, Herbert Alexander. *Administrative Behavior: A Study of Decision-Making Processes in Administrative Organization*. New York: Macmillan, 1947, 1957, 1976.

———. "The Business School: A Problem in Organizational Design." *Journal of Management Studies* 4 (1967): 1–16.

———. *The Sciences of the Artificial*. Cambridge, Mass.: MIT Press, 1969.

Sims, D., E. Morgan, J. Nicholls, K. Clarke, and J. Harris. "Between Experience and Knowledge. Learning within the MBA Programme." *Management Learning* 25, no. 2 (1994): 275–87.

Sims, David. "Mental Simulation: An Effective Vehicle for Adult Learning." *IHE* 3, no. 1 (1986): 33–35.

Singer, E. A., and L. M. Wooton. "The Triumph and Failure of Albert Spears Administrative Genius: Implication for Current Management and Practice." *Journal of Applied Behavioral Science* 12, no. 1: 79–103.

Slater, Robert, and Jack Welch. *The New GE: How Jack Welch Revived an American Institution.* Homewood, Ill.: Irwin, 1993.

Smalter, D. T., and J. L. J. Ruggles. "Six Business Lessons from the Pentagon." *Harvard Business Review* (March–April 1966) 64–75.

Smith, Douglas K., and Robert C. Alexander, *Fumbling the Future: How Xerox Invented, Then Ignored, the First Personal Computer.* New York: William Morrow and Co., Inc, 1988.

Sonnenfeld, Jeffrey. "Serial Acquirers Tend to End Badly." *International Herald Tribune,* June 14, 2002.

Spender, J. C. *Industry Recipes.* Oxford: Blackwell, 1989.

———. "Knowing, Managing and Learning: A Dynamic Managerial Epistemology." *Management Learning* 25, no. 3 (1994): 387–412.

———. "Underlying Antinomies and Perpetuated Problems: An Historical View of the Challenges Confronting Business Schools Today." Working Paper, 1997; available from home.earthlink.net/~jcspender.

Starbuck, William H. "The Origins of Organizational Theory." In *Handbook of Organizational Theory: Meta-Theoretical Perspectives,* ed. Haridimos Tsoukas and Christian Knudsen. Oxford: Oxford University Press, 2002.

Stedman, Craig. "Craig Pulling Plug on Real-Time Computing." *SNElectronique News,* December 14, 1992.

Stern, Stefan. "What Did Business School Do for Them?" *Management Today* (February 2002): 40–45.

Stevenson, Howard H. "Who Are the Harvard Self-Employed?" Wellesley, Mass: Frontiers of Entrepreneurial Research, Babson College, 1983 (also Harvard Business School, 1983).

Sturdy, Andrew, and Gabriel Yiannis. "Missionaries, Mercenaries or Car Salesmen? MBA Teaching in Malaysia." *Journal of Management Studies* 37, no. 7 (2000): 979–1002.

Summers, Colonel Harry, Jr. *On Strategy: The Vietnam War in Context.* Washington, D.C., and Carlisle Barracks, Pa.: Government Printing Office and Strategic Studies Institute, 1981.

Sutter, Stan. "Levi's Slow Fade." *Marketing Magazine* 104, no. 44 (November 22, 1999).

Syrett, Michel. "View from the Top." *Asian Business* (September 1995): 24–29.

Tate, Ralph. "The New Flexible MBA." *Business Life* (July/August 1998): 38–41.

Taylor, Frederick Winslow. *The Principles of Scientific Management.* New York: Harper, 1911.

Taylor, Alex, III. "Consultants Have a Big People Problem." *Fortune,* April 13, 1998, 162–66.

Thirunarayana, P. N. "Self Managed Learning MBA: An Enterprising Approach to Learning." *TMTC Journal of Management* (June/July 1992).

Tichy, Noel, and Ram Charan. "Speed, Simplicity, Self-Confidence: An Interview with Jack Welch." *Harvard Business Review* (September/October 1989): 2–9.

*Time.* "Back in a Tailspin." 136, no. 26 (December 17, 1990).

———. "Harvard's Waffle Case." May 4, 1981a.

————. "The Money Chase—Business School Solutions May Be Part of the U.S. Problem." May 4, 1981b, 52–59.

————. "Special Report: Business Schools and Globalization." April 7, 1997.

Turner, Arthur. "The Case Discussion Method Revisited (a)." *Exchange: The Organizational Behavior Teaching Journal*, 6, no. 3 (1981): 6–8.

Ulrich, David, Steven Kerr, and Ronald N. Ashkenas. *The GE Work-Out*. New York: McGraw-Hill, 2002.

Updike, Edith. "Ivy-Covered Halls vs. Street Smarts." *Business Week*, February 1, 1999.

*USA Today*. "Even Prestigious MBA Programs Must Change to Keep Pace." May 23, 2000.

Useem, Michael. *Liberal Education and the Corporation: The Hiring and Advancement of College Graduates*. New York: de Gruyter, 1989.

Uttal, Bro. "Behind the Fall of Steve Jobs." *Fortune*, August 5, 1985, 20–24.

Utterback, James M. *Mastering the Dynamics of Innovation*. Boston: Harvard Business School Press, 1994.

Vail, Peter. *Managing as a Performing Art: New Ideas for a World of Chaotic Change*. San Francisco: Jossey-Bass, 1989.

Van Buskirk, Bill. "Five Classroom Exercises for Sensitizing Students to Aspects of Japanese Culture and Business Practice." *Journal of Management Education* 15, no. 1 (1996): 96–112.

Vicere, Albert A. "Changes in Practices, Changes in Perspectives: The 1997 International Study of Executive Development Trends." *Journal of Management Development* 17, no. 7 (1998): 526–43.

Vogl, A J. "Making It in the '90s." *Across the Board* 32, no. 4 (1995): 27–31.

*Wall Street Journal*. "Supercomputer Maker Posts $26.5 Million 4th-Period Loss." January 21, 1993.

Wallace, Wanda T., John Gallagher, John McCann, and Blair Sheppard. *Organizational Learning and Learning Networks: The Place and Space Model in Management Development*. Duke Corporate Education, Inc. Available at www.DukeCE.com; 2003.

Warner, Melanie. "Can Merck Stand Alone?" *Fortune*, July 23, 2001, 62.

*Washington Post*. "And Now to Spending." June 6, 2001, A26.

Waters, James A. "Managerial Skill Development." *Academy of Management Review* 5, no. 3 (1980): 449–53.

Watson, Rob. "Kofi Annan's Diplomatic Style." *BBC News*, February 28, 1998.

Watson, Stephen R. "The Place for Universities in Management Education." *Journal of General Management* 19, no. 2 (1993): 14–42.

Watson, Tony J. *In Search of Management: Culture, Chaos and Control in Managerial Work*. London: Routledge, 1994.

————. "Motivation: That's Maslow, Isn't It?" *Management Learning* 27, no. 4 (1996): 447–64.

Watts, Robert. *Sunday Telegraph*. July 18, 1997, 43.

Webber, Ross. "Modern Imperatives." *Financial Post*, October 12, 1996.

Weick, Karl E. *The Social Psychology of Organizing*. Reading, Mass.: Addison-Wesley, 1969.

————. "Speaking to Practice: The Scholarship of Integration." *Journal of Management Inquiry* 5, no. 3 (1996): 251–58.

Westall, Oliver. "Don's Diary." *The Times Higher Education Supplement*, August 17, 2001.

The Wharton MBA Program. *Math Proficiency.* Available at www.wharton.upenn. edu/mba/curriculum/pre_term.html; 2003.

Wheat, Alynda. "The Anatomy of a Great Workplace." *Fortune,* February 4, 2002, 75–78.

Whetten, David A., and Kim S. Cameron. *Developing Management Skills.* Glenview, Ill.: Scott Foresman, various editions (1998, 2002).

Whetten, David A., and Sue Campbell Clark. "An Integrated Model for Teaching Management Skills." *Journal of Management Education* 20, no. 2 (1996): 151–81.

Whitehead, Alfred North. *Essays in Science and Philosophy.* New York: Philosophical Library, 1932.

Whitford, David. "A New MBA for the E-Corp: Half-Geek, Half-Manager." *Fortune,* March 15, 1999, 189–92.

Whitley, Richard. "Academic Knowledge and Work Jurisdiction in Management." *Organization Science* 16, no. 1 (1995): 81–105.

———. "The Fragmented State of Management Studies: Reasons and Consequences." *Journal of Management Studies* 21, no. 3 (1984a): 331–48.

———. "On the Nature of Managerial Tasks and Skills: Their Distinguishing Characteristics and Organization." *Journal of Management Studies* 26, no. 3 (1989): 209–24.

———. "The Scientific Status of Management Research as a Practically-Oriented Social Science." *Journal of Management Studies* 21, no. 4 (1984b): 369–90.

Whitley, Richard, Alan Thomas, and Jane Marceau. *Masters of Business? Business Schools and Business Graduates in Britain and France.* London: Tavistock, 1981.

Wiggenhorn, William. "Motorola U: When Training Becomes an Education." *Harvard Business Review* (July–August 1990): 71–83.

Wildavsky, Aaron B. *The Politics of the Budgetary Process.* 2d ed. Boston: Little, Brown, 1974.

Wilensky, Harold L. *Organizational Intelligence.* New York: Basic Books, 1967.

Williams, David. "Is This Really a Passport to Mastering the Universe?" *The Guardian,* February 23, 2002.

Wind, Jerry. "Reinventing the Business School for the Global Information Age." Philadelphia: Wharton School, University of Pennsylvania, 1999. Presented at the EFMD Conference, Helsinki, 2000.

Wood, Lisa. "Bringing Practicality to the Table: Management Consultants." *Financial Times,* May 23, 2000.

———. "Integration Pays Off." *Financial Times,* October 21, 2001.

Yoshida, Junko. "Zenith Rebounding from Nadir?" *Electronic Engineering Times* 888 (February 12, 1996).

Zalaznick, Sheldon. "The MBA, the Man, the Myth, and the Method." *Fortune* (May 1968): 168–206.

Zaleznik, Abraham. "Managers and Leaders: Are They Different?" *Harvard Business Review* (May–June 1977): 67–78.

# INDEX

# ABOUT THE AUTHOR

HENRY MINTZBERG joined the Faculty of Management at McGill University in 1968, where he taught the MBA course in management policy until the mid-1980s, after which he has concentrated on education for practicing managers and doctoral students. He holds an M.S. (basically an MBA) as well as a Ph.D. from the MIT Sloan School of Management and has been a visiting professor at Insead, London Business School, Université d'Aix-Marseille, Carnegie-Mellon University, and École des Hautes Études Commercial de Montréal. He is currently the Cleghorn Professor of Management Studies at McGill.

This is his twelfth book, and it links most closely to his first, *The Nature of Managerial Work*. It builds on the conclusions of that book while advancing his views of the management process and the implication of these for the development of managers. Aspects of his other books, particularly on organization design and strategy formation, are drawn upon here as well.

Starting in 1980, Mintzberg taught a two-day program for practicing managers for many years, particularly with the Management Centre Europe. After creating the International Masters Program in Practicing Management with colleagues from Canada, England, France, India, and Japan in 1996, he directed the program for its first four years and has remained close to it ever since.

Mintzberg was named an Officer of the Order of Canada and l'Ordre National du Québec in 1998, has been a fellow of the Royal Society of Canada since 1980 (the first from a management faculty), and received the Distinguished Scholar Award for Contributions to Management from the Academy of Management in 2000 as well as its George R. Terry Award for the best book of 1995 (*The Rise and Fall of Strategic Planning*).

This book marks a transition in his writing, from describing management and organization to addressing broader social issues. An "electronic pamphlet" under the title *Getting Past Smith and Marx: Toward a Balanced Society*, which he has been preparing for several years, will be his next major effort.

Mintzberg is married to Saša Sadilova and is the father of Susie and Lisa. He is particularly enthusiastic about getting off the usual track, whether on a bicycle, in a canoe or hiking boots, bushwhacking atop cross-country skis, or with his pen, writing short stories about his experiences.

### Strategy Safari
*The complete guide through the wilds of strategic management*

0273 656368

The word strategy has been around for a long time. It is considered to be the high point of managerial activity, and managers use the word both freely and fondly. But what does the word really mean? *Strategy Safari* sets out to provide an answer.

In this colourful primer, Henry Mintzberg, Bruce Ahlstrand and Joseph Lampel draw togeth diverse strands of strategic thought into ten distinct schools. In a final chapter they see to blend the schools together; pointing out however that a truly unified theory may not be possible or desirable. The result is a thoughtful and readable guide to the wilds of strategic management.

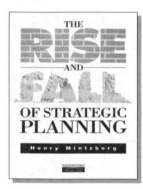

### The Rise and Fall of Strategic Planning

0273 650378

*"My favourite management book of the last 25 years? No contest. The Rise & Fall of Strategic Planning by Henry Mintzberg."* **Tom Peters**

In this definitive and revealing history, Henry Mintzberg unmasks the process that has mesmerised so many organisations since 1965 ... strategic planning.

Mintzberg traces the origin and history of strategic planning and proposes new definition of planning and strategy, arguing that we must reconceive the process by which strategie are created by emphasising informal learning and personal vision.

Essential reading for anyone influenced by the planning or strategy-making process and students undertaking corporate strategy, strategic management and business policy courses.

Available at all good bookshops and online at
**www.pearson-books.com**

**FT** Prentice Hall
FINANCIAL TIMES

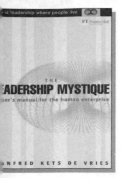

### The Leadership Mystique
Manfred Kets de Vries

0273 656201

Whether you work on the shop floor or in a corner office, what have you done today to be more effective as a leader?

In *The Leadership Mystique*, management and psychology guru Manfred Kets de Vries unpicks the many layers that underlie effective leadership, and gets to the heart of the day-to-day behaviour of leading people in the human enterprise.

### Living Strategy
*Putting People at the heart of corporate purpose*
Lynda Gratton

0273 650157

*Living Strategy* is the book that puts the human in human capital.

*Living Strategy* demonstrates that the companies who will be most successful in the 21st century will be those that are capable of gathering and bonding talented, creative, motivated people, who trust the company and are inspired by what they do.

*Living Strategy* takes the reader through the why and the how of thinking and acting differently to create organizations that have meaning and soul.

### Business Minds
*Management Wisdom, Direct from the World's Greatest Thinkers*
Tom Brown, Stuart Crainer, Des Dearlove, Jorge N Rodrigues

0273 656600

The more you know; the faster you go. So whose ideas are you listening to?

*Business Minds* brings you the latest and greatest management ideas live and direct from the leading thinkers. The management gurus, unplugged. From the gurus of the old world - Peter Drucker, Tom Peters, Peter Senge et al. to the gurus of the new world - Jonas Ridderstrale, Don Tapscott, and Patty Seybold.

converse with the best brains in business; arm yourself with the biggest ideas.

---

available at all good bookshops and online at
www.pearson-books.com

**FT** Prentice Hall
FINANCIAL TIMES